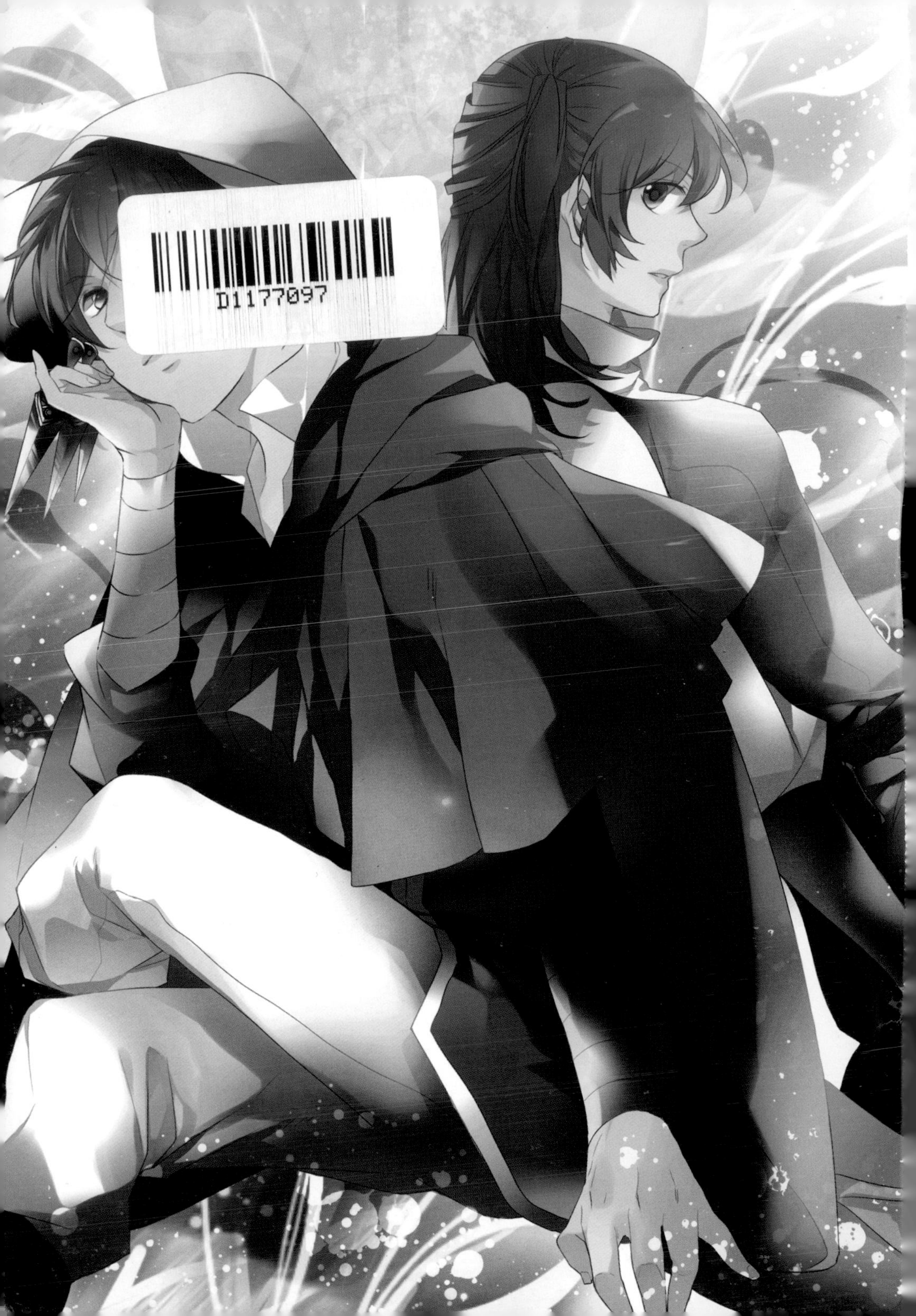

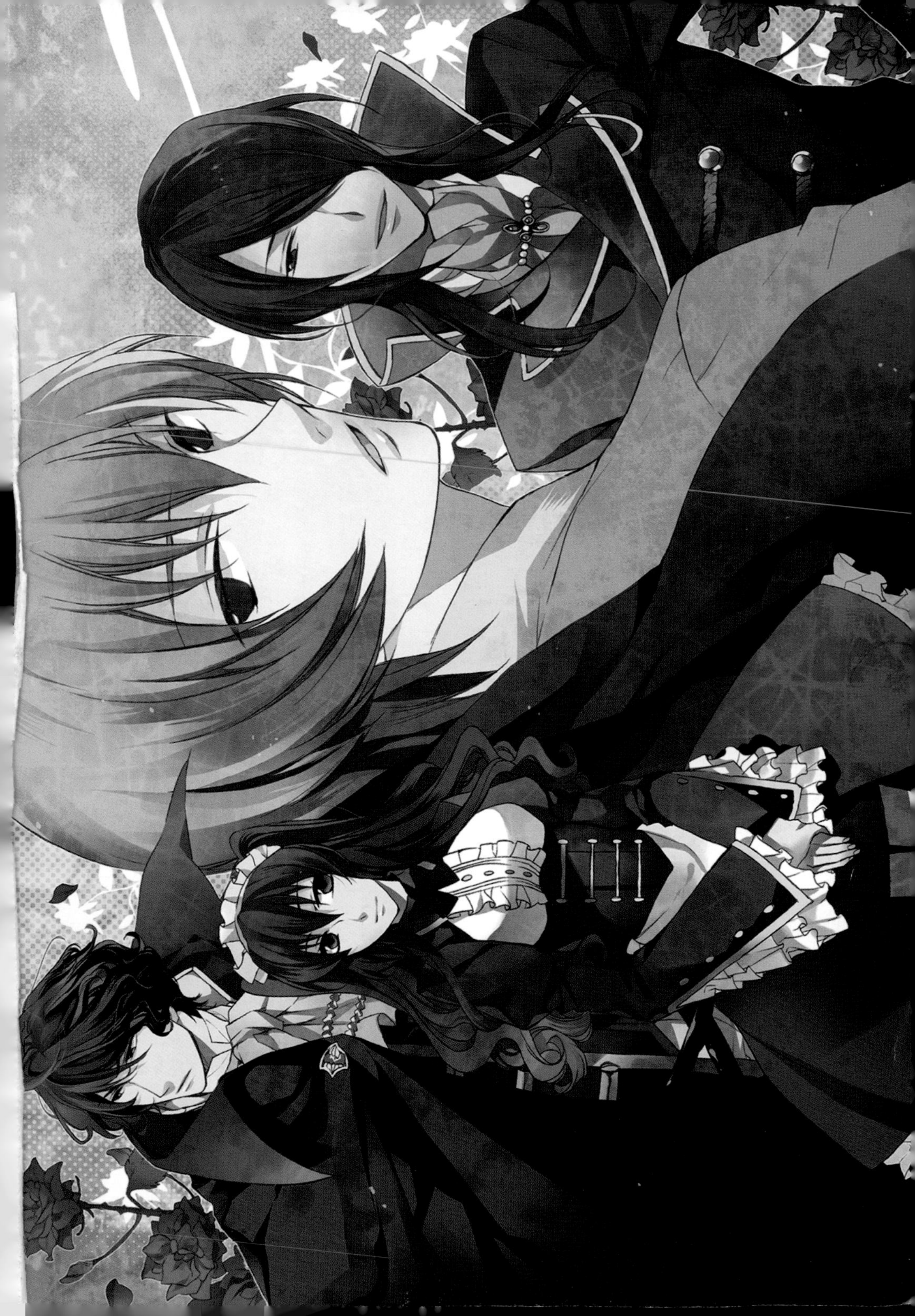

CRIMSON EMPIRE

クリムゾン・エンパイア

~ Circumstances to serve a noble ~

We devote our life proudly.
my life for you. For all you.

Quin Rose 2008

- STORY -

The setting is a country of aristocrats: a tributary nation for Luxonne. *Crimson Empire* is a love adventure game about a maid, Sheila, who works in the luxurious royal castle. But behind the lavish façade, the castle is home to a savage—and bloody—political war.

Strong and skilled, Sheila uses her position as a maid to hide her true profession: bodyguard to Prince Edvard. Sheila carries a dark past of enslavement and murder. Now she survives day to day, with only a small wish in her heart.

While navigating the power struggle between Prince Edvard and his brother, the deceptive Prince Justin, Sheila must understand and use the dangerous people who surround her. But although a brilliant fighter and tactician, Sheila is unskilled when it comes to love and friendships. Such a gap between her power and her heart could lead to a dire ending indeed!

Crimson Empire Character Information

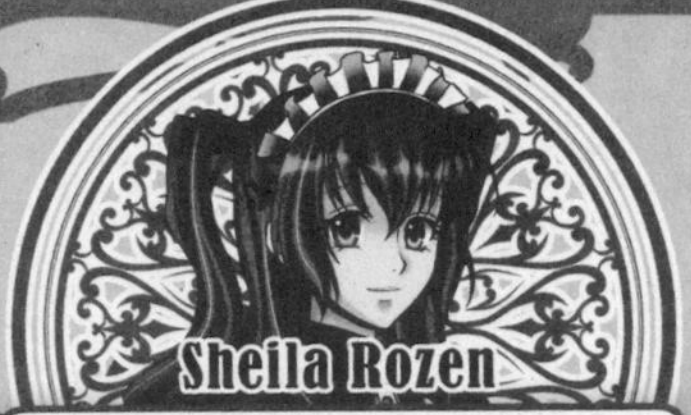

Sheila Rozen

The intensely loyal head maid to Prince Edvard—and his secret bodyguard. She's a skilled leader and shrewdly political, in addition to being fierce in combat. She doesn't hide her roots as a slave.

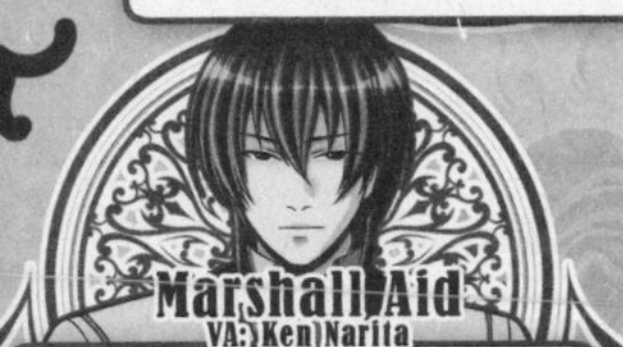

Marshall Aid

VA: Ken Narita

Prince Justin's head servant. He argues with Sheila in public but doesn't dislike her. In private, they're intimate enough to spar peacefully.

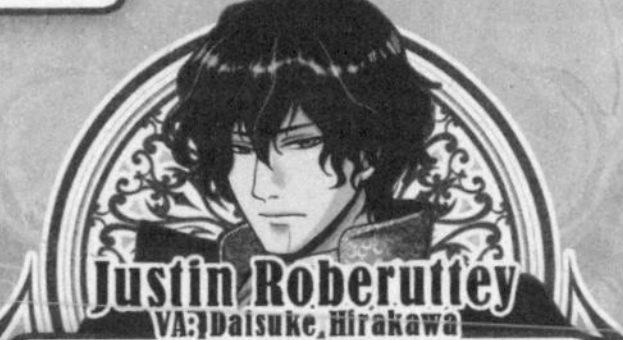

Justin Roberuttey

VA: Daisuke Hirakawa

The eldest prince, and Edvard's older half-brother. Since his mother is of lower status, Justin falls below his younger brother in line for the throne.

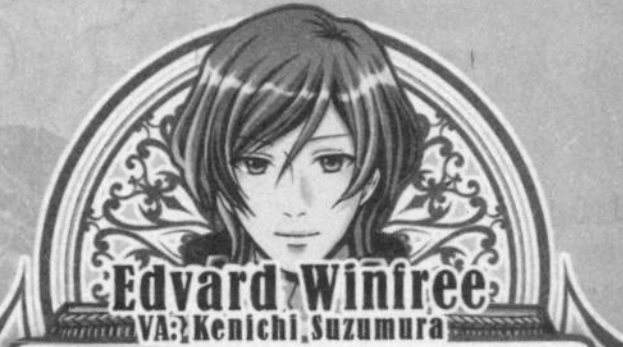

Edvard Winfree

VA: Kenichi Suzumura

Sheila's master. While friendly and regal on the surface, he's very condescending. He thinks of Sheila as more than a subordinate and loves her more than his own family... or so he *claims*.

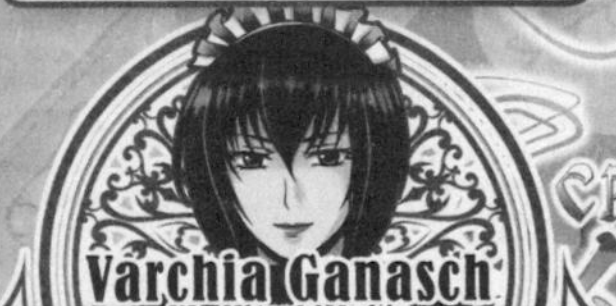

Varchia Ganasch

VA: Mitsuki Saiga

Varchia, the vice-maid, is a close friend of Sheila's, and is a former slave. Her actions and words are always painfully neutral. She's trustworthy and helps Sheila in both public and private.

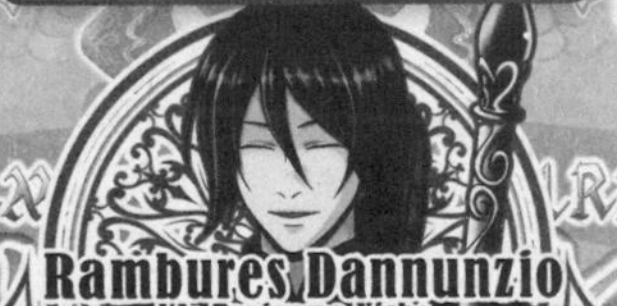

Rambures Dannunzio

VA: Taniyama Kisho

A commoner who was knighted after saving the king. He loves to lurk in his room and brew concoctions—which often stink and explode—instead of interacting with the nobility.

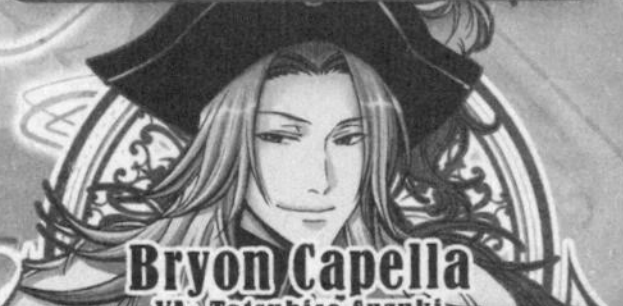

Bryon Capella

VA: Tatsuhisa Suzuki

Son of the marquis who one day will inherit the position and become an important pillar of the country. He seems cheerful and carefree, but rather guarded. Like his sister, he adores Sheila.

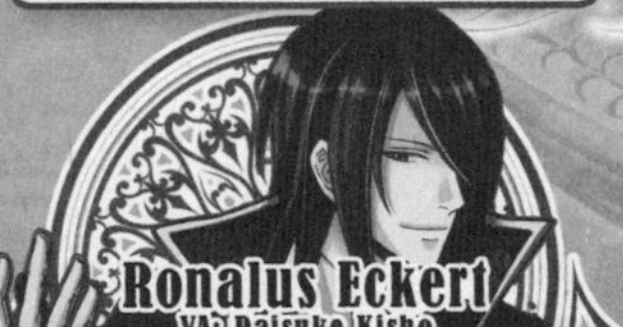

Ronalus Eckert

VA: Daisuke Kisho

Another guest in the royal castle, Ronalus is the servant to the Queen of Luxonne. Although he enjoys a higher status by serving the queen, he has a good relationship with other servants. His role is to monitor Meissen.

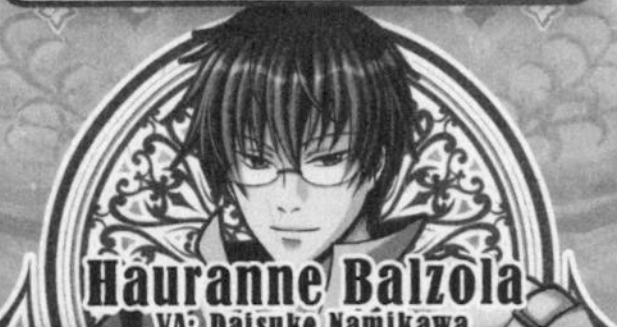

Hauranne Balzola

VA: Daisuke Namikawa

A wizard staying in the royal castle who is treated as a guest, but he's been in the castle longer than anyone. He's lived a *long* life...and his real age doesn't match his looks.

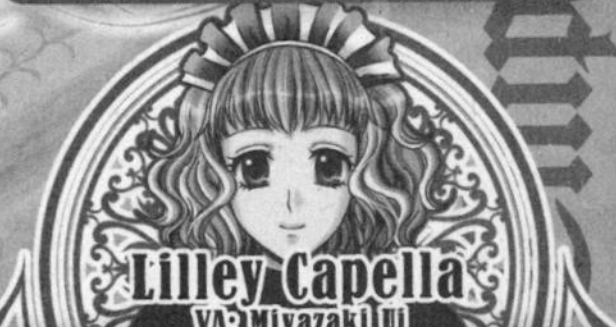

Lilley Capella

VA: Miyazaki Ui

Another battle maid, but of noble birth, Lilley is fiercely loyal to Sheila. She has innate skill, and her strength is second only to Sheila's. She and her brother Bryon are very close.

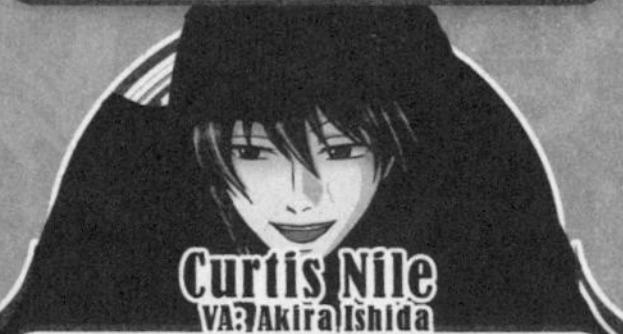

Curtis Nile

VA: Akira Ishida

A deadly assassin who specializes in poisons. He raised Sheila, and nearly killed her with his vicious training. Ever since, their relationship has been strained, to say the least.

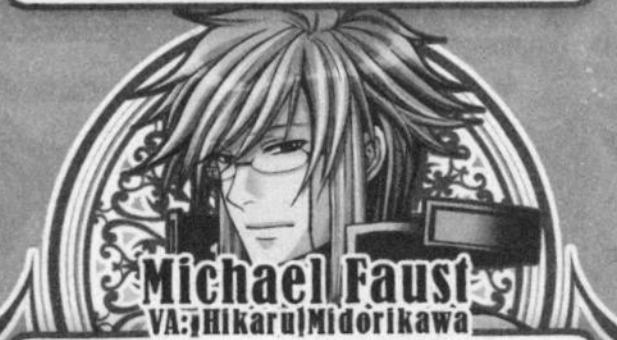

Michael Faust

VA: Hikaru Midorikawa

A demon who made a contract with Meissen. He's dangerously strong, monologues frequently, and is oddly nervous. His mental instability feeds his pessimism.

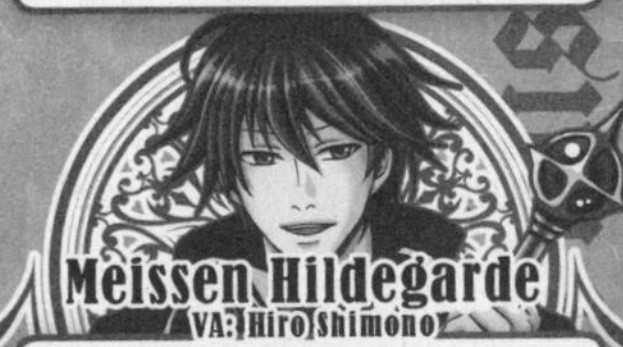

Meissen Hildegarde

VA: Hiro Shimono

Meissen has a tendency to wander, and he's traveled all over the world. His ladykiller persona hides a powerful wizard. He's searching for the truth and is trying to become a sage...supposedly.

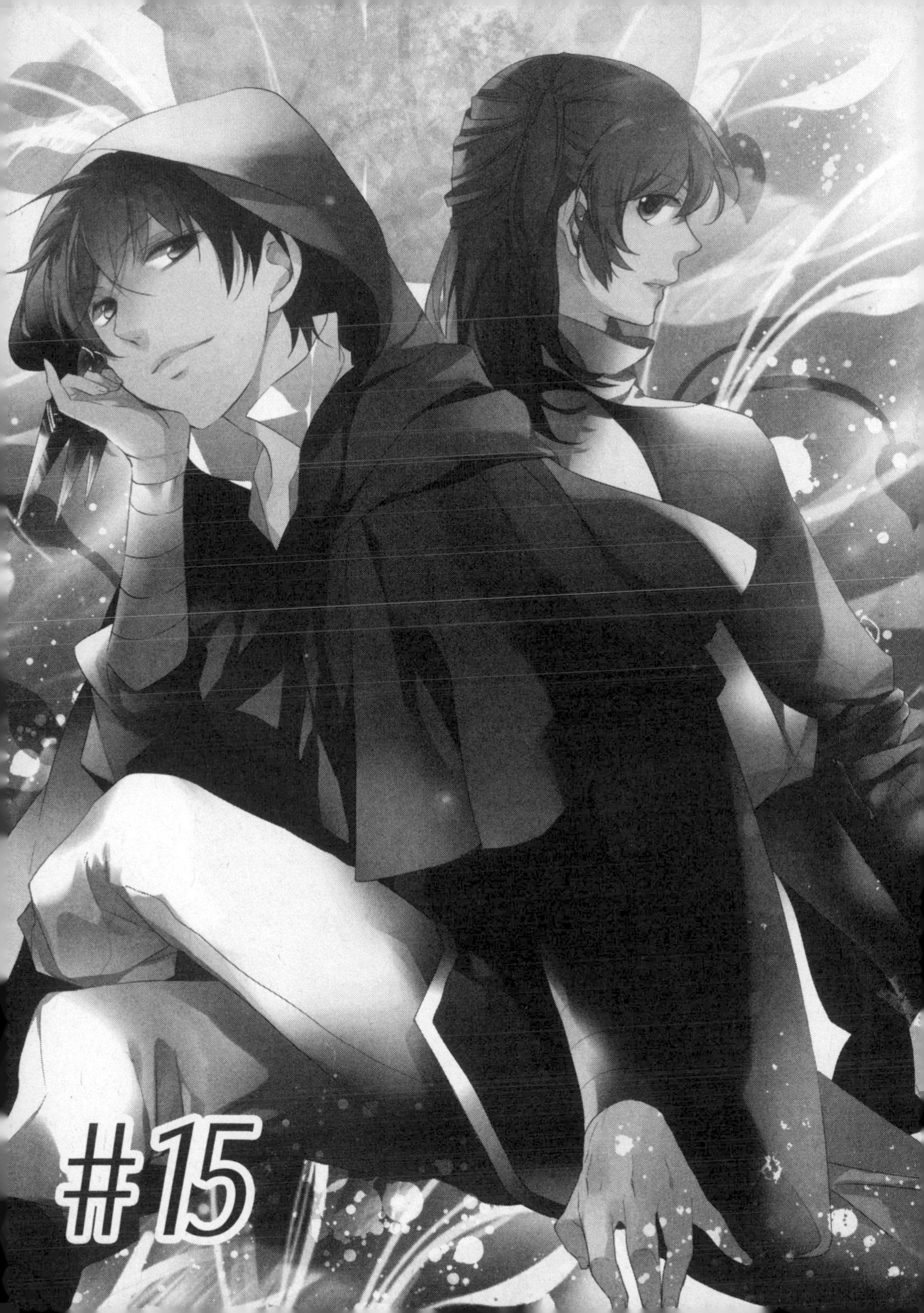
#15

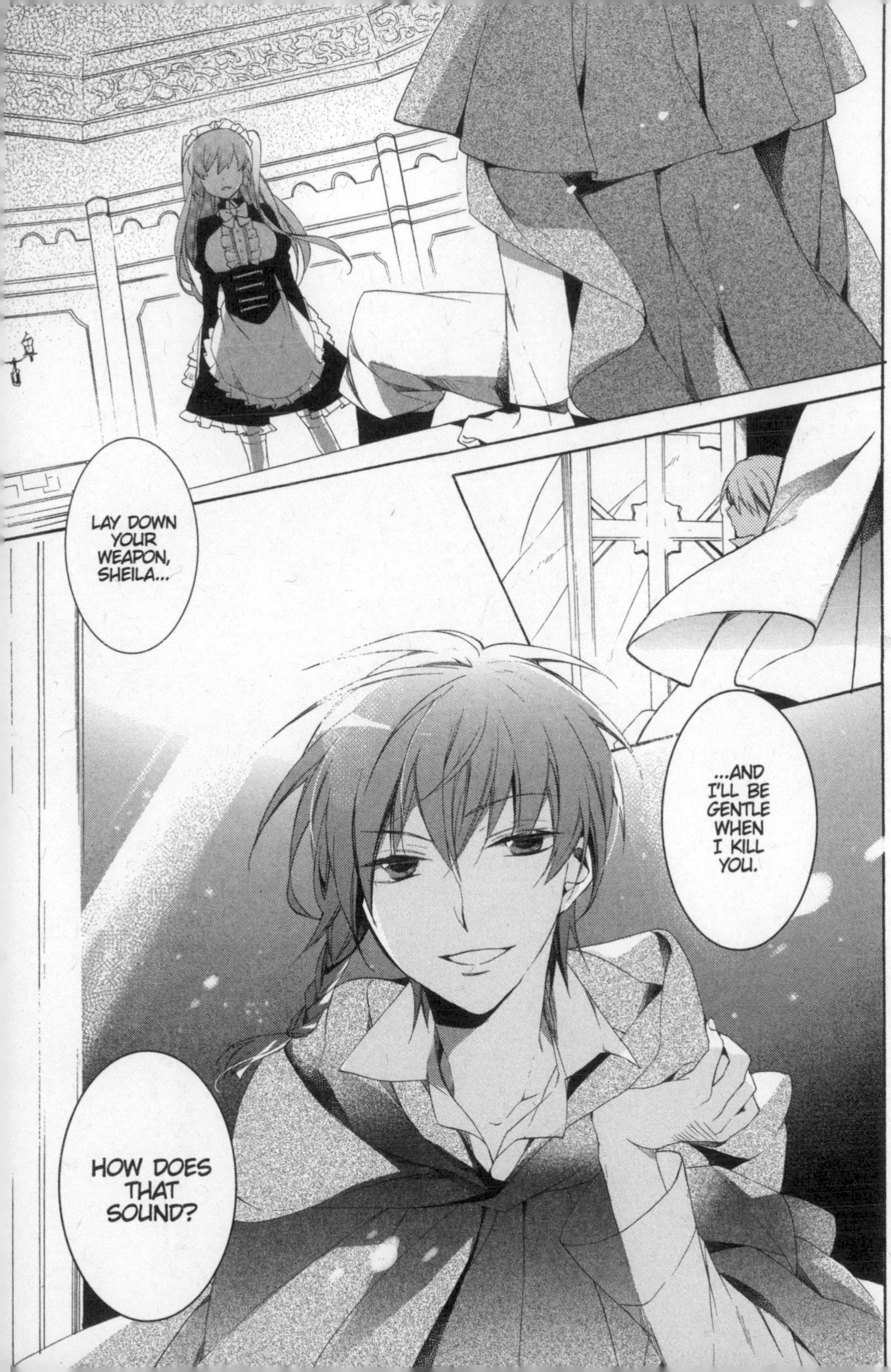
LAY DOWN YOUR WEAPON, SHEILA...
...AND I'LL BE GENTLE WHEN I KILL YOU.
HOW DOES THAT SOUND?

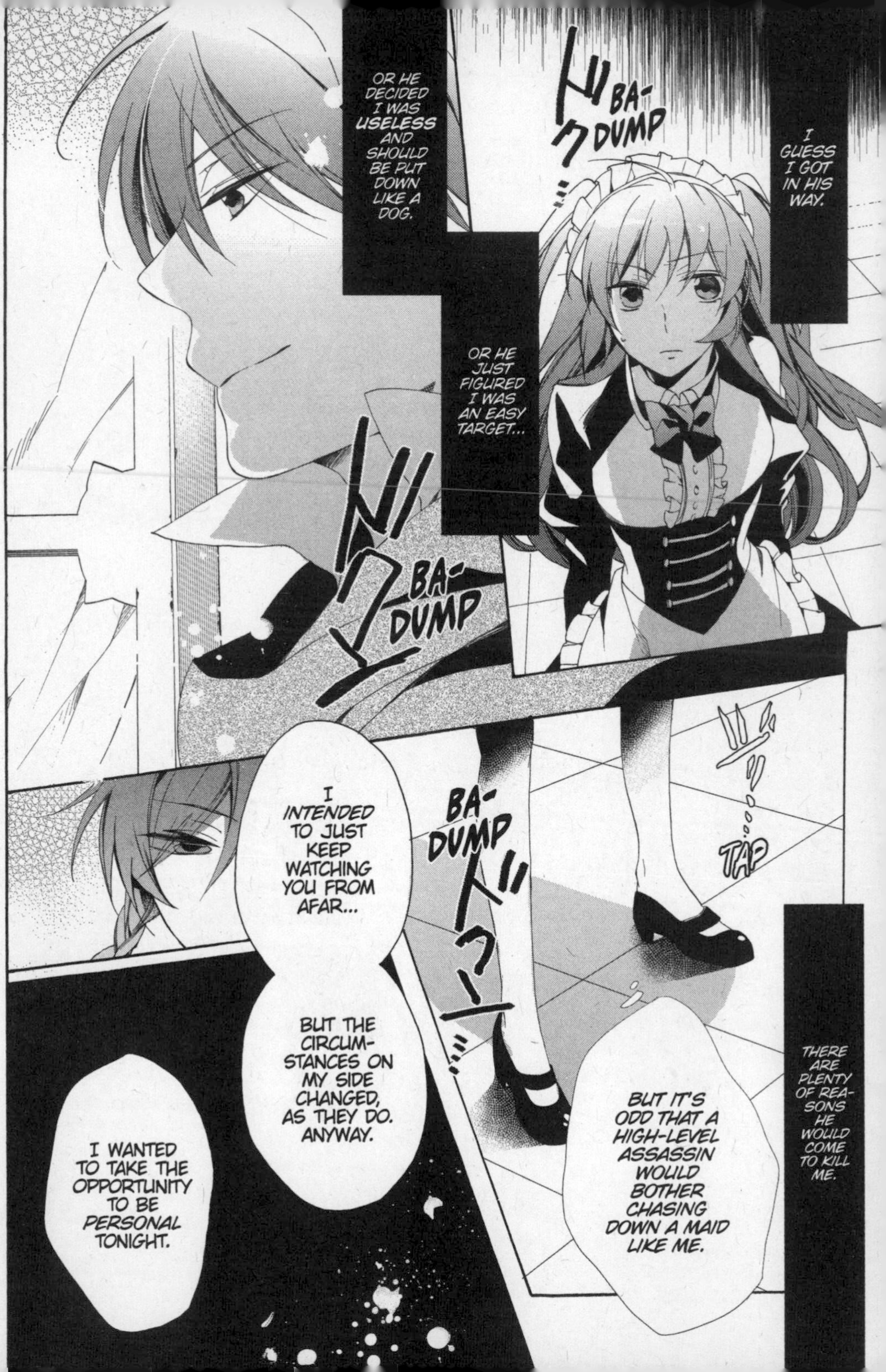

I GUESS I GOT IN HIS WAY.
BA-DUMP
OR HE DECIDED I WAS USELESS AND SHOULD BE PUT DOWN LIKE A DOG.
OR HE JUST FIGURED I WAS AN EASY TARGET...
BA-DUMP
THERE ARE PLENTY OF REA-SONS HE WOULD COME TO KILL ME.
BUT IT'S ODD THAT A HIGH-LEVEL ASSASSIN WOULD BOTHER CHASING DOWN A MAID LIKE ME.
TAP
BA-DUMP
I INTENDED TO JUST KEEP WATCHING YOU FROM AFAR...
BUT THE CIRCUM-STANCES ON MY SIDE CHANGED, AS THEY DO. ANYWAY.
I WANTED TO TAKE THE OPPORTUNITY TO BE PERSONAL TONIGHT.

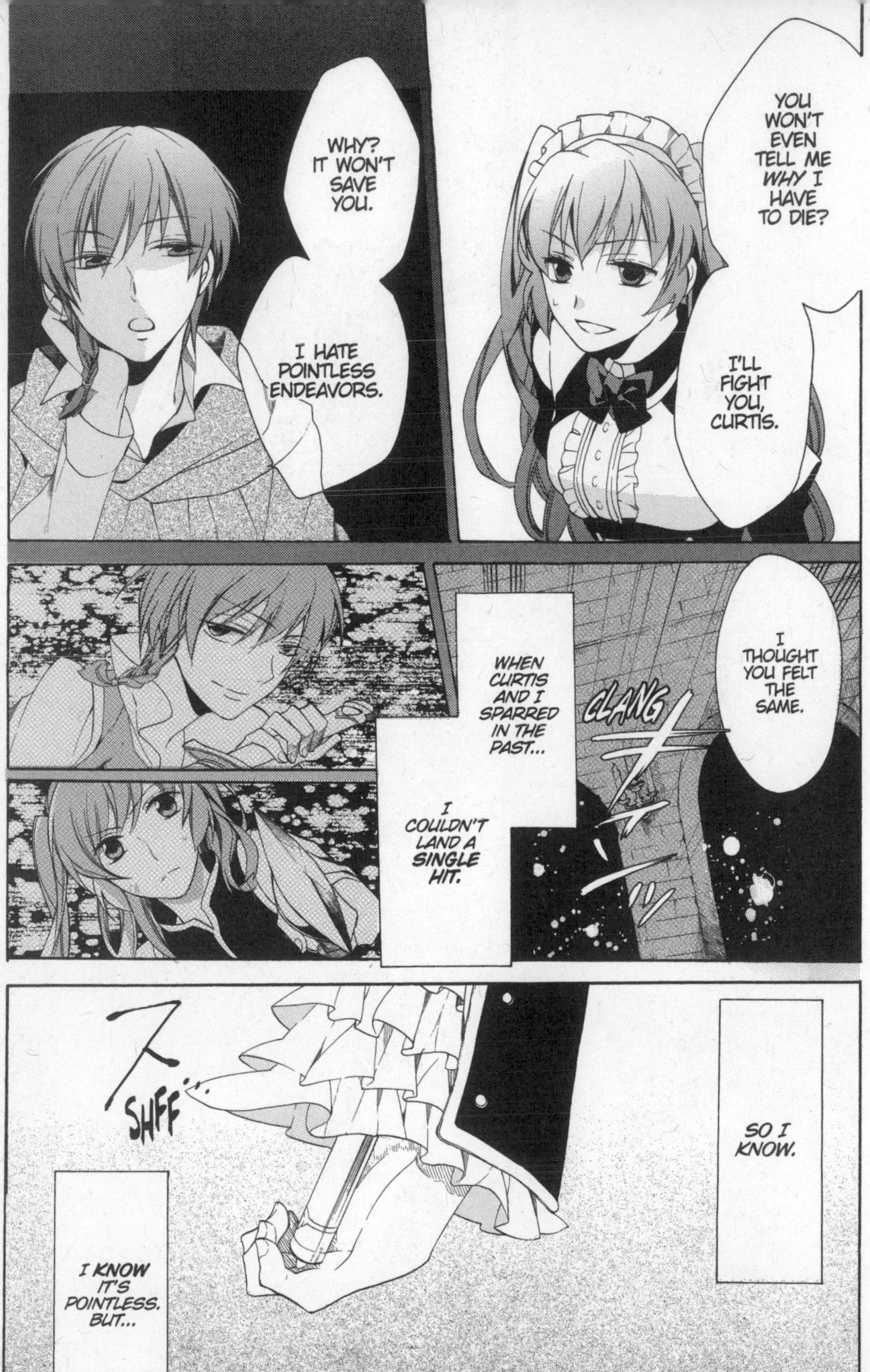
YOU WON'T EVEN TELL ME *WHY* I HAVE TO DIE?
I'LL FIGHT YOU, CURTIS.
WHY? IT WON'T SAVE YOU.
I HATE POINTLESS ENDEAVORS.
I THOUGHT YOU FELT THE SAME.
CLANG
WHEN CURTIS AND I SPARRED IN THE PAST...
I COULDN'T LAND A SINGLE HIT.
SO I KNOW.
SHFF
I KNOW IT'S POINTLESS. BUT...

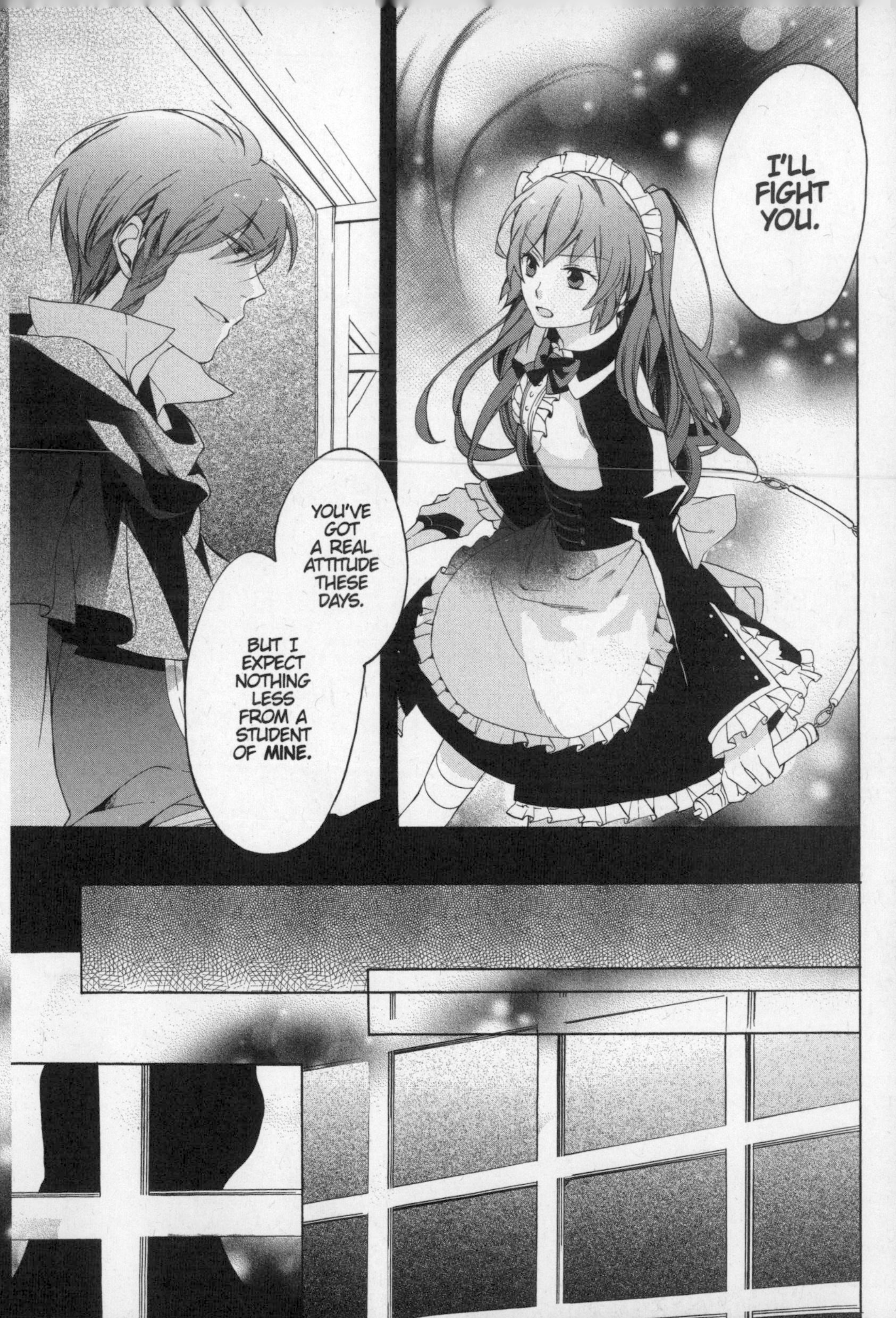
I'LL FIGHT YOU.
YOU'VE GOT A REAL ATTITUDE THESE DAYS.
BUT I EXPECT NOTHING LESS FROM A STUDENT OF MINE.

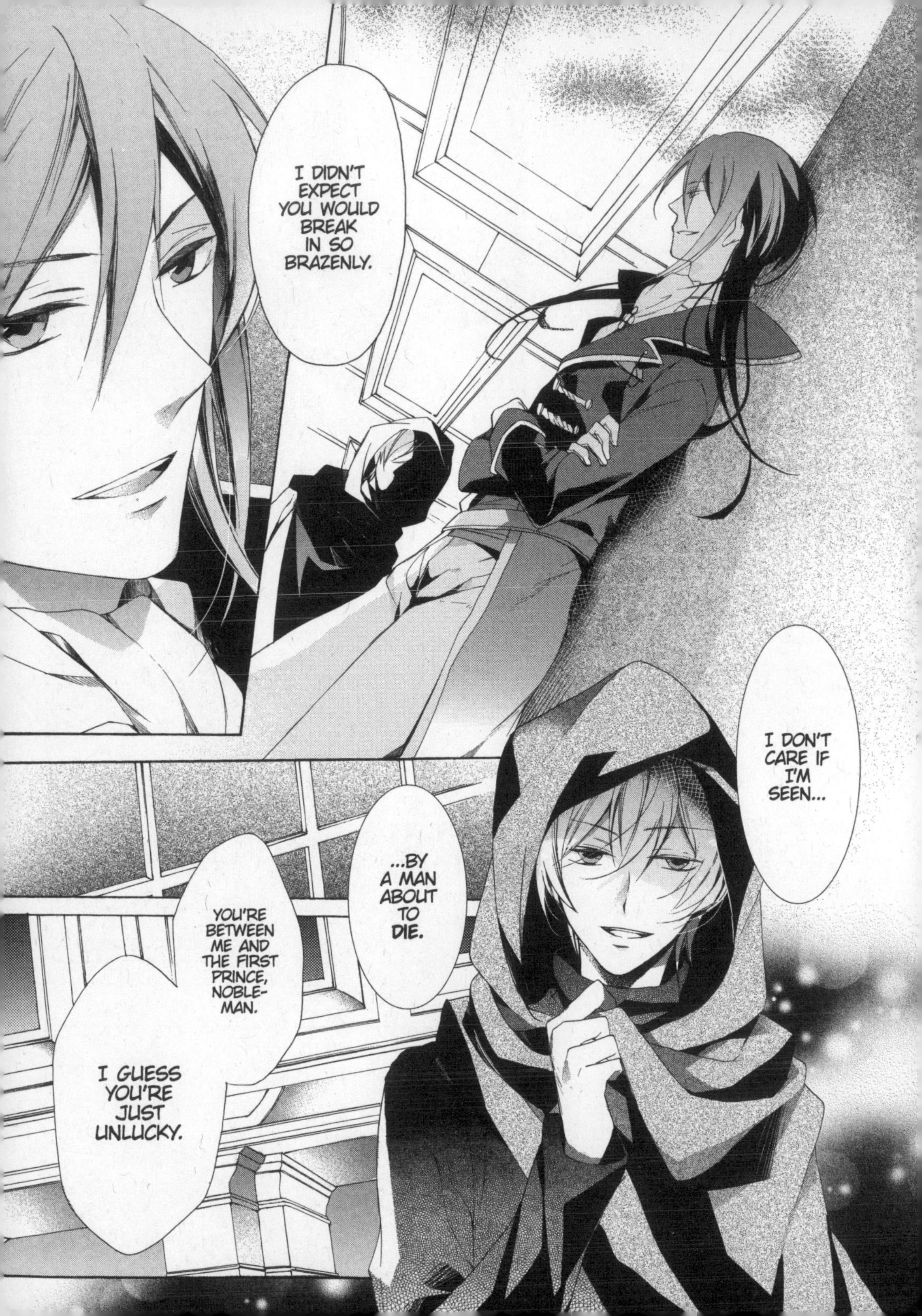
I DIDN'T EXPECT YOU WOULD BREAK IN SO BRAZENLY.
I DON'T CARE IF I'M SEEN...
...BY A MAN ABOUT TO DIE.
YOU'RE BETWEEN ME AND THE FIRST PRINCE, NOBLE-MAN.
I GUESS YOU'RE JUST UNLUCKY.

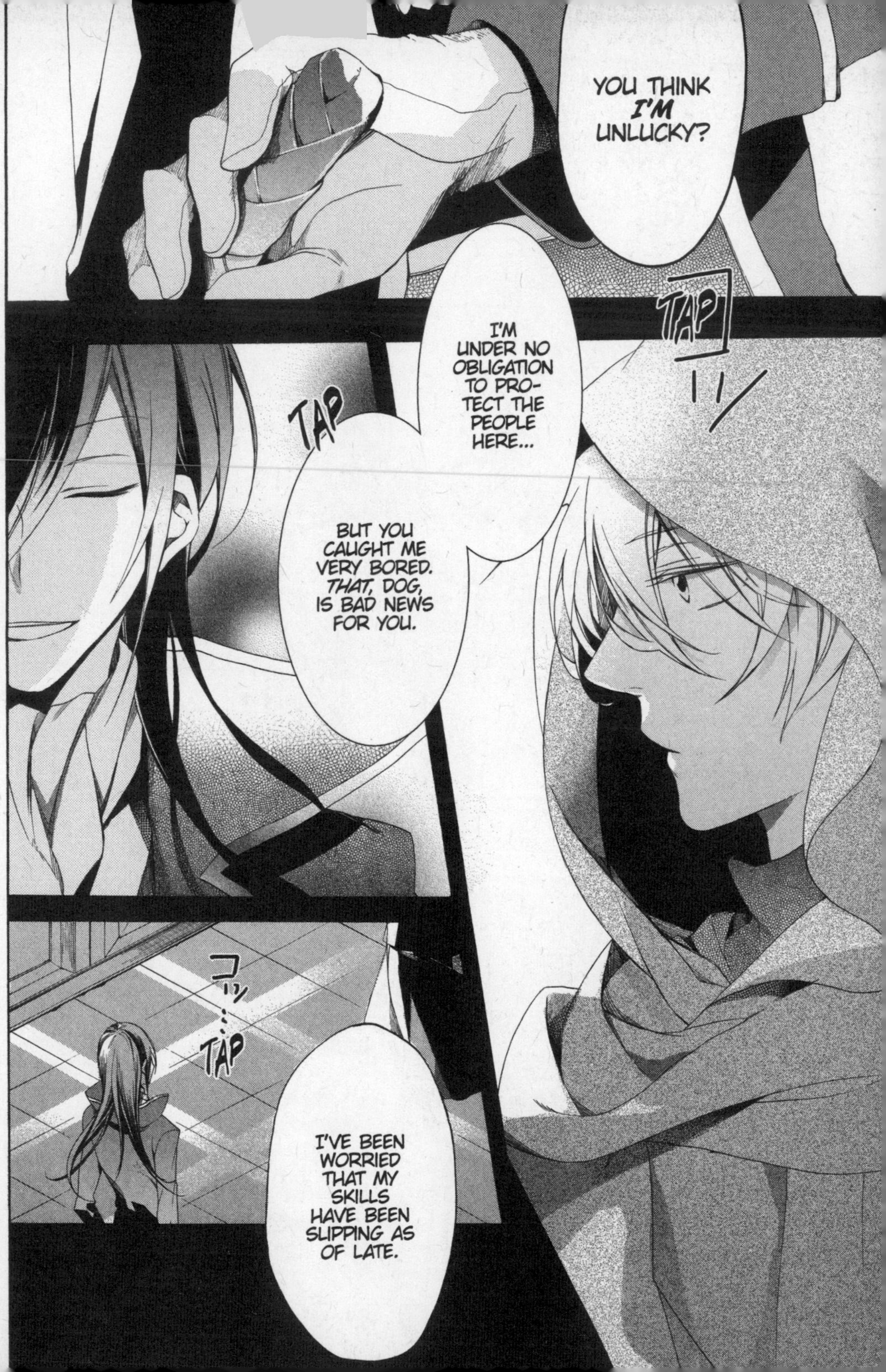
YOU THINK *I'M* UNLUCKY?
TAP
I'M UNDER NO OBLIGATION TO PRO-TECT THE PEOPLE HERE...
TAP
BUT YOU CAUGHT ME VERY BORED. *THAT*, DOG, IS BAD NEWS FOR YOU.
コッ
TAP
I'VE BEEN WORRIED THAT MY SKILLS HAVE BEEN SLIPPING AS OF LATE.

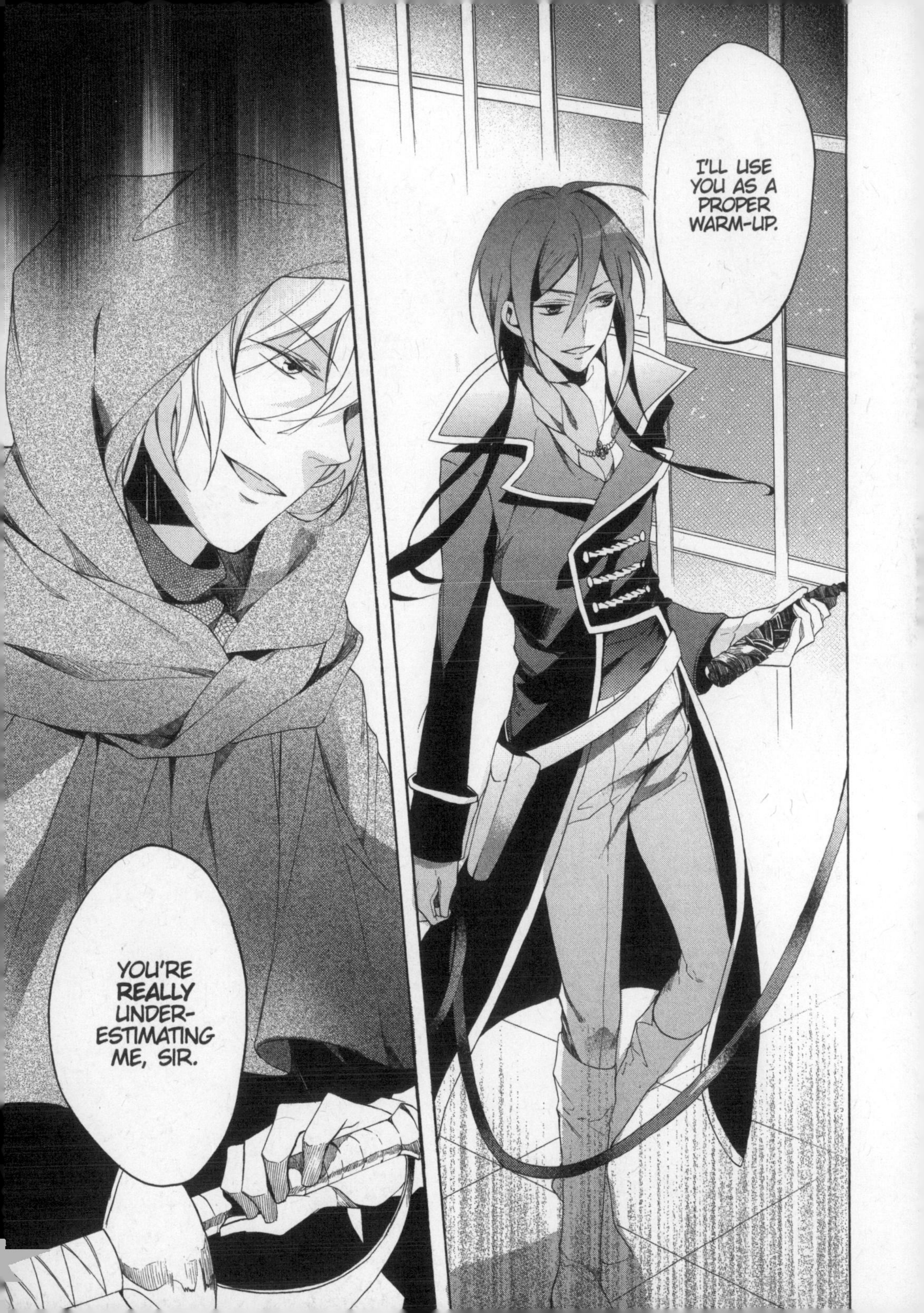
I'LL USE YOU AS A PROPER WARM-UP.
YOU'RE REALLY UNDER-ESTIMATING ME, SIR.

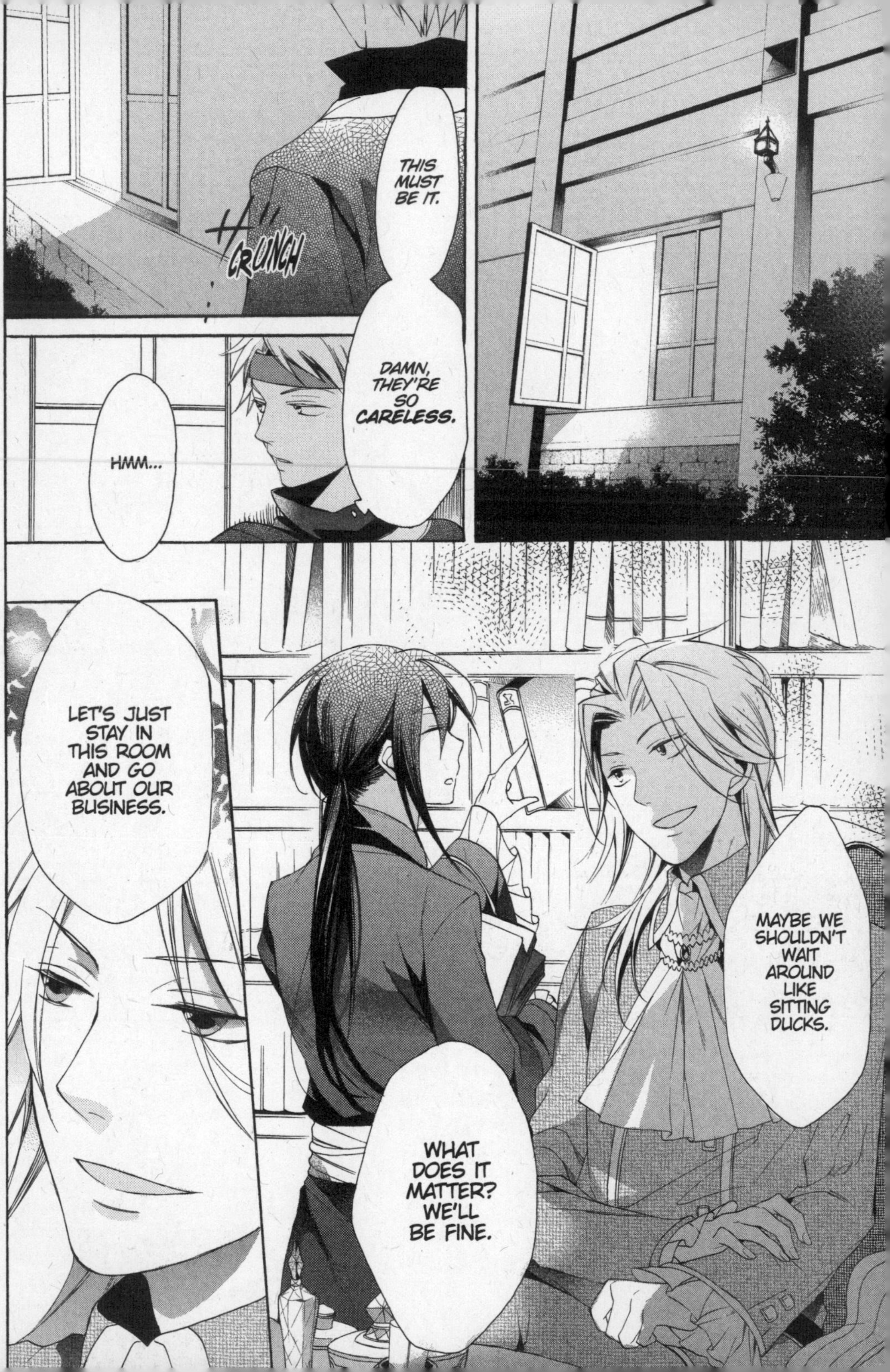
THIS MUST BE IT.
CRUNCH
DAMN, THEY'RE SO CARELESS.
HMM...
MAYBE WE SHOULDN'T WAIT AROUND LIKE SITTING DUCKS.
WHAT DOES IT MATTER? WE'LL BE FINE.
LET'S JUST STAY IN THIS ROOM AND GO ABOUT OUR BUSINESS.

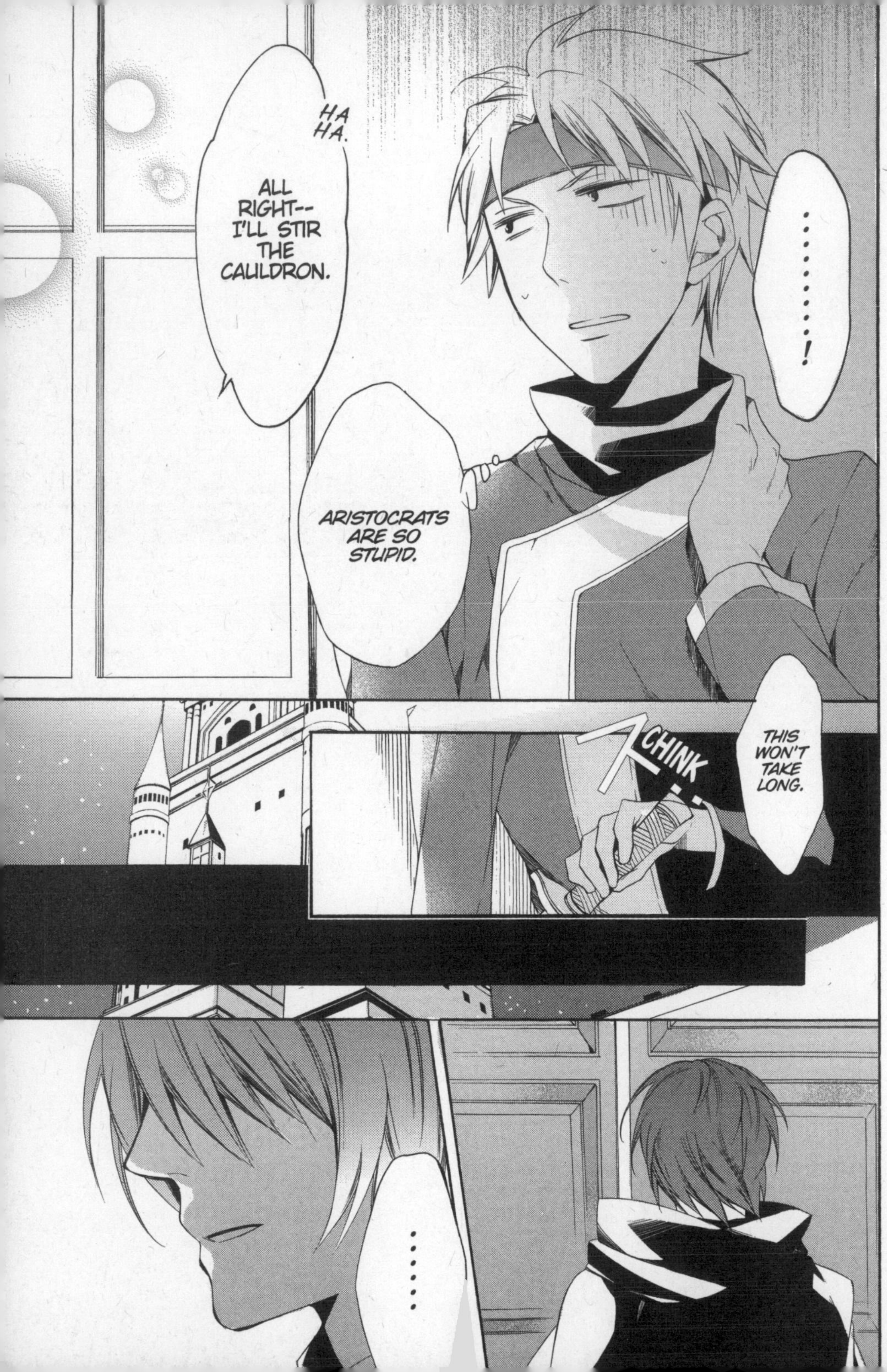

……!
ARISTOCRATS ARE SO STUPID.
HA HA.
ALL RIGHT-- I'LL STIR THE CAULDRON.
THIS WON'T TAKE LONG.
CHINK
……

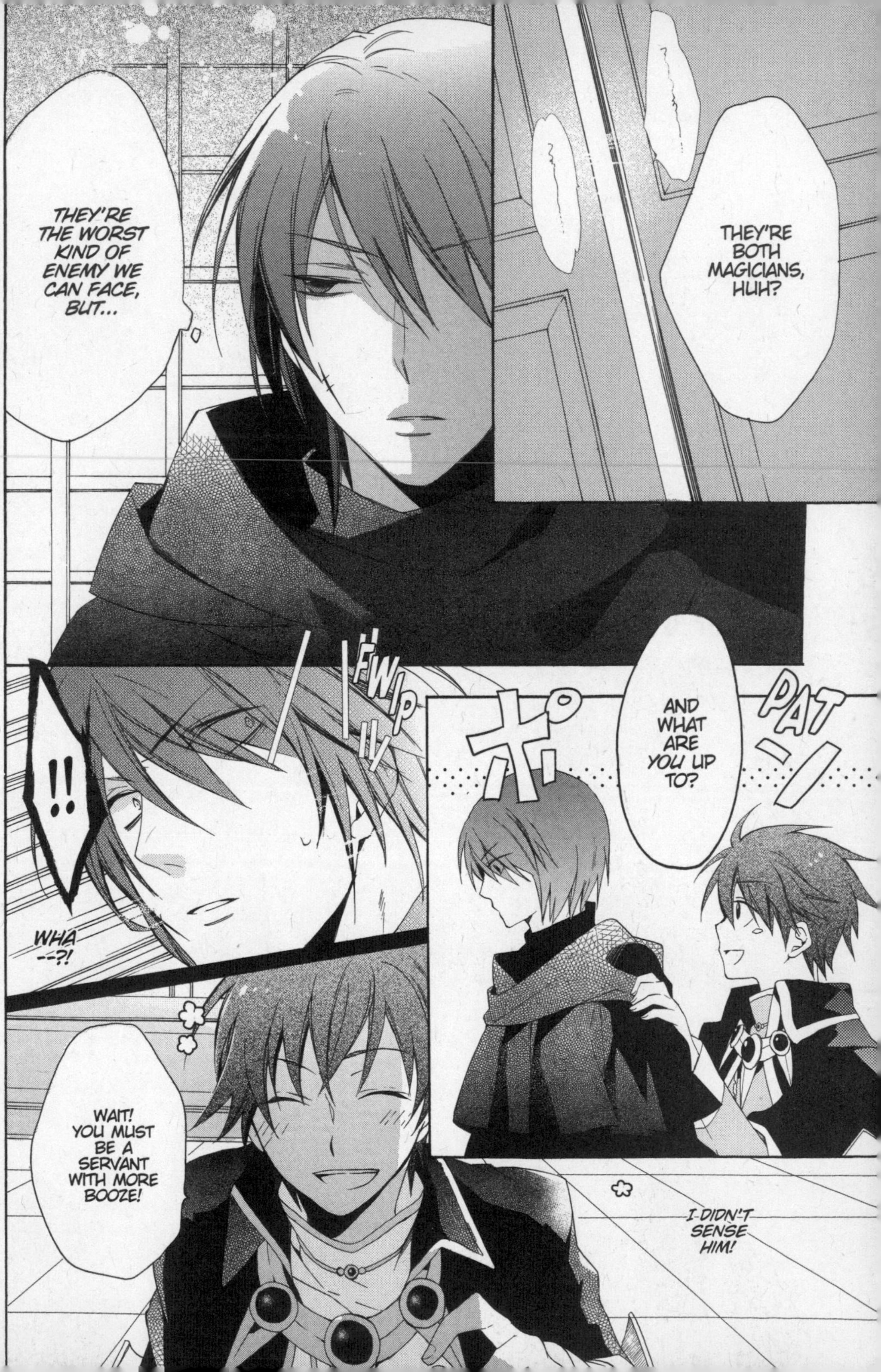

THEY'RE BOTH MAGICIANS, HUH?
THEY'RE THE WORST KIND OF ENEMY WE CAN FACE, BUT...
AND WHAT ARE YOU UP TO?
PAT
ポン
FWIP
!!
WHA--?!
I-DIDN'T SENSE HIM!
WAIT! YOU MUST BE A SERVANT WITH MORE BOOZE!

LEARN MORE

$35 million
raised for literacy

38 million
books donated

475 million
books reused or recycled

87 million
customers served

BUY BOOKS · DO GOOD · BUY BOOKS · DO GOOD ·

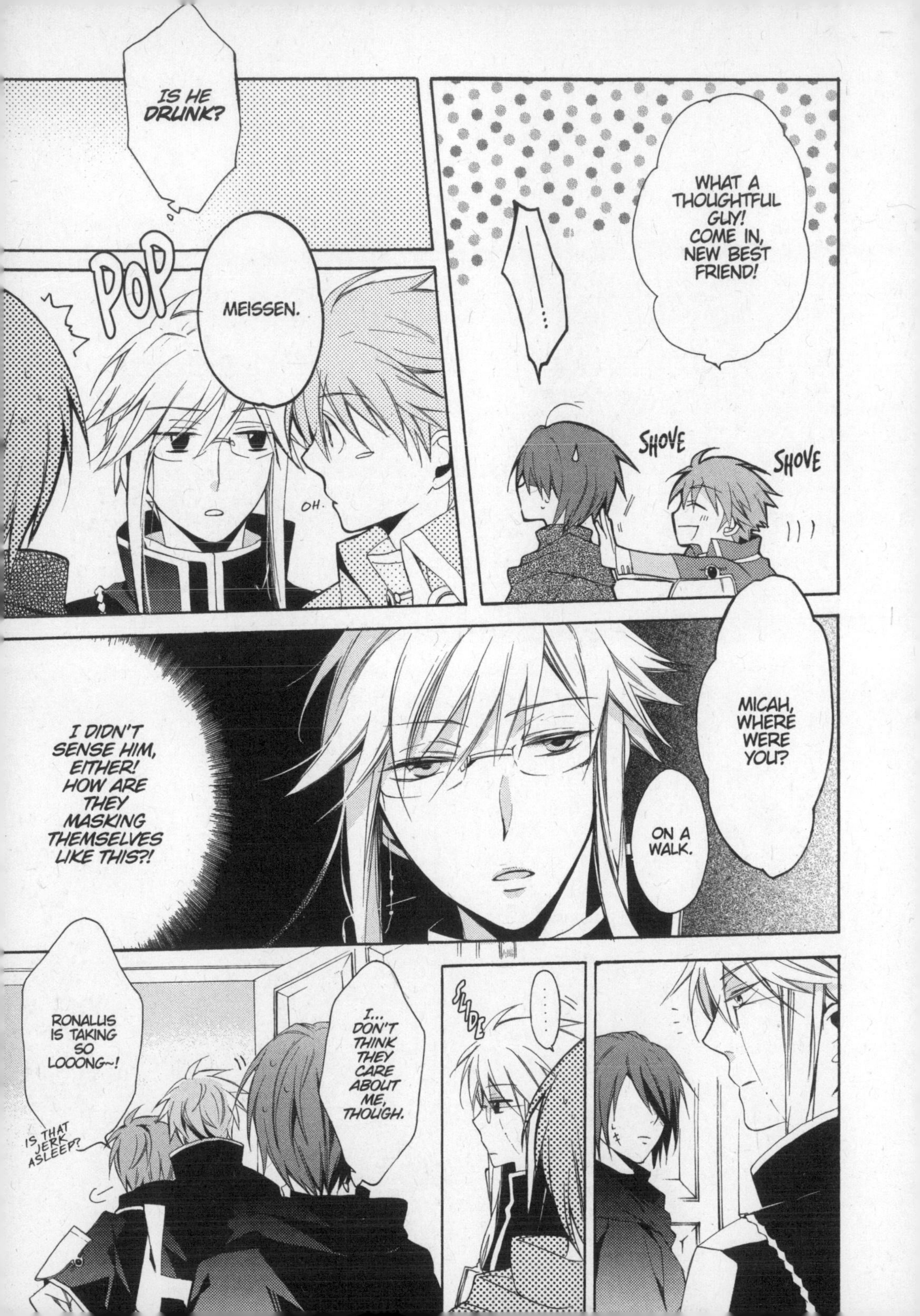
WHAT A THOUGHTFUL GUY! COME IN, NEW BEST FRIEND!
!
SHOVE
SHOVE
IS HE DRUNK?
POP
MEISSEN.
OH.
MICAH, WHERE WERE YOU?
ON A WALK.
I DIDN'T SENSE HIM, EITHER! HOW ARE THEY MASKING THEMSELVES LIKE THIS?!
......
SLIDE
I... DON'T THINK THEY CARE ABOUT ME, THOUGH.
RONALUS IS TAKING SO LOOONG~!
IS THAT JERK ASLEEP?

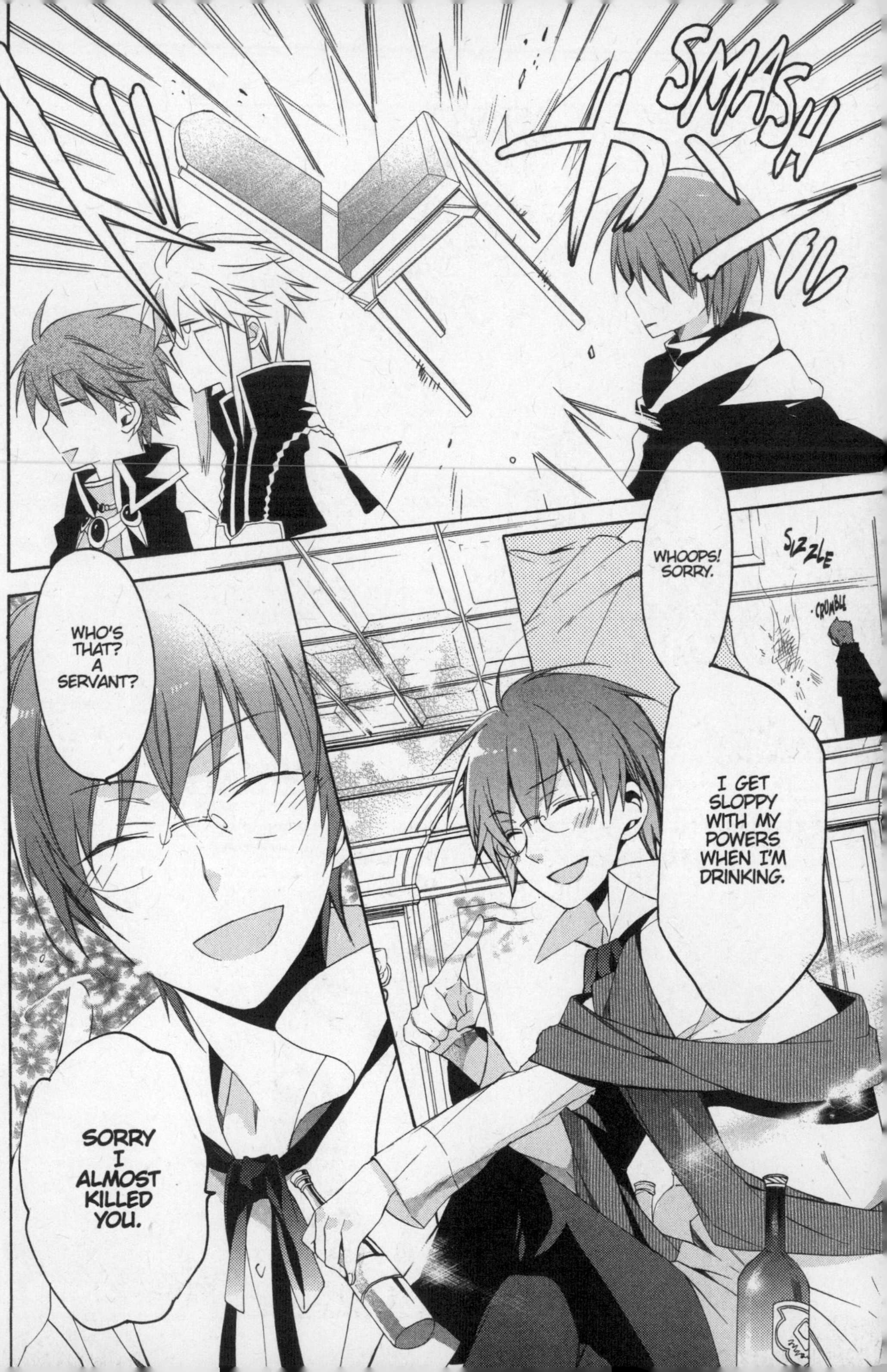
SMASH
WHOOPS! SORRY.
SIZZLE
CRUMBLE
I GET SLOPPY WITH MY POWERS WHEN I'M DRINKING.
WHO'S THAT? A SERVANT?
SORRY I ALMOST KILLED YOU.

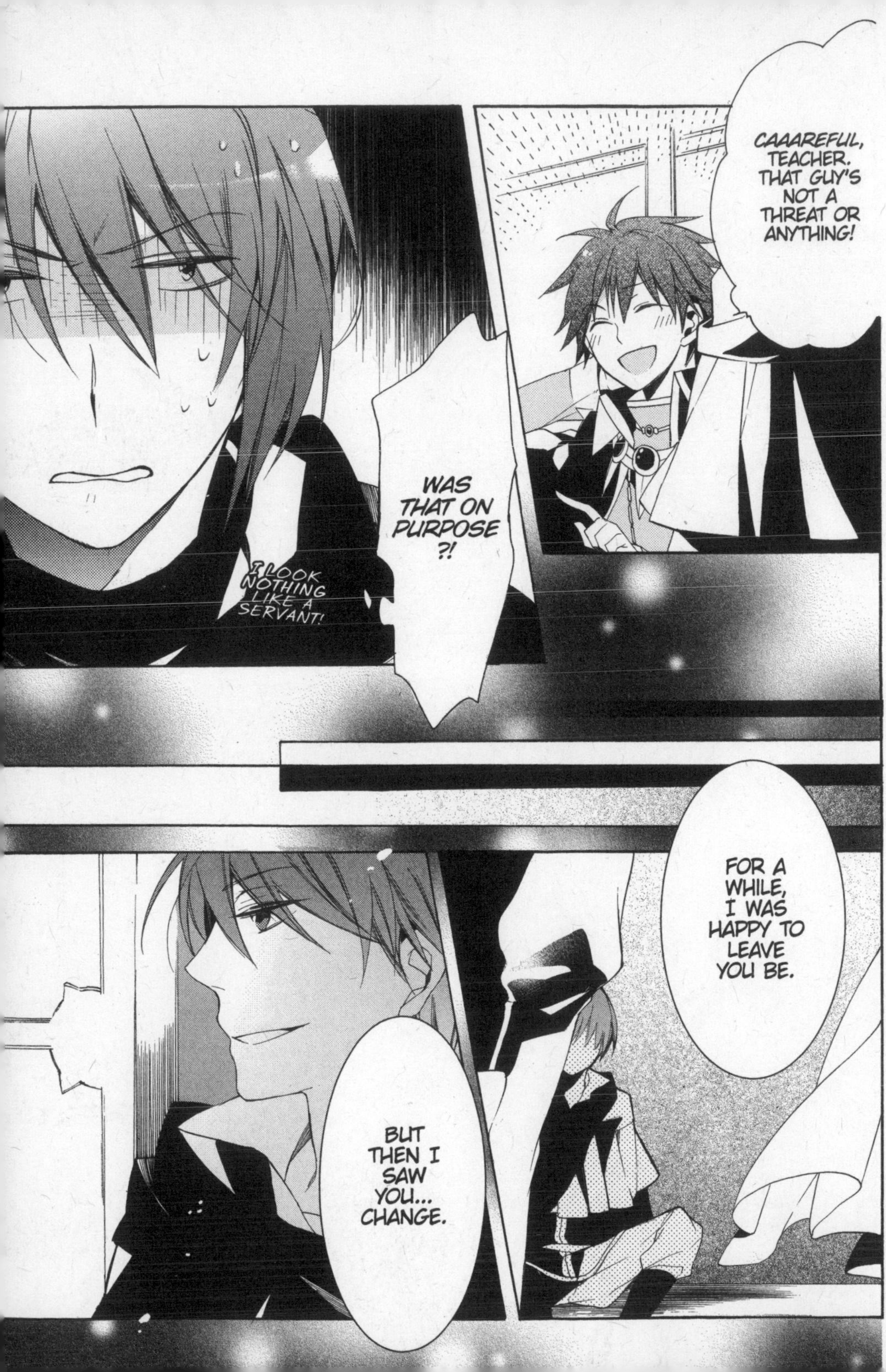
CAAAREFUL, TEACHER. THAT GUY'S NOT A THREAT OR ANYTHING!
WAS THAT ON PURPOSE ?!
I LOOK NOTHING LIKE A SERVANT!
FOR A WHILE, I WAS HAPPY TO LEAVE YOU BE.
BUT THEN I SAW YOU... CHANGE.

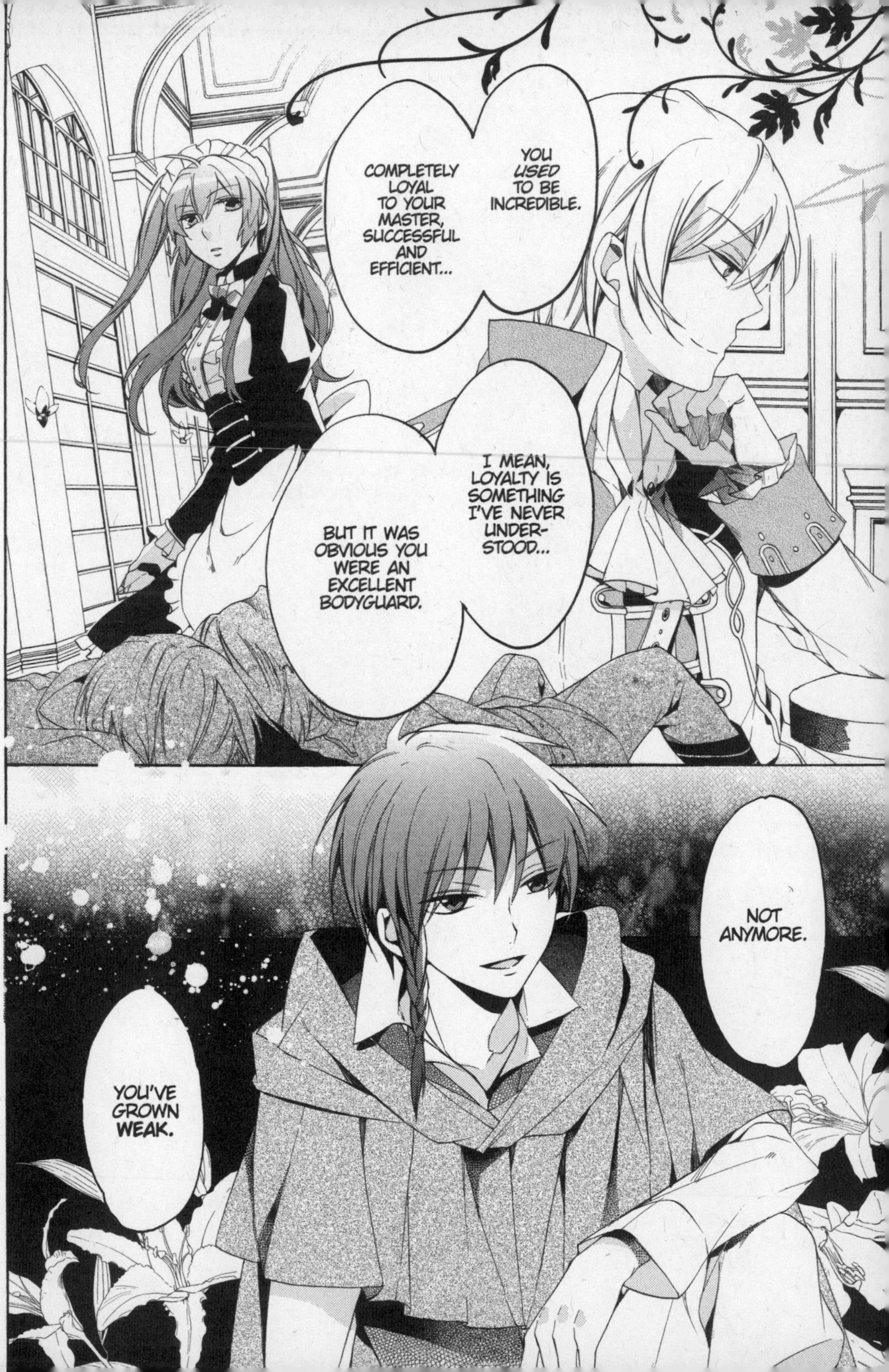
YOU USED TO BE INCREDIBLE.
COMPLETELY LOYAL TO YOUR MASTER, SUCCESSFUL AND EFFICIENT...
I MEAN, LOYALTY IS SOMETHING I'VE NEVER UNDER-STOOD...
BUT IT WAS OBVIOUS YOU WERE AN EXCELLENT BODYGUARD.
NOT ANYMORE.
YOU'VE GROWN WEAK.

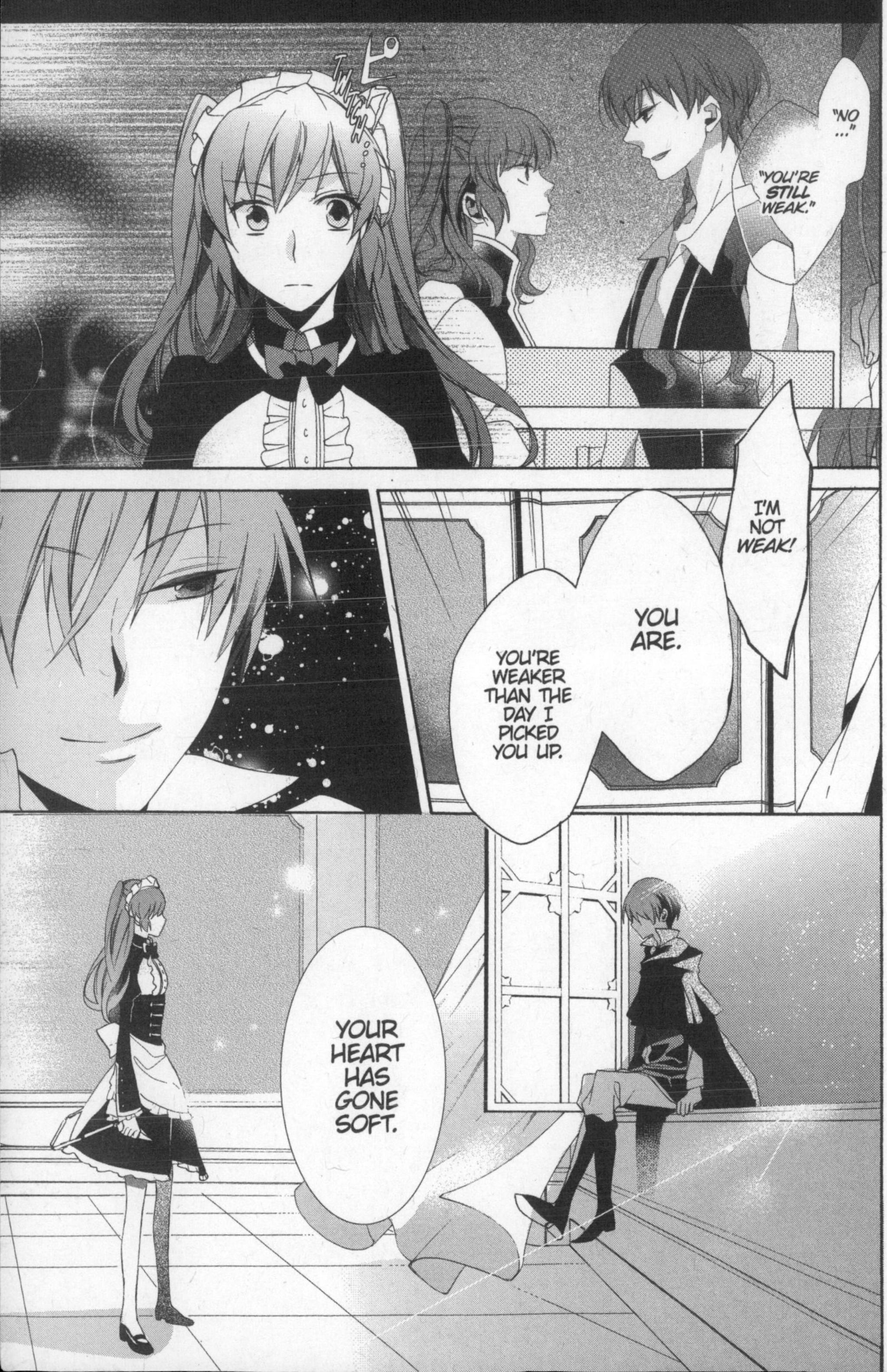
"NO..."
"YOU'RE STILL WEAK."
ピ
TWITCH
I'M NOT WEAK!
YOU ARE.
YOU'RE WEAKER THAN THE DAY I PICKED YOU UP.
YOUR HEART HAS GONE SOFT.

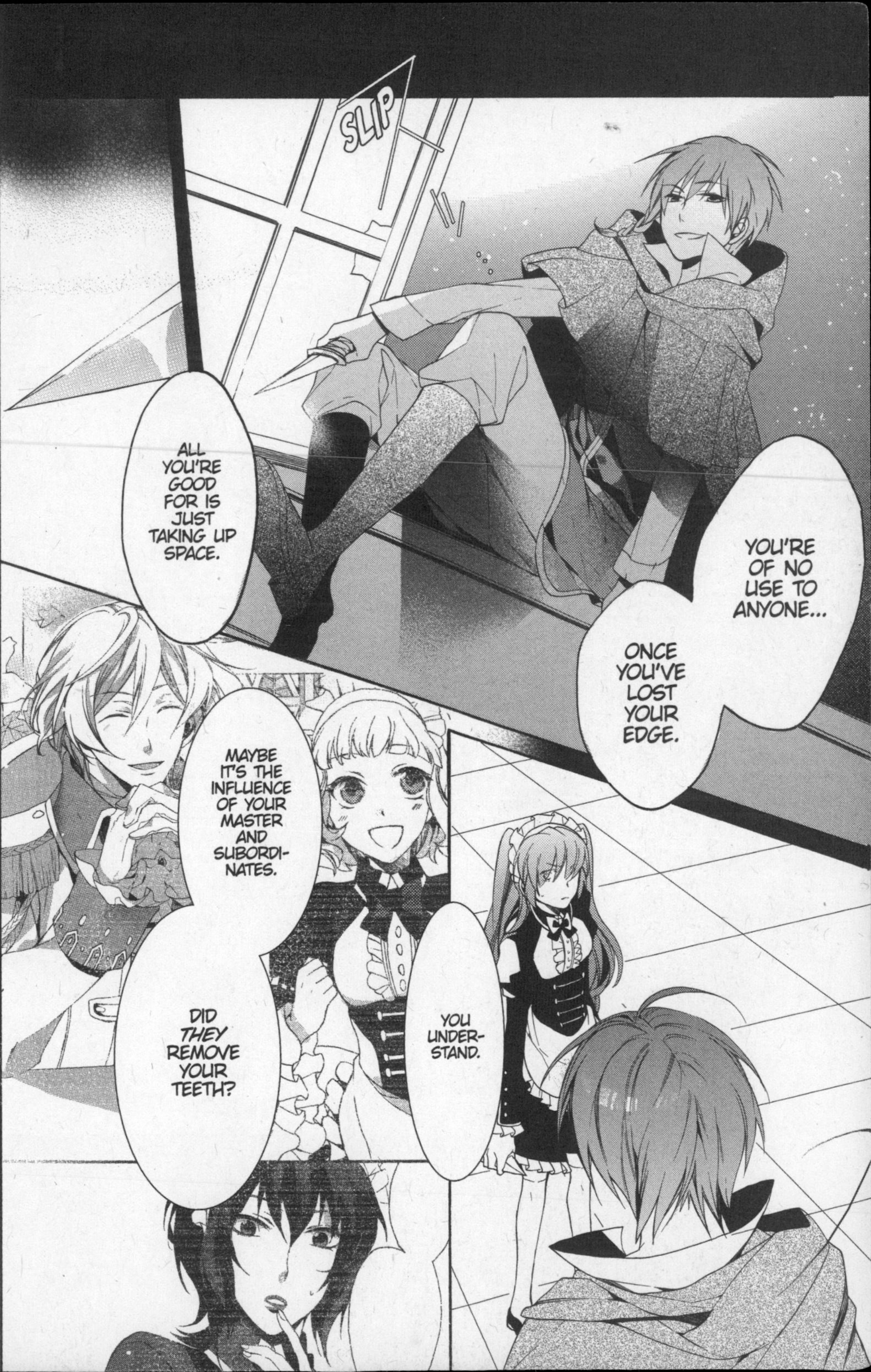
SLIP
YOU'RE OF NO USE TO ANYONE...
ONCE YOU'VE LOST YOUR EDGE.
ALL YOU'RE GOOD FOR IS JUST TAKING UP SPACE.
YOU UNDERSTAND.
MAYBE IT'S THE INFLUENCE OF YOUR MASTER AND SUBORDINATES.
DID *THEY* REMOVE YOUR TEETH?

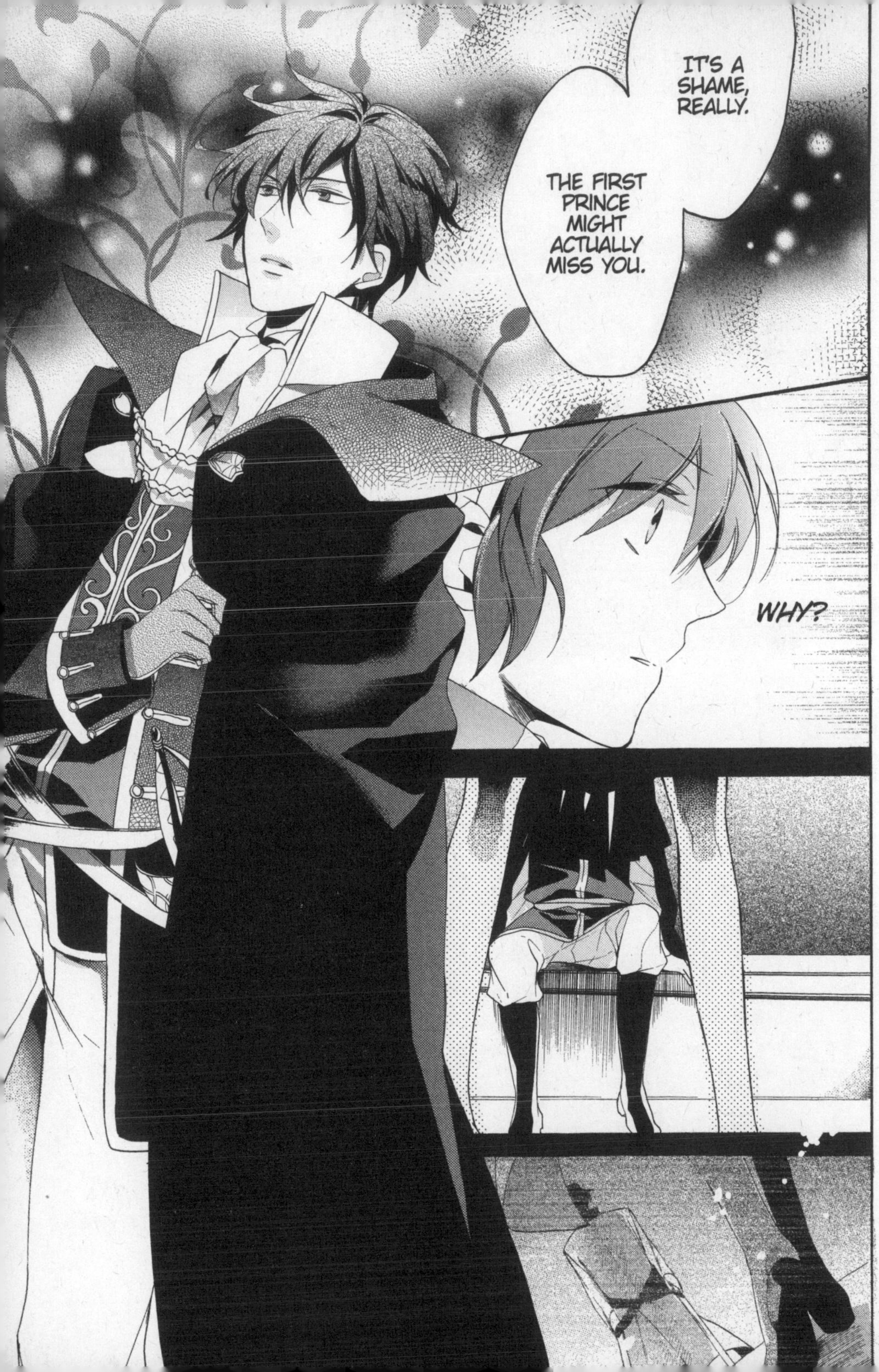
IT'S A SHAME, REALLY.
THE FIRST PRINCE MIGHT ACTUALLY MISS YOU.
WHY?

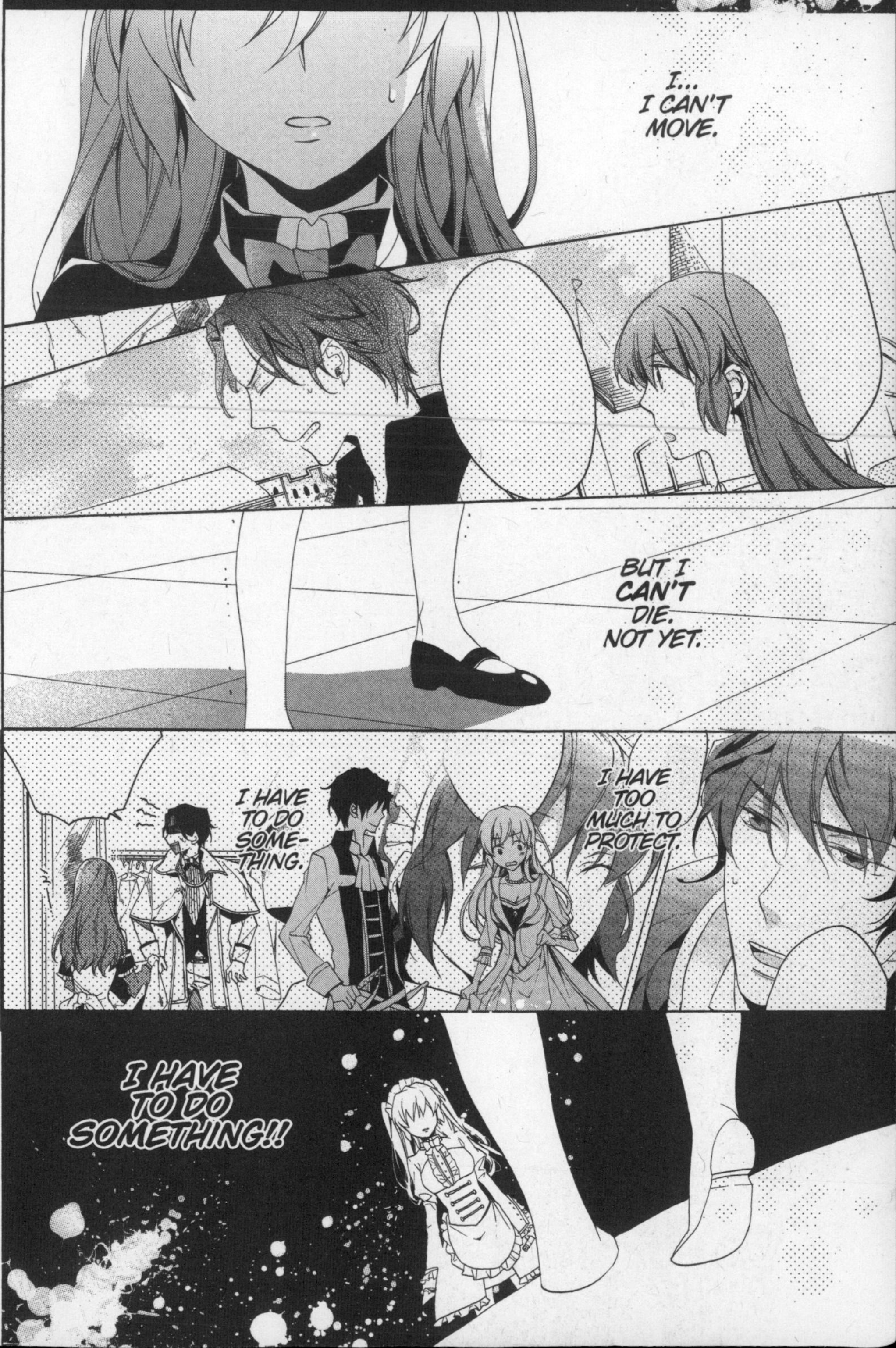
I... I CAN'T MOVE.
BUT I CAN'T DIE. NOT YET.
I HAVE TOO MUCH TO PROTECT.
I HAVE TO DO SOME-THING.
I HAVE TO DO SOMETHING!!

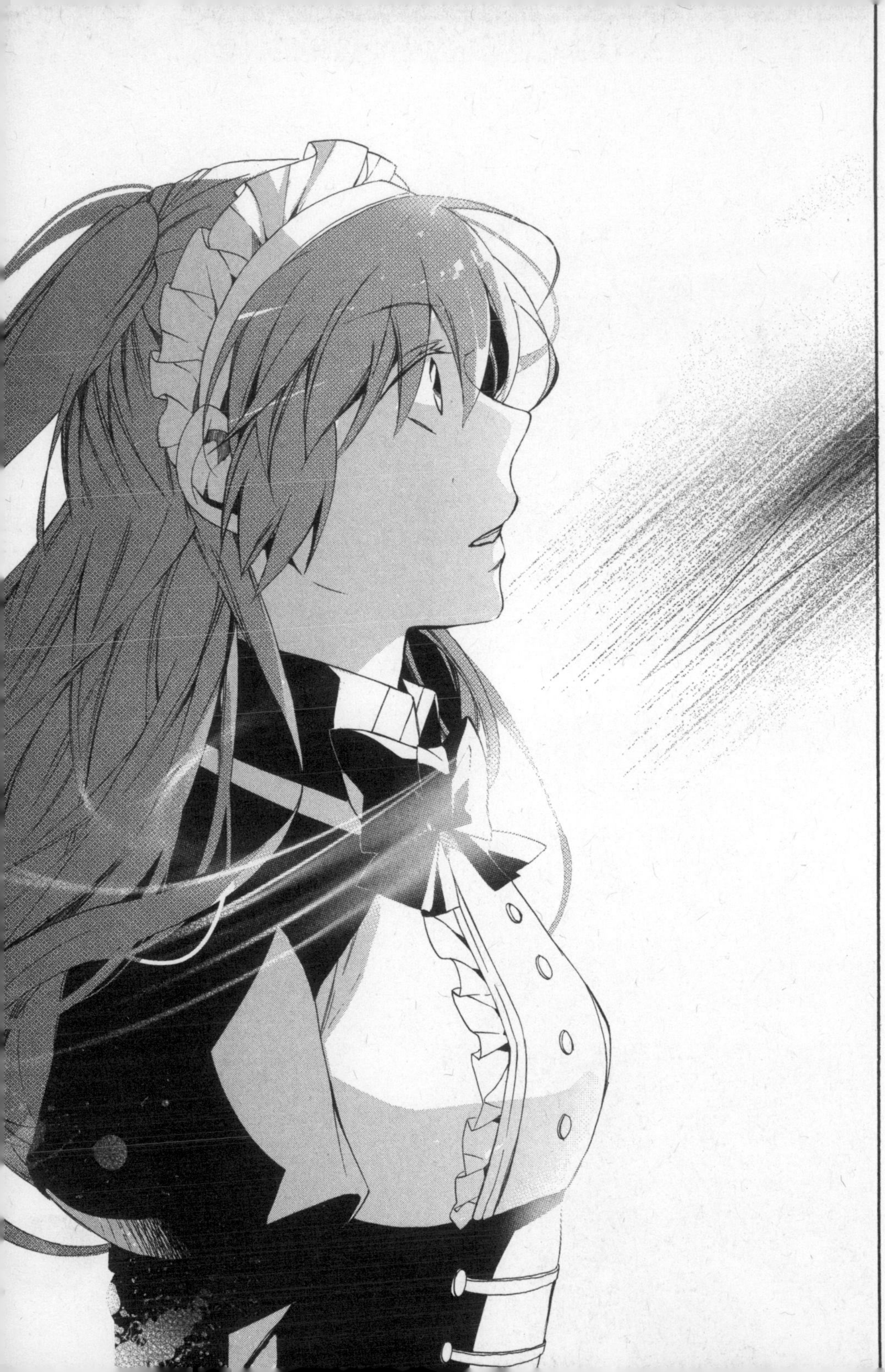

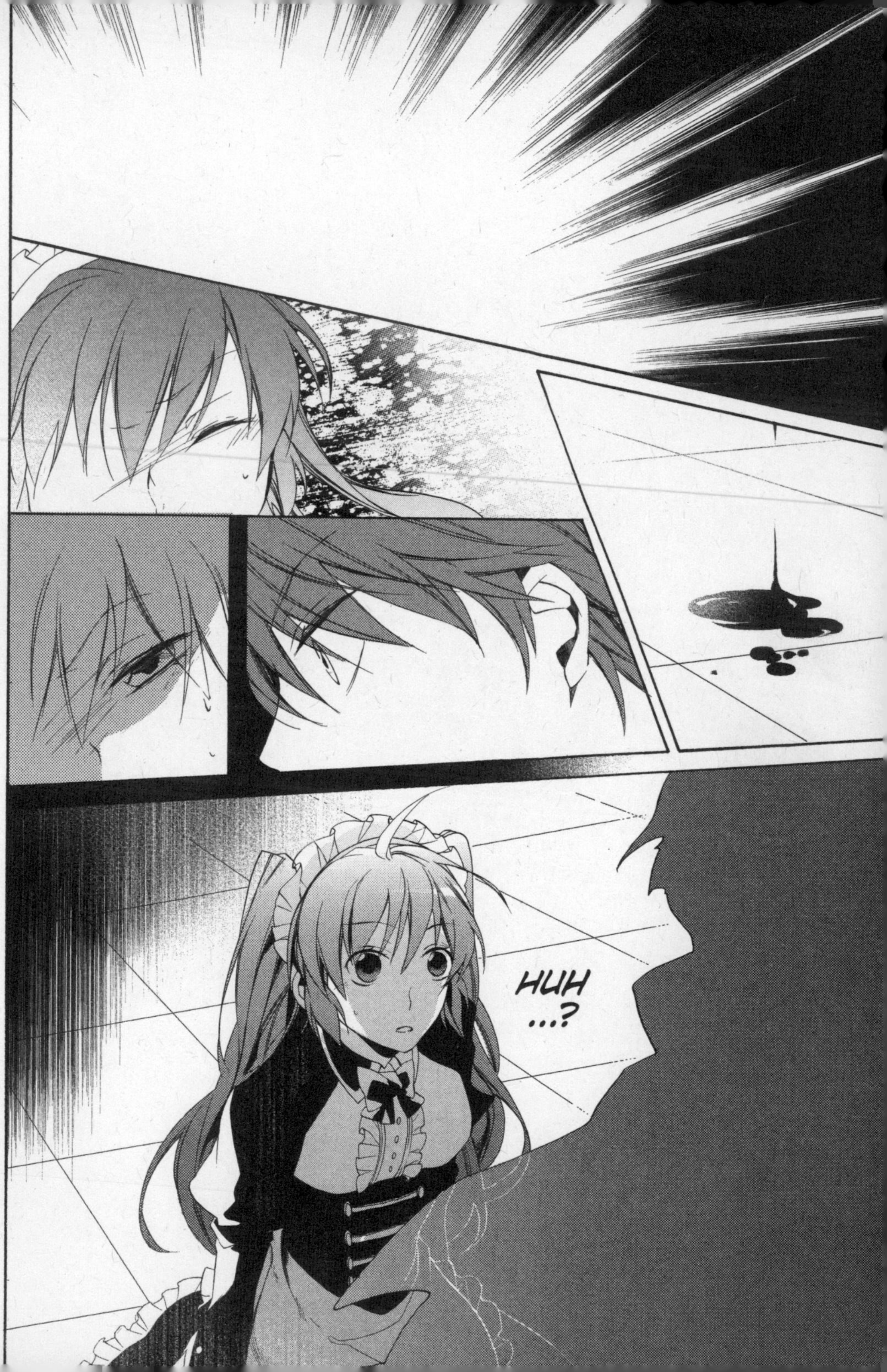
HUH ...?

CRIMSON EMPIRE

Circumstances to serve a noble

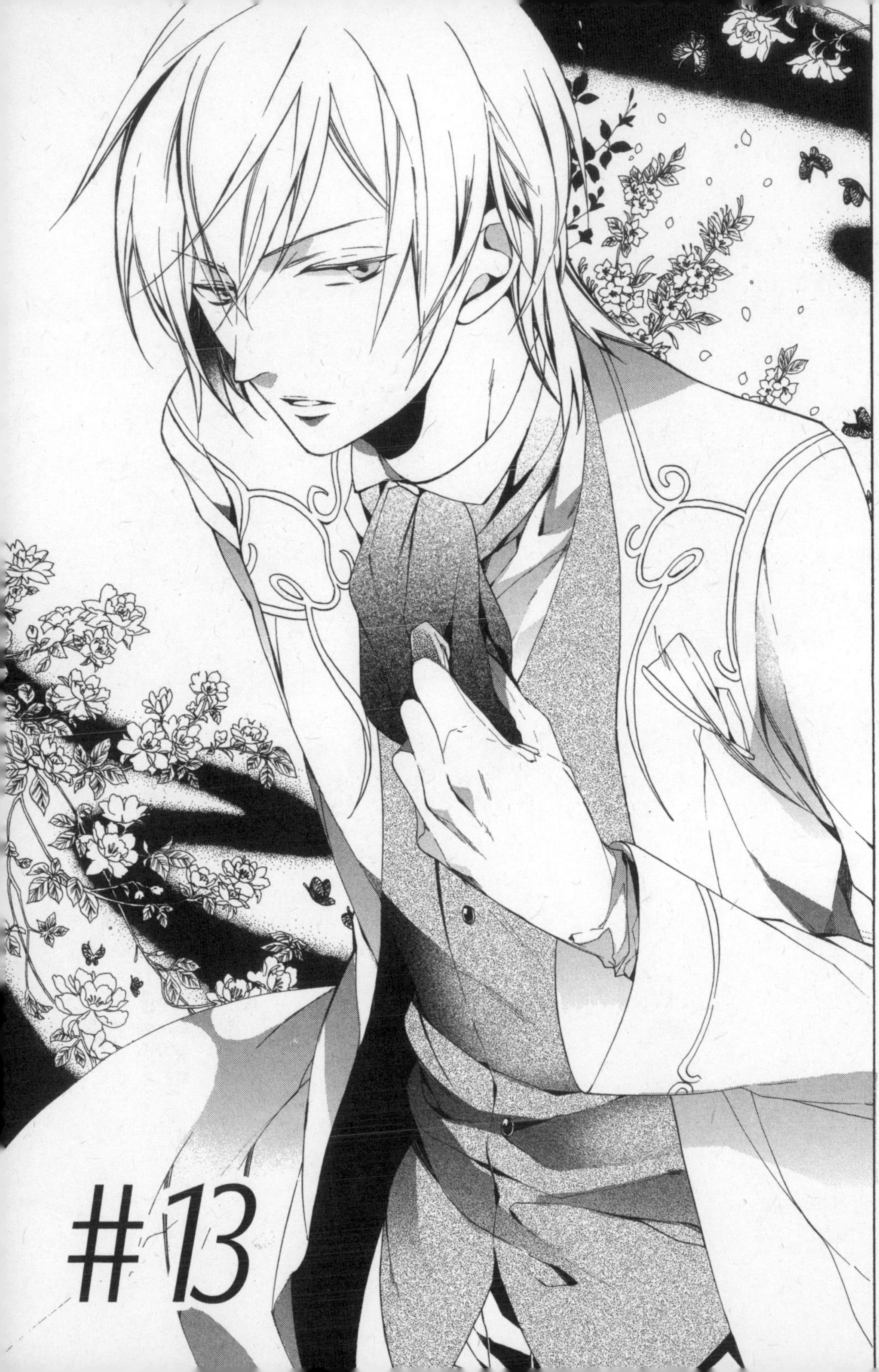
#13

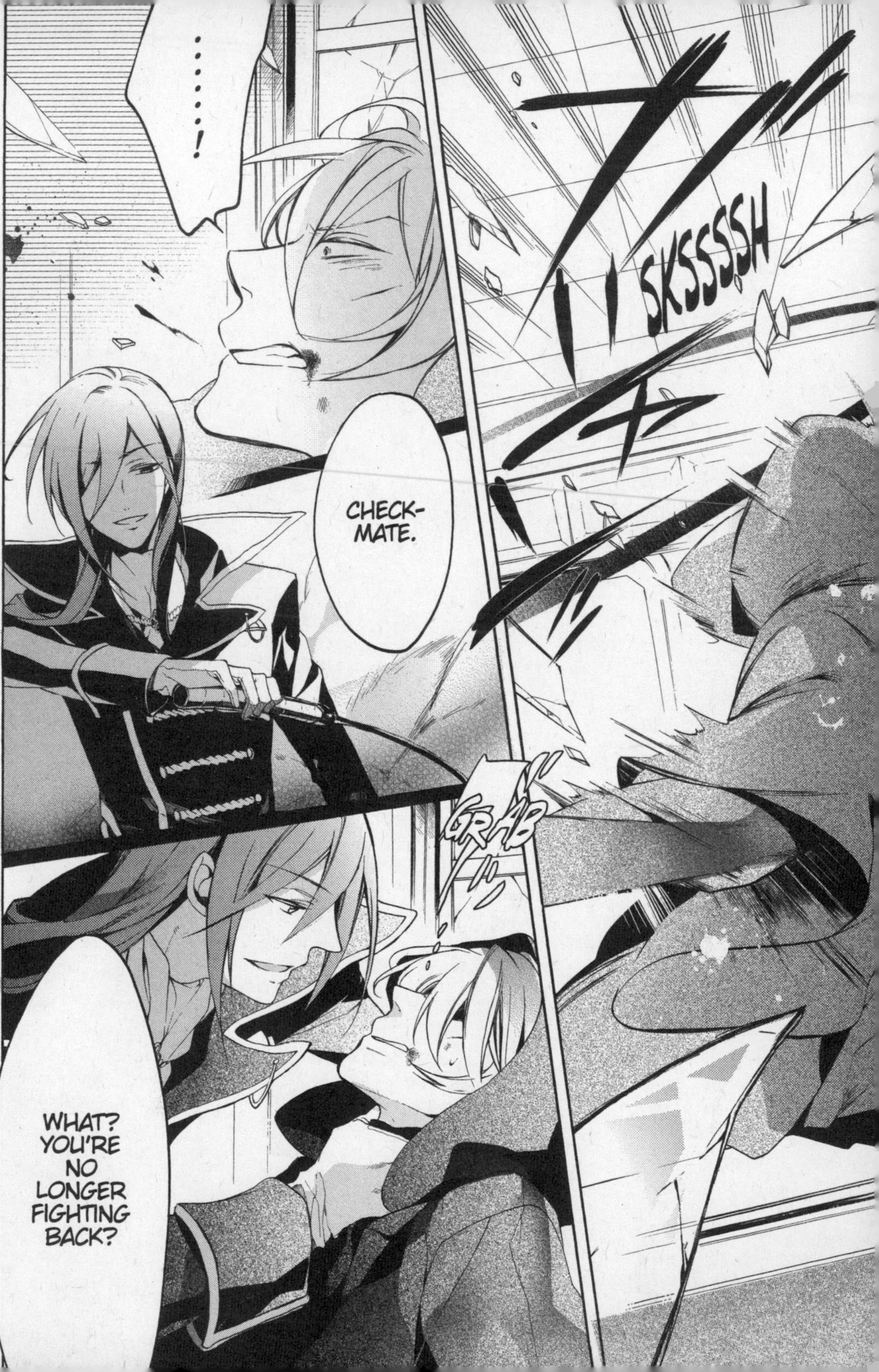
SKSSSSH
......!
CHECK-MATE.
GRAB
WHAT? YOU'RE NO LONGER FIGHTING BACK?

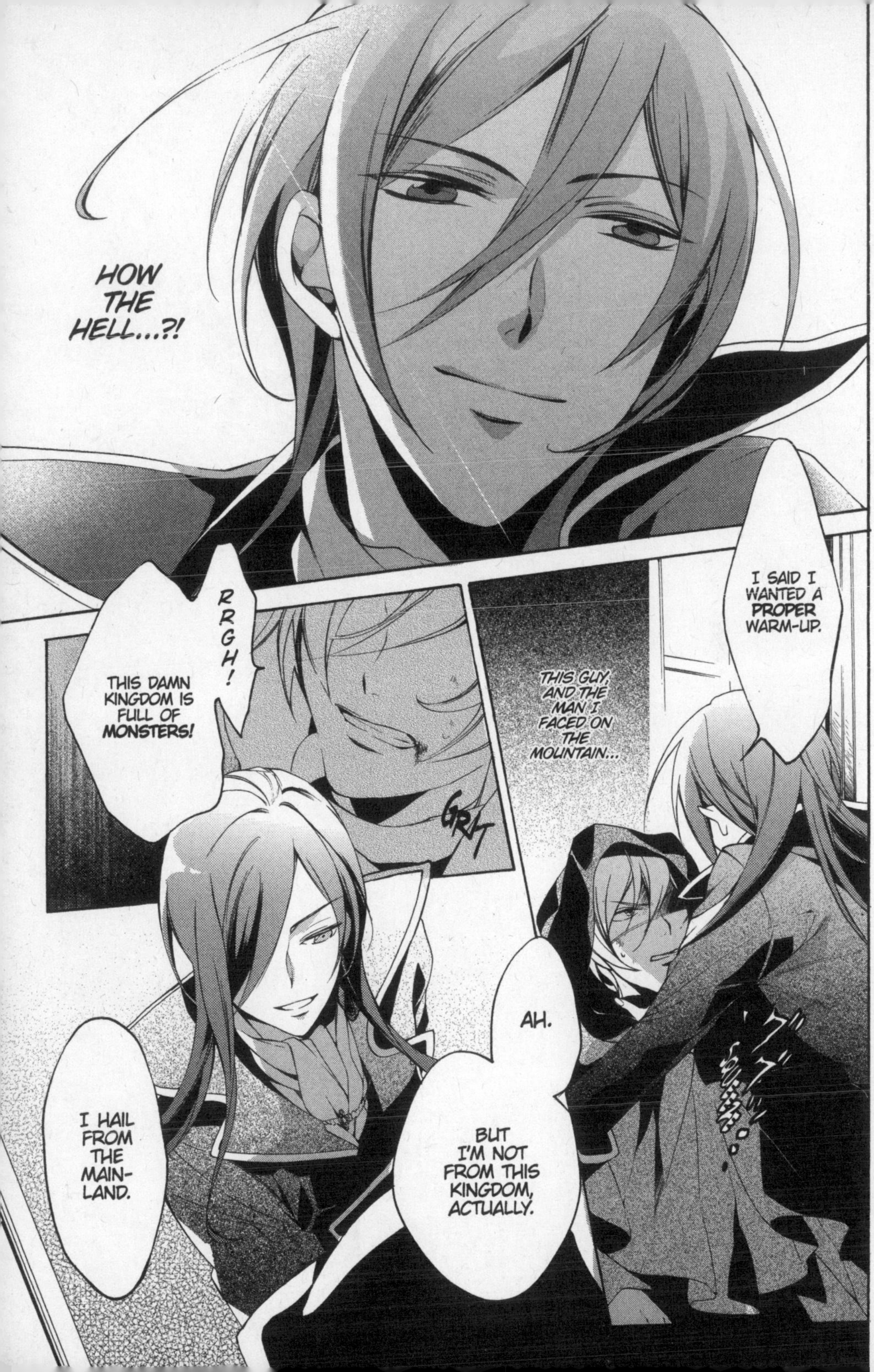
HOW THE HELL...?!
I SAID I WANTED A PROPER WARM-UP.
THIS GUY, AND THE MAN I FACED ON THE MOUNTAIN...
RRGH!
THIS DAMN KINGDOM IS FULL OF MONSTERS!
GRIT
AH.
BUT I'M NOT FROM THIS KINGDOM, ACTUALLY.
I HAIL FROM THE MAIN-LAND.

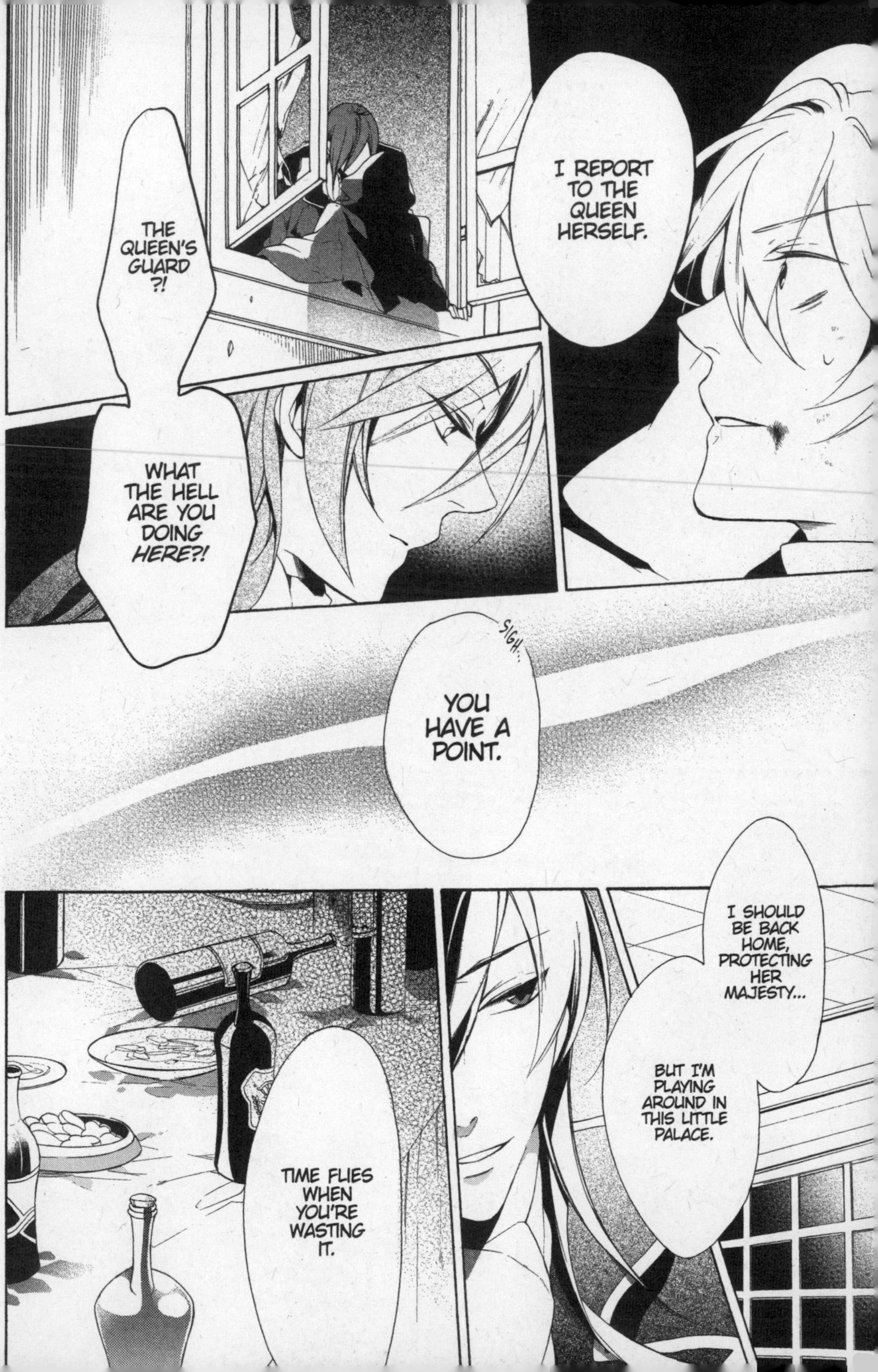
I REPORT TO THE QUEEN HERSELF.
THE QUEEN'S GUARD ?!
WHAT THE HELL ARE YOU DOING HERE?!
SIGH...
YOU HAVE A POINT.
I SHOULD BE BACK HOME, PROTECTING HER MAJESTY...
BUT I'M PLAYING AROUND IN THIS LITTLE PALACE.
TIME FLIES WHEN YOU'RE WASTING IT.

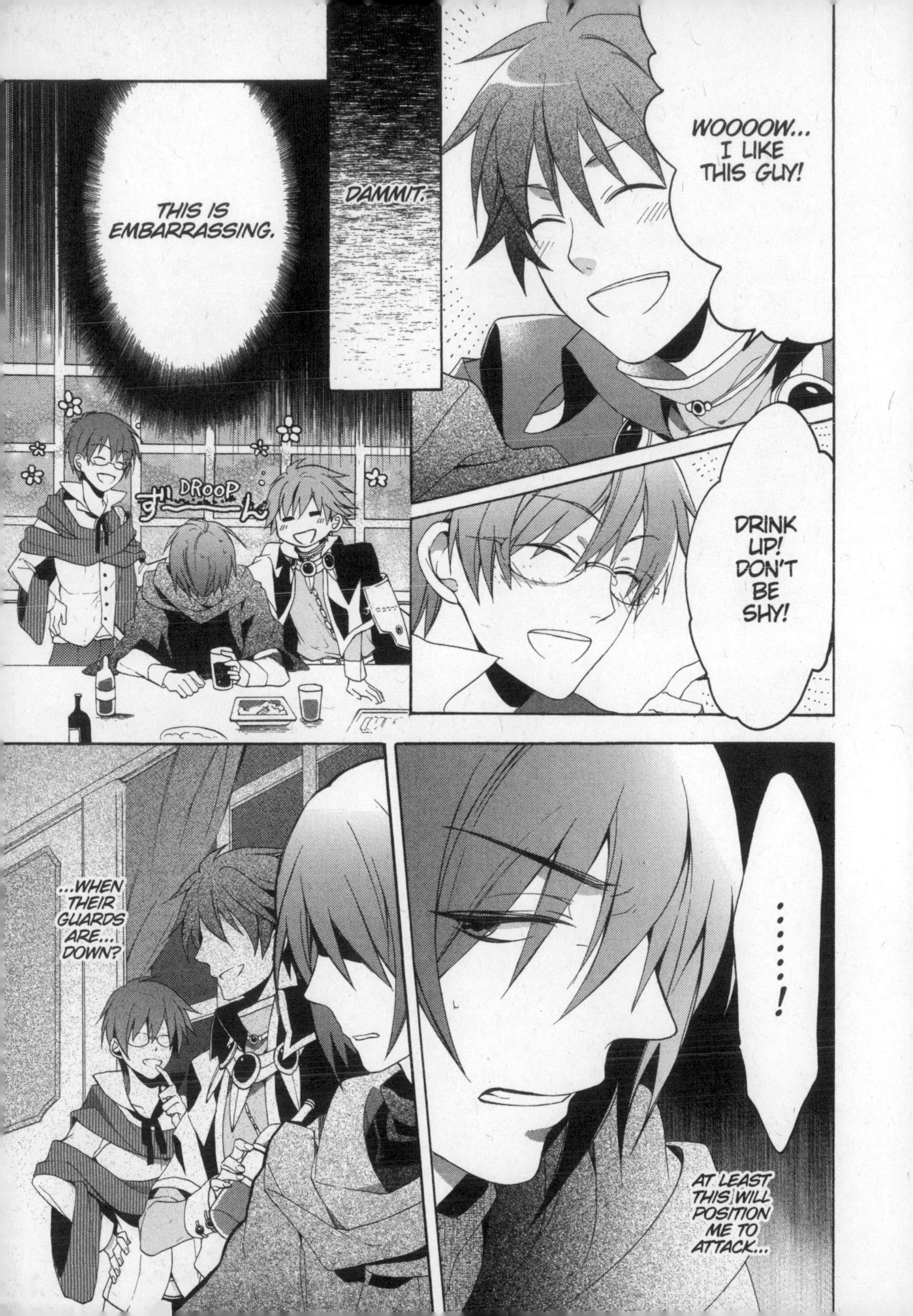
WOOOOW... I LIKE THIS GUY!
DRINK UP! DON'T BE SHY!
DAMMIT.
THIS IS EMBARRASSING.
ずーん
DROOP
......!
AT LEAST THIS WILL POSITION ME TO ATTACK...
...WHEN THEIR GUARDS ARE... DOWN?

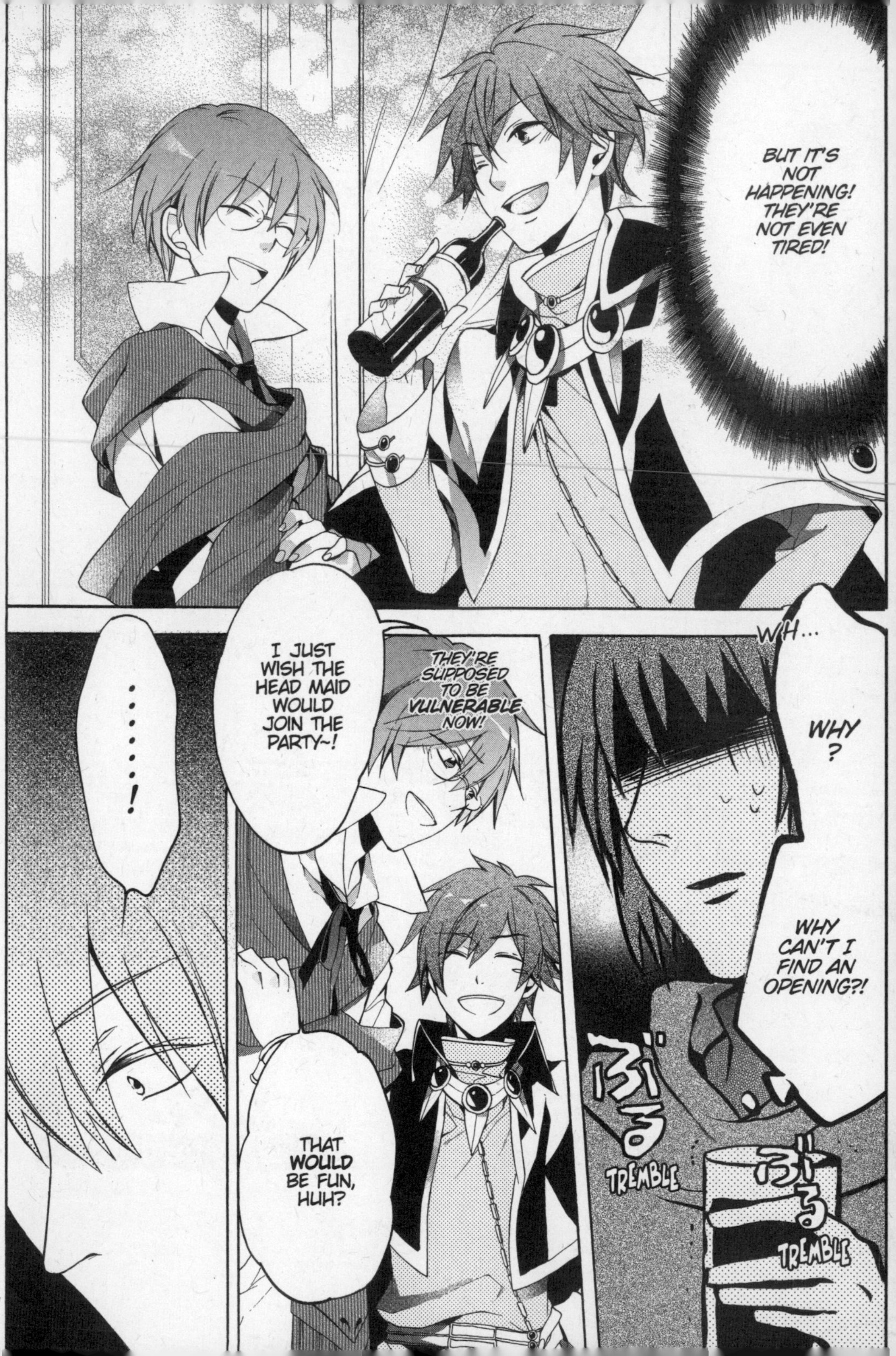
BUT IT'S NOT HAPPENING! THEY'RE NOT EVEN TIRED!
WH...
WHY?
WHY CAN'T I FIND AN OPENING?!
ぶる
TREMBLE
ぶる
TREMBLE
THEY'RE SUPPOSED TO BE VULNERABLE NOW!
I JUST WISH THE HEAD MAID WOULD JOIN THE PARTY~!
THAT WOULD BE FUN, HUH?
......!

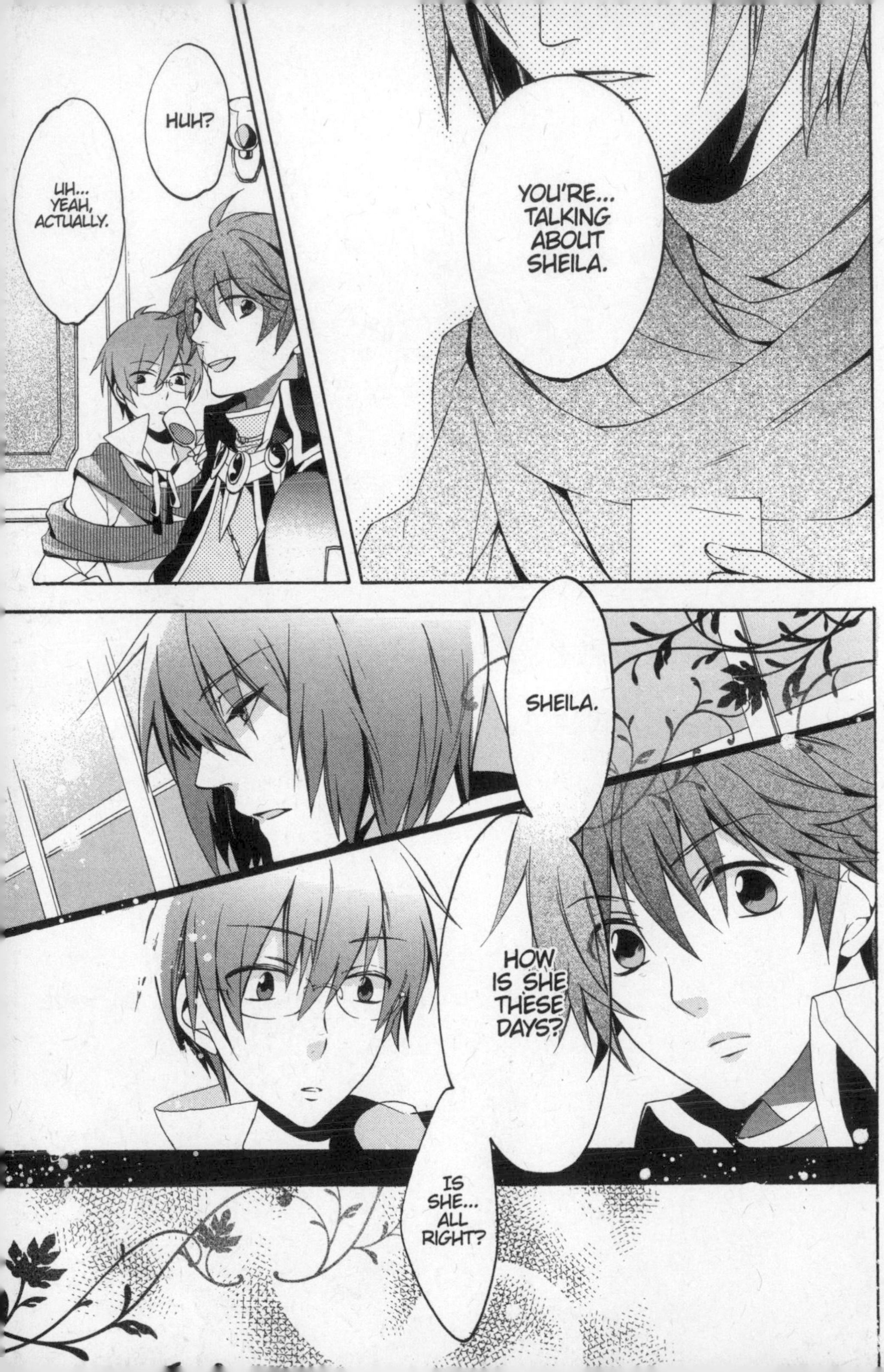
YOU'RE... TALKING ABOUT SHEILA.
HUH?
UH... YEAH, ACTUALLY.
SHEILA.
HOW IS SHE THESE DAYS?
IS SHE... ALL RIGHT?

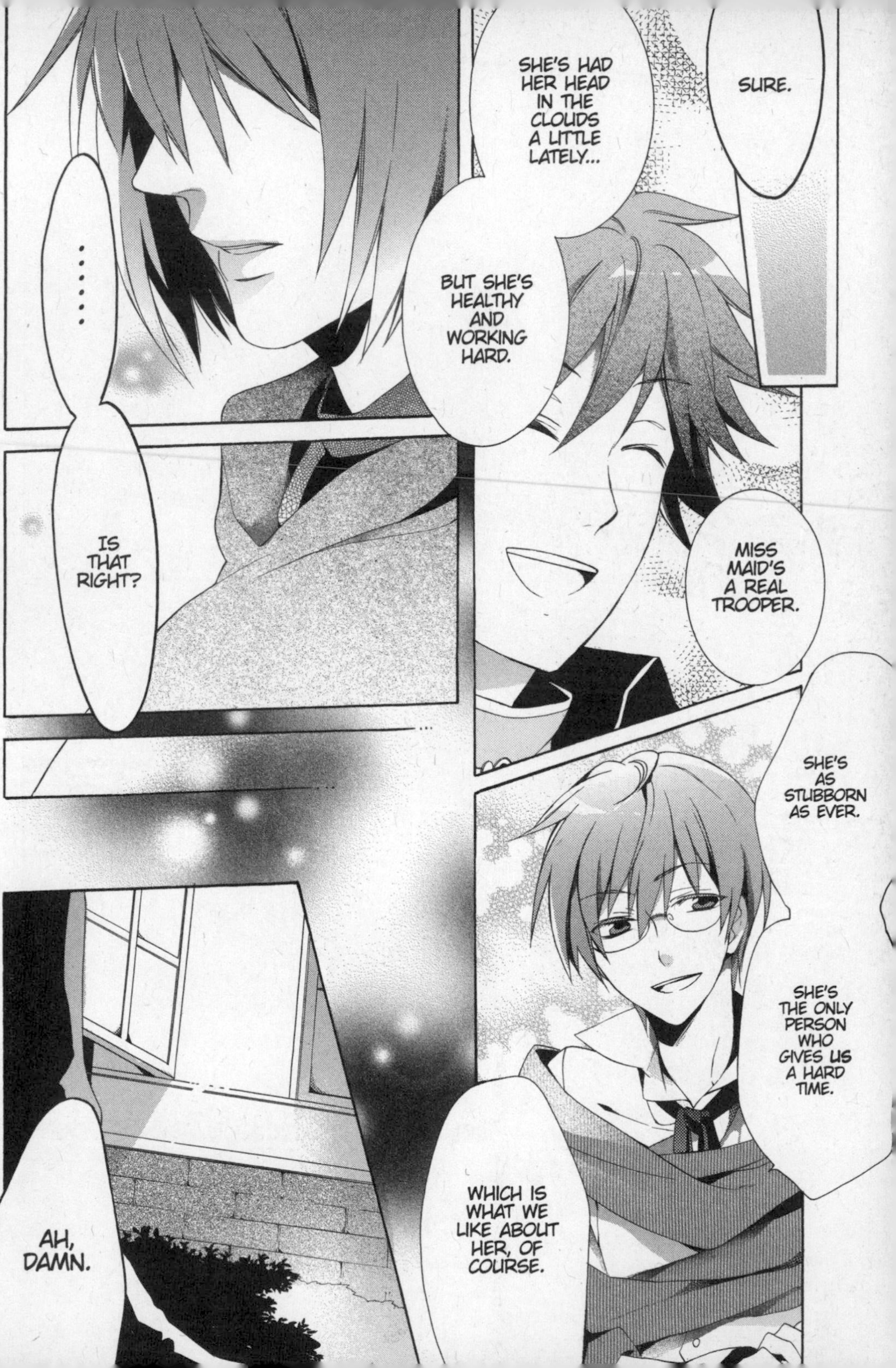
SURE.
SHE'S HAD HER HEAD IN THE CLOUDS A LITTLE LATELY...
BUT SHE'S HEALTHY AND WORKING HARD.
......
MISS MAID'S A REAL TROOPER.
IS THAT RIGHT?
SHE'S AS STUBBORN AS EVER.
SHE'S THE ONLY PERSON WHO GIVES US A HARD TIME.
WHICH IS WHAT WE LIKE ABOUT HER, OF COURSE.
AH, DAMN.

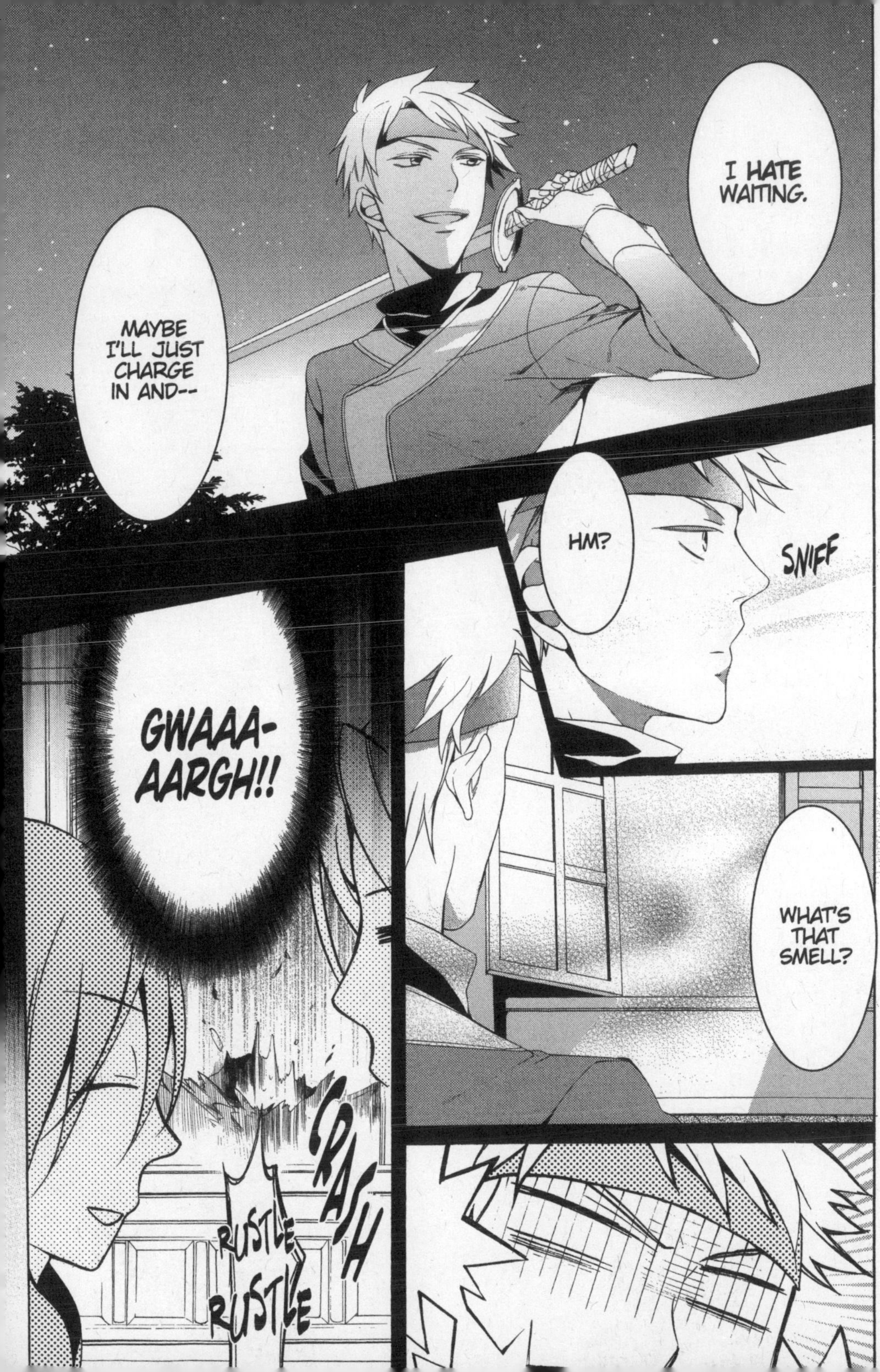
I HATE WAITING.
MAYBE I'LL JUST CHARGE IN AND--
HM?
SNIFF
WHAT'S THAT SMELL?
GWAAA-AARGH!!
CRASH
RUSTLE RUSTLE

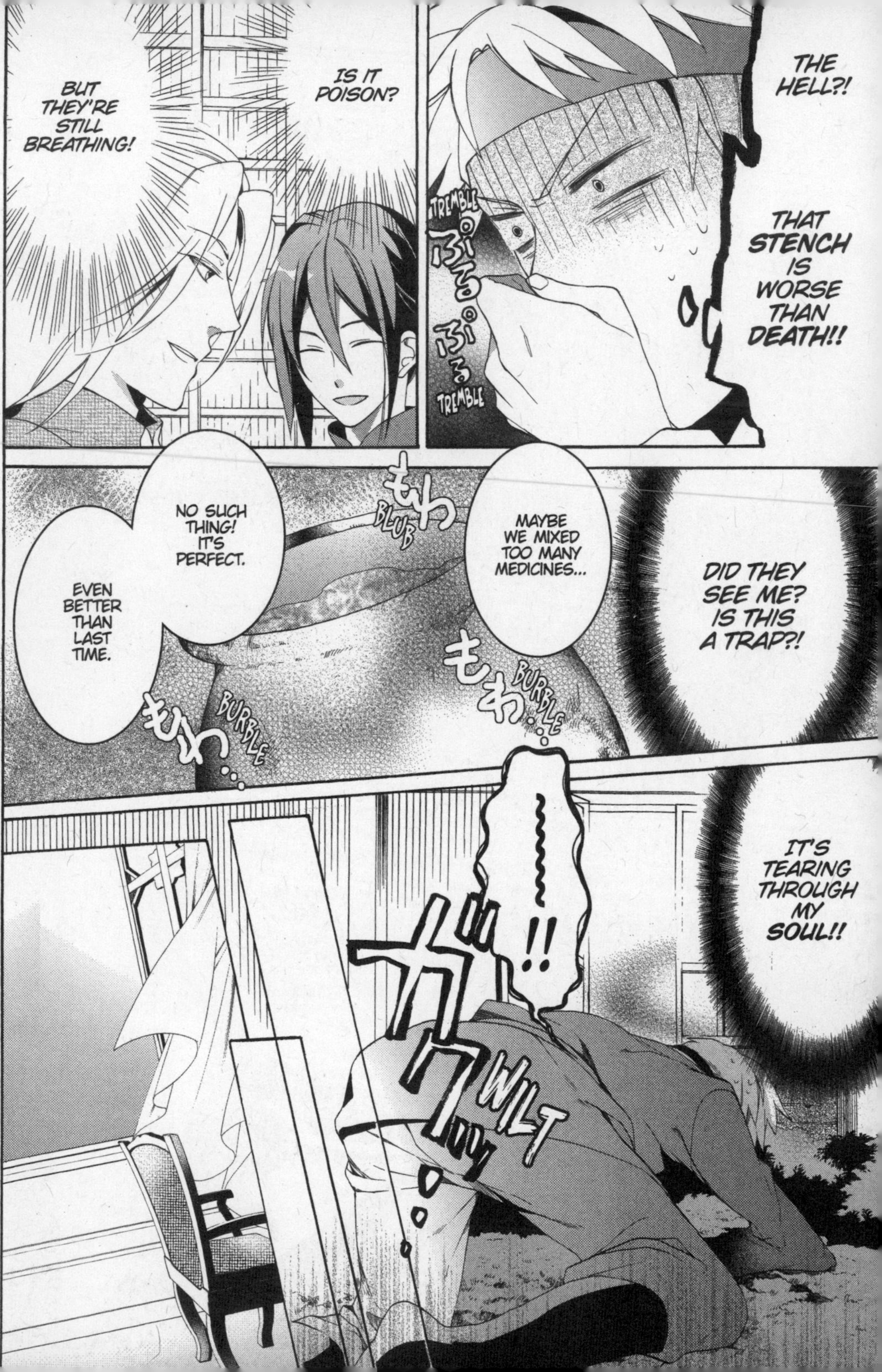
THE HELL?!
THAT STENCH IS WORSE THAN DEATH!!
TREMBLE ぷるぷる TREMBLE
IS IT POISON?
BUT THEY'RE STILL BREATHING!
DID THEY SEE ME? IS THIS A TRAP?!
MAYBE WE MIXED TOO MANY MEDICINES...
もわ BLUB
NO SUCH THING! IT'S PERFECT.
EVEN BETTER THAN LAST TIME.
もわ... BURBLE
もわ... BURBLE
IT'S TEARING THROUGH MY SOUL!!
~~~~!!
ガク... WILT
~~~~

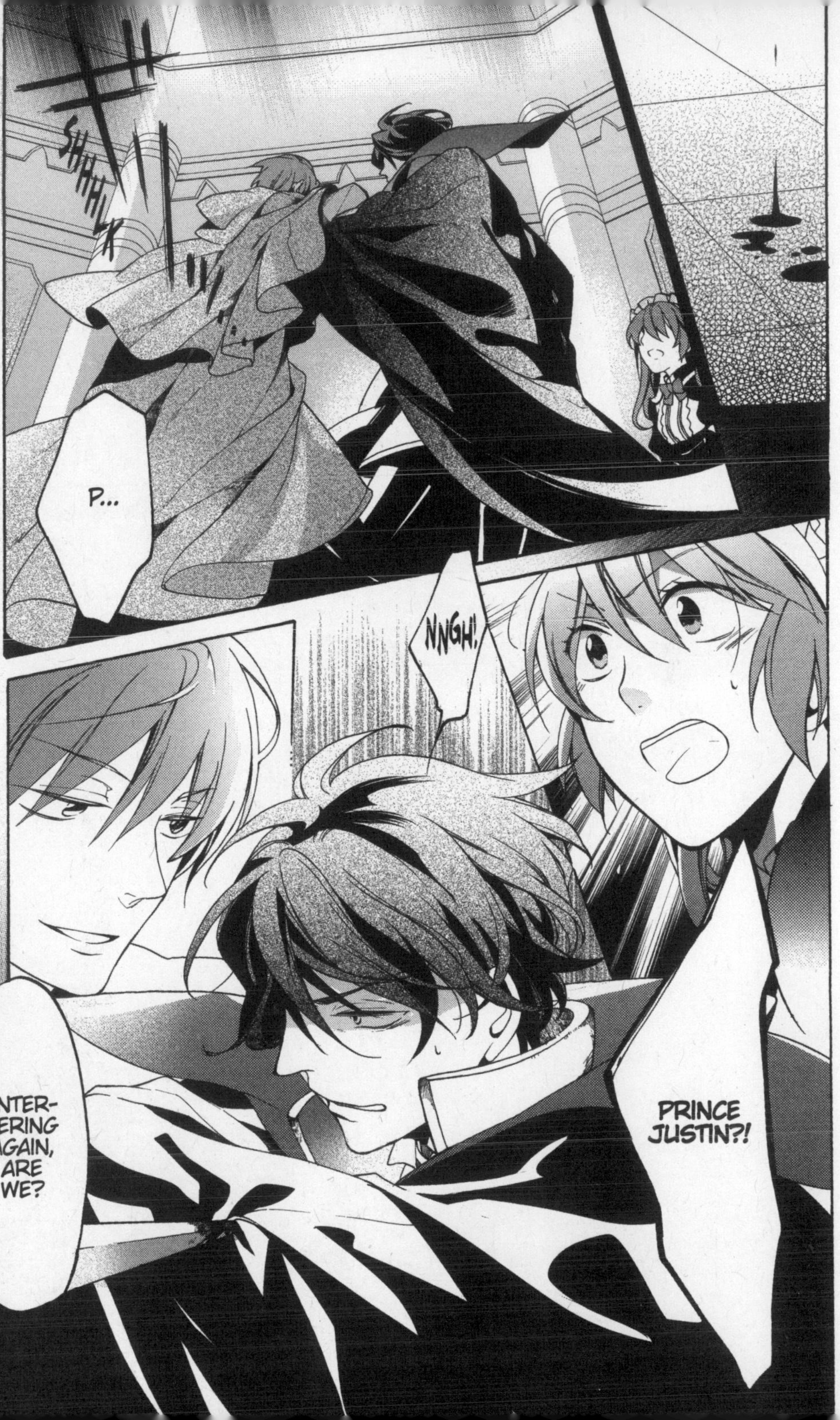
SHHHLK
P...
NNGH!
PRINCE JUSTIN?!
INTER-FERING AGAIN, ARE WE?

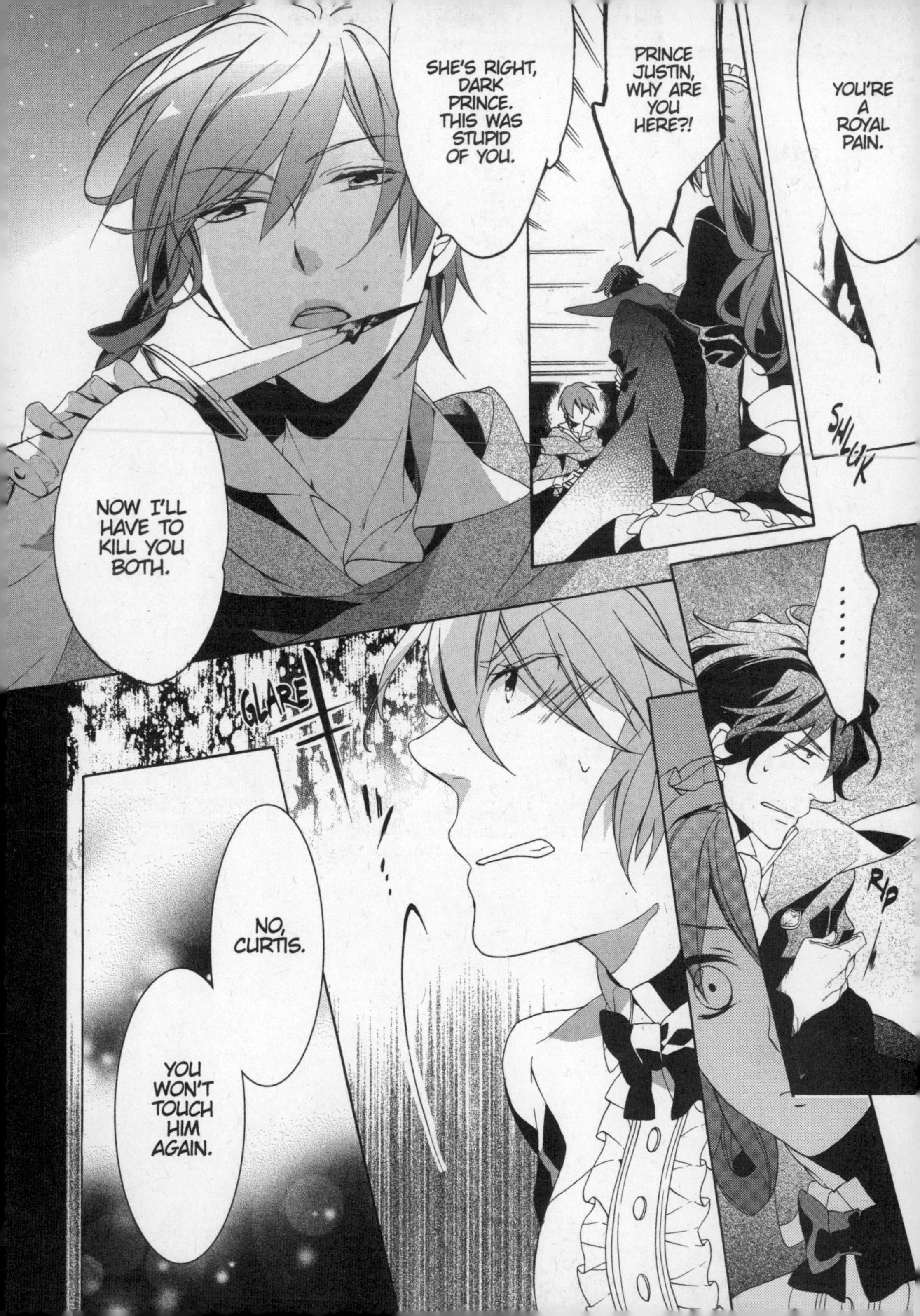

YOU'RE A ROYAL PAIN.
SHLUK
PRINCE JUSTIN, WHY ARE YOU HERE?!
SHE'S RIGHT, DARK PRINCE. THIS WAS STUPID OF YOU.
NOW I'LL HAVE TO KILL YOU BOTH.
......
RIP
GLARE
NO, CURTIS.
YOU WON'T TOUCH HIM AGAIN.

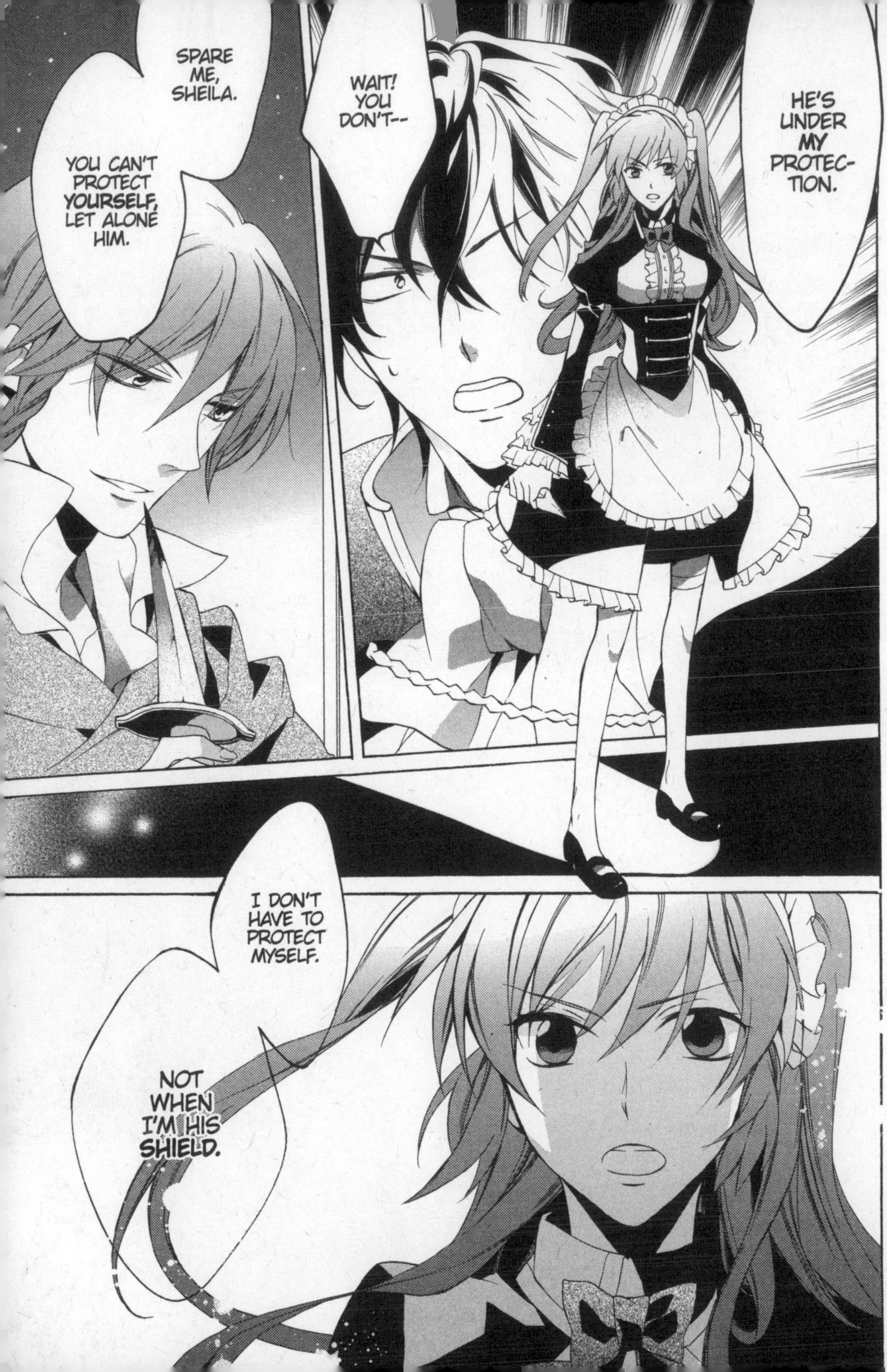
HE'S UNDER MY PROTEC-TION.
WAIT! YOU DON'T--
SPARE ME, SHEILA.
YOU CAN'T PROTECT YOURSELF, LET ALONE HIM.
I DON'T HAVE TO PROTECT MYSELF.
NOT WHEN I'M HIS SHIELD.

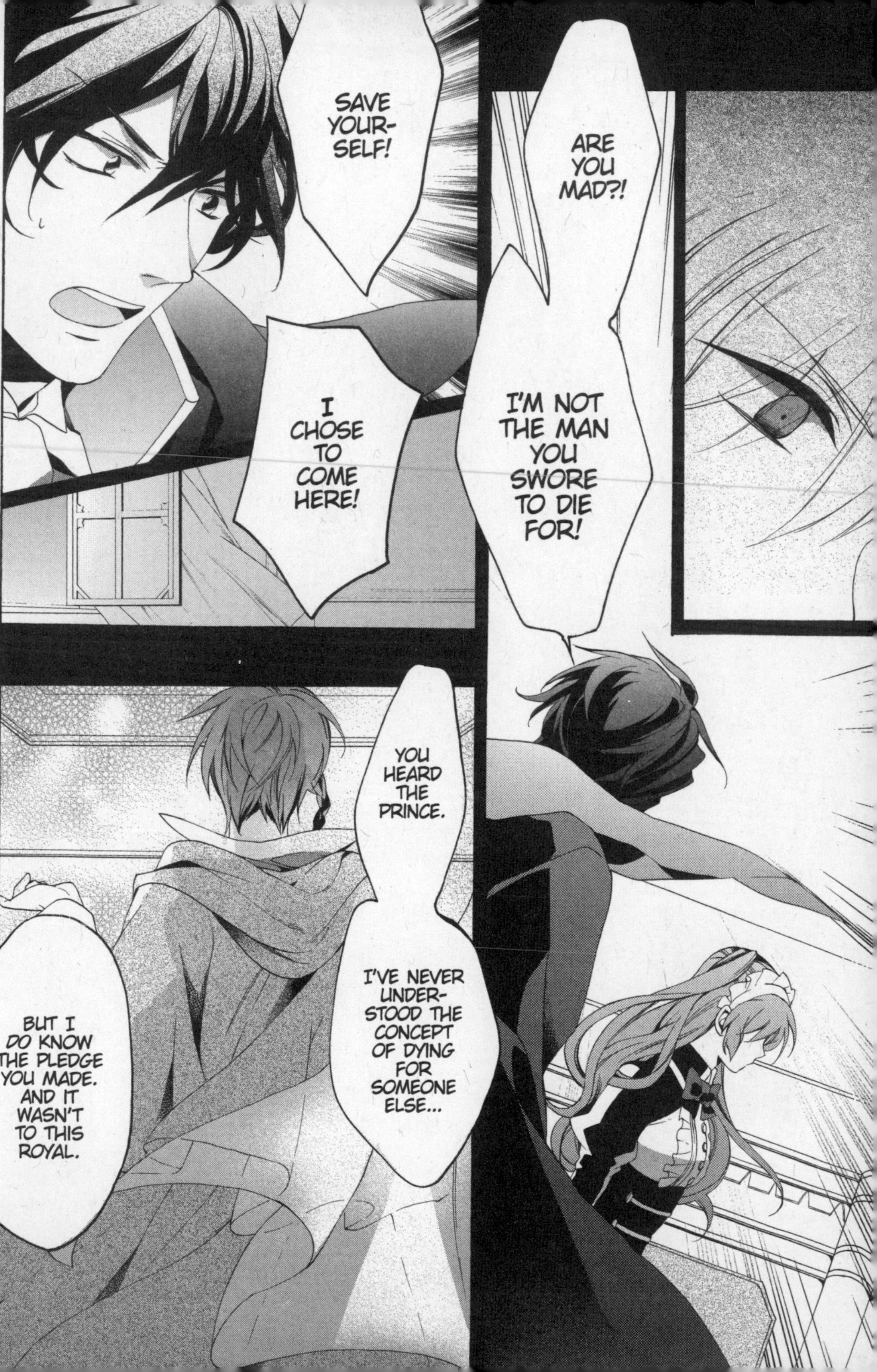
ARE YOU MAD?!
I'M NOT THE MAN YOU SWORE TO DIE FOR!
SAVE YOURSELF!
I CHOSE TO COME HERE!
YOU HEARD THE PRINCE.
I'VE NEVER UNDERSTOOD THE CONCEPT OF DYING FOR SOMEONE ELSE...
BUT I DO KNOW THE PLEDGE YOU MADE. AND IT WASN'T TO THIS ROYAL.

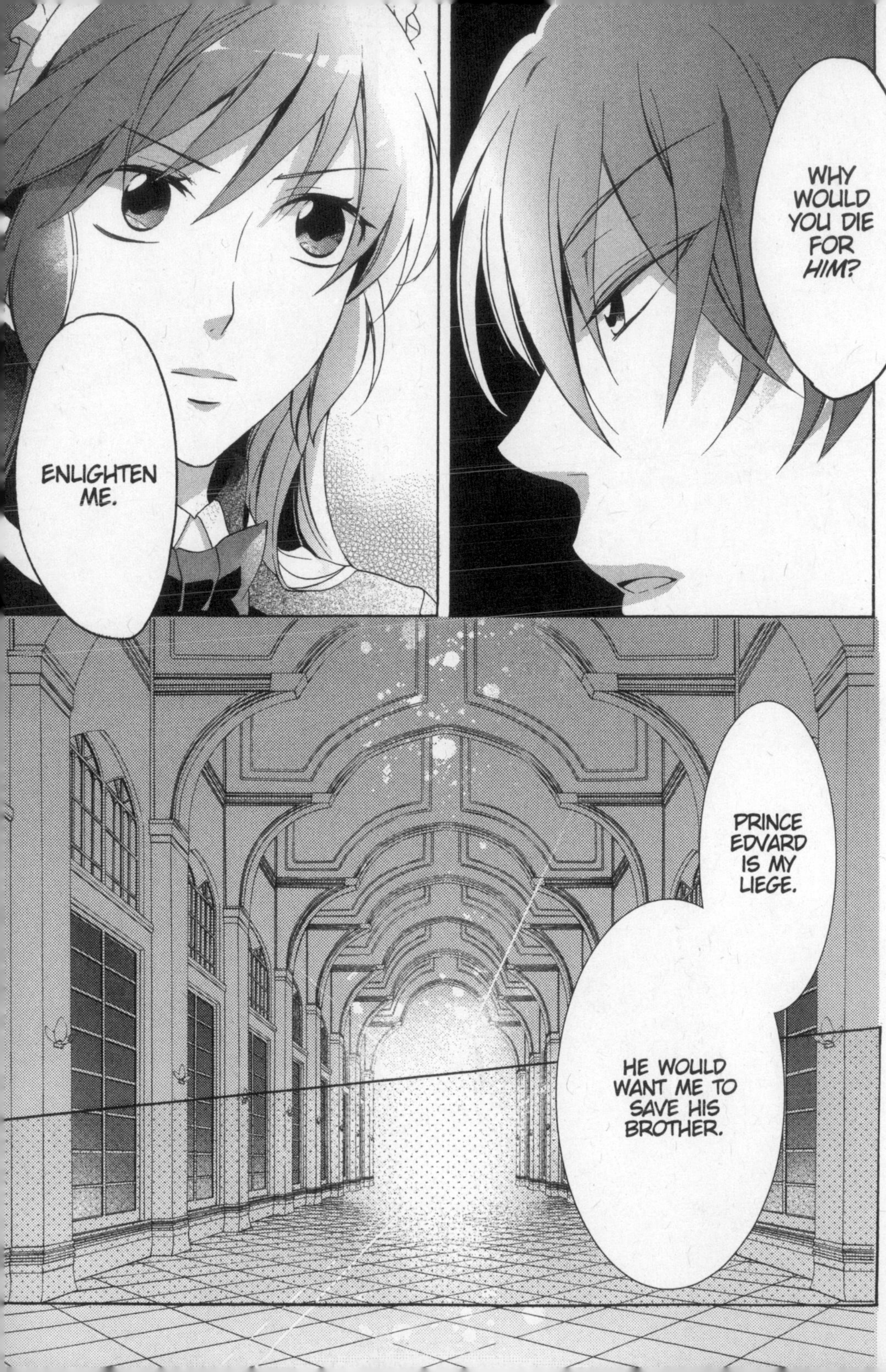
WHY WOULD YOU DIE FOR HIM?
ENLIGHTEN ME.
PRINCE EDVARD IS MY LIEGE.
HE WOULD WANT ME TO SAVE HIS BROTHER.

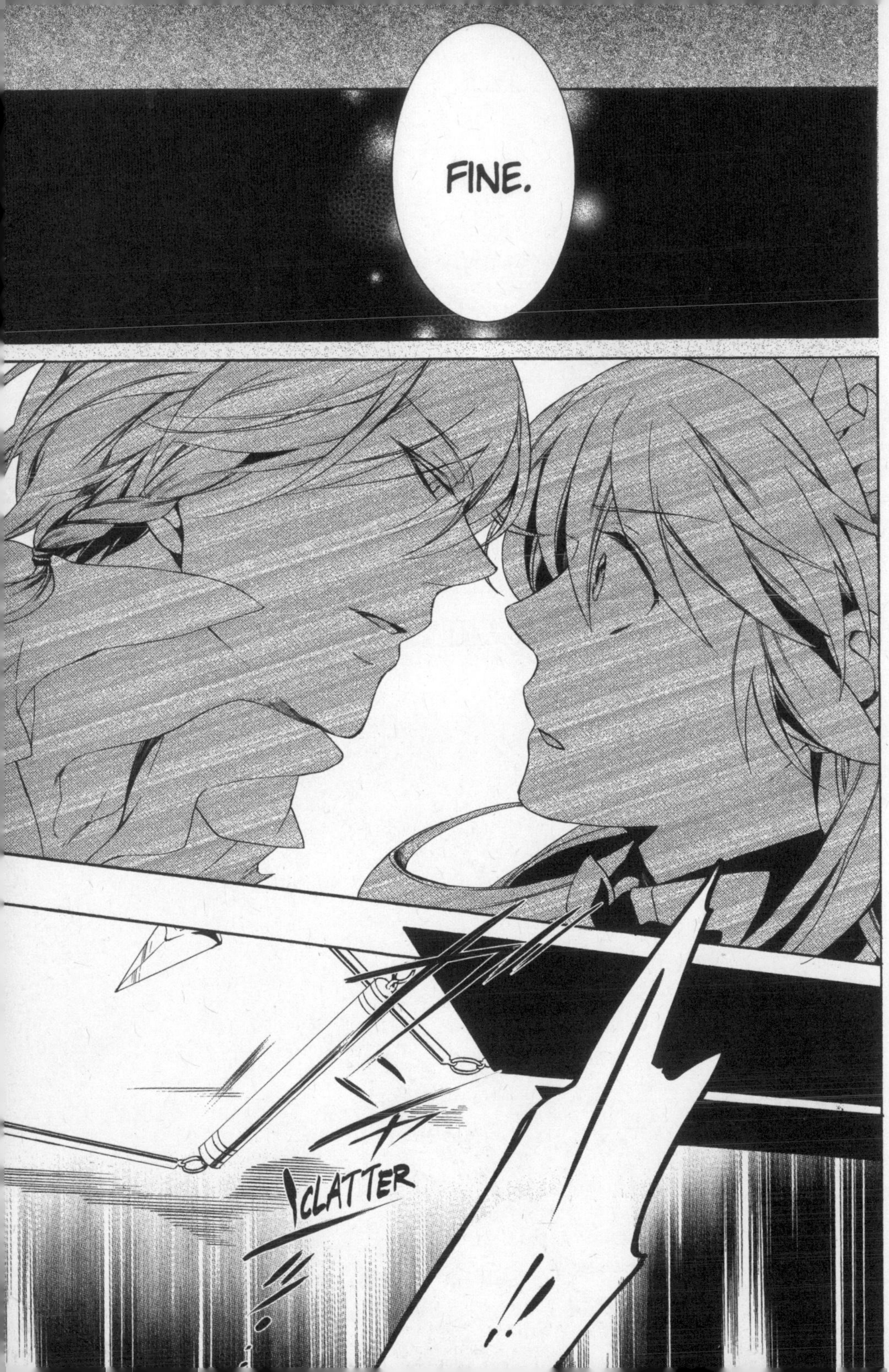
FINE.
CLATTER

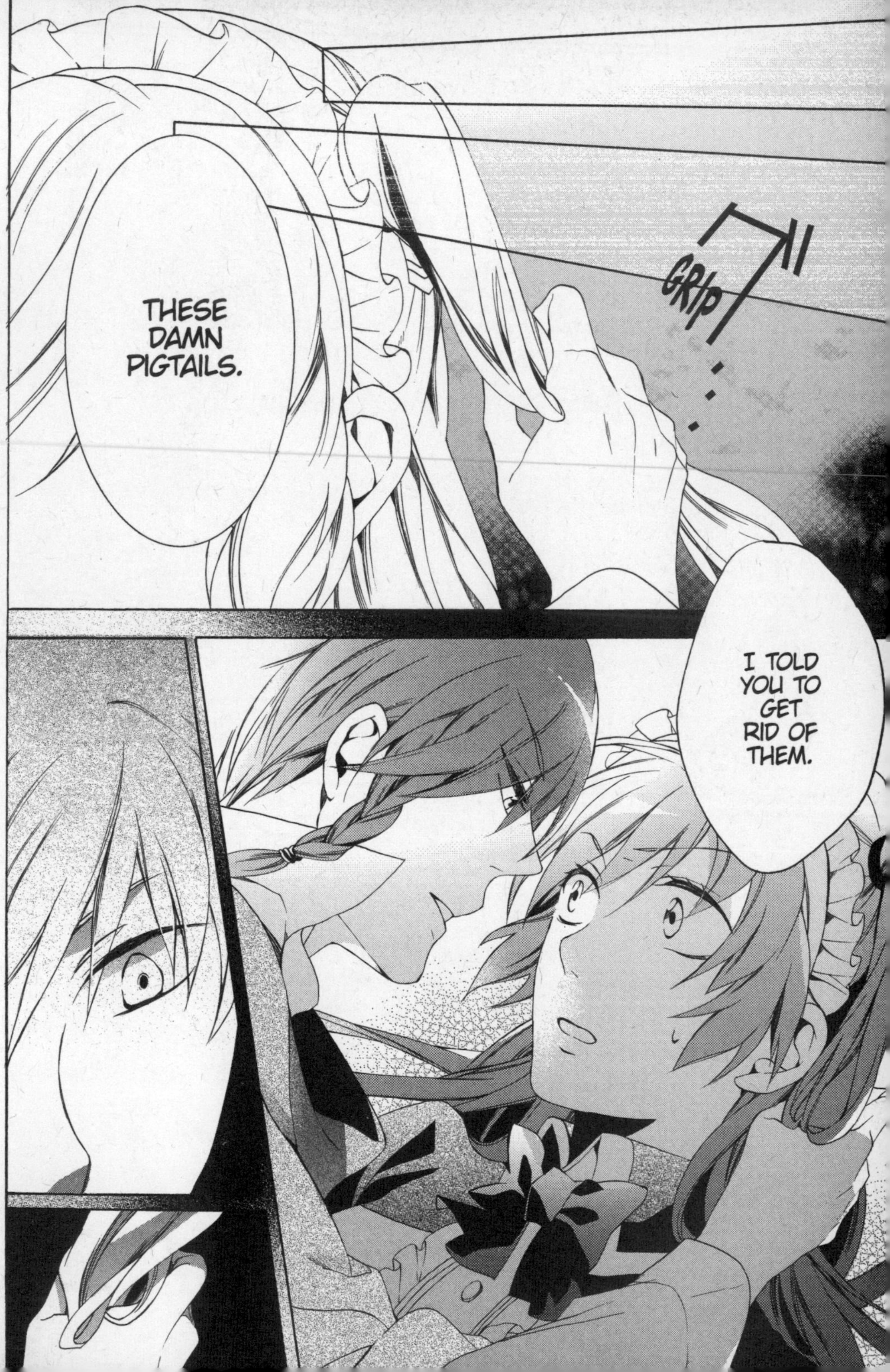
GRIP
THESE DAMN PIGTAILS.
I TOLD YOU TO GET RID OF THEM.

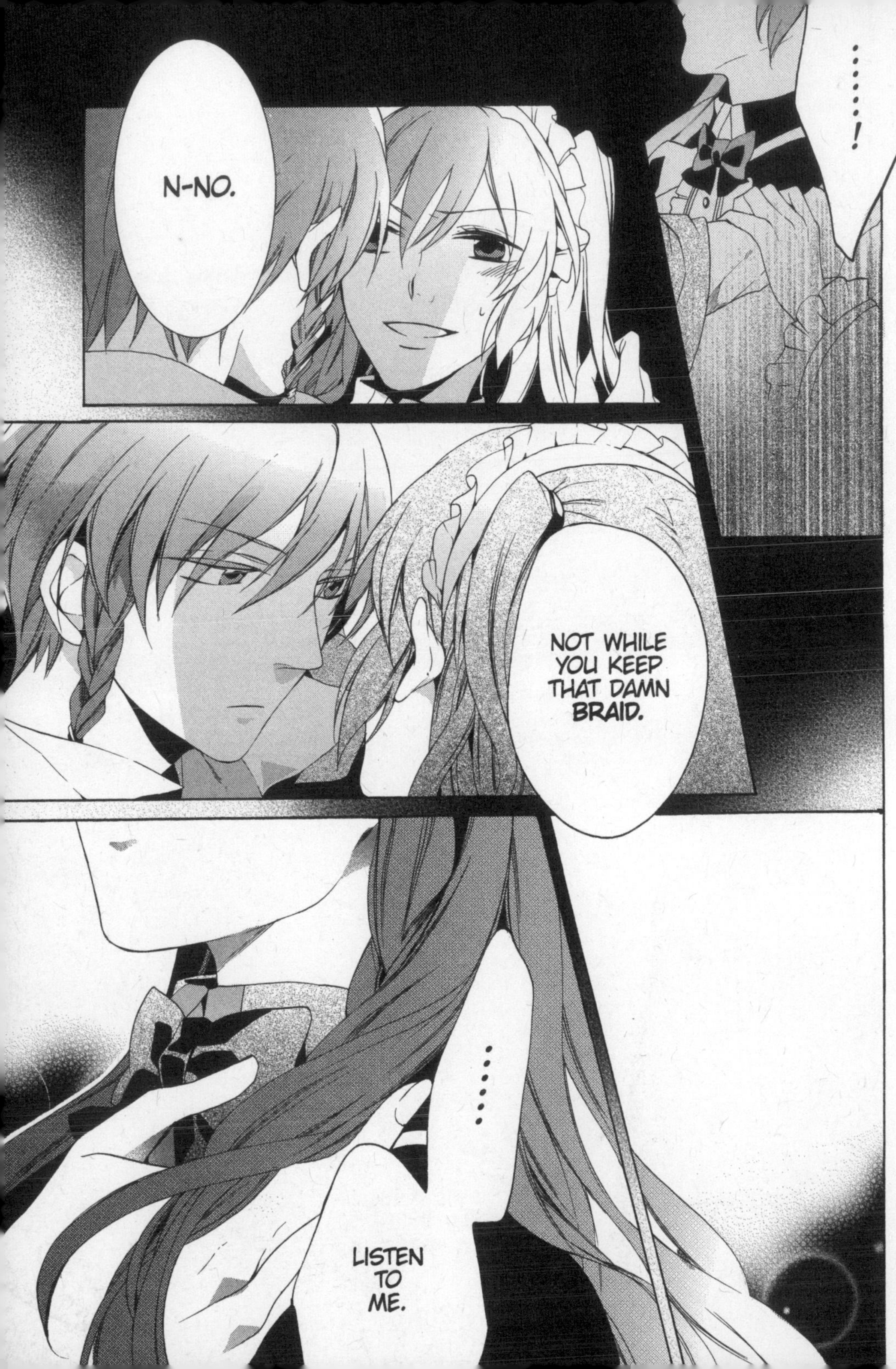
……!
N-NO.
NOT WHILE YOU KEEP THAT DAMN BRAID.
……
LISTEN TO ME.

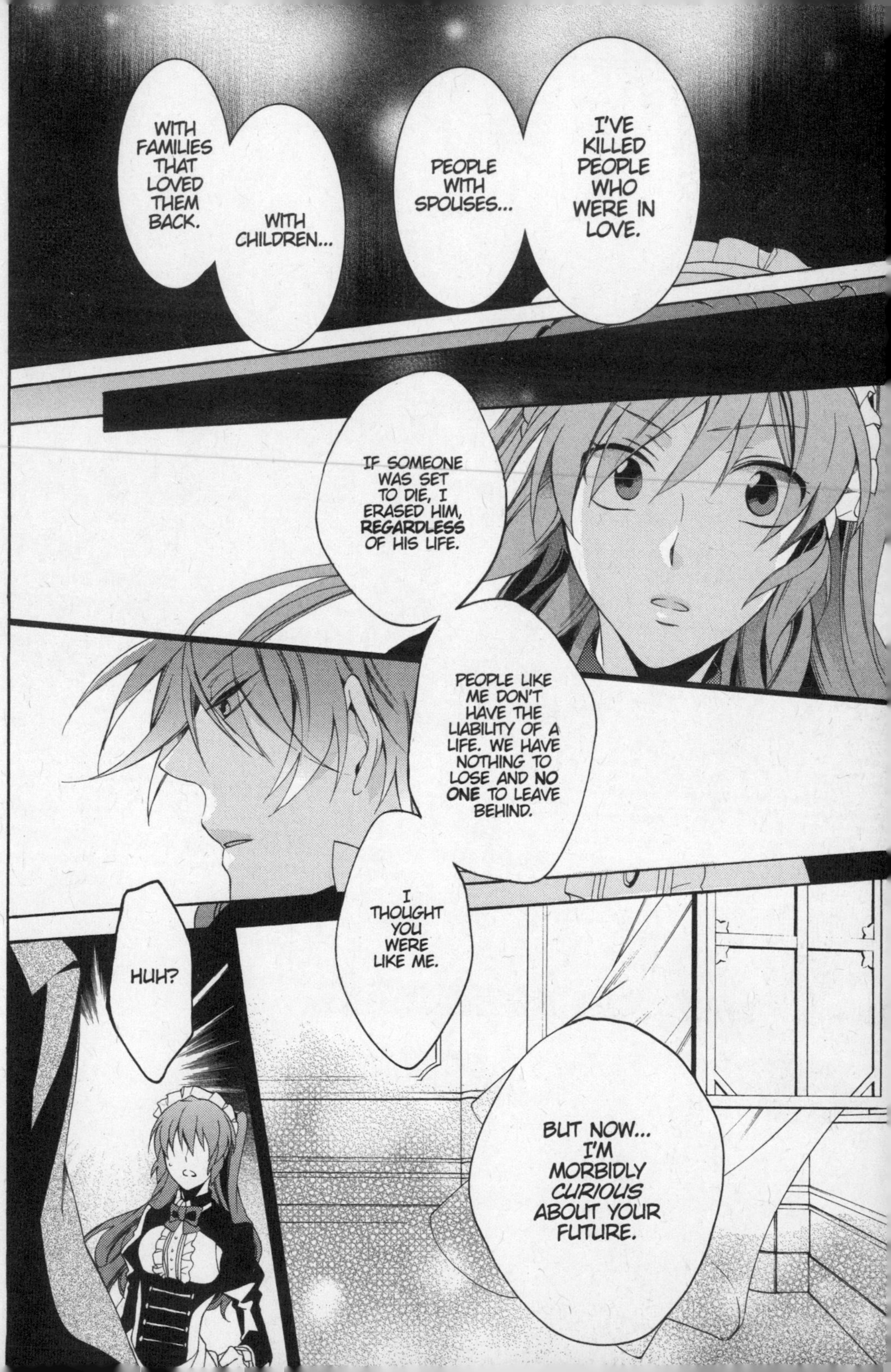
I'VE KILLED PEOPLE WHO WERE IN LOVE.
PEOPLE WITH SPOUSES...
WITH CHILDREN...
WITH FAMILIES THAT LOVED THEM BACK.
IF SOMEONE WAS SET TO DIE, I ERASED HIM, REGARDLESS OF HIS LIFE.
PEOPLE LIKE ME DON'T HAVE THE LIABILITY OF A LIFE. WE HAVE NOTHING TO LOSE AND NO ONE TO LEAVE BEHIND.
I THOUGHT YOU WERE LIKE ME.
HUH?
BUT NOW... I'M MORBIDLY *CURIOUS* ABOUT YOUR FUTURE.

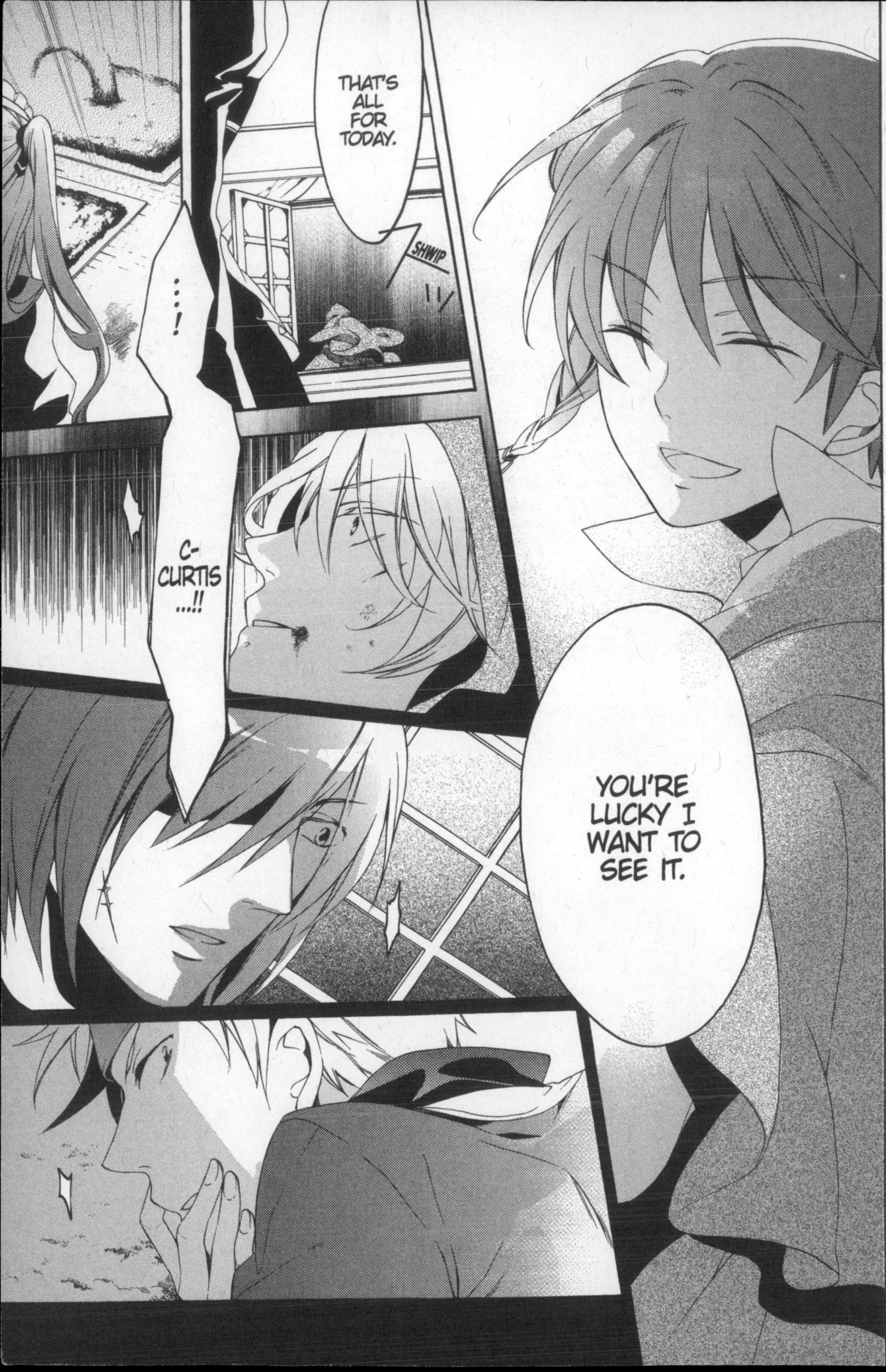

YOU'RE LUCKY I WANT TO SEE IT.
THAT'S ALL FOR TODAY.
SHWIP
...!
C-CURTIS ...!!

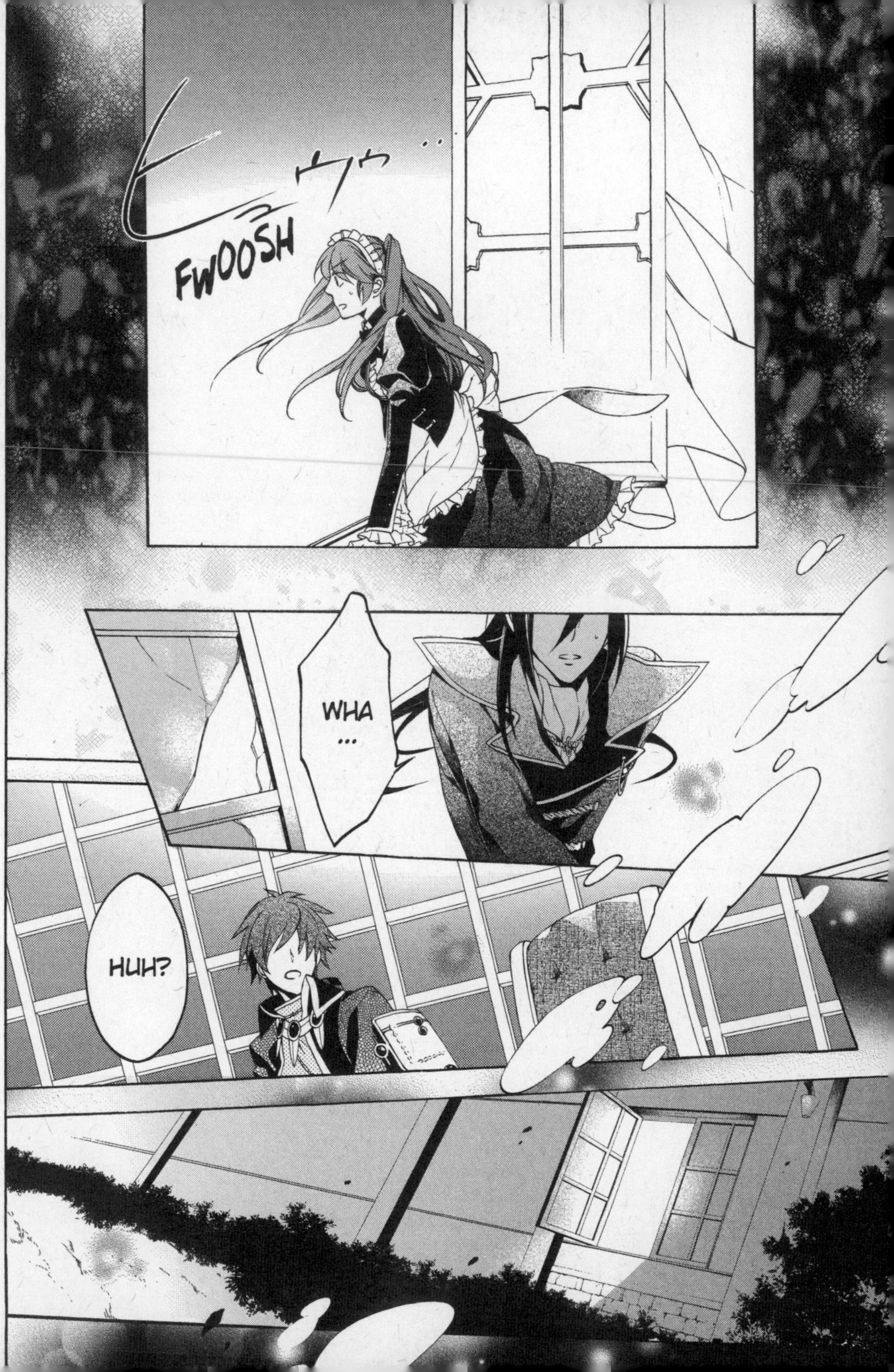
ヒュゥゥ‥
FWOOSH
WHA ...
HUH?

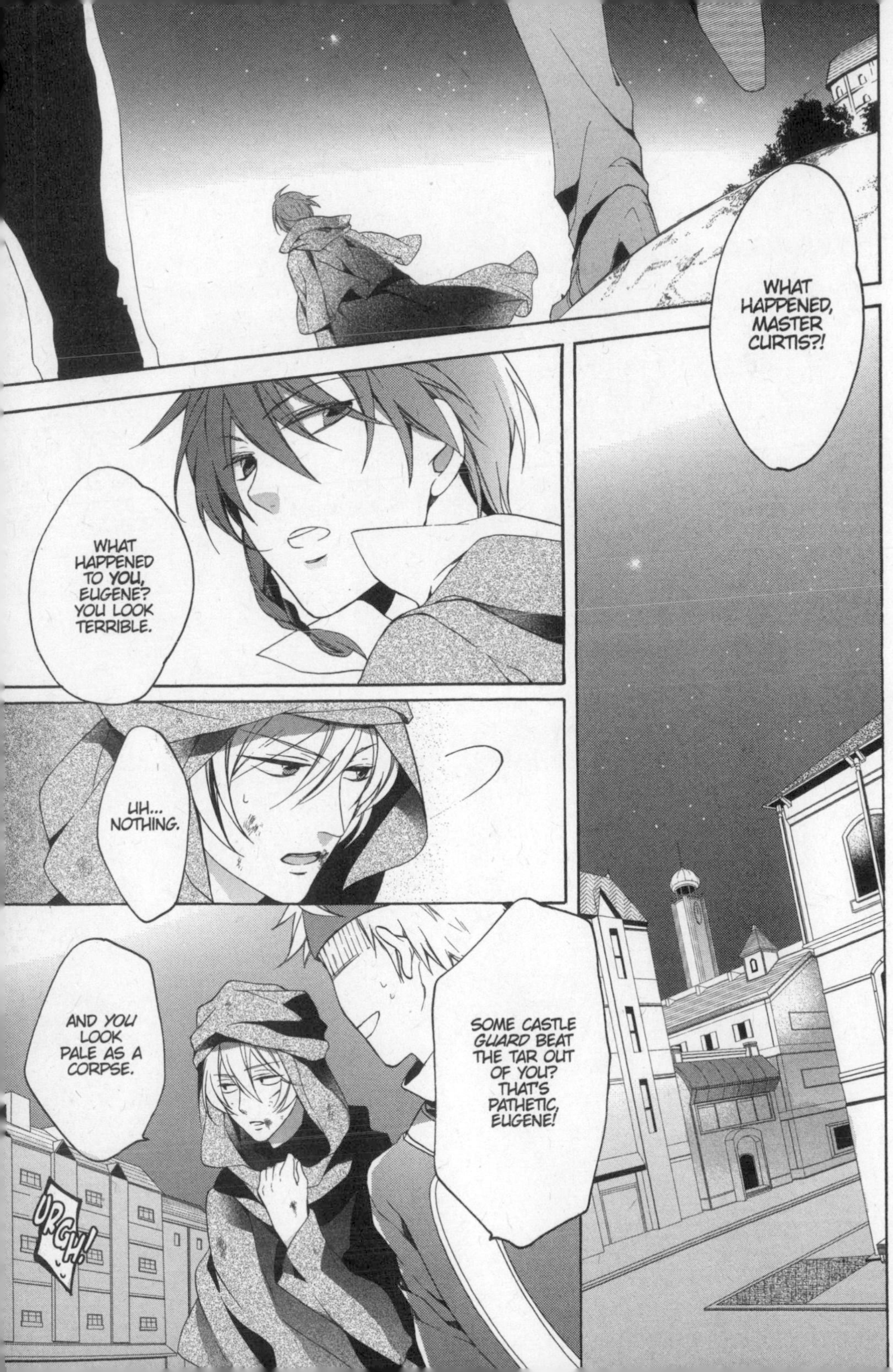
WHAT HAPPENED, MASTER CURTIS?!
WHAT HAPPENED TO YOU, EUGENE? YOU LOOK TERRIBLE.
UH... NOTHING.
SOME CASTLE *GUARD* BEAT THE TAR OUT OF YOU? THAT'S PATHETIC, EUGENE!
AND *YOU* LOOK PALE AS A CORPSE.
URGH!

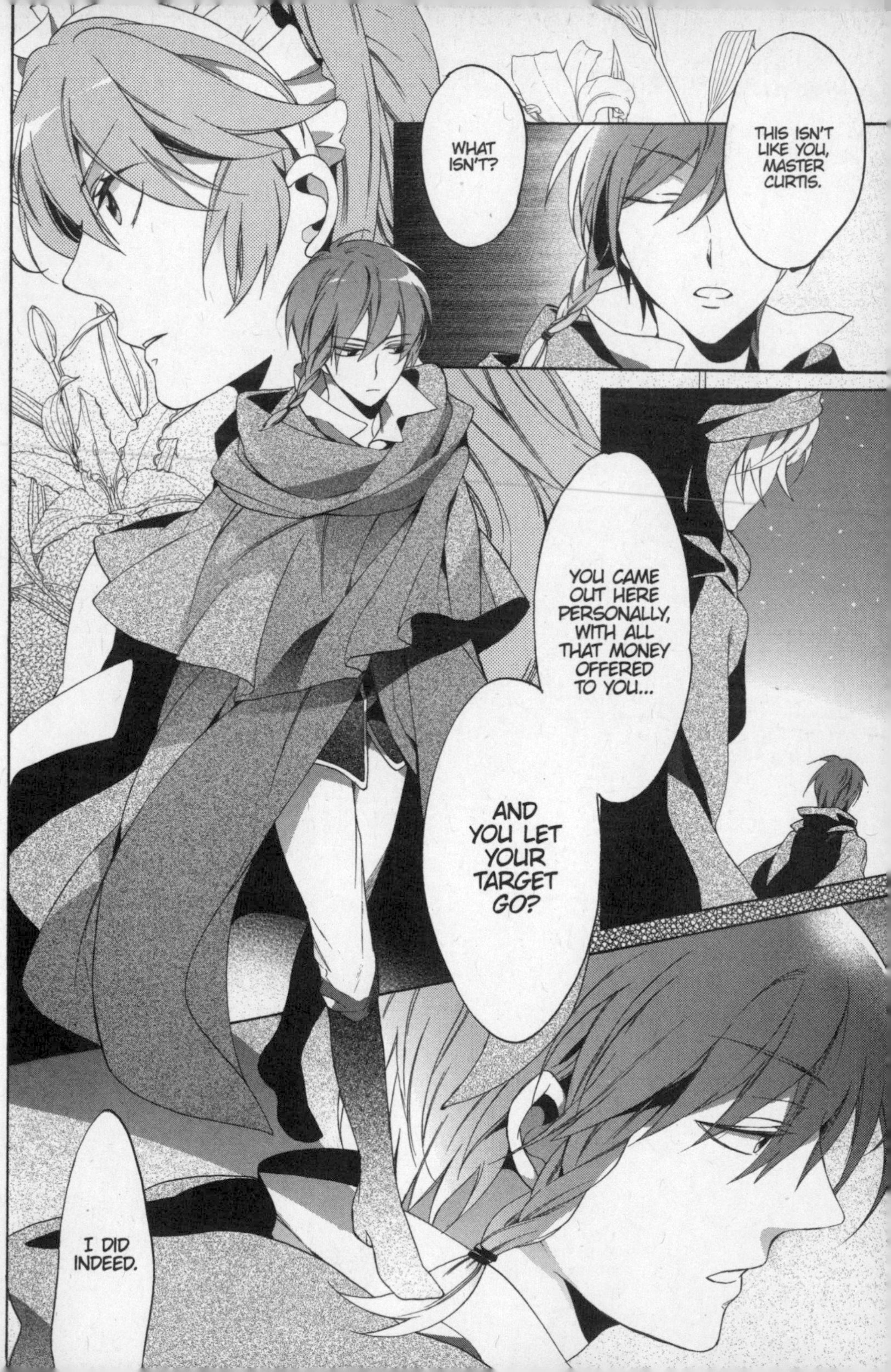
THIS ISN'T LIKE YOU, MASTER CURTIS.
WHAT ISN'T?
YOU CAME OUT HERE PERSONALLY, WITH ALL THAT MONEY OFFERED TO YOU...
AND YOU LET YOUR TARGET GO?
I DID INDEED.

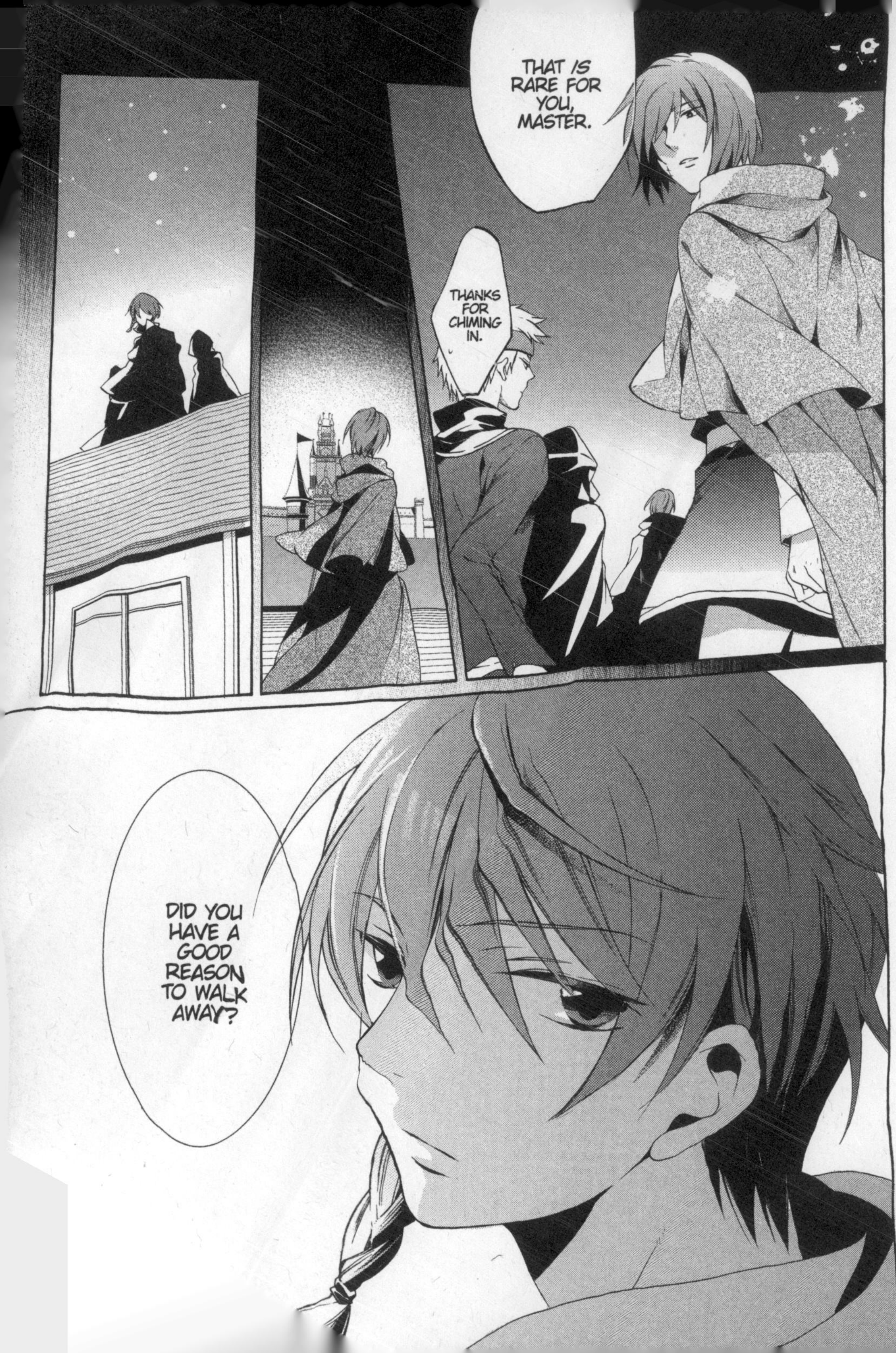
THAT IS RARE FOR YOU, MASTER.
THANKS FOR CHIMING IN.
DID YOU HAVE A GOOD REASON TO WALK AWAY?

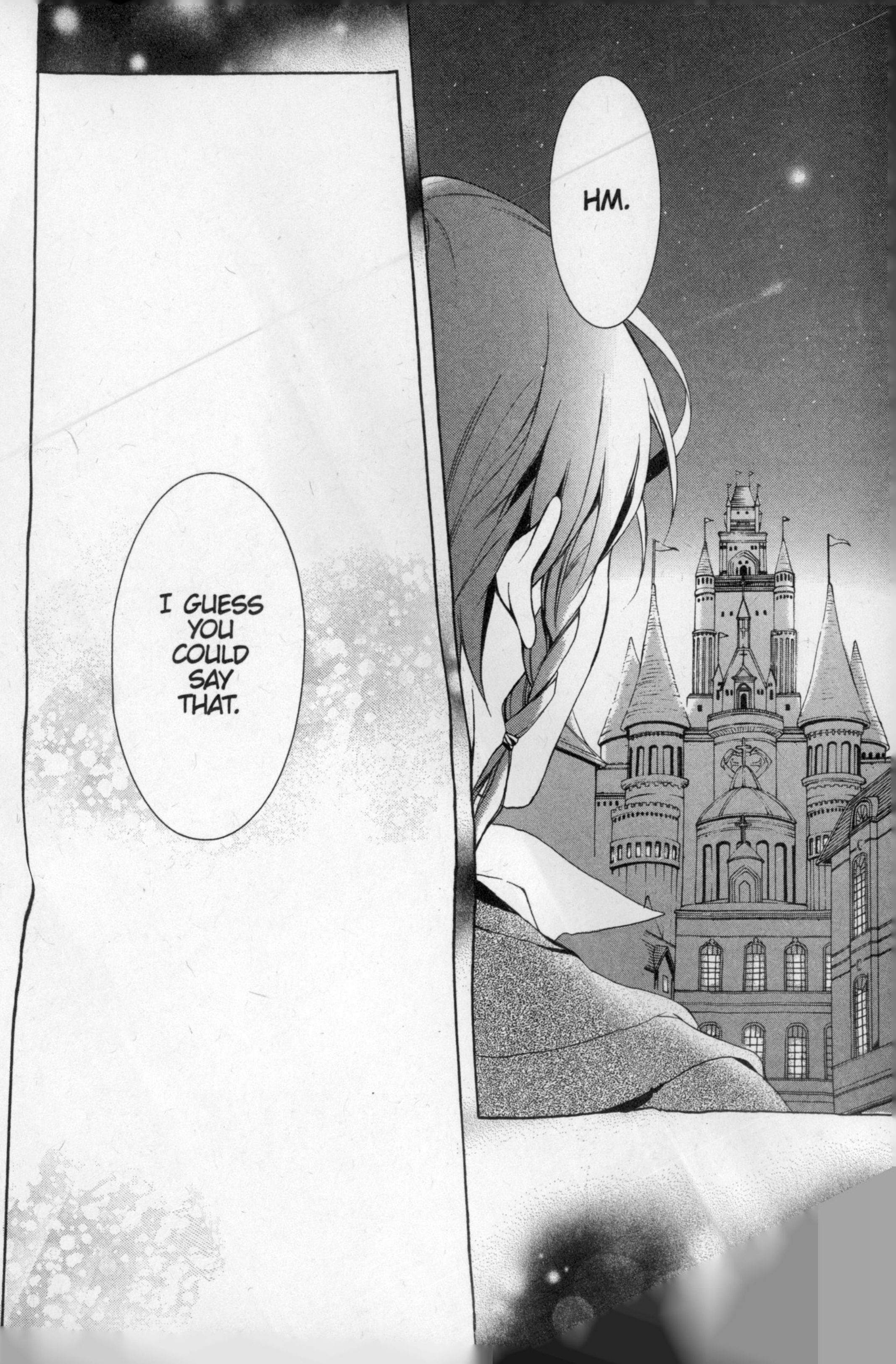
HM.
I GUESS YOU COULD SAY THAT.

CRIMSON EMPIRE

Circumstances to serve a noble

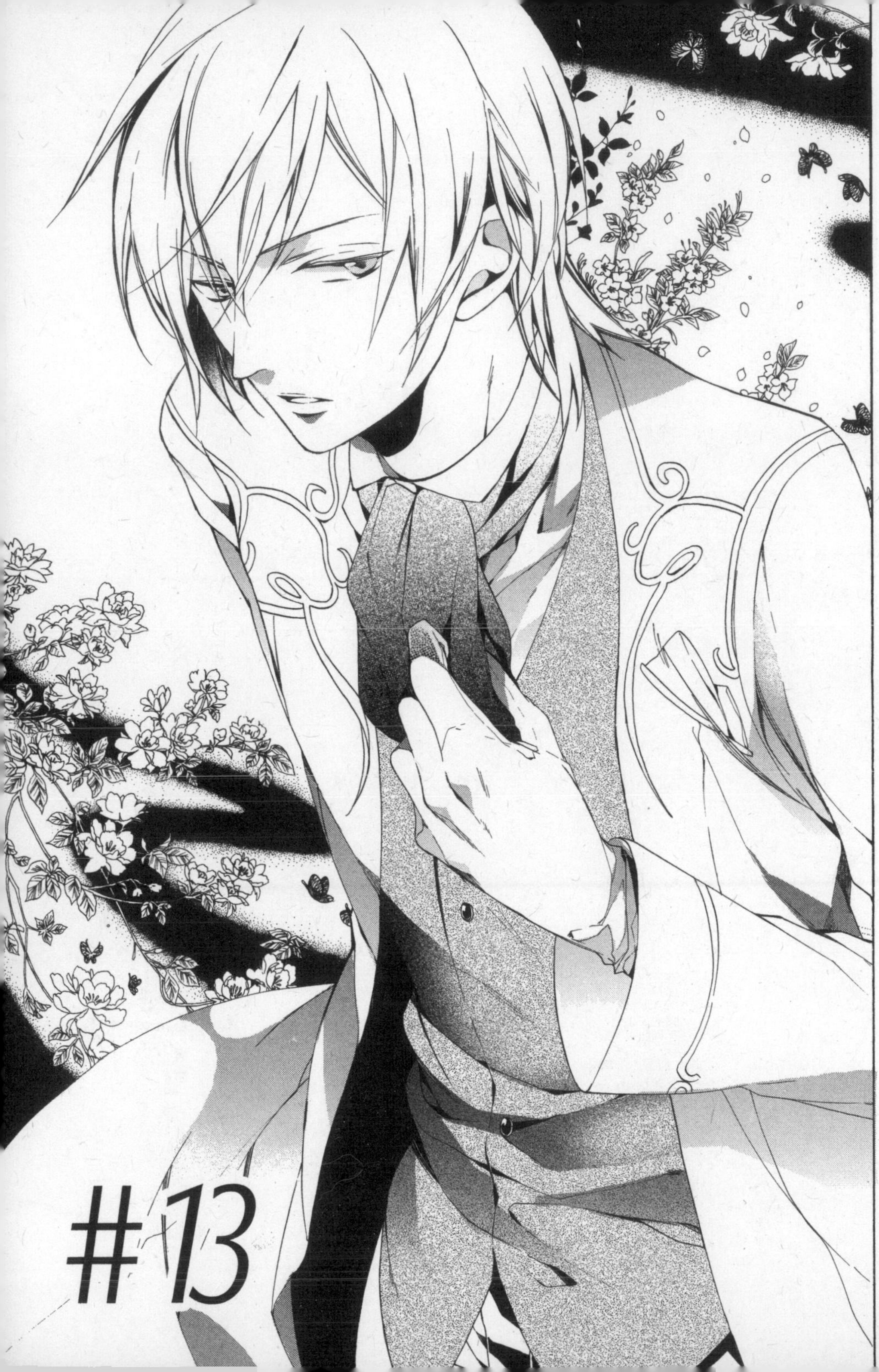
#13

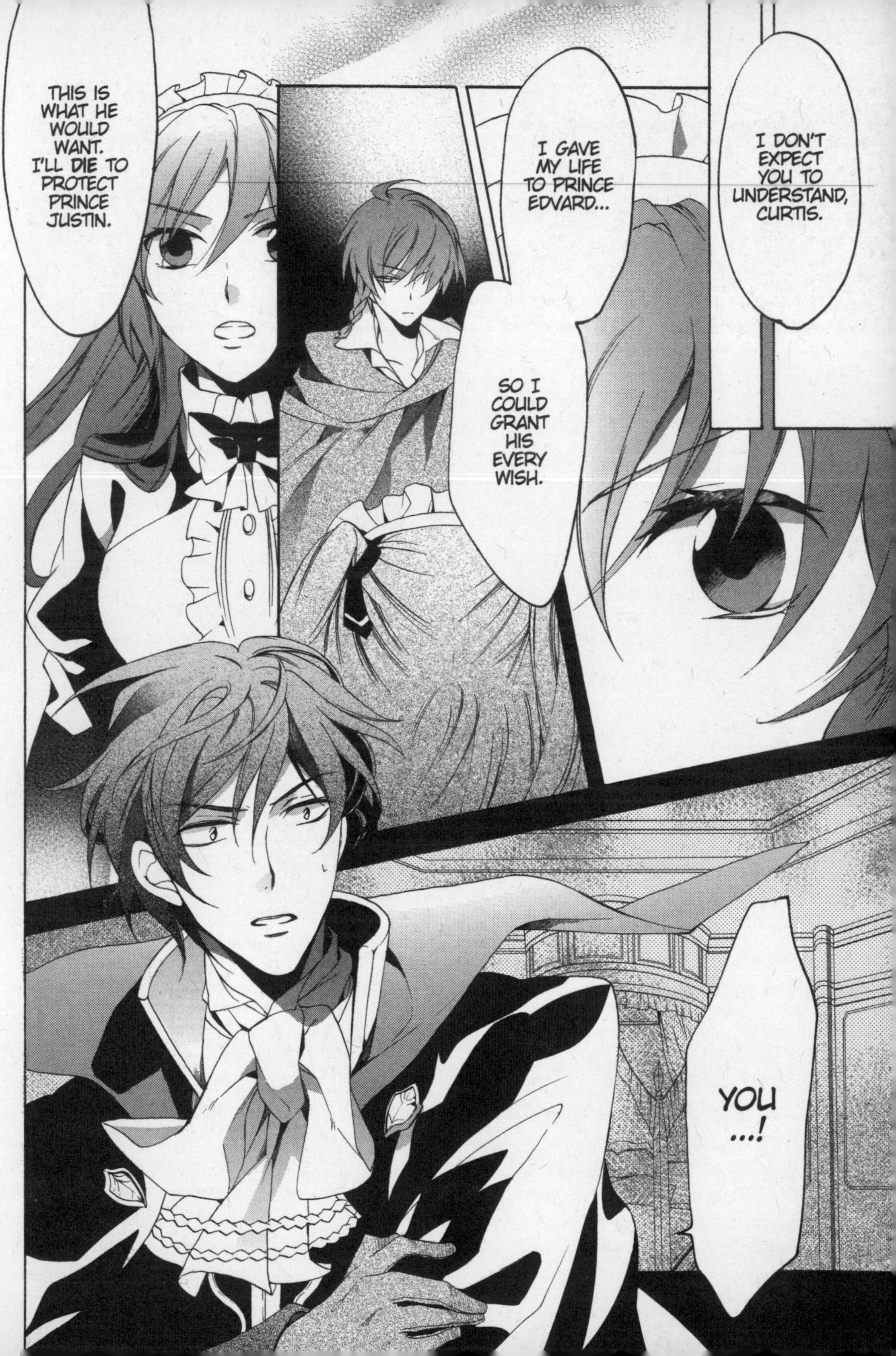
I DON'T EXPECT YOU TO UNDERSTAND, CURTIS.
I GAVE MY LIFE TO PRINCE EDVARD...
SO I COULD GRANT HIS EVERY WISH.
THIS IS WHAT HE WOULD WANT. I'LL DIE TO PROTECT PRINCE JUSTIN.
YOU ...!

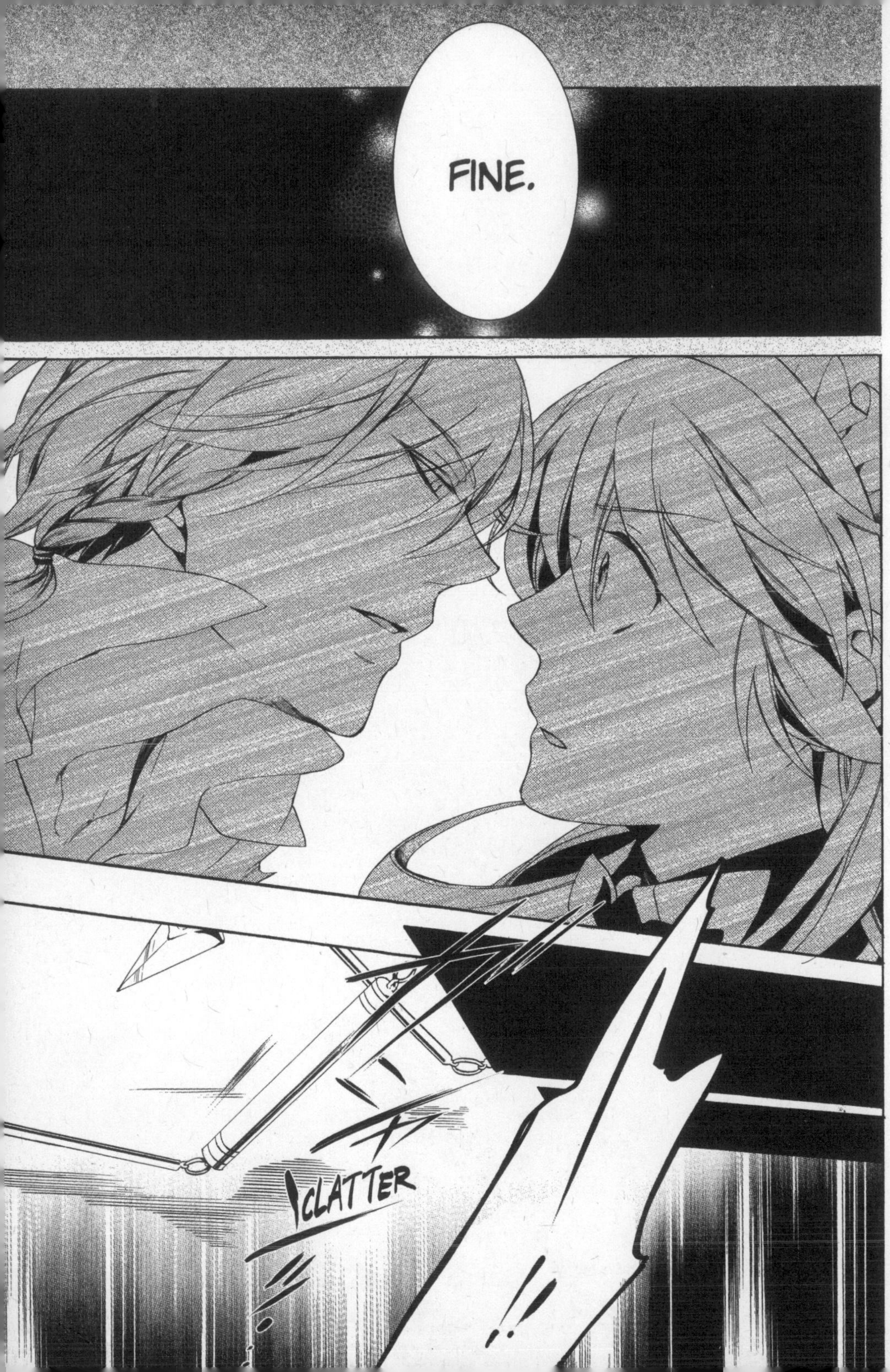
FINE.
CLATTER

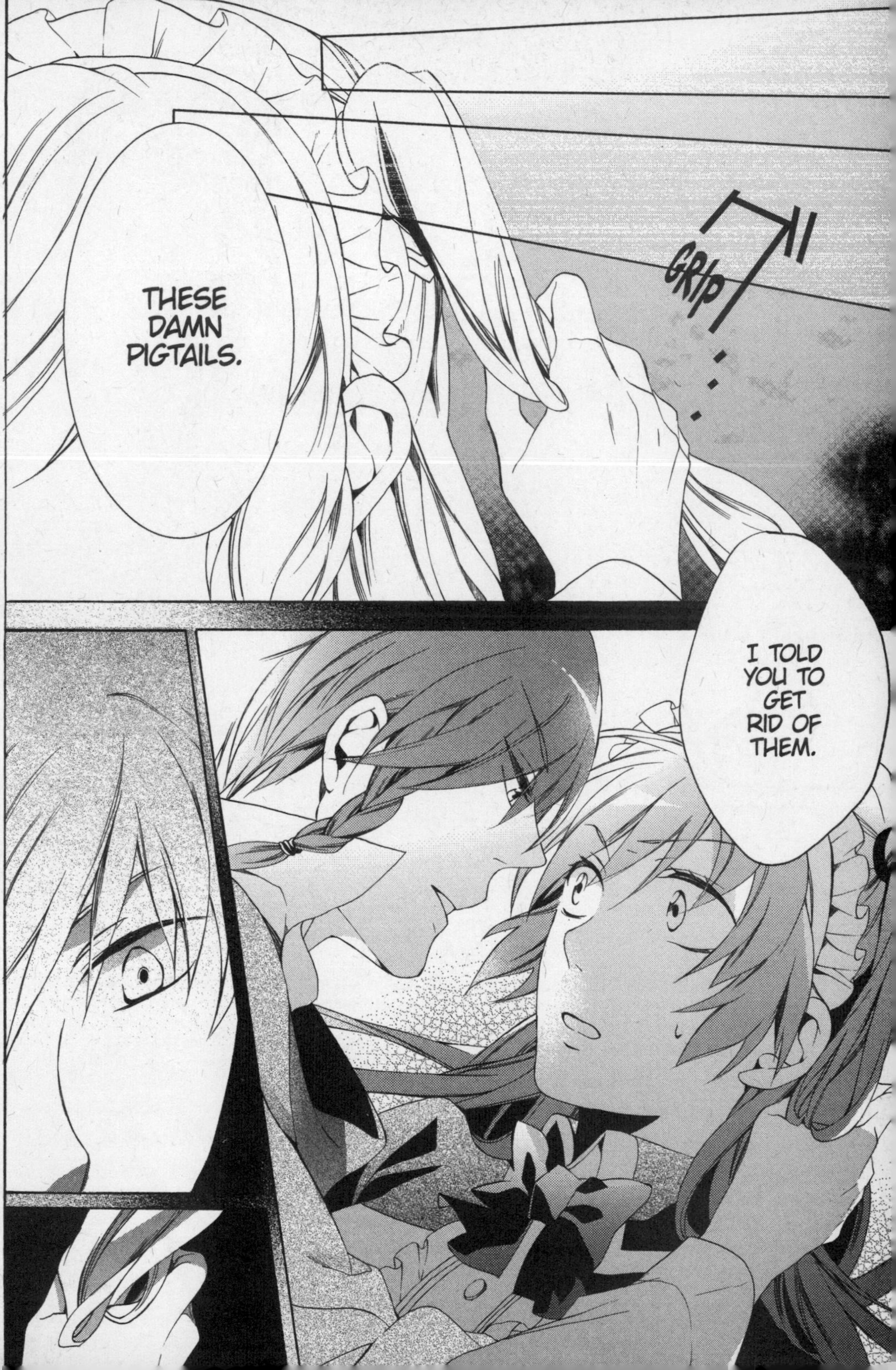
GRIP
THESE DAMN PIGTAILS.
I TOLD YOU TO GET RID OF THEM.

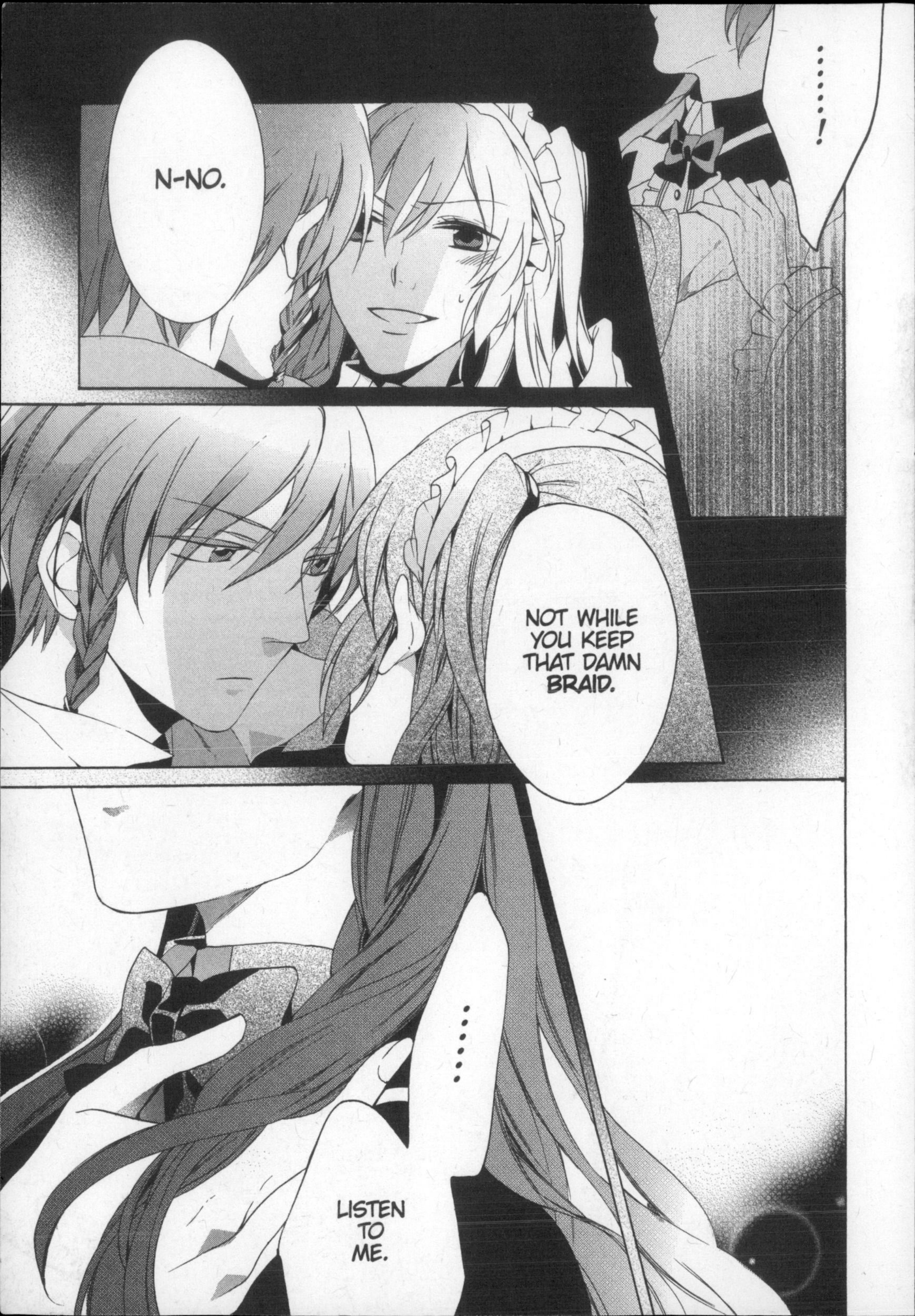
......!
N-NO.
NOT WHILE YOU KEEP THAT DAMN BRAID.
......
LISTEN TO ME.

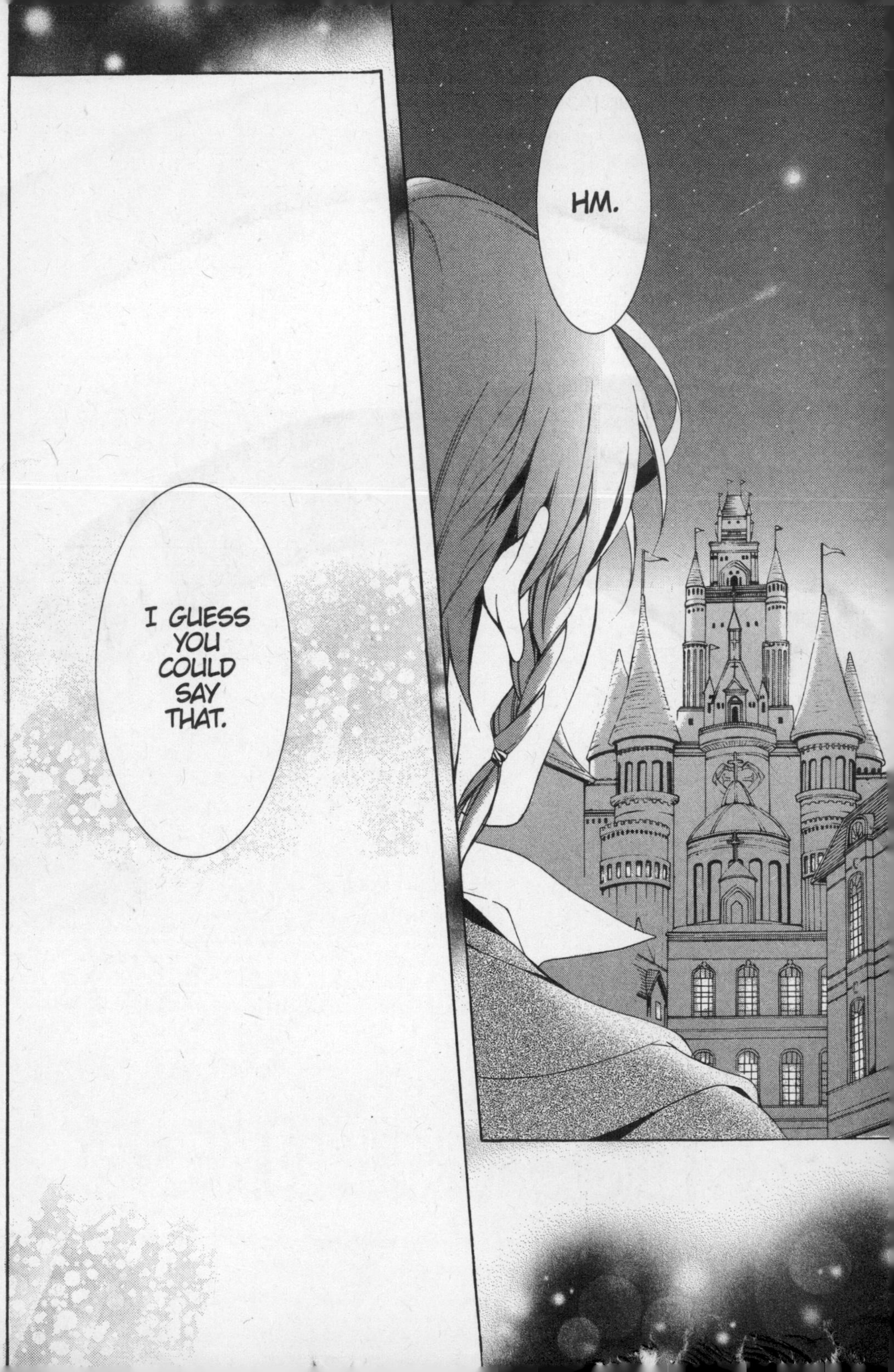
HM.
I GUESS YOU COULD SAY THAT.

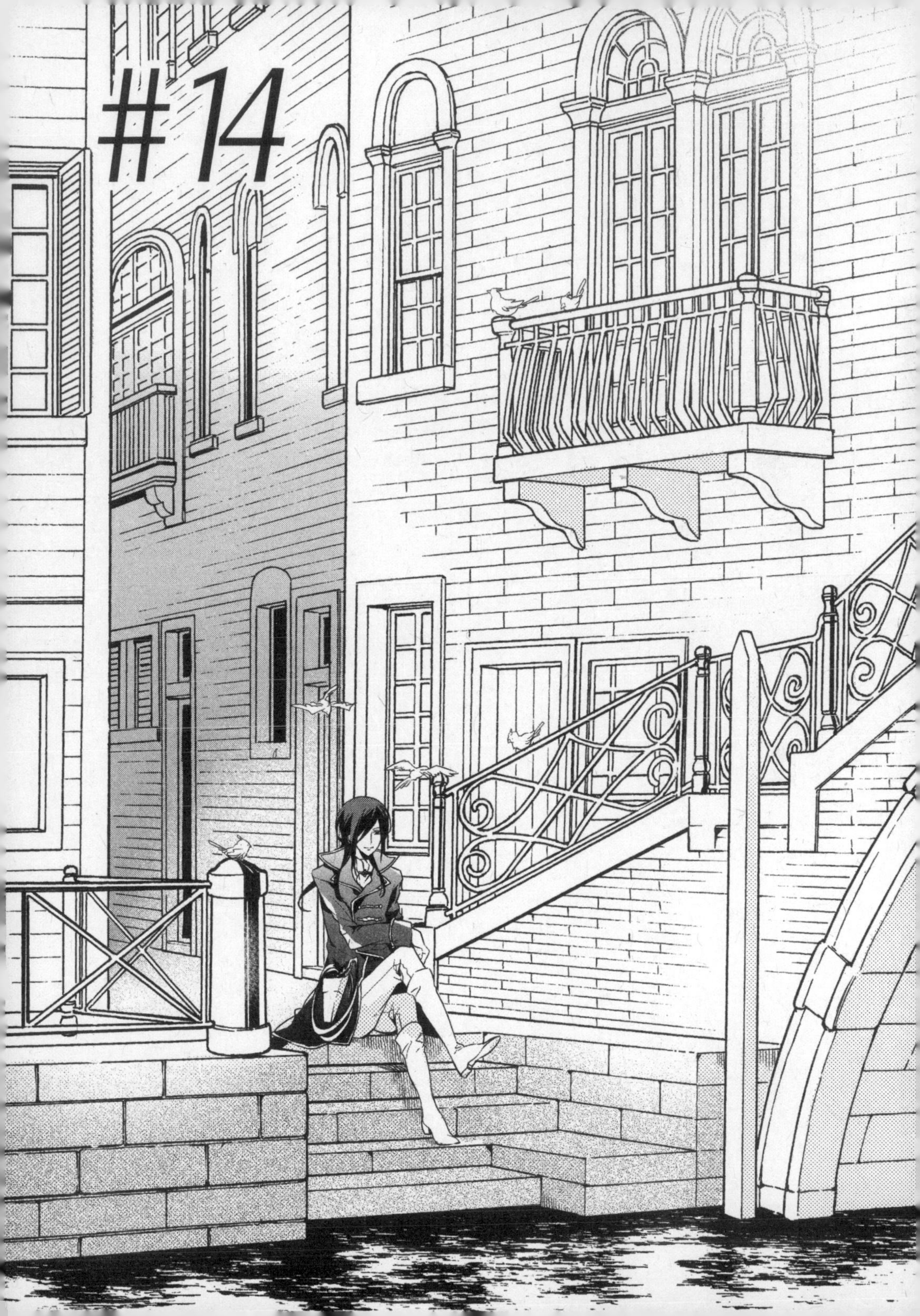
#14

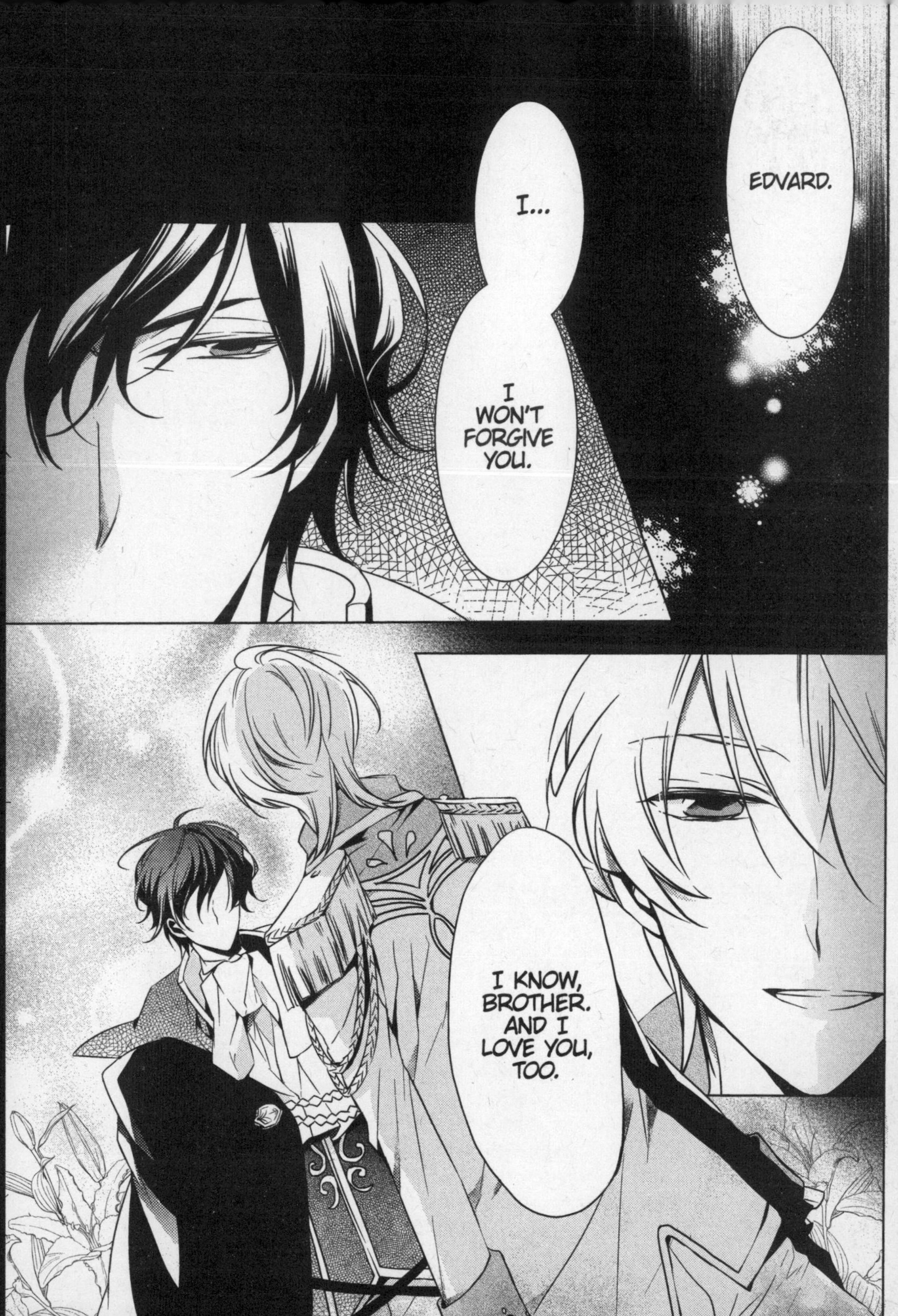
EDVARD.
I...
I WON'T FORGIVE YOU.
I KNOW, BROTHER. AND I LOVE YOU, TOO.

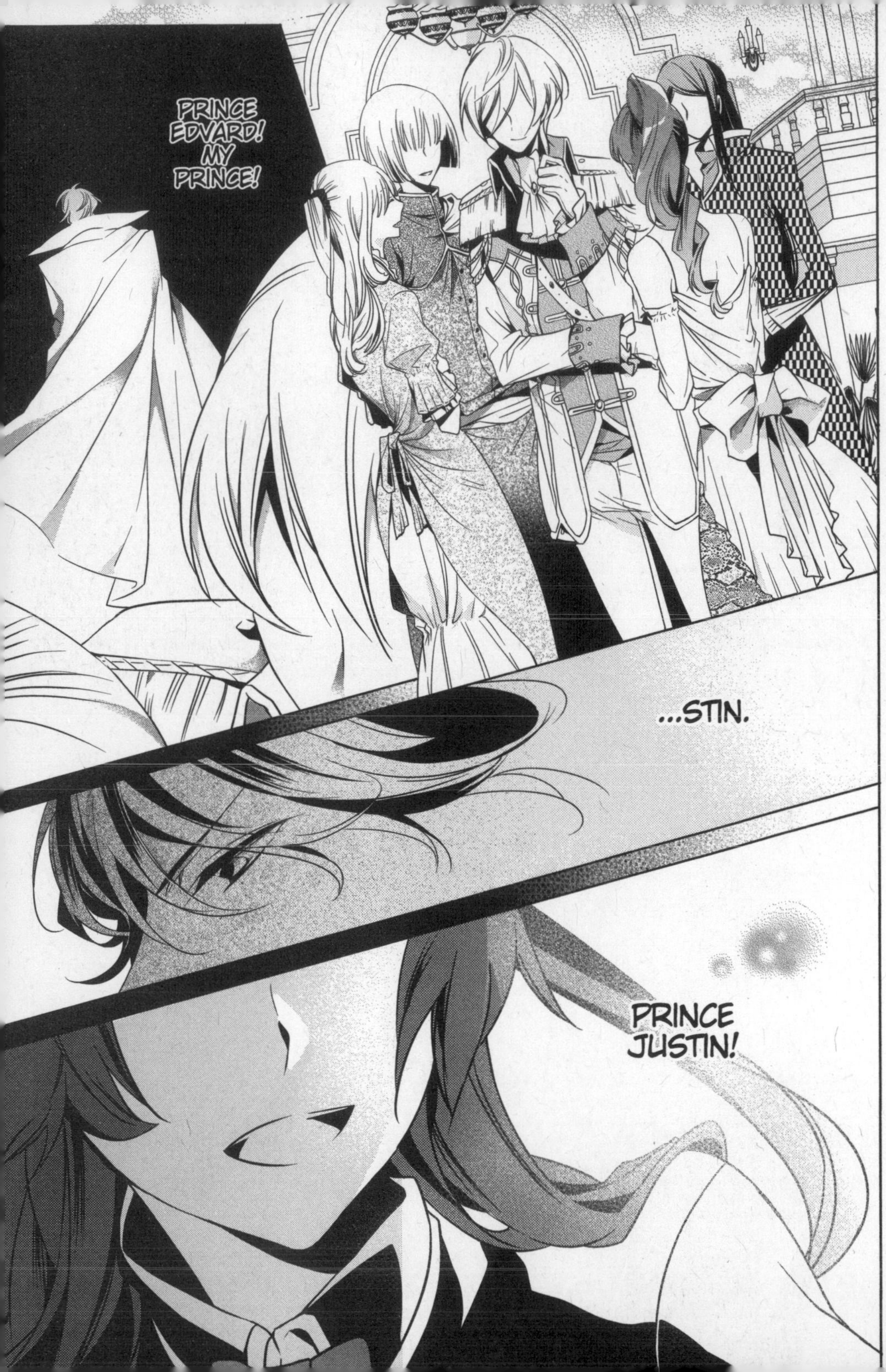
PRINCE EDVARD! MY PRINCE!
...STIN.
PRINCE JUSTIN!

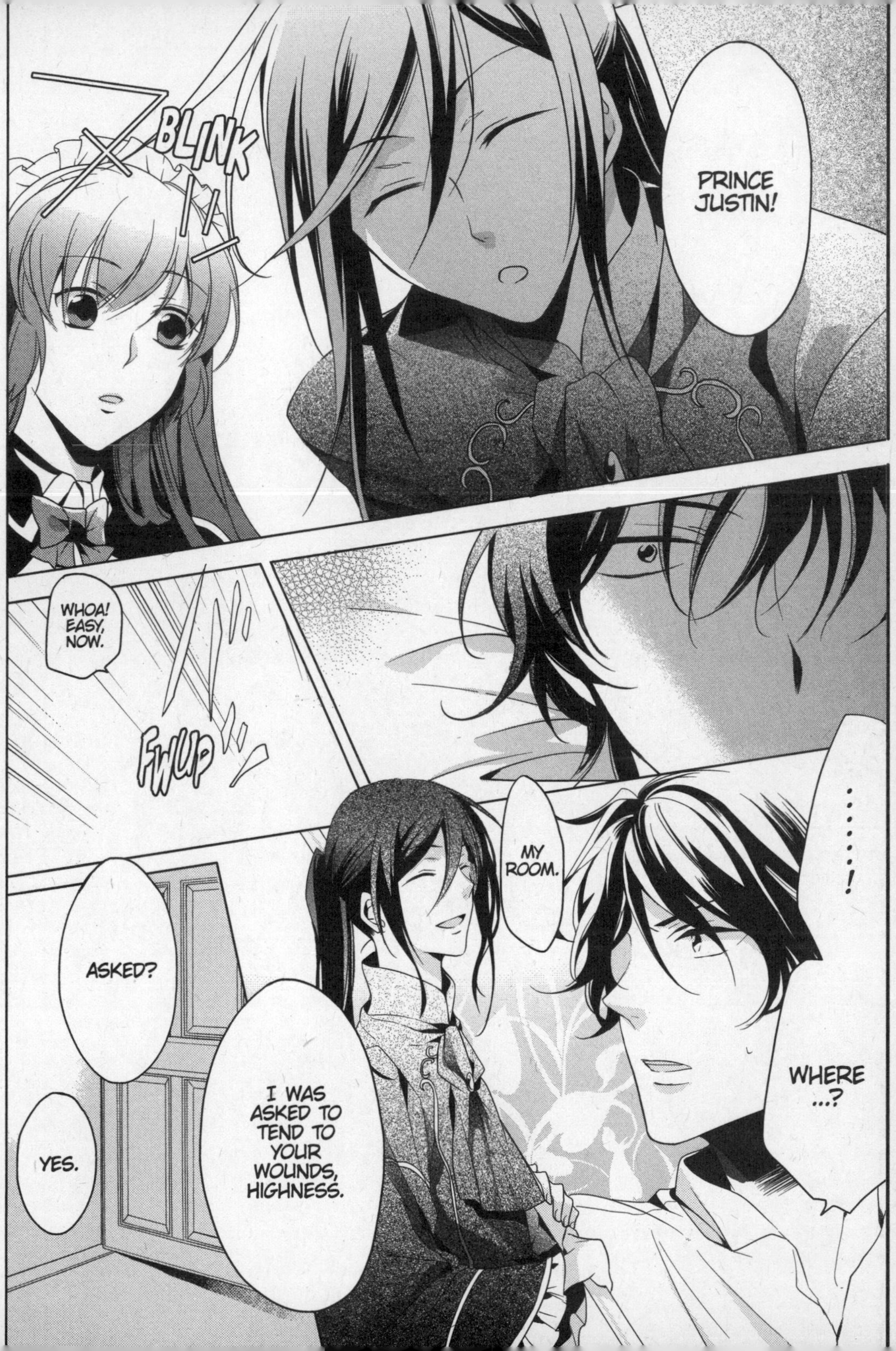
PRINCE JUSTIN!
BLINK
WHOA! EASY, NOW.
FWUP
......!
WHERE ...?
MY ROOM.
I WAS ASKED TO TEND TO YOUR WOUNDS, HIGHNESS.
ASKED?
YES.

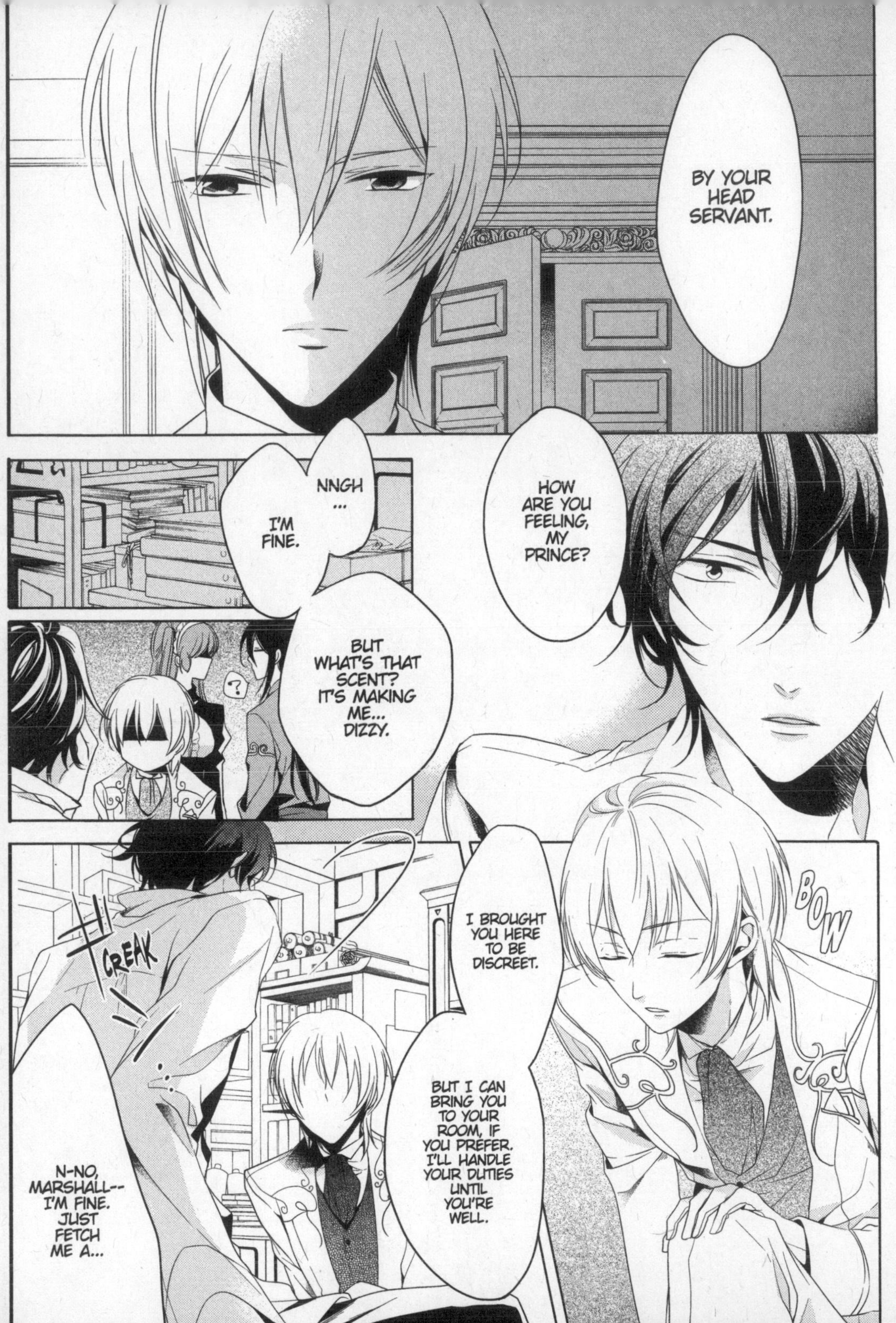
BY YOUR HEAD SERVANT.
HOW ARE YOU FEELING, MY PRINCE?
NNGH ... I'M FINE.
BUT WHAT'S THAT SCENT? IT'S MAKING ME... DIZZY.
?
BOW
I BROUGHT YOU HERE TO BE DISCREET.
BUT I CAN BRING YOU TO YOUR ROOM, IF YOU PREFER. I'LL HANDLE YOUR DUTIES UNTIL YOU'RE WELL.
CREAK
...
N-NO, MARSHALL-- I'M FINE. JUST FETCH ME A...

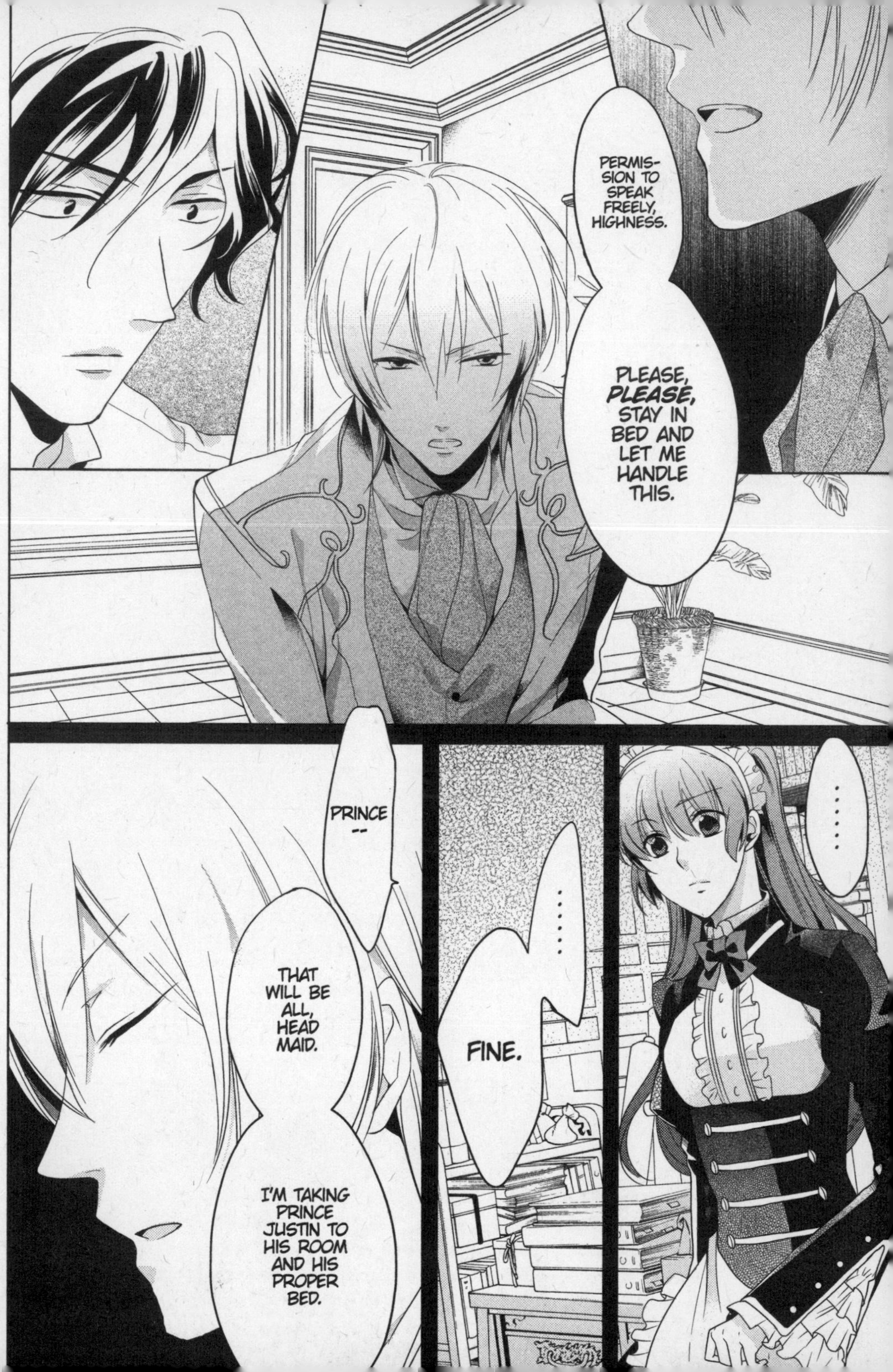
PERMISSION TO SPEAK FREELY, HIGHNESS.
PLEASE, *PLEASE*, STAY IN BED AND LET ME HANDLE THIS.
......
......
FINE.
PRINCE --
THAT WILL BE ALL, HEAD MAID.
I'M TAKING PRINCE JUSTIN TO HIS ROOM AND HIS PROPER BED.

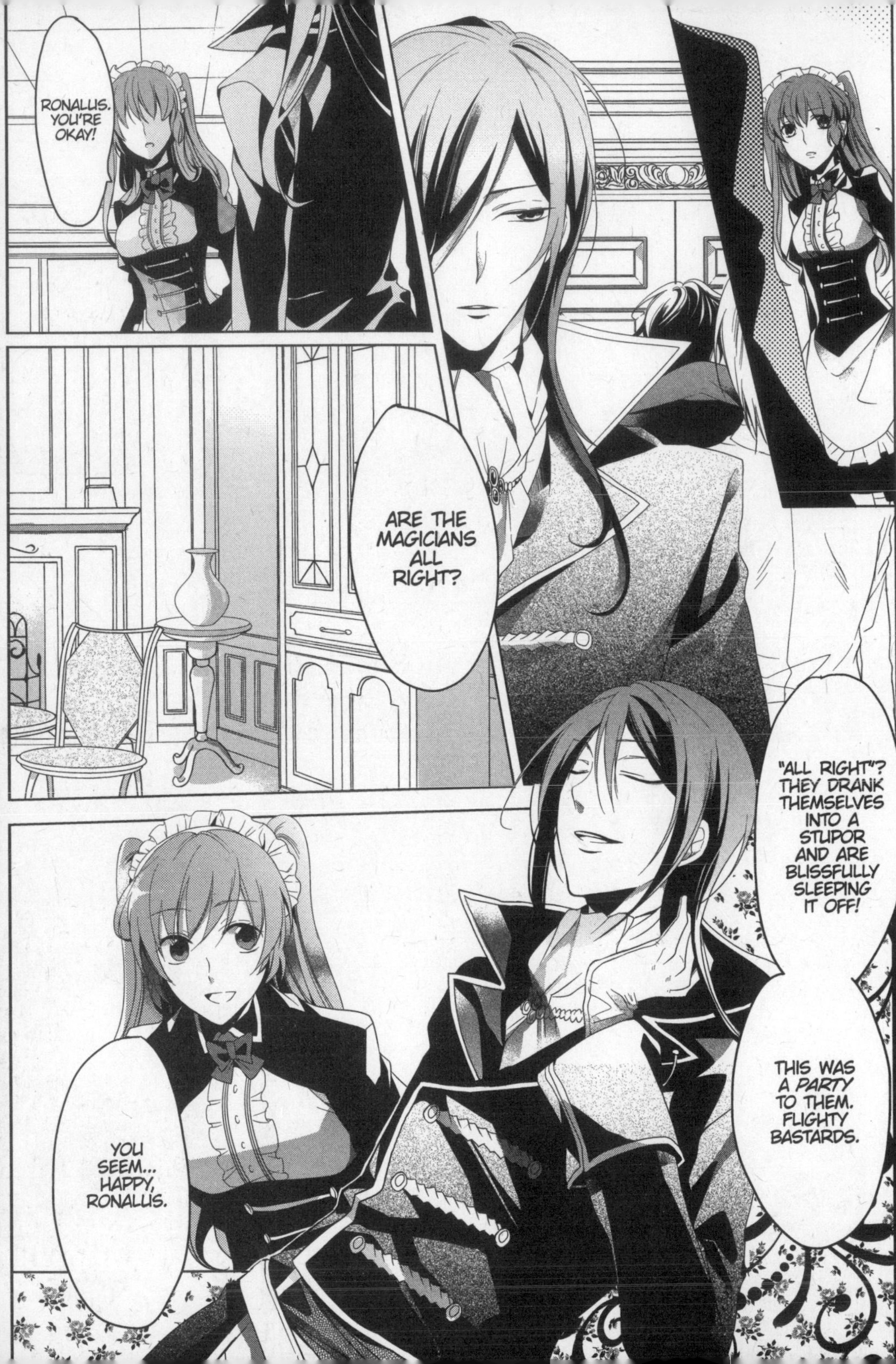
RONALUS. YOU'RE OKAY!
ARE THE MAGICIANS ALL RIGHT?
"ALL RIGHT"? THEY DRANK THEMSELVES INTO A STUPOR AND ARE BLISSFULLY SLEEPING IT OFF!
THIS WAS A *PARTY* TO THEM. FLIGHTY BASTARDS.
YOU SEEM... HAPPY, RONALUS.

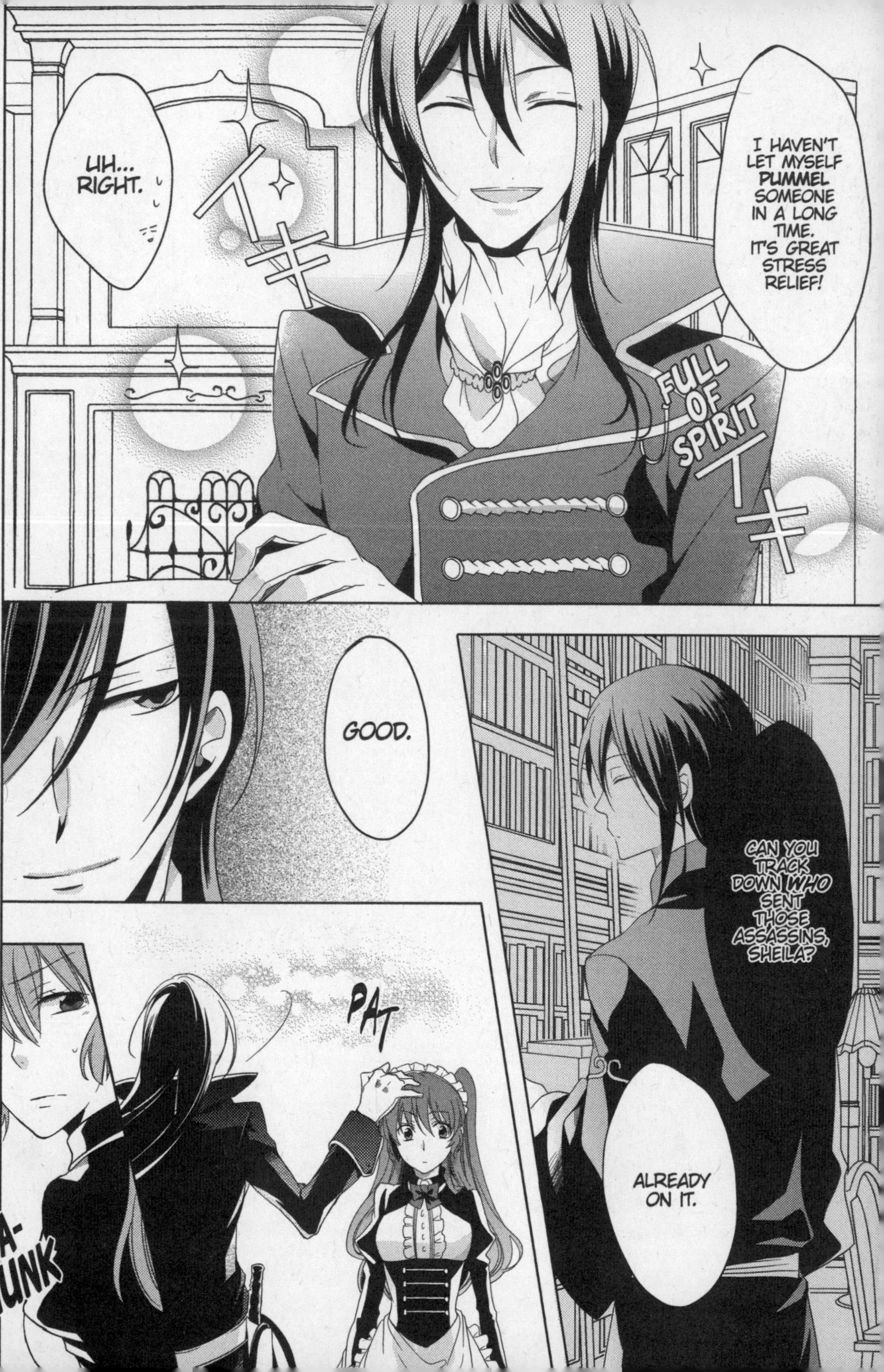
I HAVEN'T LET MYSELF PUMMEL SOMEONE IN A LONG TIME. IT'S GREAT STRESS RELIEF!
FULL OF SPIRIT
UH... RIGHT.
CAN YOU TRACK DOWN WHO SENT THOSE ASSASSINS, SHEILA?
ALREADY ON IT.
GOOD.
PAT
KA-CHUNK

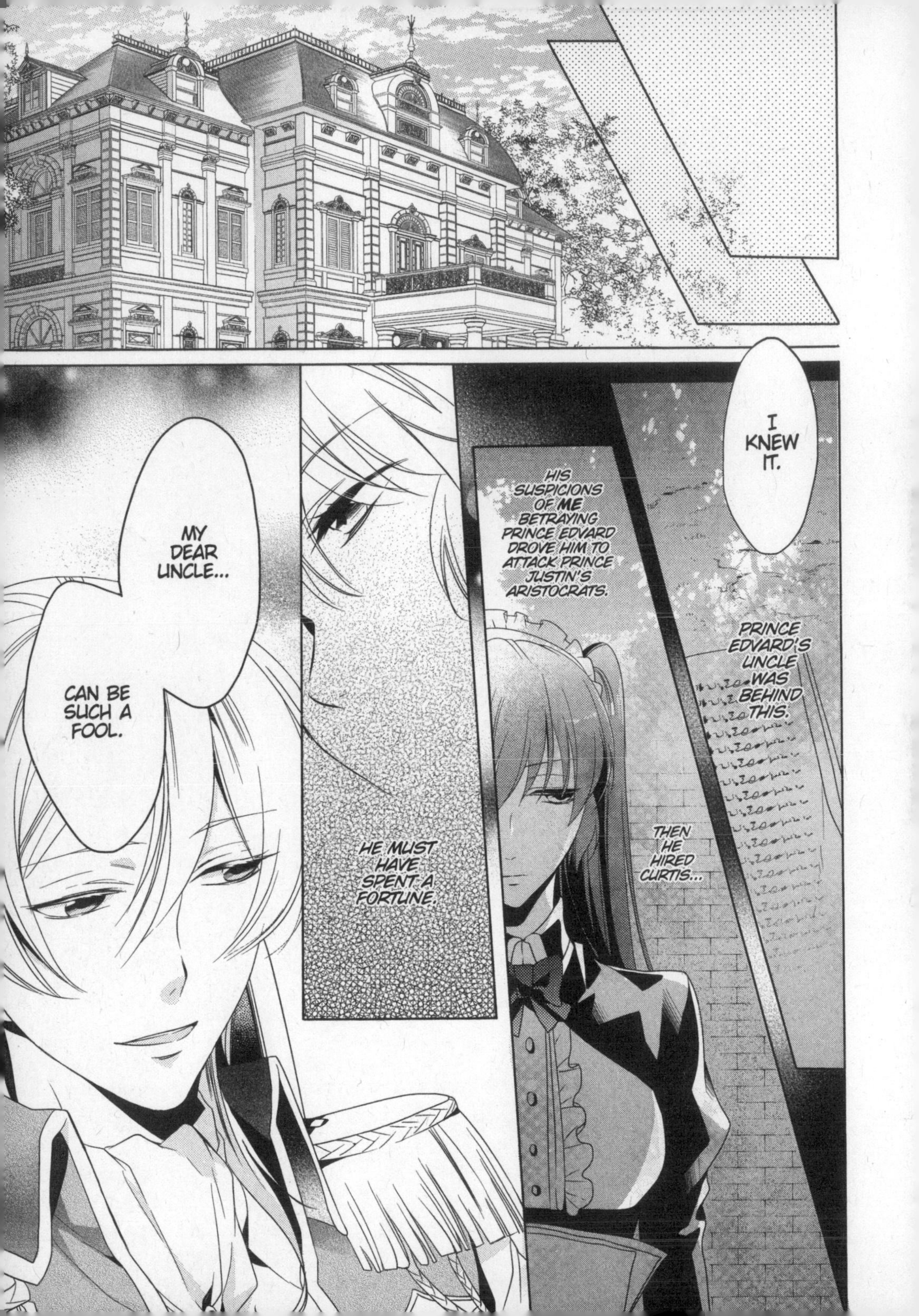

I KNEW IT.
PRINCE EDVARD'S UNCLE WAS BEHIND THIS.
THEN HE HIRED CURTIS...
HIS SUSPICIONS OF ME BETRAYING PRINCE EDVARD DROVE HIM TO ATTACK PRINCE JUSTIN'S ARISTOCRATS.
HE MUST HAVE SPENT A FORTUNE.
MY DEAR UNCLE...
CAN BE SUCH A FOOL.

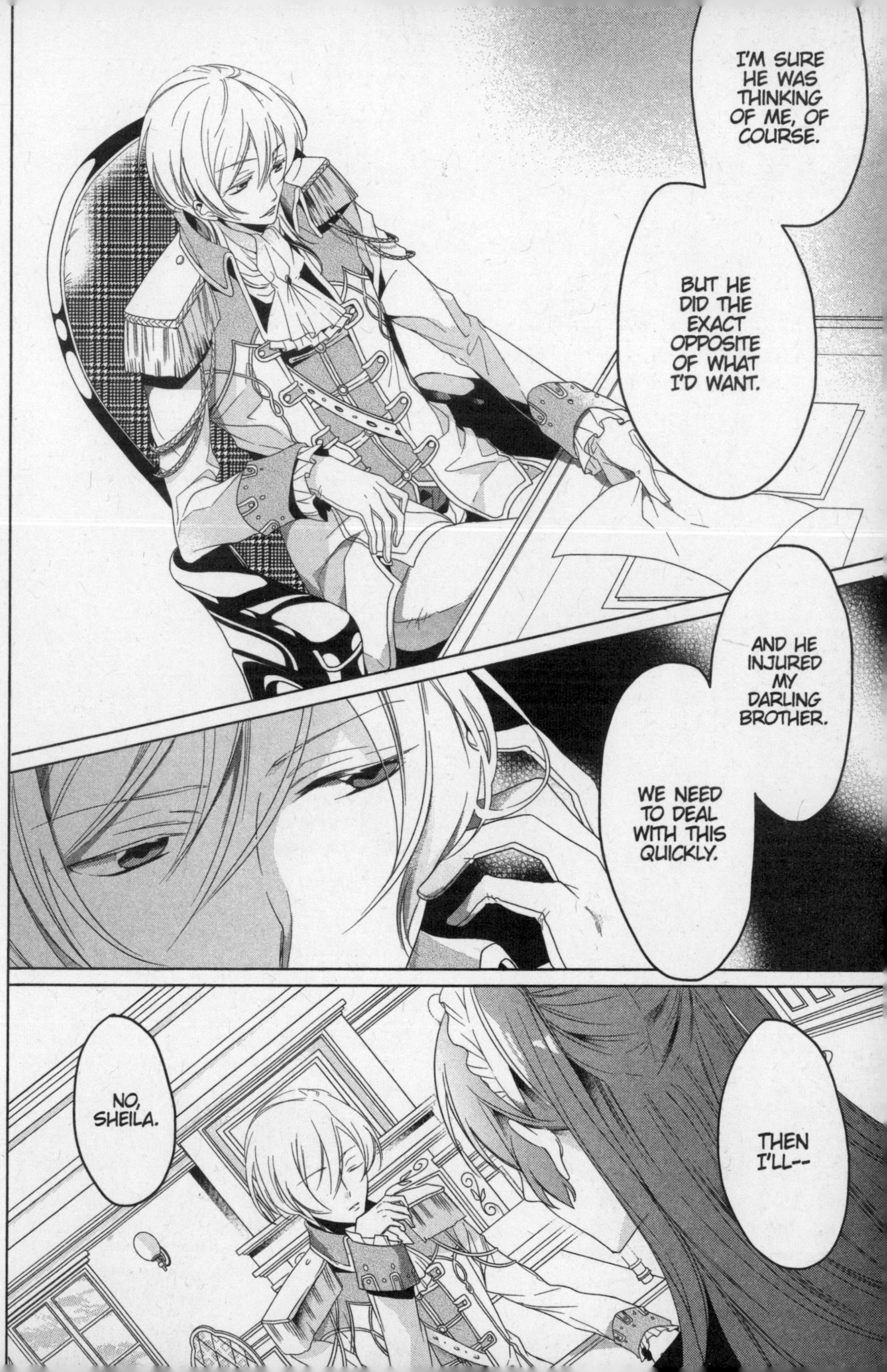
I'M SURE HE WAS THINKING OF ME, OF COURSE.
BUT HE DID THE EXACT OPPOSITE OF WHAT I'D WANT.
AND HE INJURED MY DARLING BROTHER.
WE NEED TO DEAL WITH THIS QUICKLY.
THEN I'LL--
NO, SHEILA.

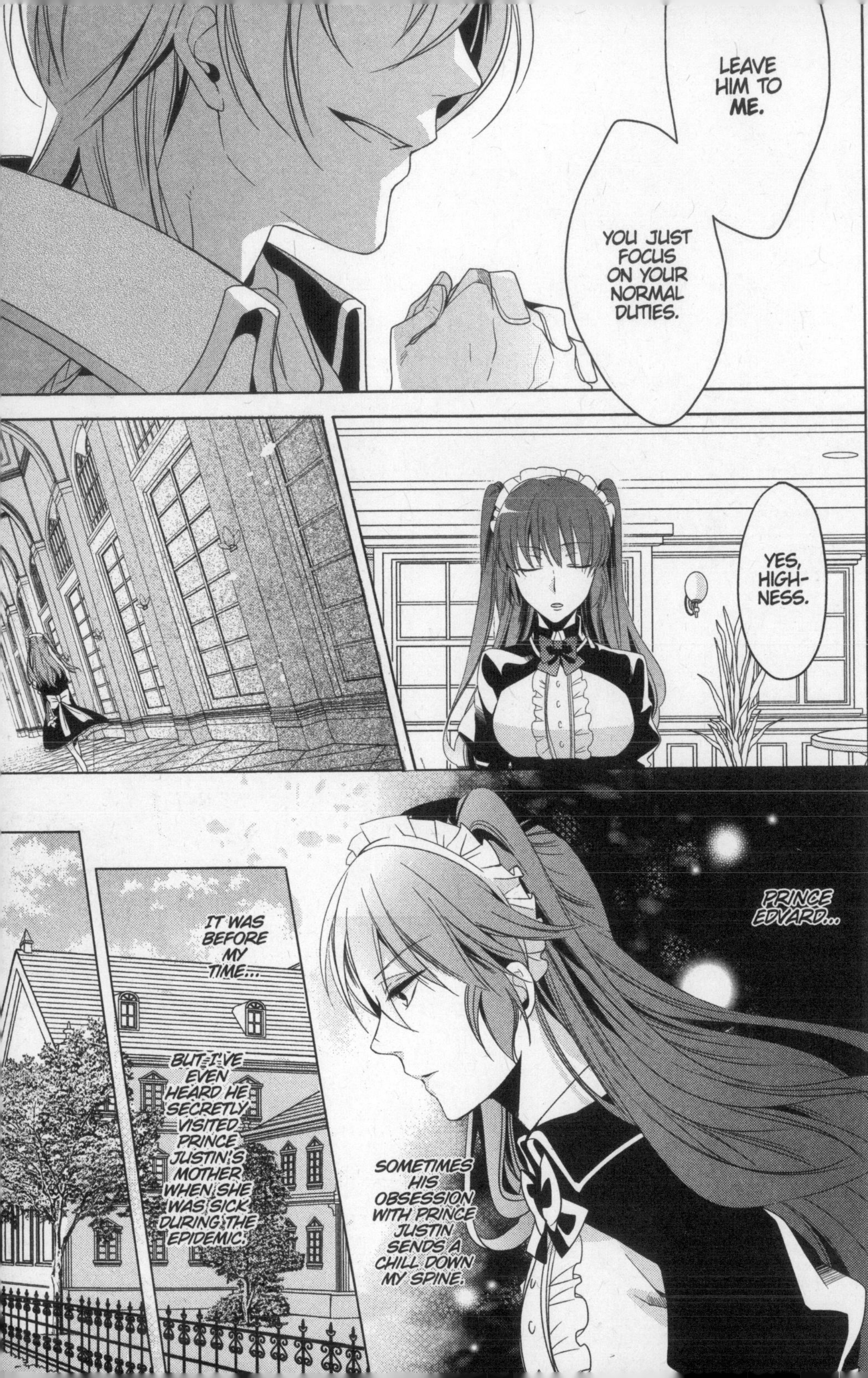
LEAVE HIM TO ME.
YOU JUST FOCUS ON YOUR NORMAL DUTIES.
YES, HIGH-NESS.
PRINCE EDVARD...
SOMETIMES HIS OBSESSION WITH PRINCE JUSTIN SENDS A CHILL DOWN MY SPINE.
IT WAS BEFORE MY TIME...
BUT I'VE EVEN HEARD HE SECRETLY VISITED PRINCE JUSTIN'S MOTHER WHEN SHE WAS SICK DURING THE EPIDEMIC.

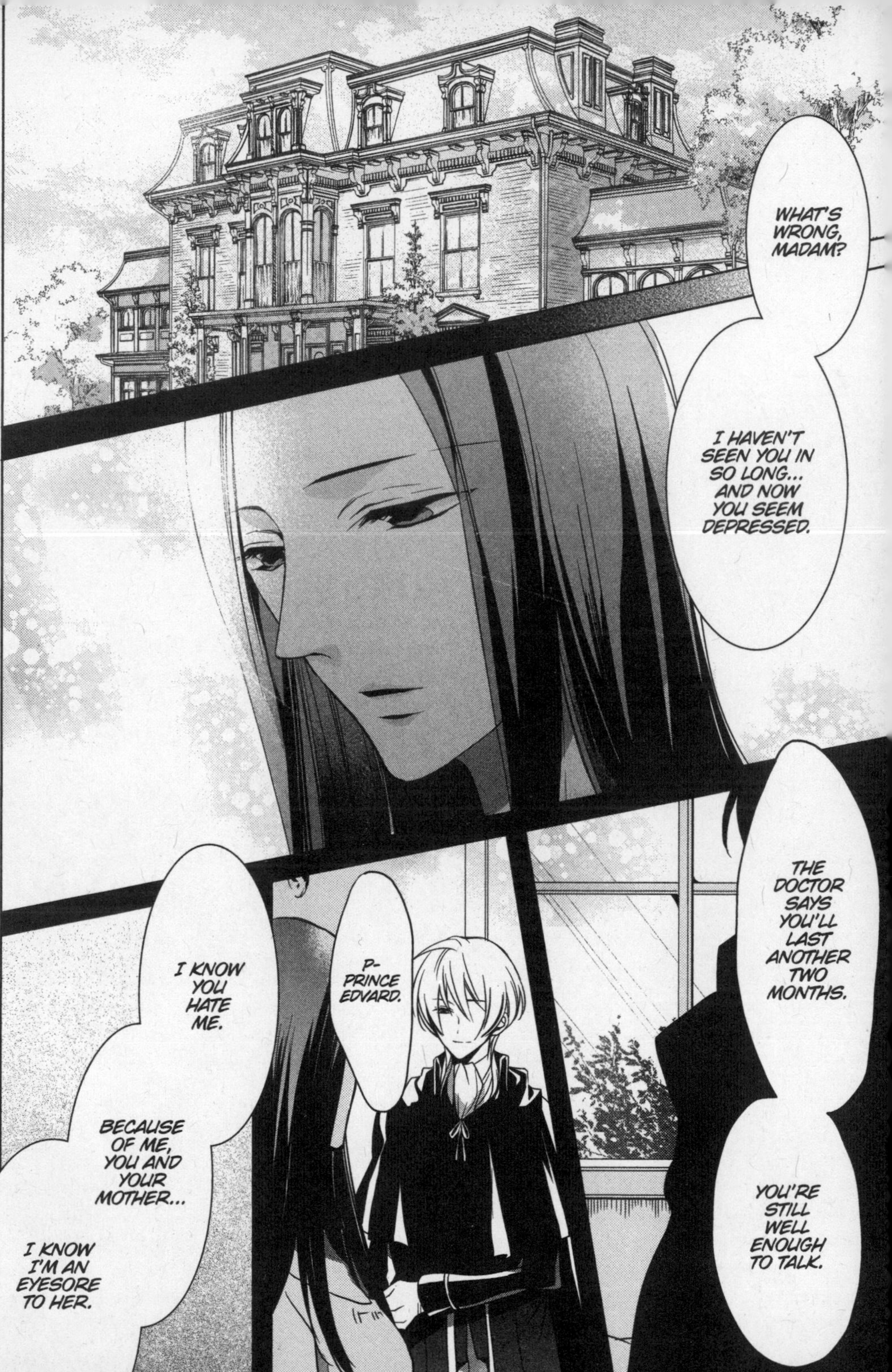
WHAT'S WRONG, MADAM?
I HAVEN'T SEEN YOU IN SO LONG... AND NOW YOU SEEM DEPRESSED.
THE DOCTOR SAYS YOU'LL LAST ANOTHER TWO MONTHS.
YOU'RE STILL WELL ENOUGH TO TALK.
P-PRINCE EDVARD.
I KNOW YOU HATE ME.
BECAUSE OF ME, YOU AND YOUR MOTHER...
I KNOW I'M AN EYESORE TO HER.

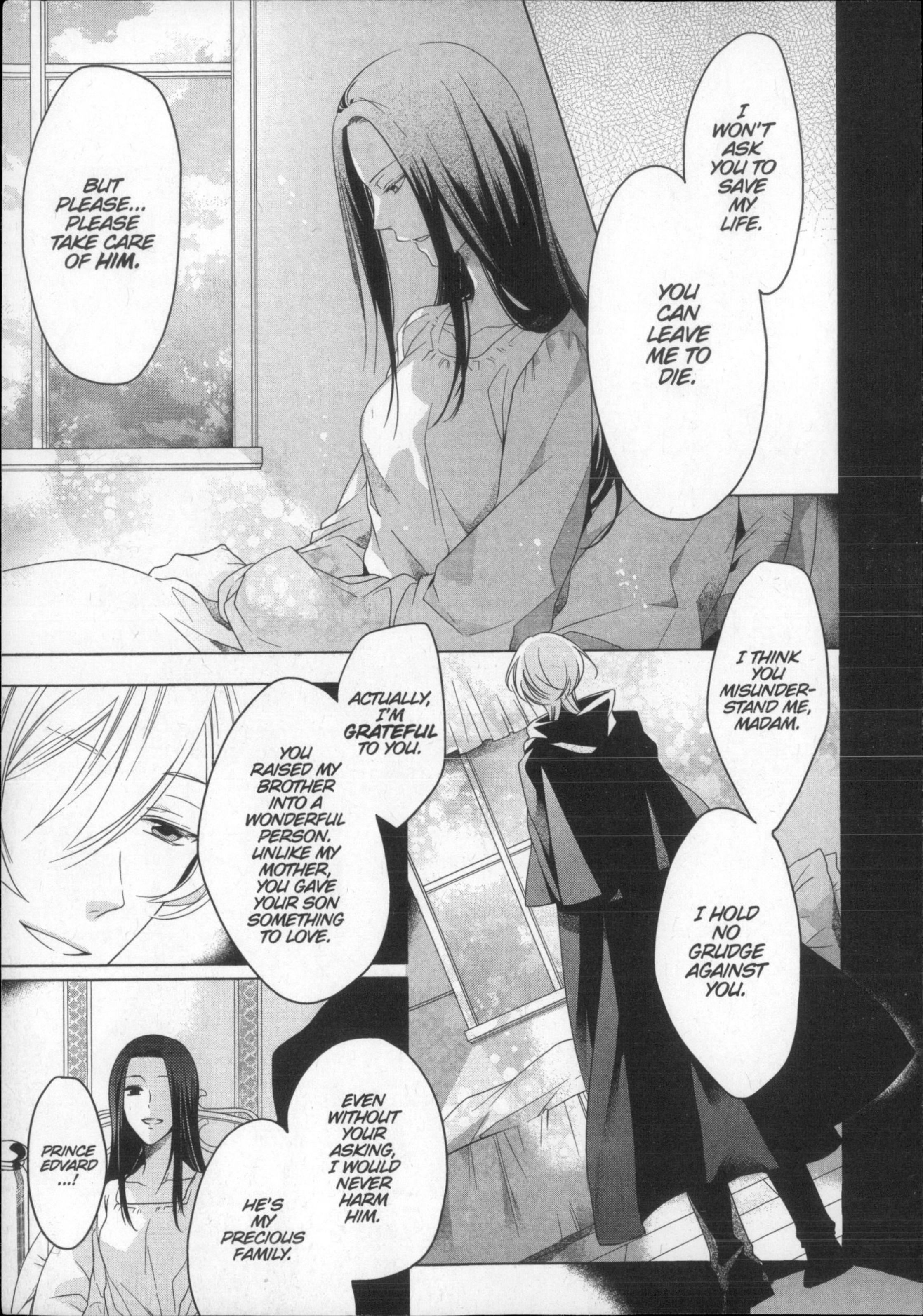
I WON'T ASK YOU TO SAVE MY LIFE.
YOU CAN LEAVE ME TO DIE.
BUT PLEASE... PLEASE TAKE CARE OF **HIM.**
I THINK YOU MISUNDERSTAND ME, MADAM.
I HOLD NO GRUDGE AGAINST YOU.
ACTUALLY, I'M **GRATEFUL** TO YOU.
YOU RAISED MY BROTHER INTO A WONDERFUL PERSON. UNLIKE MY MOTHER, YOU GAVE YOUR SON SOMETHING TO LOVE.
EVEN WITHOUT YOUR ASKING, I WOULD NEVER HARM HIM.
HE'S MY PRECIOUS FAMILY.
PRINCE EDVARD ...!

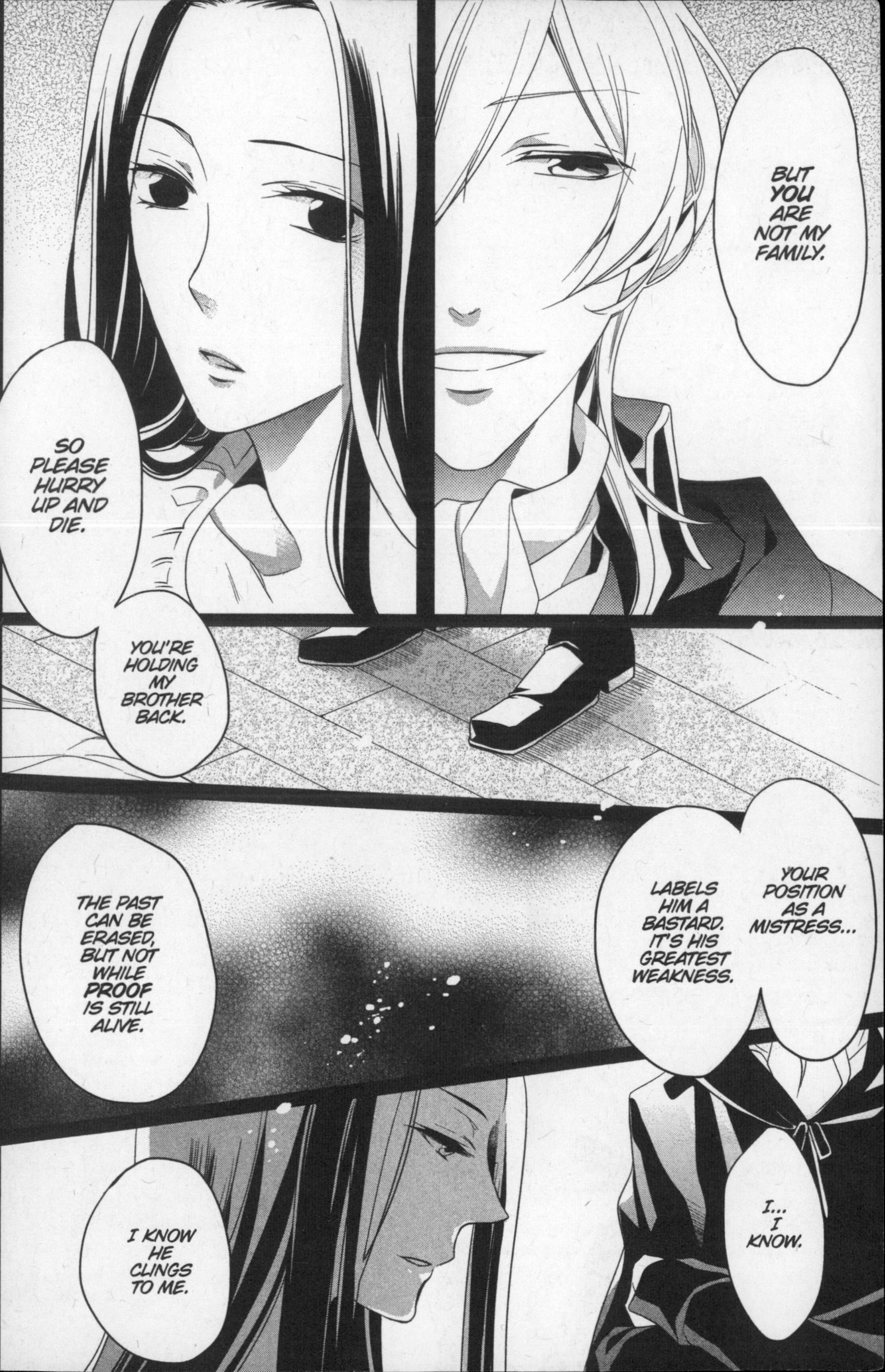
BUT YOU ARE NOT MY FAMILY.
SO PLEASE HURRY UP AND DIE.
YOU'RE HOLDING MY BROTHER BACK.
YOUR POSITION AS A MISTRESS...
LABELS HIM A BASTARD. IT'S HIS GREATEST WEAKNESS.
THE PAST CAN BE ERASED, BUT NOT WHILE PROOF IS STILL ALIVE.
I... I KNOW.
I KNOW HE CLINGS TO ME.

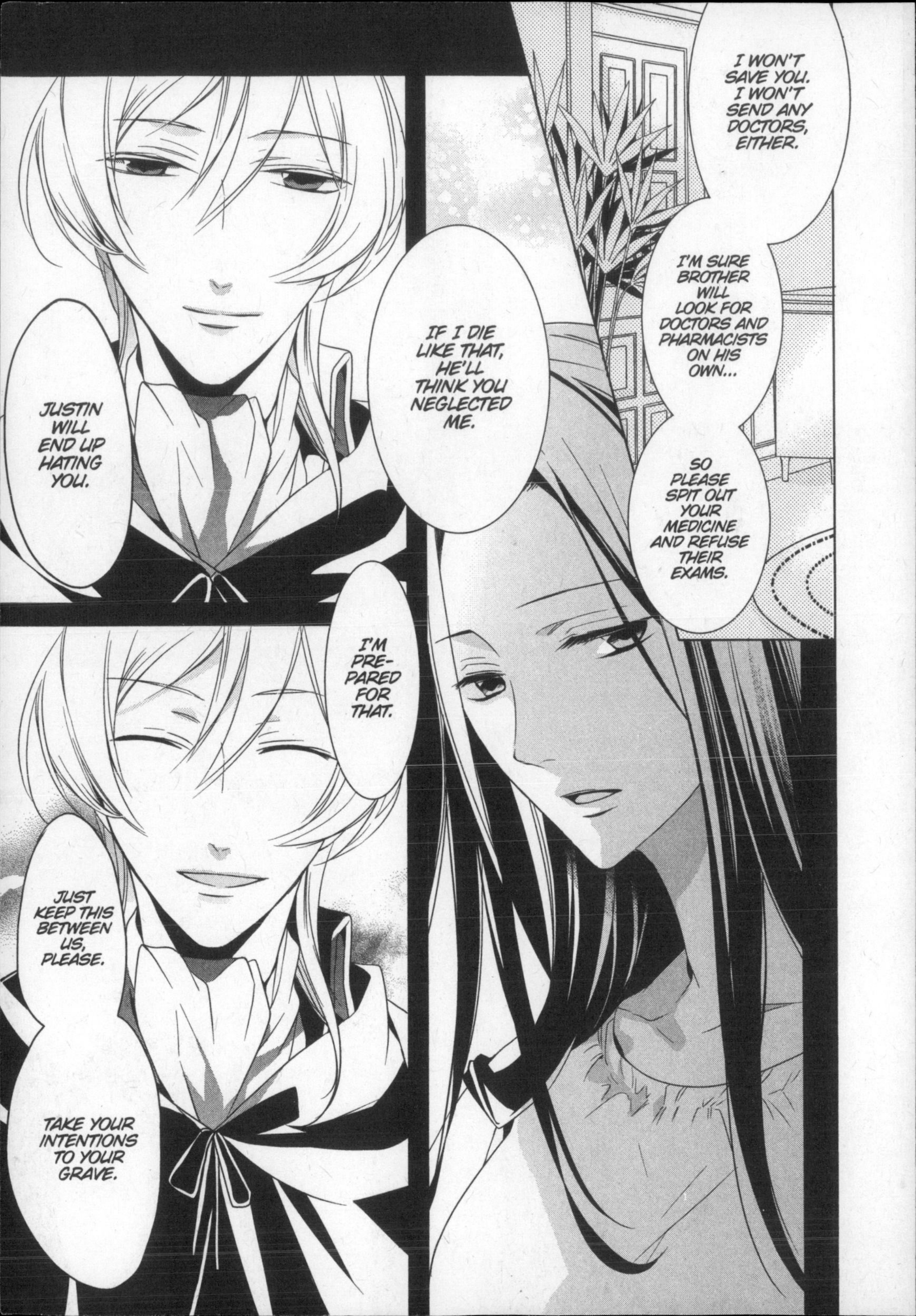
I WON'T SAVE YOU. I WON'T SEND ANY DOCTORS, EITHER.
I'M SURE BROTHER WILL LOOK FOR DOCTORS AND PHARMACISTS ON HIS OWN...
SO PLEASE SPIT OUT YOUR MEDICINE AND REFUSE THEIR EXAMS.
IF I DIE LIKE THAT, HE'LL THINK YOU NEGLECTED ME.
JUSTIN WILL END UP HATING YOU.
I'M PRE-PARED FOR THAT.
JUST KEEP THIS BETWEEN US, PLEASE.
TAKE YOUR INTENTIONS TO YOUR GRAVE.

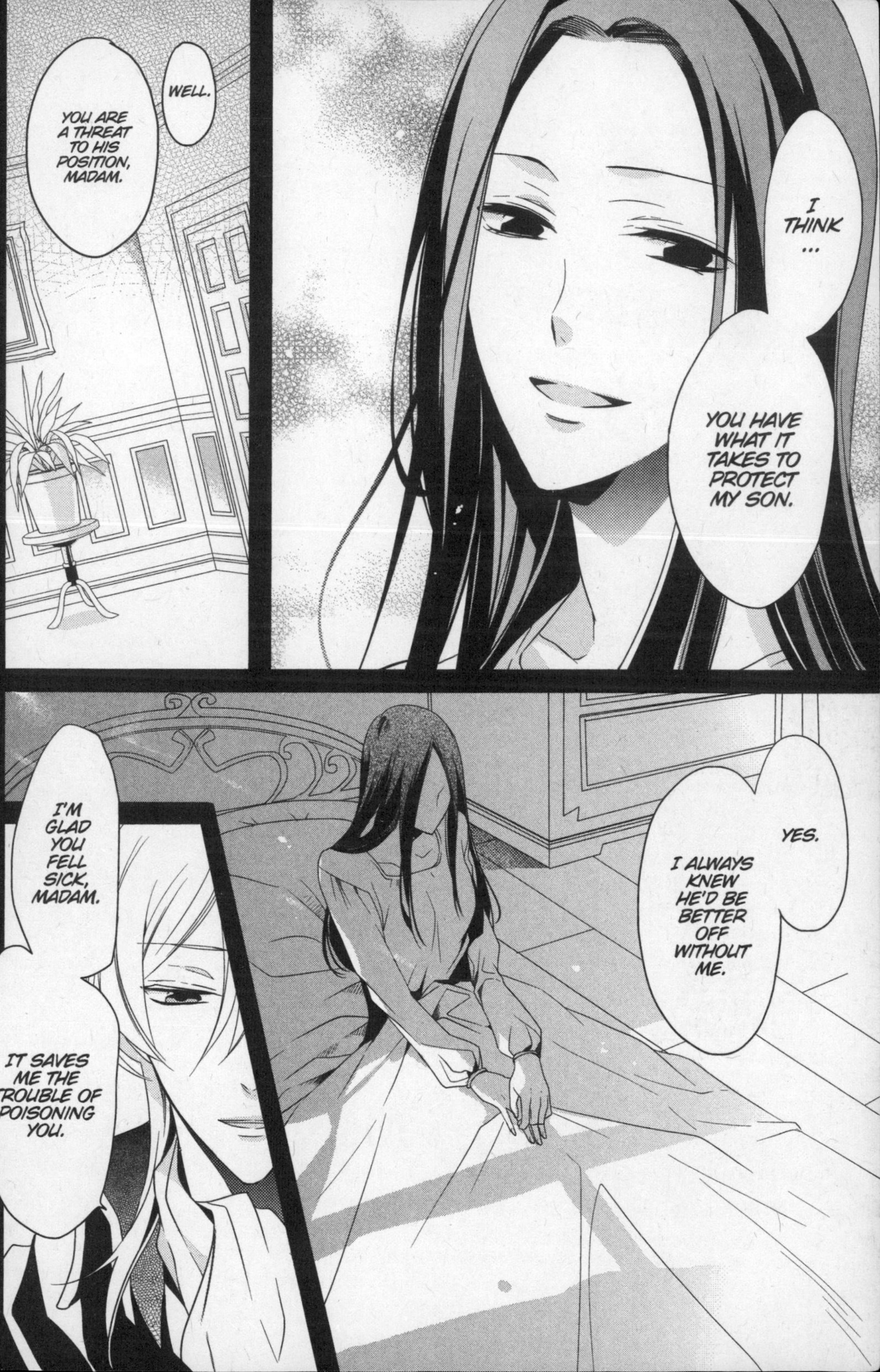
I THINK ...
YOU HAVE WHAT IT TAKES TO PROTECT MY SON.
WELL.
YOU ARE A THREAT TO HIS POSITION, MADAM.
YES.
I ALWAYS KNEW HE'D BE BETTER OFF WITHOUT ME.
I'M GLAD YOU FELL SICK, MADAM.
IT SAVES ME THE TROUBLE OF POISONING YOU.

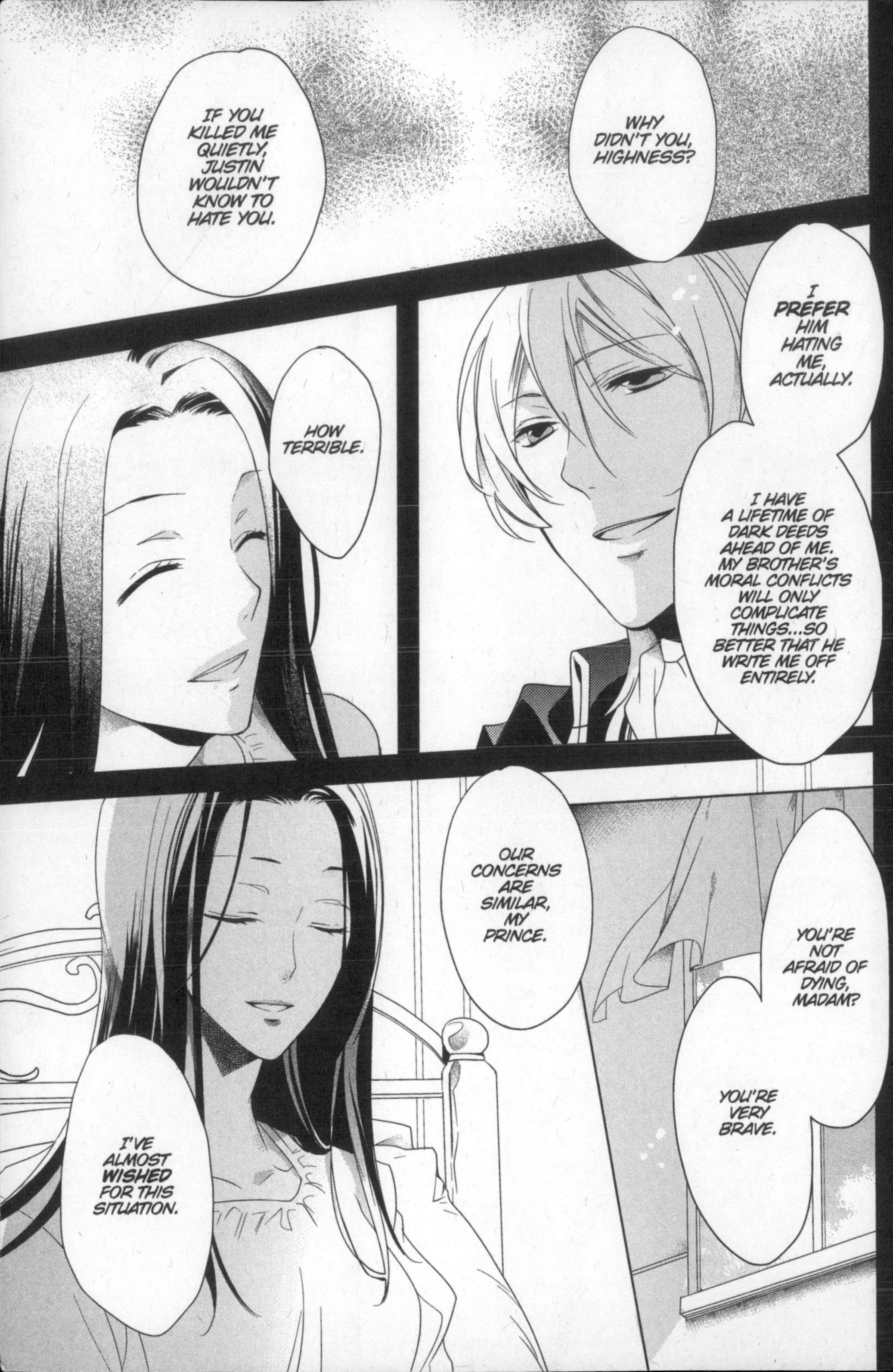
WHY DIDN'T YOU, HIGHNESS?
IF YOU KILLED ME QUIETLY, JUSTIN WOULDN'T KNOW TO HATE YOU.
I PREFER HIM HATING ME, ACTUALLY.
I HAVE A LIFETIME OF DARK DEEDS AHEAD OF ME. MY BROTHER'S MORAL CONFLICTS WILL ONLY COMPLICATE THINGS...SO BETTER THAT HE WRITE ME OFF ENTIRELY.
HOW TERRIBLE.
YOU'RE NOT AFRAID OF DYING, MADAM?
YOU'RE VERY BRAVE.
OUR CONCERNS ARE SIMILAR, MY PRINCE.
I'VE ALMOST WISHED FOR THIS SITUATION.

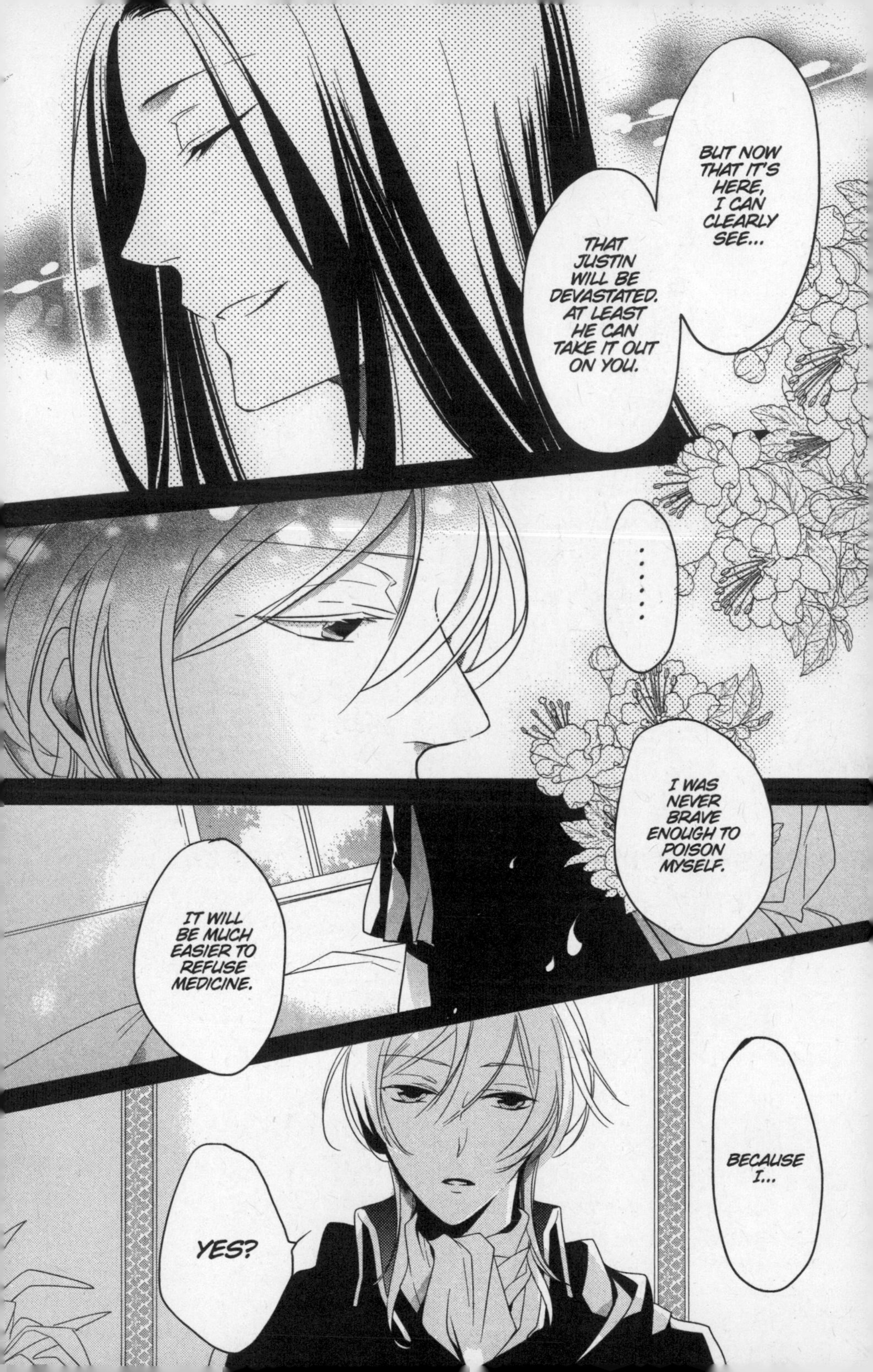
BUT NOW THAT IT'S HERE, I CAN CLEARLY SEE...
THAT JUSTIN WILL BE DEVASTATED. AT LEAST HE CAN TAKE IT OUT ON YOU.
......
I WAS NEVER BRAVE ENOUGH TO POISON MYSELF.
IT WILL BE MUCH EASIER TO REFUSE MEDICINE.
BECAUSE I...
YES?

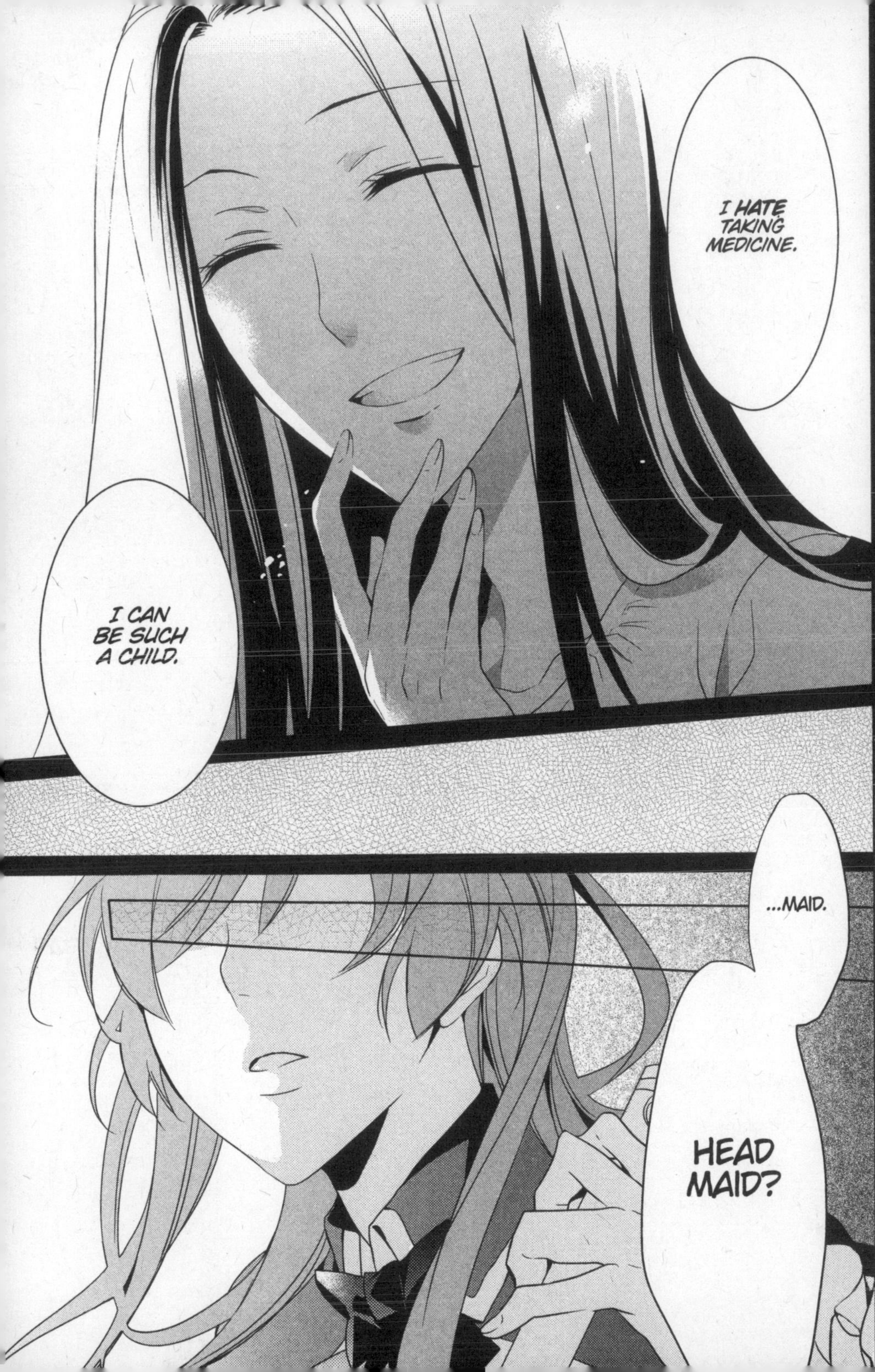
I HATE TAKING MEDICINE.
I CAN BE SUCH A CHILD.
...MAID.
HEAD MAID?

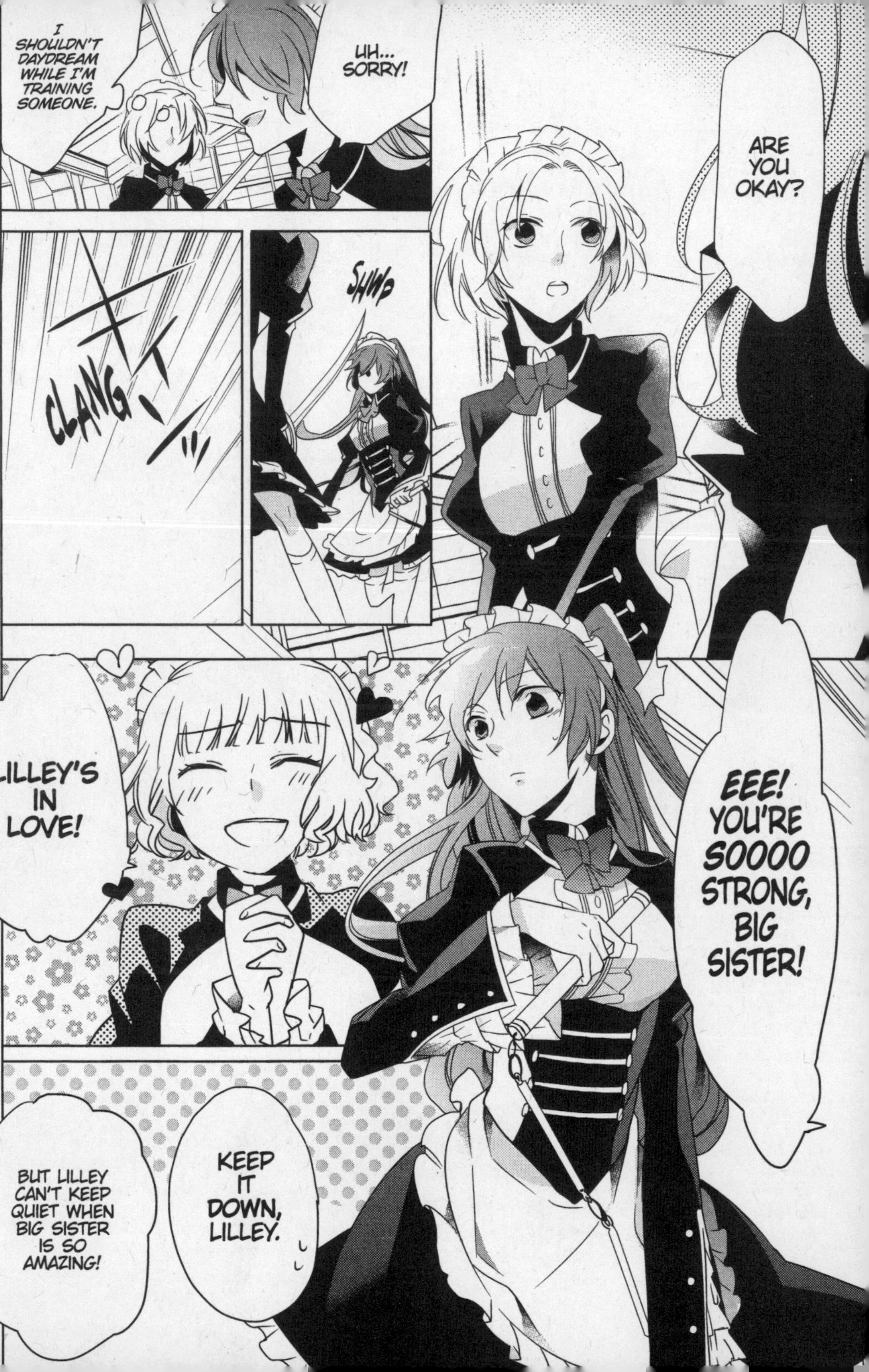
ARE YOU OKAY?
UH... SORRY!
I SHOULDN'T DAYDREAM WHILE I'M TRAINING SOMEONE.
SHWP
CLANG
EEE! YOU'RE SOOOO STRONG, BIG SISTER!
LILLEY'S IN LOVE!
KEEP IT DOWN, LILLEY.
BUT LILLEY CAN'T KEEP QUIET WHEN BIG SISTER IS SO AMAZING!

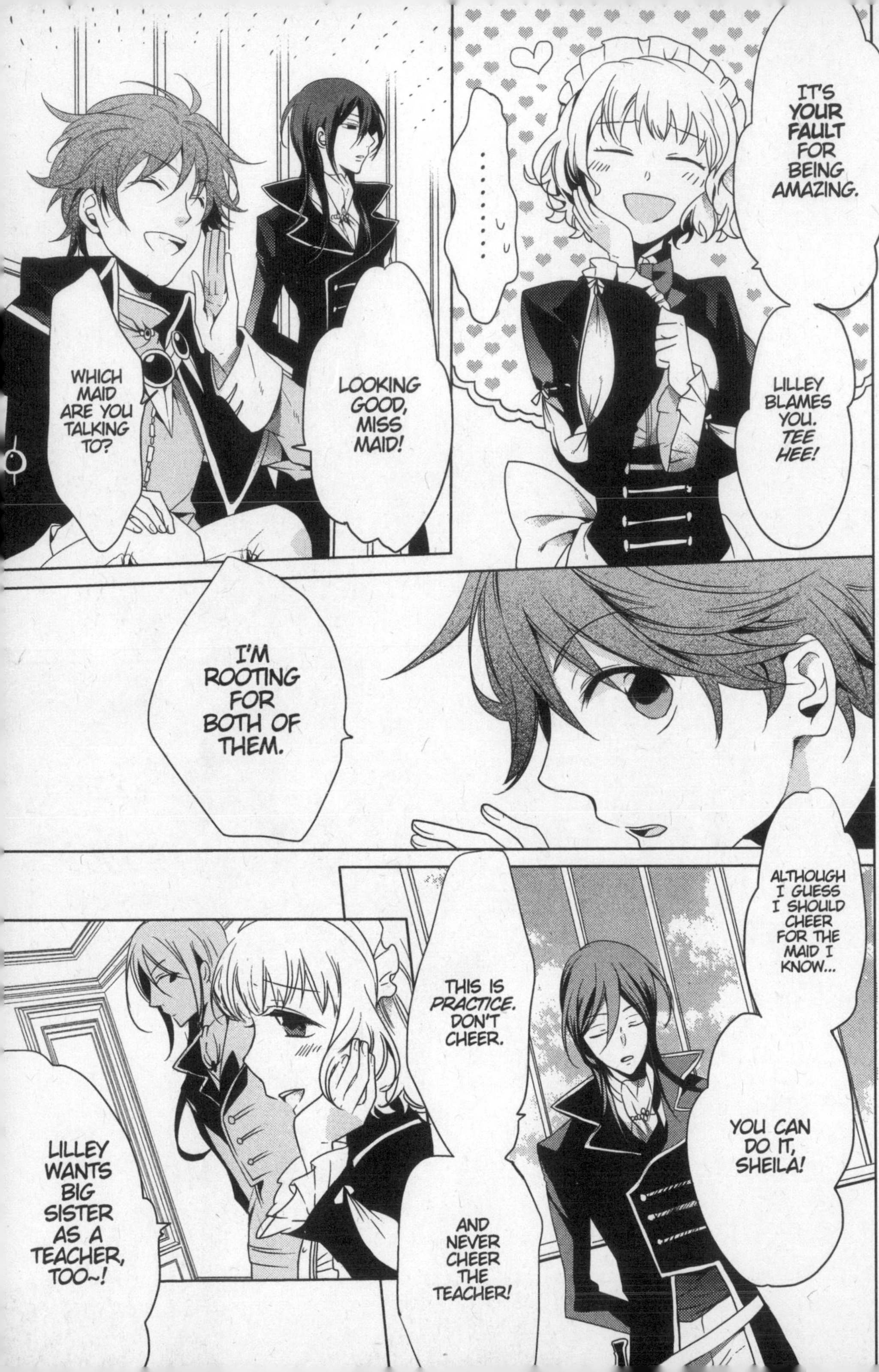
IT'S YOUR FAULT FOR BEING AMAZING.
.....
LILLEY BLAMES YOU. *TEE HEE!*
LOOKING GOOD, MISS MAID!
WHICH MAID ARE YOU TALKING TO?
I'M ROOTING FOR BOTH OF THEM.
ALTHOUGH I GUESS I SHOULD CHEER FOR THE MAID I KNOW...
YOU CAN DO IT, SHEILA!
THIS IS *PRACTICE.* DON'T CHEER.
AND NEVER CHEER THE TEACHER!
LILLEY WANTS BIG SISTER AS A TEACHER, TOO~!

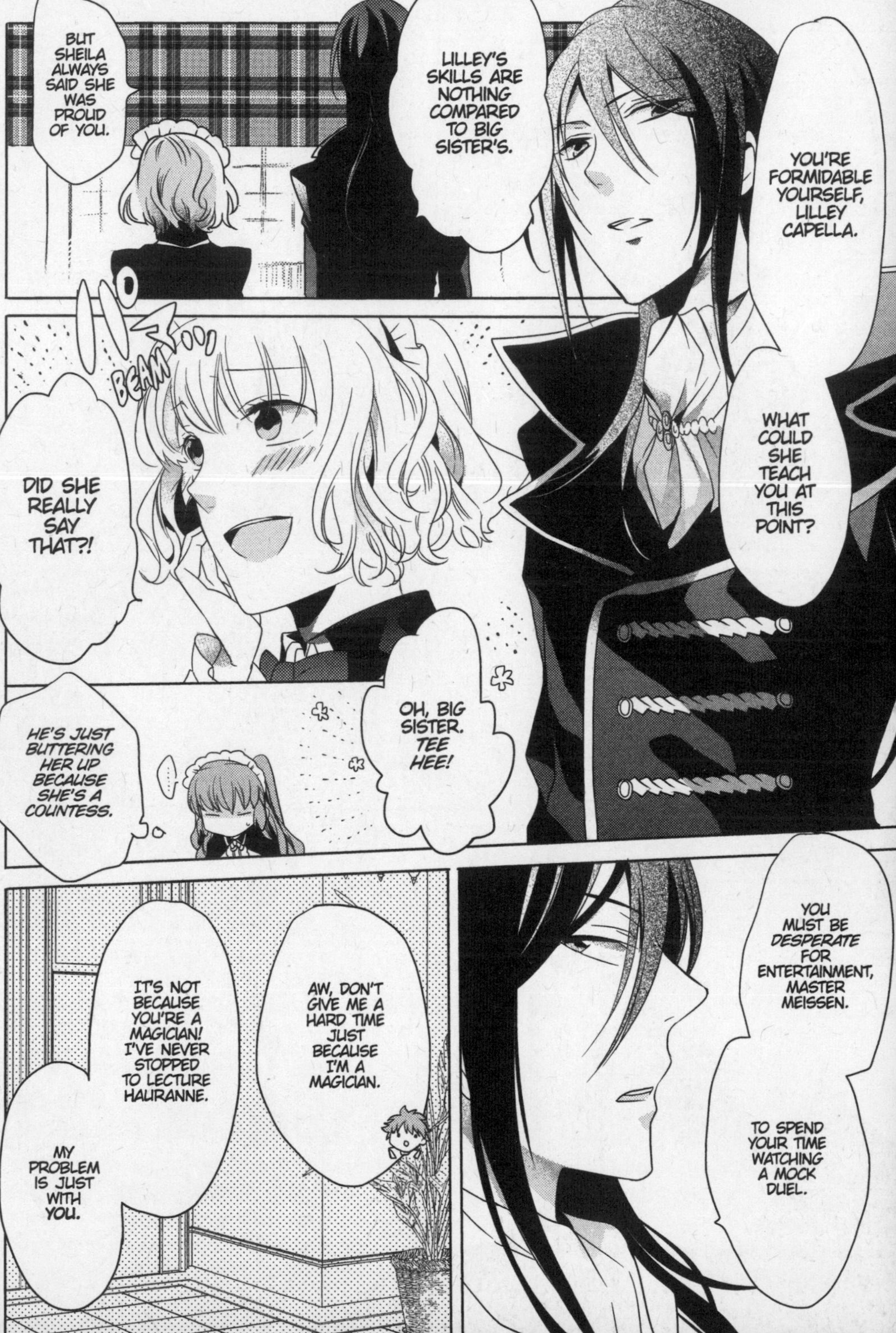
YOU'RE FORMIDABLE YOURSELF, LILLEY CAPELLA.
LILLEY'S SKILLS ARE NOTHING COMPARED TO BIG SISTER'S.
BUT SHEILA ALWAYS SAID SHE WAS PROUD OF YOU.
WHAT COULD SHE TEACH YOU AT THIS POINT?
BEAM
DID SHE REALLY SAY THAT?!
OH, BIG SISTER. TEE HEE!
HE'S JUST BUTTERING HER UP BECAUSE SHE'S A COUNTESS.
...
YOU MUST BE DESPERATE FOR ENTERTAINMENT, MASTER MEISSEN.
TO SPEND YOUR TIME WATCHING A MOCK DUEL.
AW, DON'T GIVE ME A HARD TIME JUST BECAUSE I'M A MAGICIAN.
IT'S NOT BECAUSE YOU'RE A MAGICIAN! I'VE NEVER STOPPED TO LECTURE HAURANNE.
MY PROBLEM IS JUST WITH YOU.

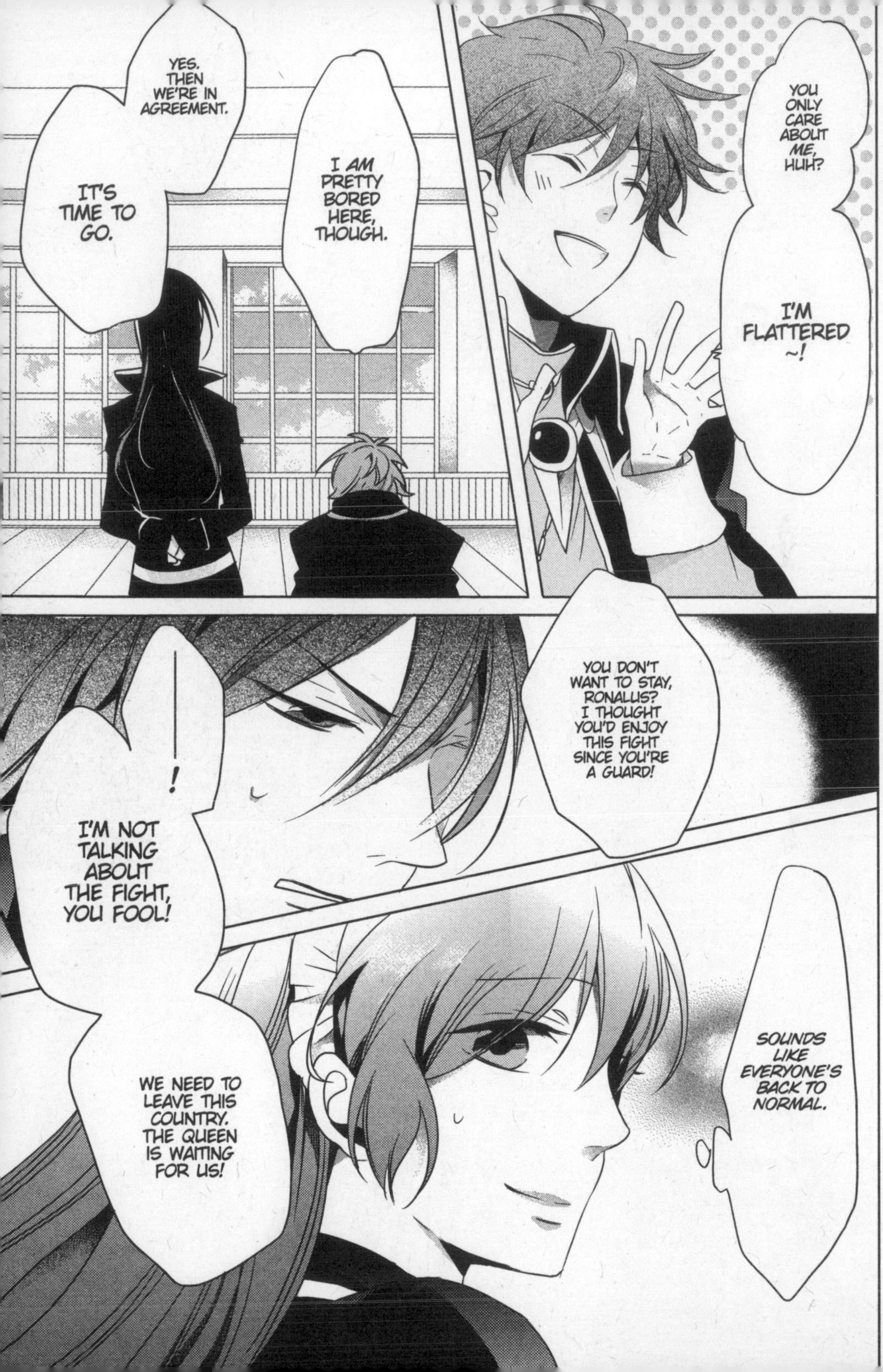
YOU ONLY CARE ABOUT ME, HUH?
I'M FLATTERED ~!
I AM PRETTY BORED HERE, THOUGH.
YES. THEN WE'RE IN AGREEMENT.
IT'S TIME TO GO.
YOU DON'T WANT TO STAY, RONALLUS? I THOUGHT YOU'D ENJOY THIS FIGHT SINCE YOU'RE A GUARD!
...!
I'M NOT TALKING ABOUT THE FIGHT, YOU FOOL!
WE NEED TO LEAVE THIS COUNTRY. THE QUEEN IS WAITING FOR US!
SOUNDS LIKE EVERYONE'S BACK TO NORMAL.

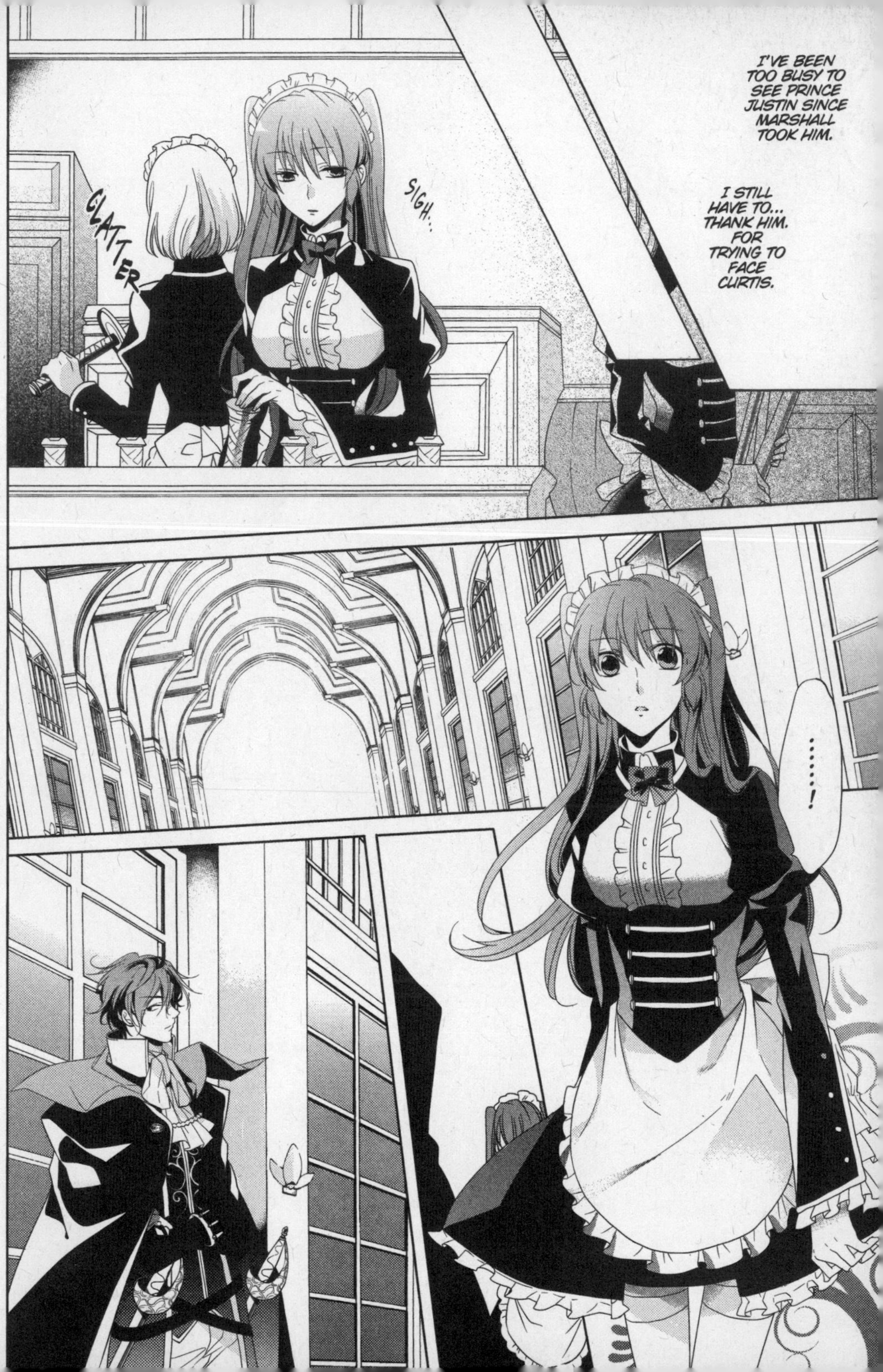
I'VE BEEN TOO BUSY TO SEE PRINCE JUSTIN SINCE MARSHALL TOOK HIM.
I STILL HAVE TO... THANK HIM. FOR TRYING TO FACE CURTIS.
SIGH...
CLATTER
......!

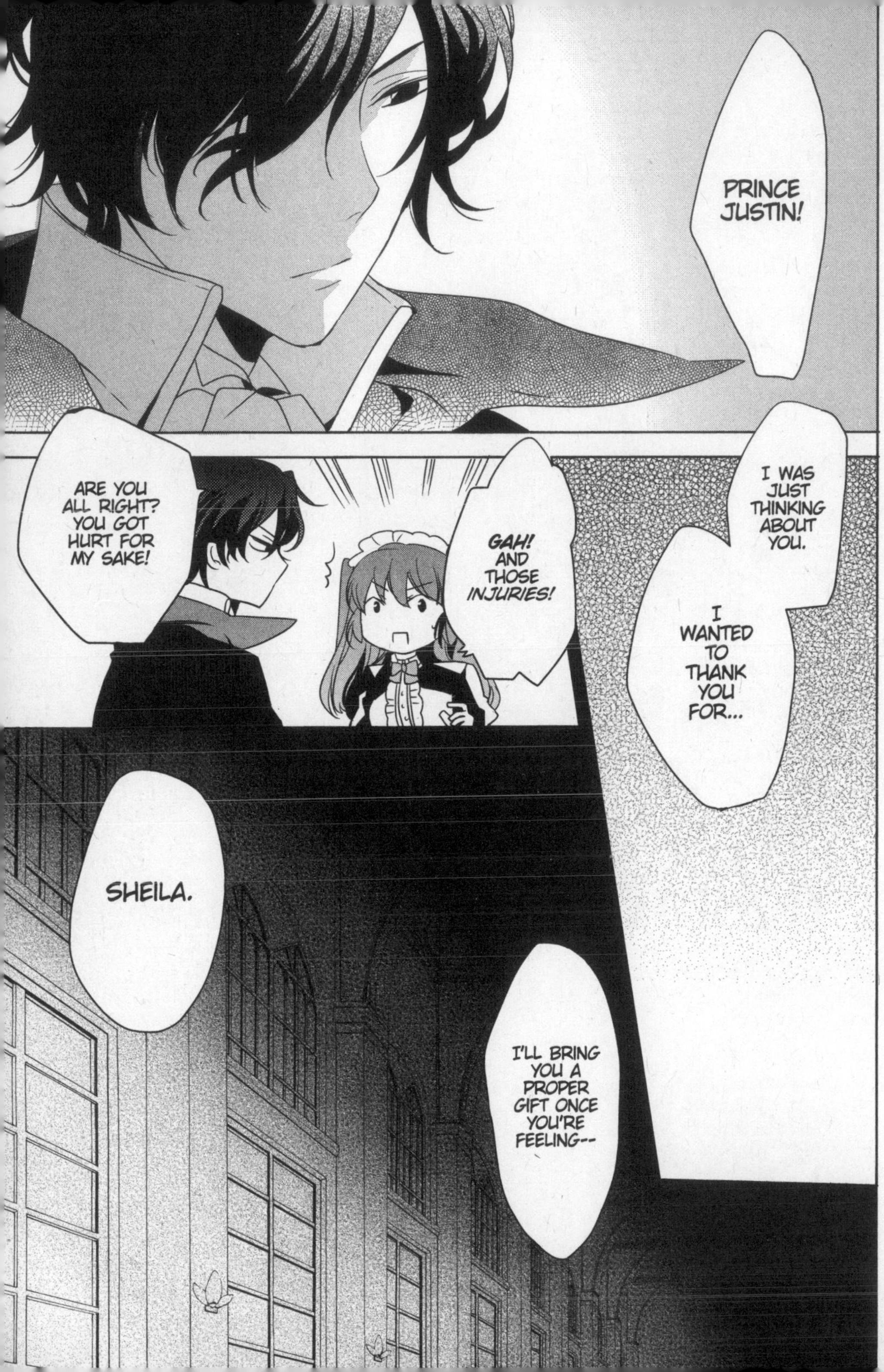
PRINCE JUSTIN!
I WAS JUST THINKING ABOUT YOU.
I WANTED TO THANK YOU FOR...
GAH! AND THOSE INJURIES!
ARE YOU ALL RIGHT? YOU GOT HURT FOR MY SAKE!
SHEILA.
I'LL BRING YOU A PROPER GIFT ONCE YOU'RE FEELING--

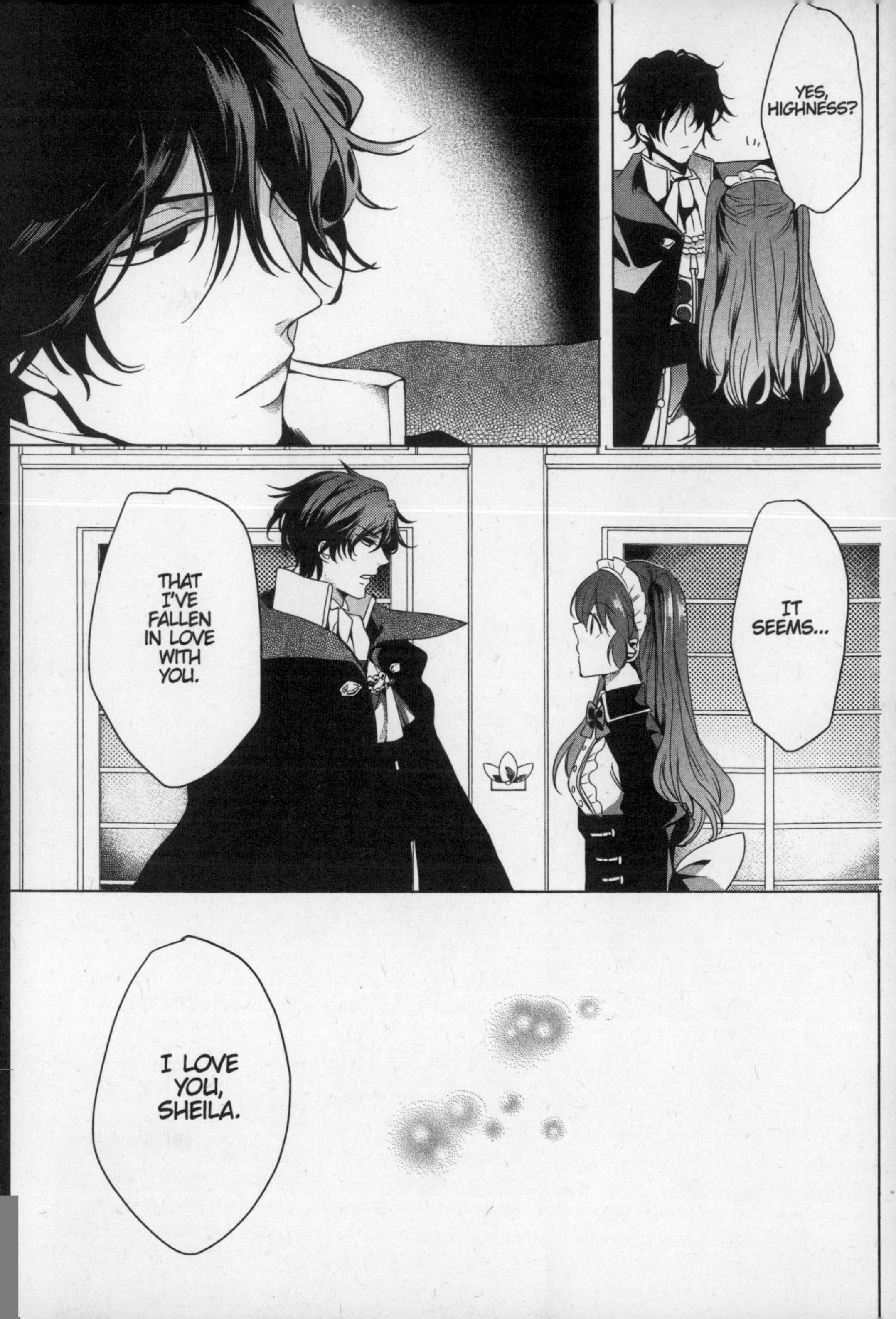
YES, HIGHNESS?
IT SEEMS...
THAT I'VE FALLEN IN LOVE WITH YOU.
I LOVE YOU, SHEILA.

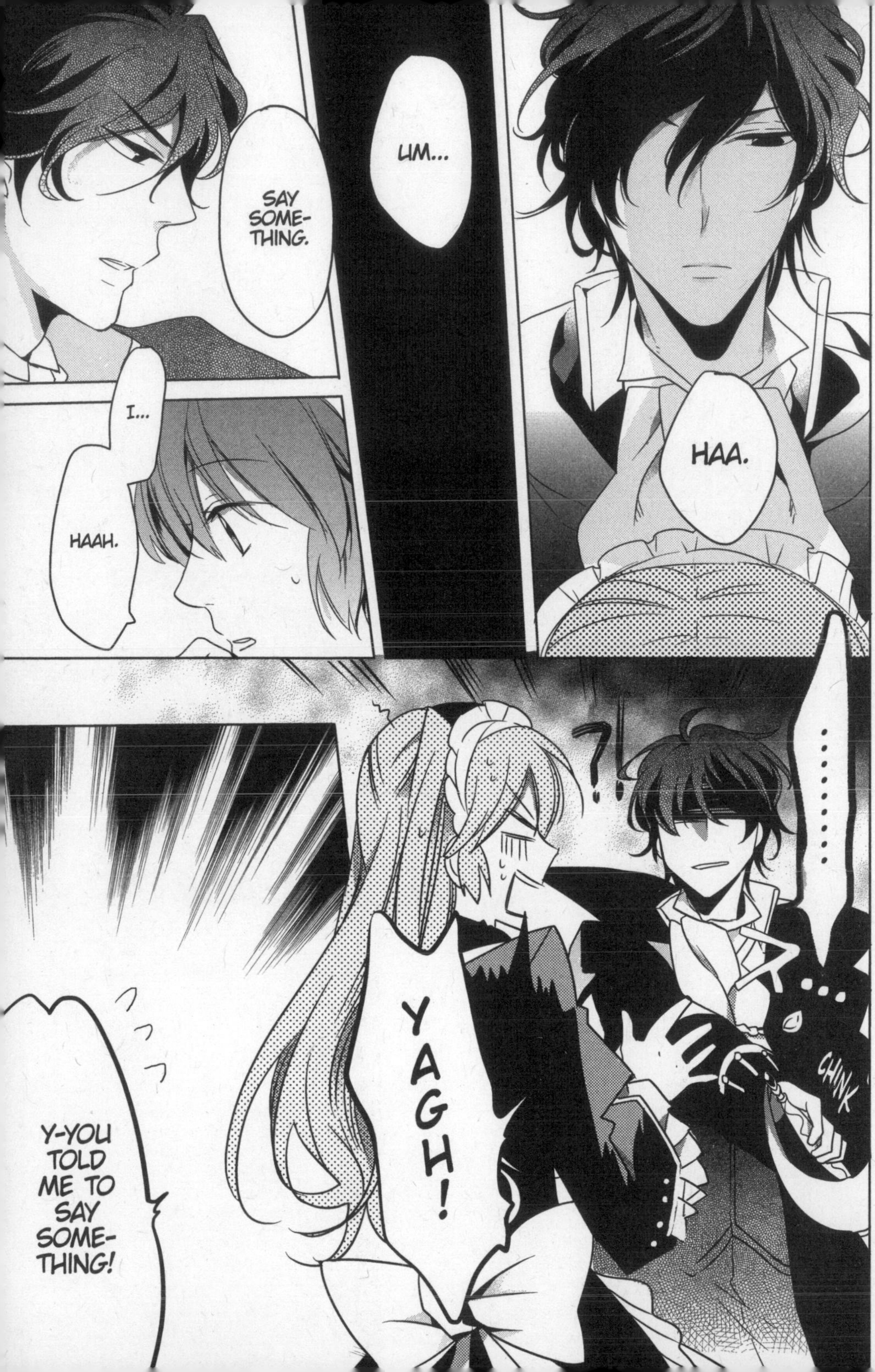
HAA.
UM...
SAY SOMETHING.
I... HAAH.
......
?!
CHINK
YAGH!
Y-YOU TOLD ME TO SAY SOMETHING!

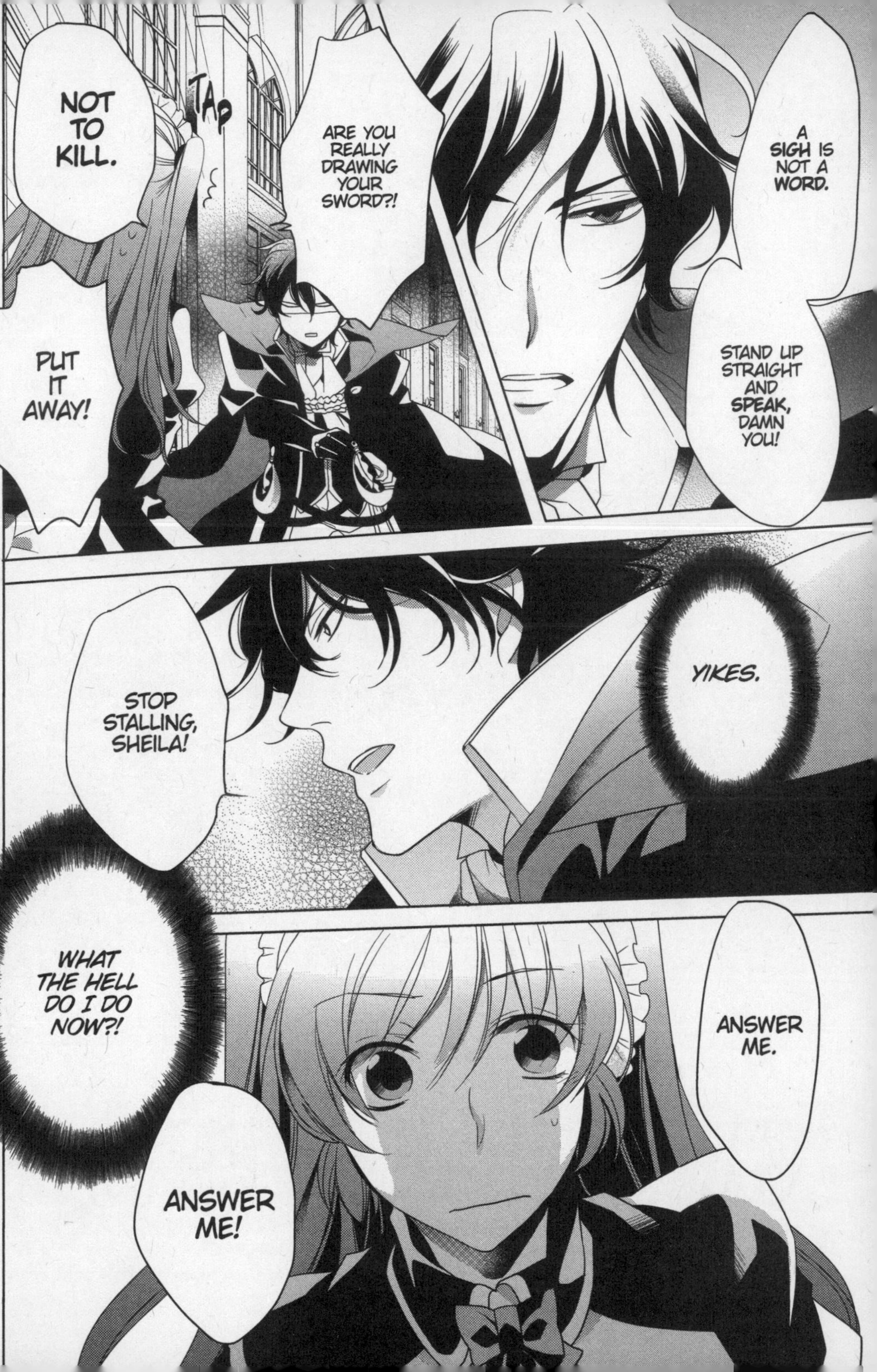
A SIGH IS NOT A WORD.
STAND UP STRAIGHT AND SPEAK, DAMN YOU!
ARE YOU REALLY DRAWING YOUR SWORD?!
NOT TO KILL.
TAP
PUT IT AWAY!
YIKES.
STOP STALLING, SHEILA!
ANSWER ME.
WHAT THE HELL DO I DO NOW?!
ANSWER ME!

CRIMSON EMPIRE

Circumstances to serve a noble

#15

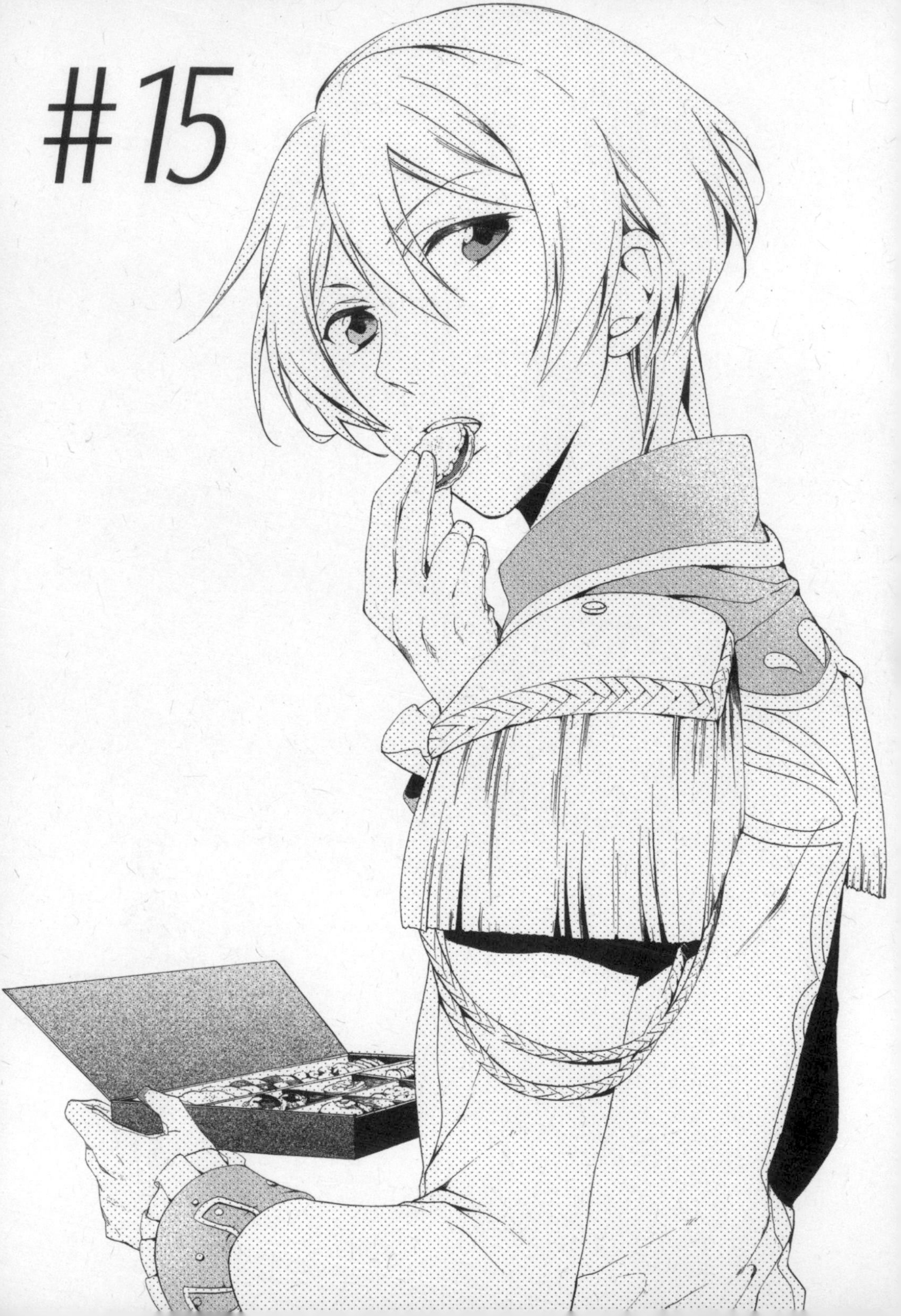

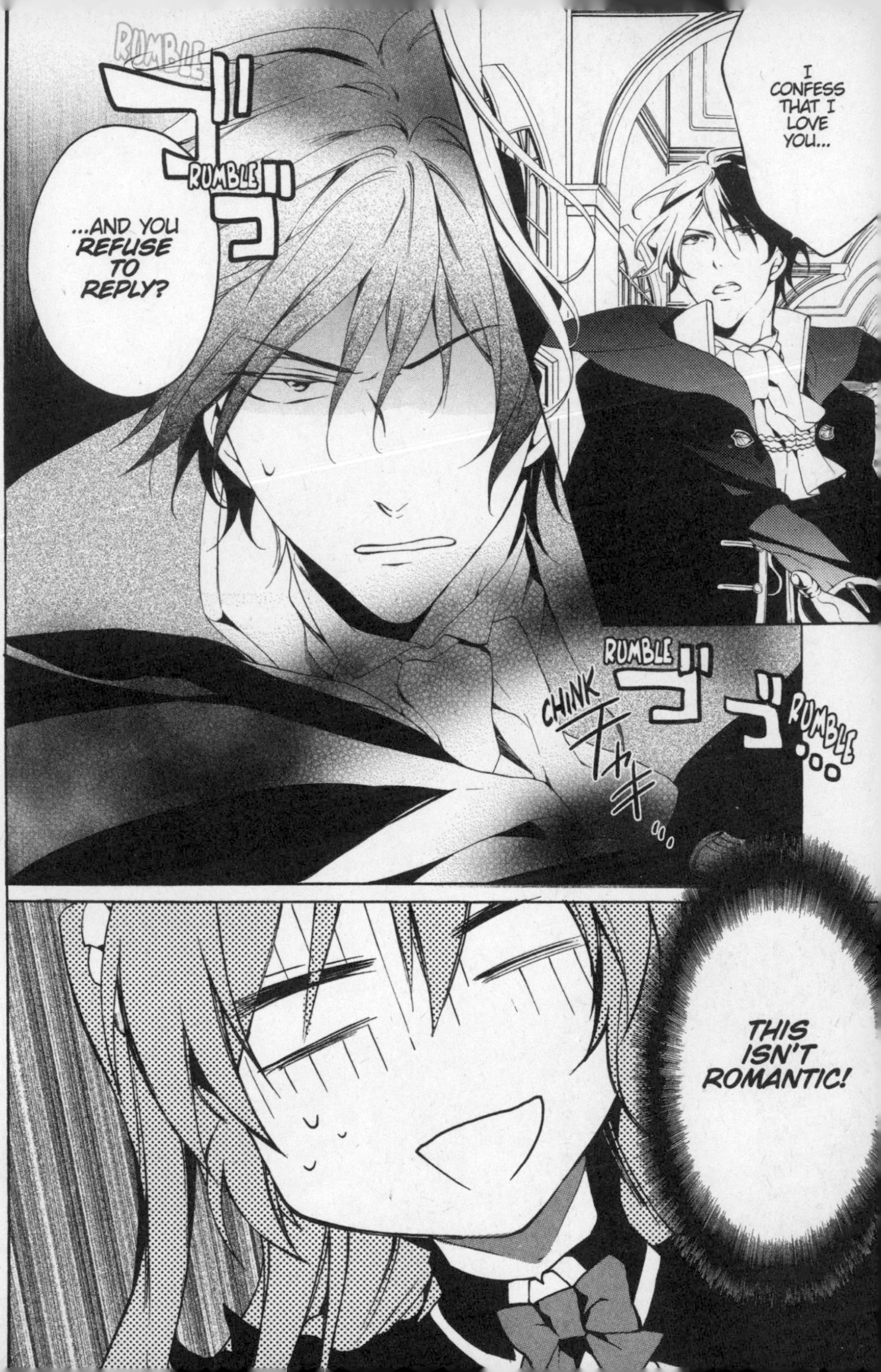
I CONFESS THAT I LOVE YOU...
RUMBLE
RUMBLE
...AND YOU REFUSE TO REPLY?
RUMBLE
RUMBLE
CHINK
THIS ISN'T ROMANTIC!

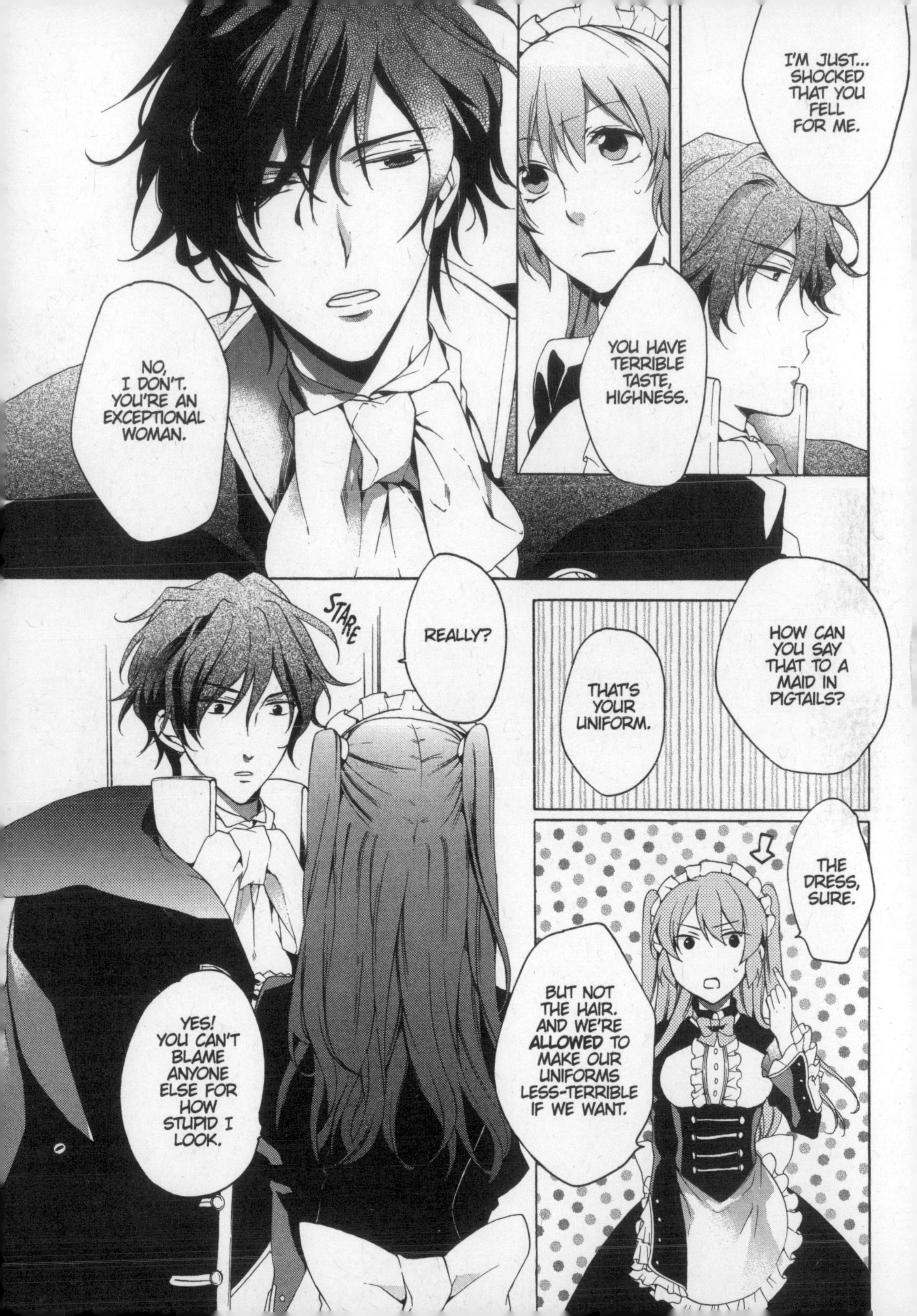
I'M JUST... SHOCKED THAT YOU FELL FOR ME.
YOU HAVE TERRIBLE TASTE, HIGHNESS.
NO, I DON'T. YOU'RE AN EXCEPTIONAL WOMAN.
HOW CAN YOU SAY THAT TO A MAID IN PIGTAILS?
THAT'S YOUR UNIFORM.
THE DRESS, SURE.
BUT NOT THE HAIR. AND WE'RE **ALLOWED** TO MAKE OUR UNIFORMS LESS-TERRIBLE IF WE WANT.
STARE
REALLY?
YES! YOU CAN'T BLAME ANYONE ELSE FOR HOW STUPID I LOOK.

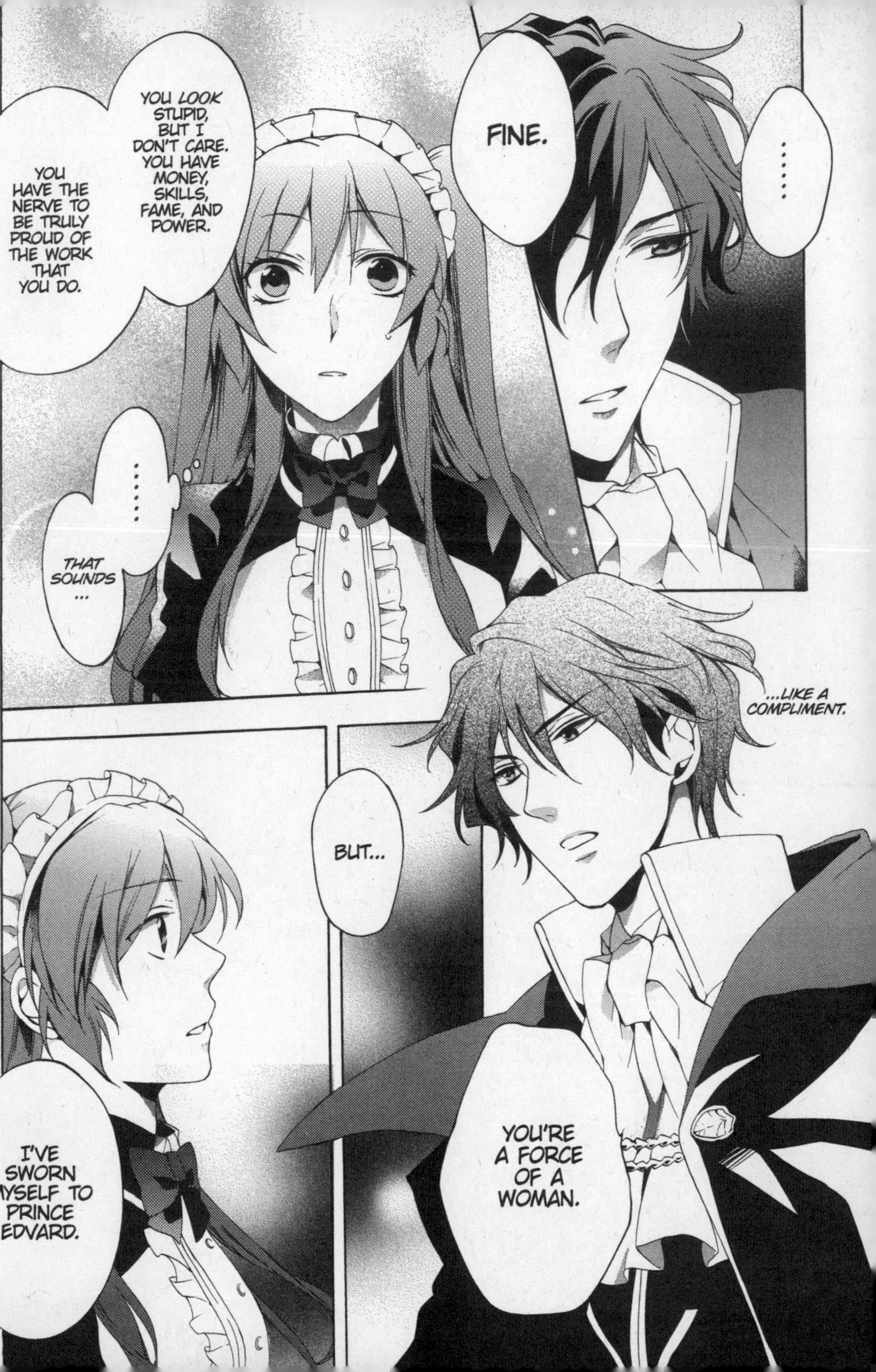
......
FINE.
YOU LOOK STUPID, BUT I DON'T CARE. YOU HAVE MONEY, SKILLS, FAME, AND POWER.
YOU HAVE THE NERVE TO BE TRULY PROUD OF THE WORK THAT YOU DO.
......
THAT SOUNDS ...
...LIKE A COMPLIMENT.
BUT...
YOU'RE A FORCE OF A WOMAN.
I'VE SWORN MYSELF TO PRINCE EDVARD.

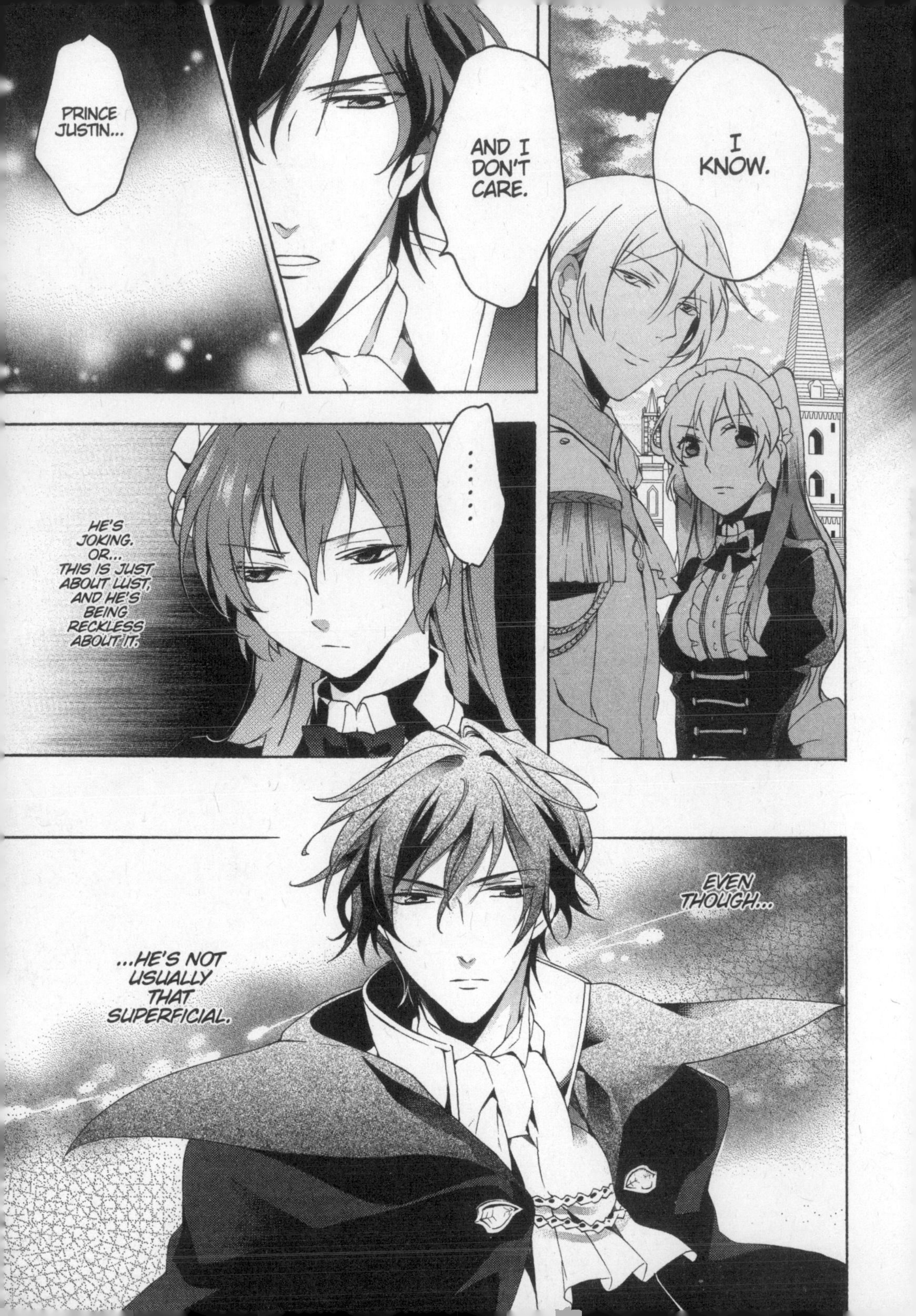
I KNOW.
AND I DON'T CARE.
PRINCE JUSTIN...
......
HE'S JOKING. OR... THIS IS JUST ABOUT LUST, AND HE'S BEING RECKLESS ABOUT IT.
EVEN THOUGH...
...HE'S NOT USUALLY THAT SUPERFICIAL.

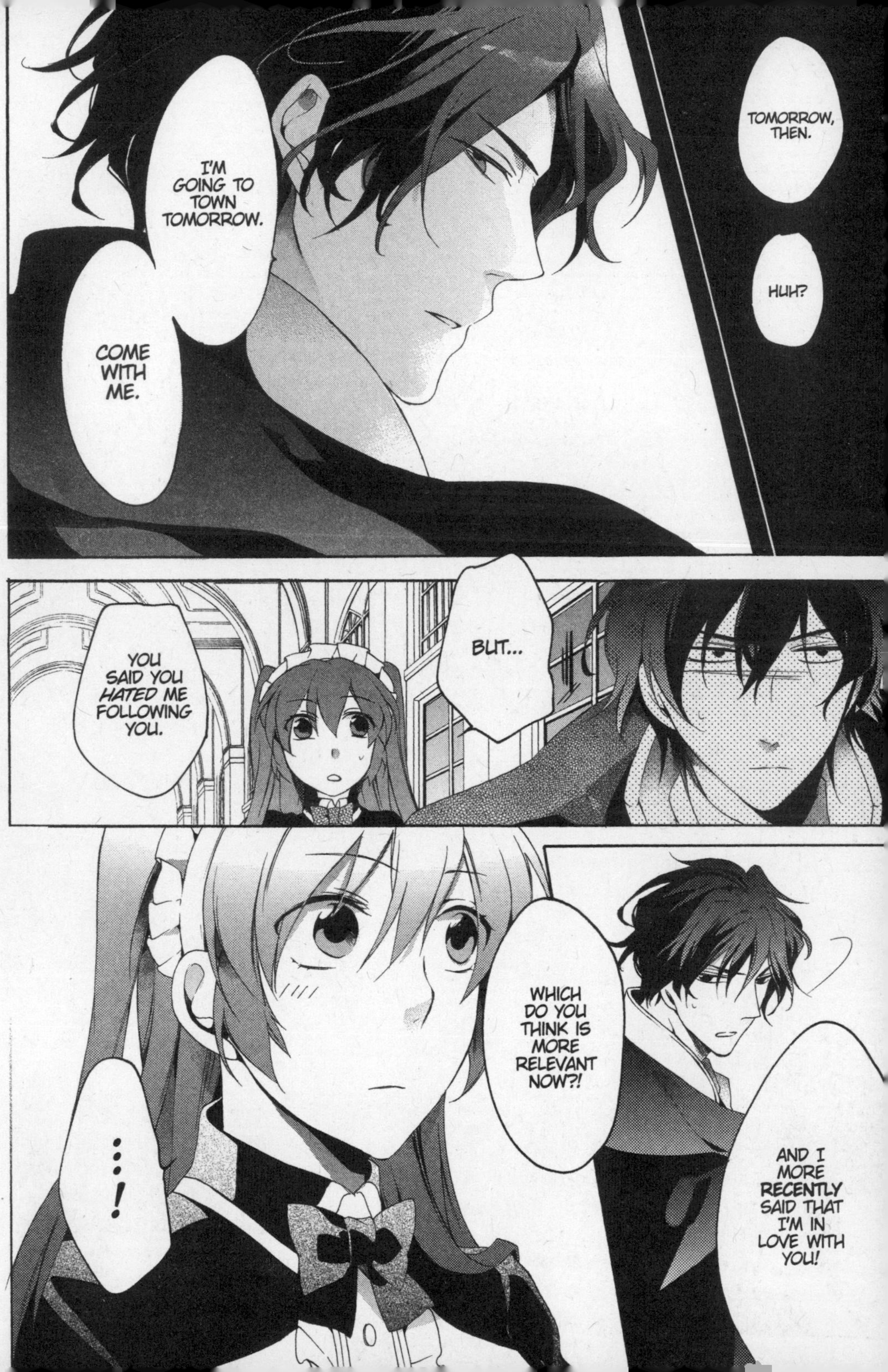
TOMORROW, THEN.
HUH?
I'M GOING TO TOWN TOMORROW.
COME WITH ME.
BUT...
YOU SAID YOU *HATED* ME FOLLOWING YOU.
AND I MORE **RECENTLY** SAID THAT I'M IN LOVE WITH YOU!
WHICH DO YOU THINK IS MORE RELEVANT NOW?!
...!

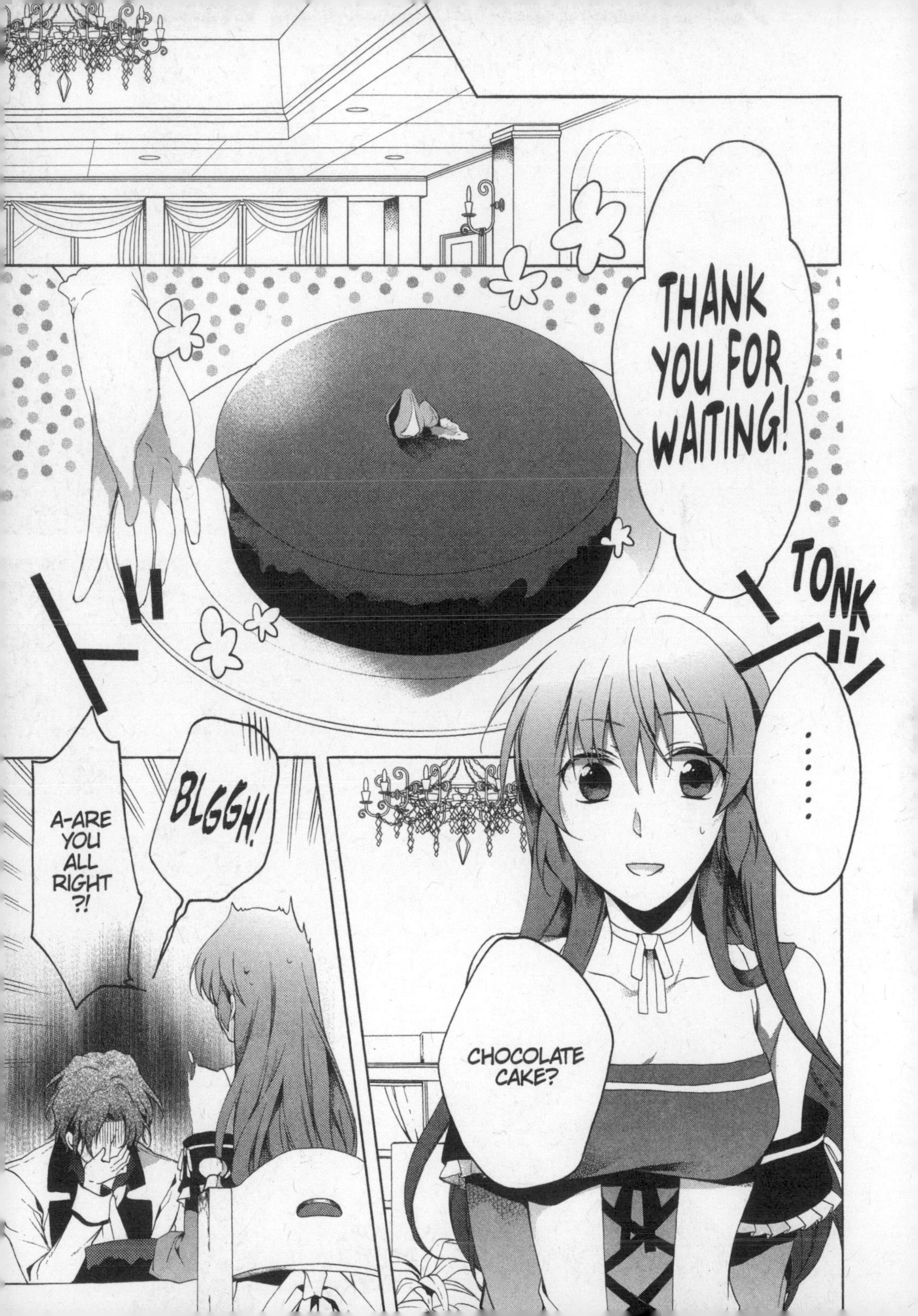

THANK YOU FOR WAITING!
TONK
......
CHOCOLATE CAKE?
BLGGH!
A-ARE YOU ALL RIGHT ?!

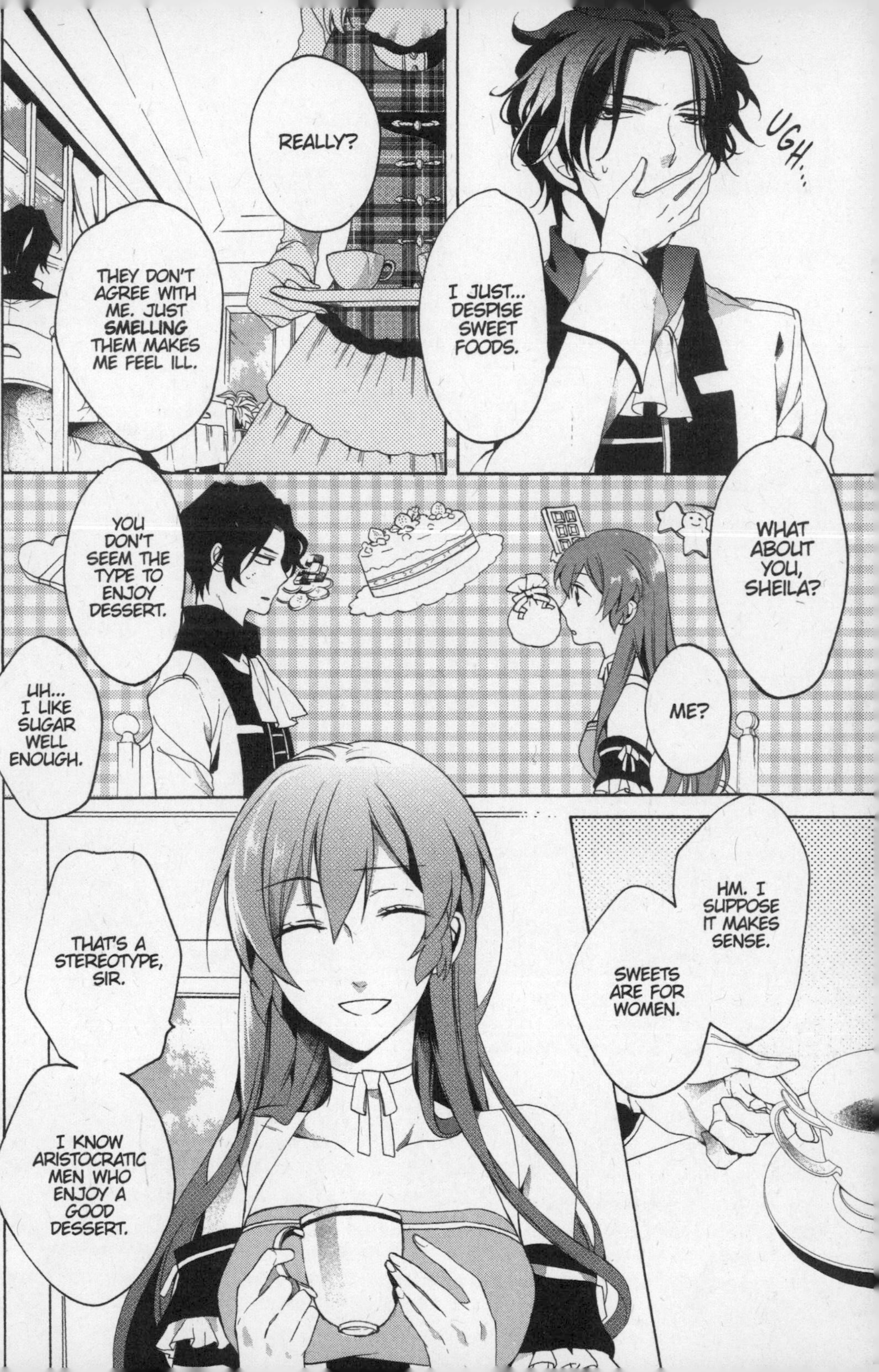
UGH...
I JUST... DESPISE SWEET FOODS.
REALLY?
THEY DON'T AGREE WITH ME. JUST SMELLING THEM MAKES ME FEEL ILL.
WHAT ABOUT YOU, SHEILA?
ME?
YOU DON'T SEEM THE TYPE TO ENJOY DESSERT.
UH... I LIKE SUGAR WELL ENOUGH.
HM. I SUPPOSE IT MAKES SENSE.
SWEETS ARE FOR WOMEN.
THAT'S A STEREOTYPE, SIR.
I KNOW ARISTOCRATIC MEN WHO ENJOY A GOOD DESSERT.

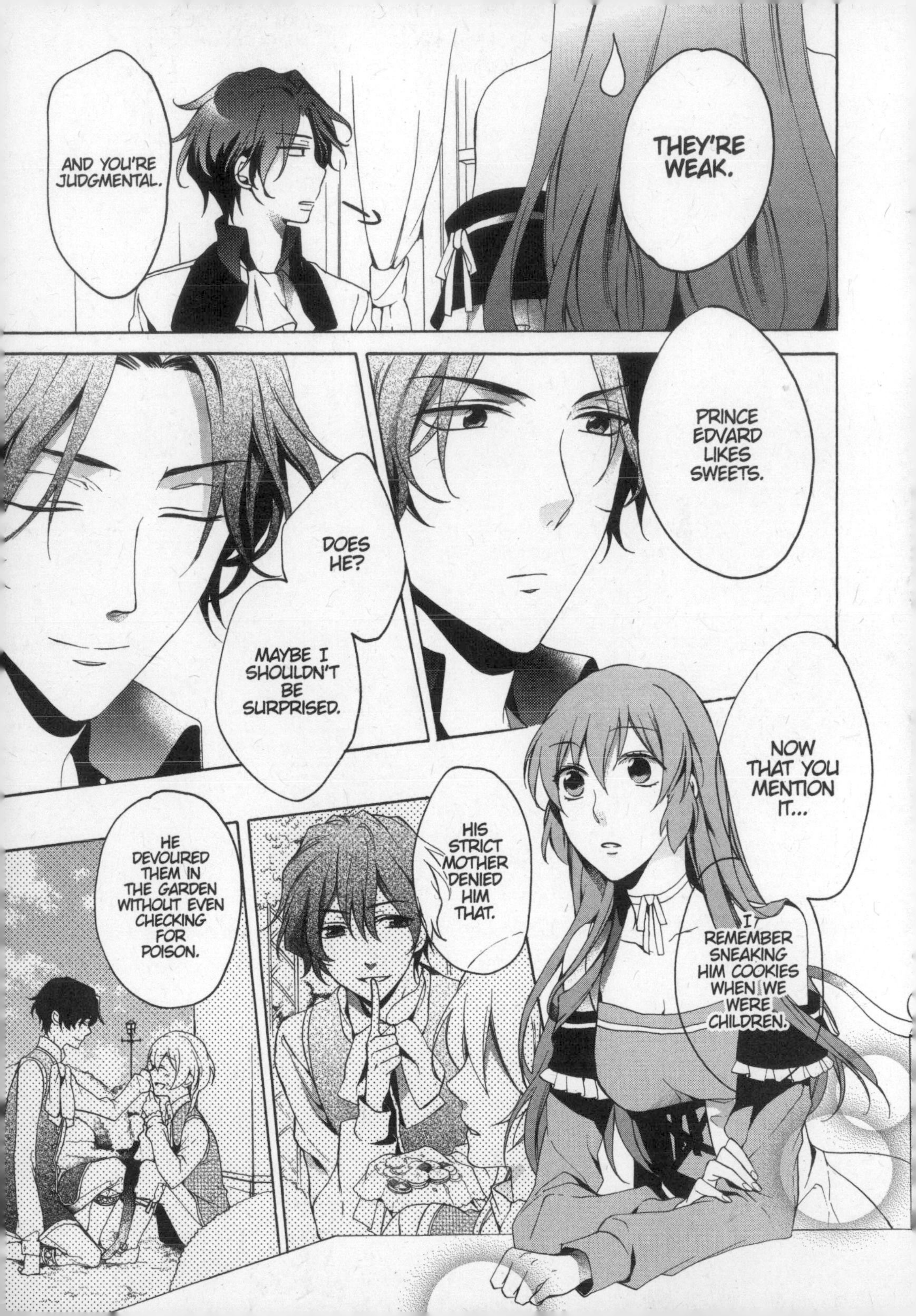
THEY'RE WEAK.
AND YOU'RE JUDGMENTAL.
PRINCE EDVARD LIKES SWEETS.
DOES HE?
MAYBE I SHOULDN'T BE SURPRISED.
NOW THAT YOU MENTION IT...
I REMEMBER SNEAKING HIM COOKIES WHEN WE WERE CHILDREN.
HIS STRICT MOTHER DENIED HIM THAT.
HE DEVOURED THEM IN THE GARDEN WITHOUT EVEN CHECKING FOR POISON.

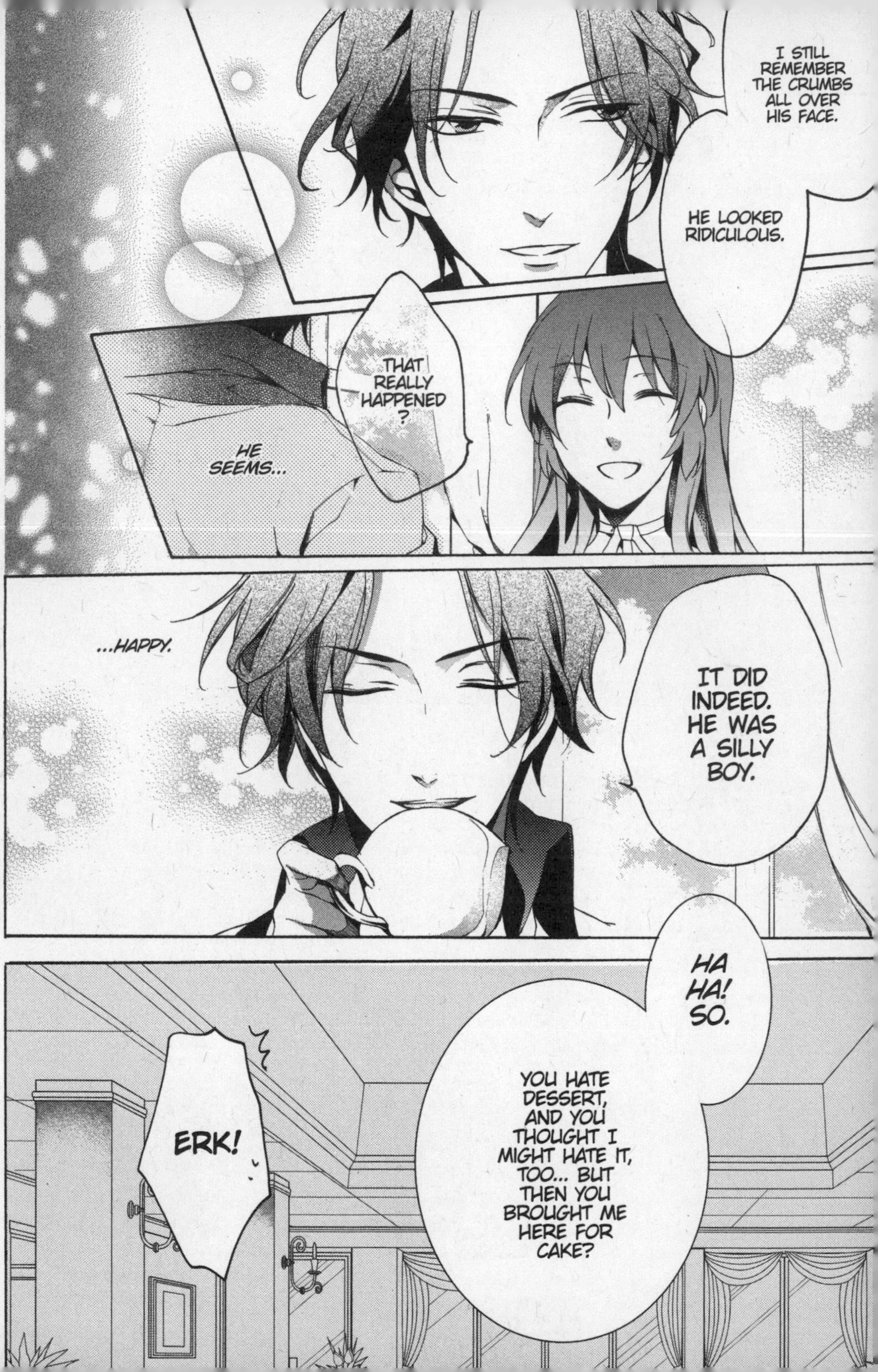
I STILL REMEMBER THE CRUMBS ALL OVER HIS FACE.
HE LOOKED RIDICULOUS.
THAT REALLY HAPPENED?
HE SEEMS...
IT DID INDEED. HE WAS A SILLY BOY.
...HAPPY.
HA HA! SO.
YOU HATE DESSERT, AND YOU THOUGHT I MIGHT HATE IT, TOO... BUT THEN YOU BROUGHT ME HERE FOR CAKE?
ERK!

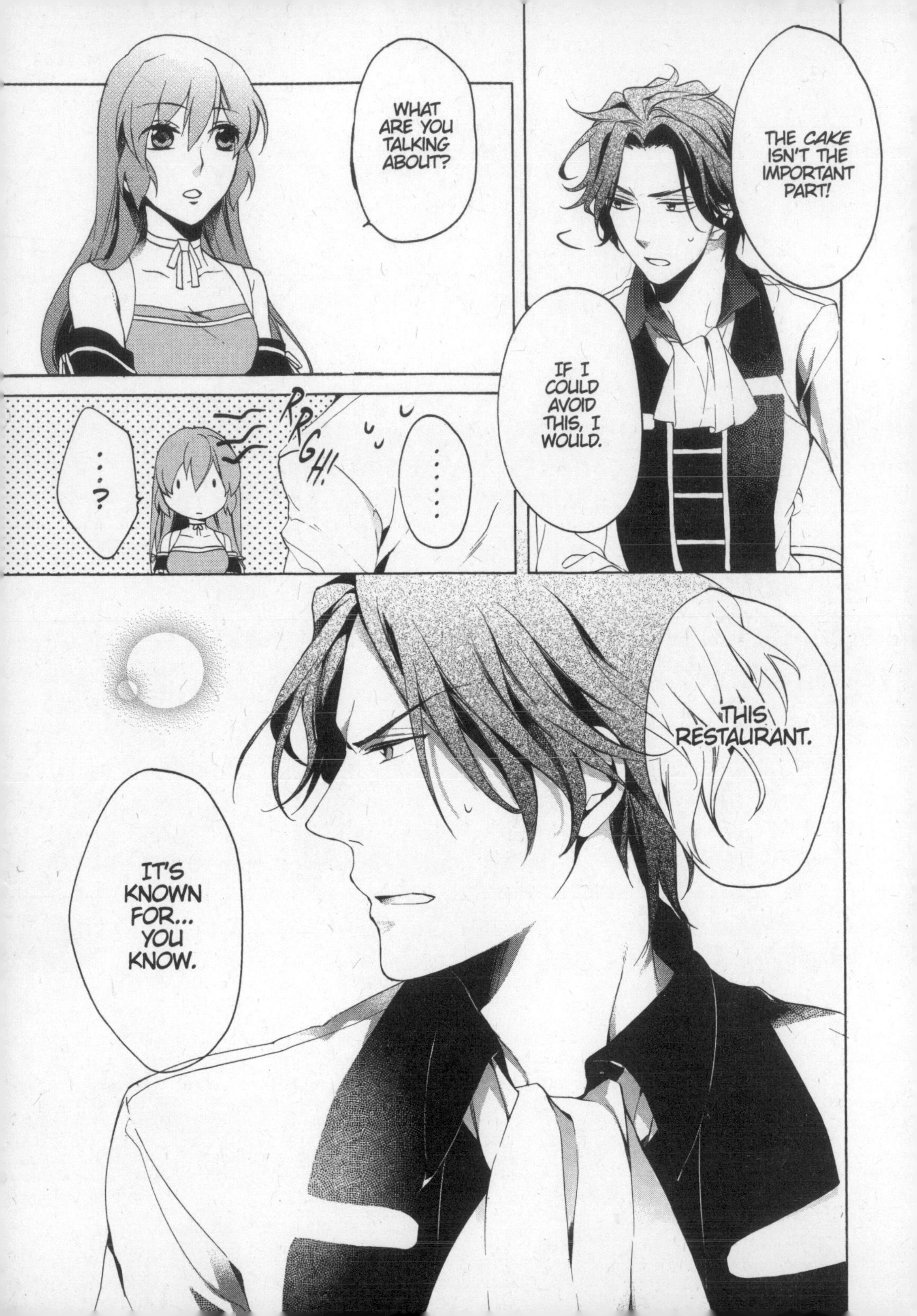
THE CAKE ISN'T THE IMPORTANT PART!
IF I COULD AVOID THIS, I WOULD.
WHAT ARE YOU TALKING ABOUT?
......
RRGH!
...?
THIS RESTAURANT.
IT'S KNOWN FOR... YOU KNOW.

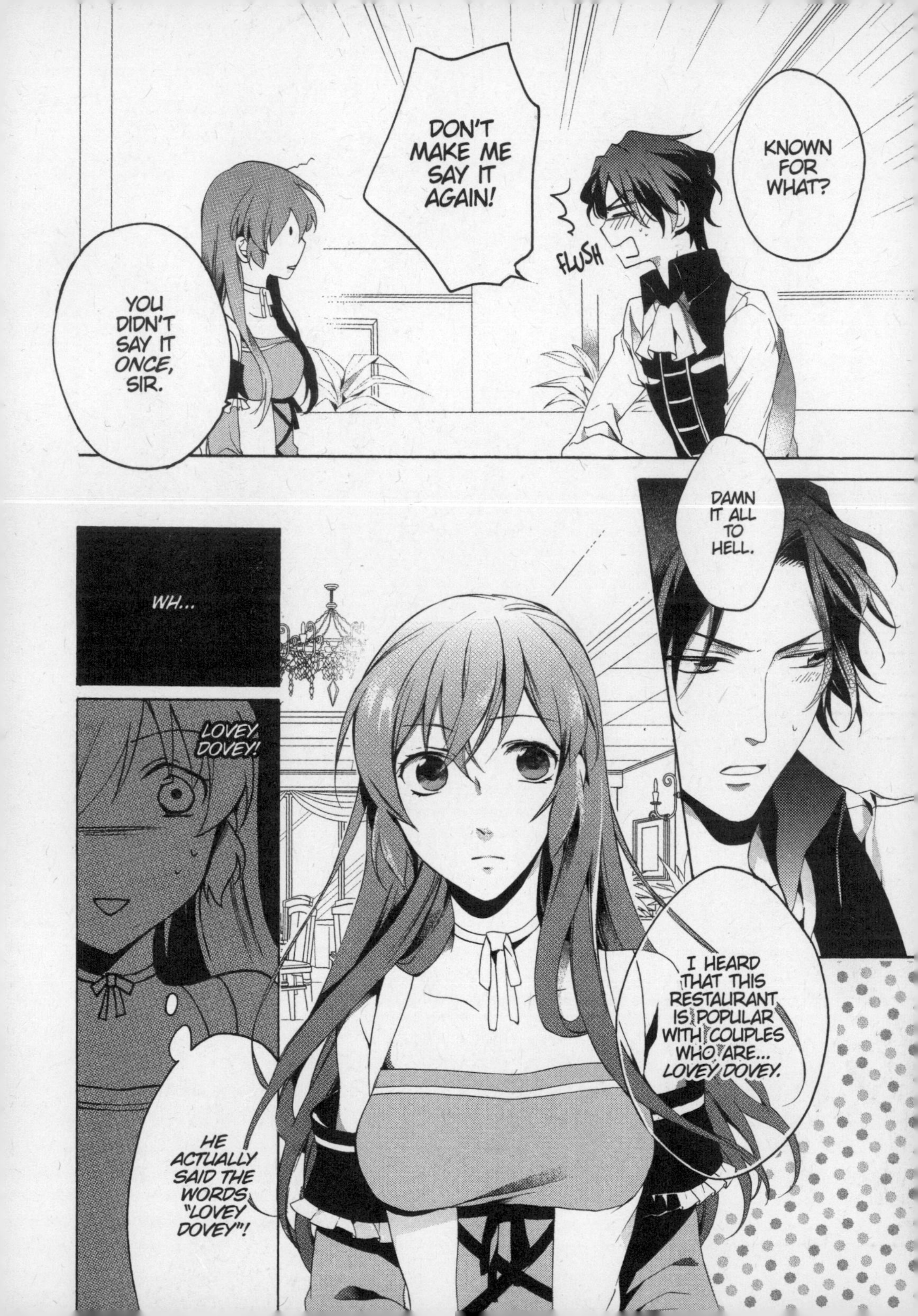
KNOWN FOR WHAT?
FLUSH
DON'T MAKE ME SAY IT AGAIN!
YOU DIDN'T SAY IT ONCE, SIR.
DAMN IT ALL TO HELL.
I HEARD THAT THIS RESTAURANT IS POPULAR WITH COUPLES WHO ARE... LOVEY DOVEY.
WH...
LOVEY DOVEY!
HE ACTUALLY SAID THE WORDS "LOVEY DOVEY"!

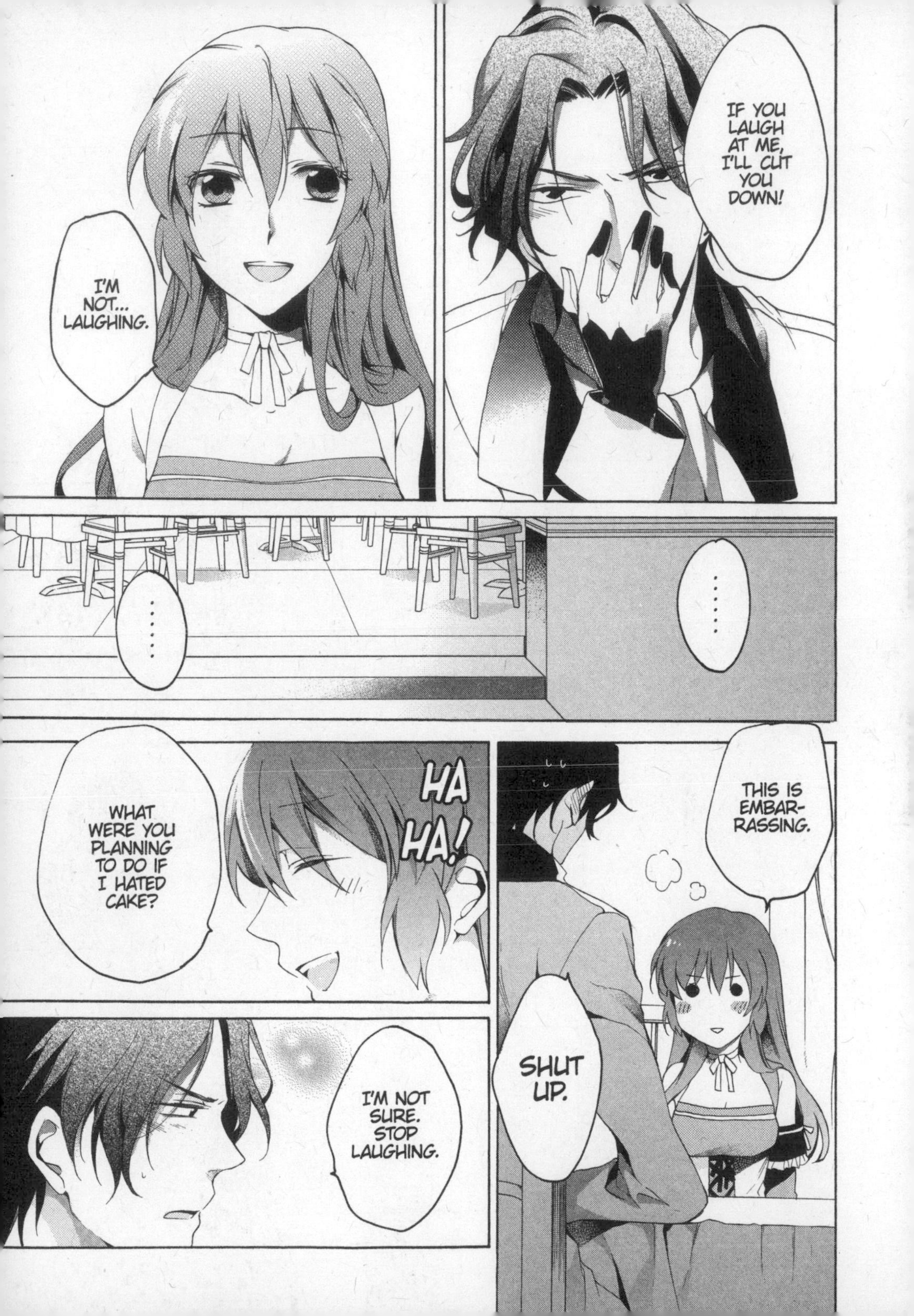
IF YOU LAUGH AT ME, I'LL CUT YOU DOWN!
I'M NOT... LAUGHING.
......
......
THIS IS EMBAR-RASSING.
SHUT UP.
WHAT WERE YOU PLANNING TO DO IF I HATED CAKE?
HA HA!
I'M NOT SURE. STOP LAUGHING.

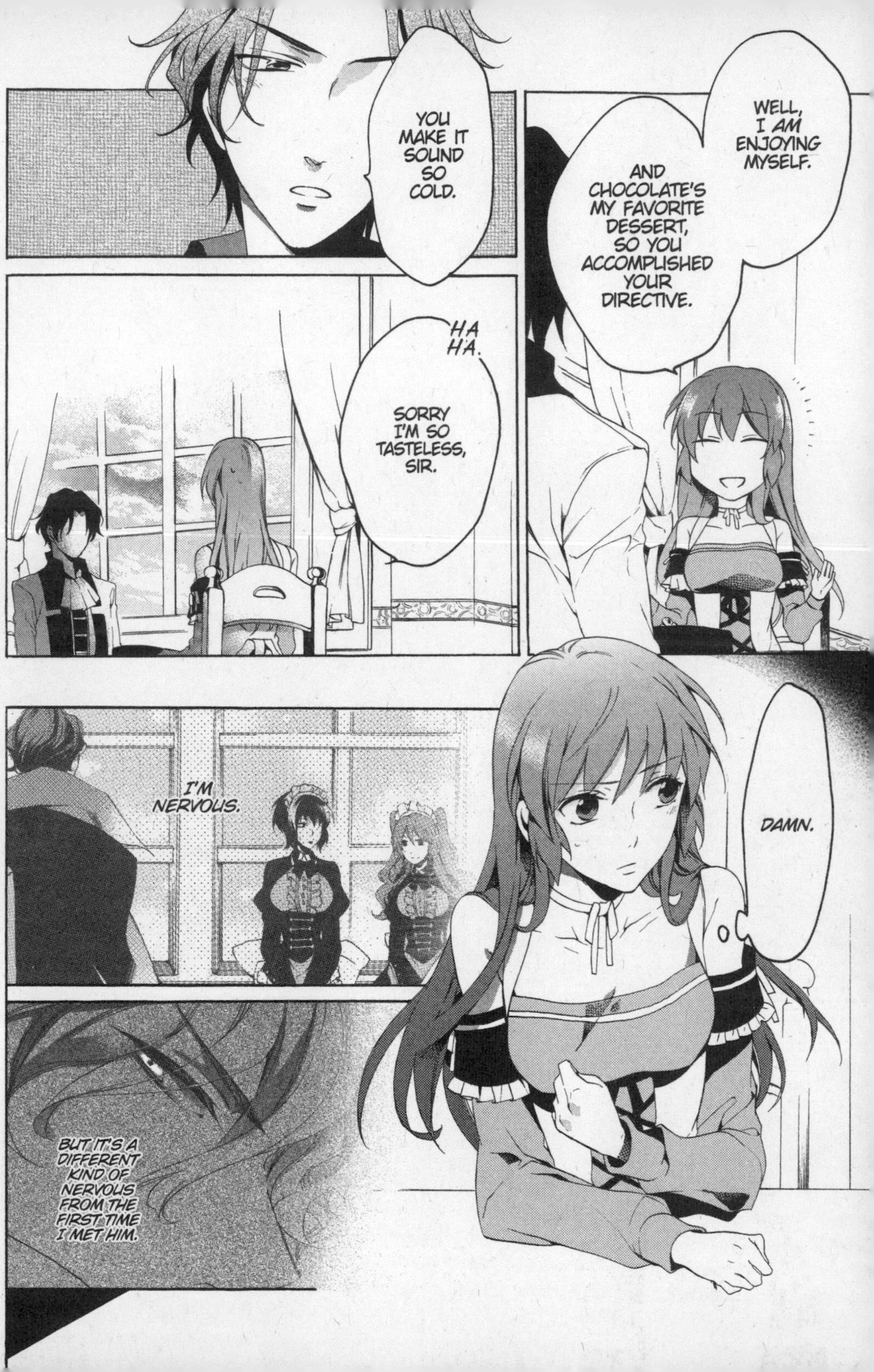
WELL, I AM ENJOYING MYSELF.
AND CHOCOLATE'S MY FAVORITE DESSERT, SO YOU ACCOMPLISHED YOUR DIRECTIVE.
YOU MAKE IT SOUND SO COLD.
HA HA.
SORRY I'M SO TASTELESS, SIR.
DAMN.
I'M NERVOUS.
BUT IT'S A DIFFERENT KIND OF NERVOUS FROM THE FIRST TIME I MET HIM.

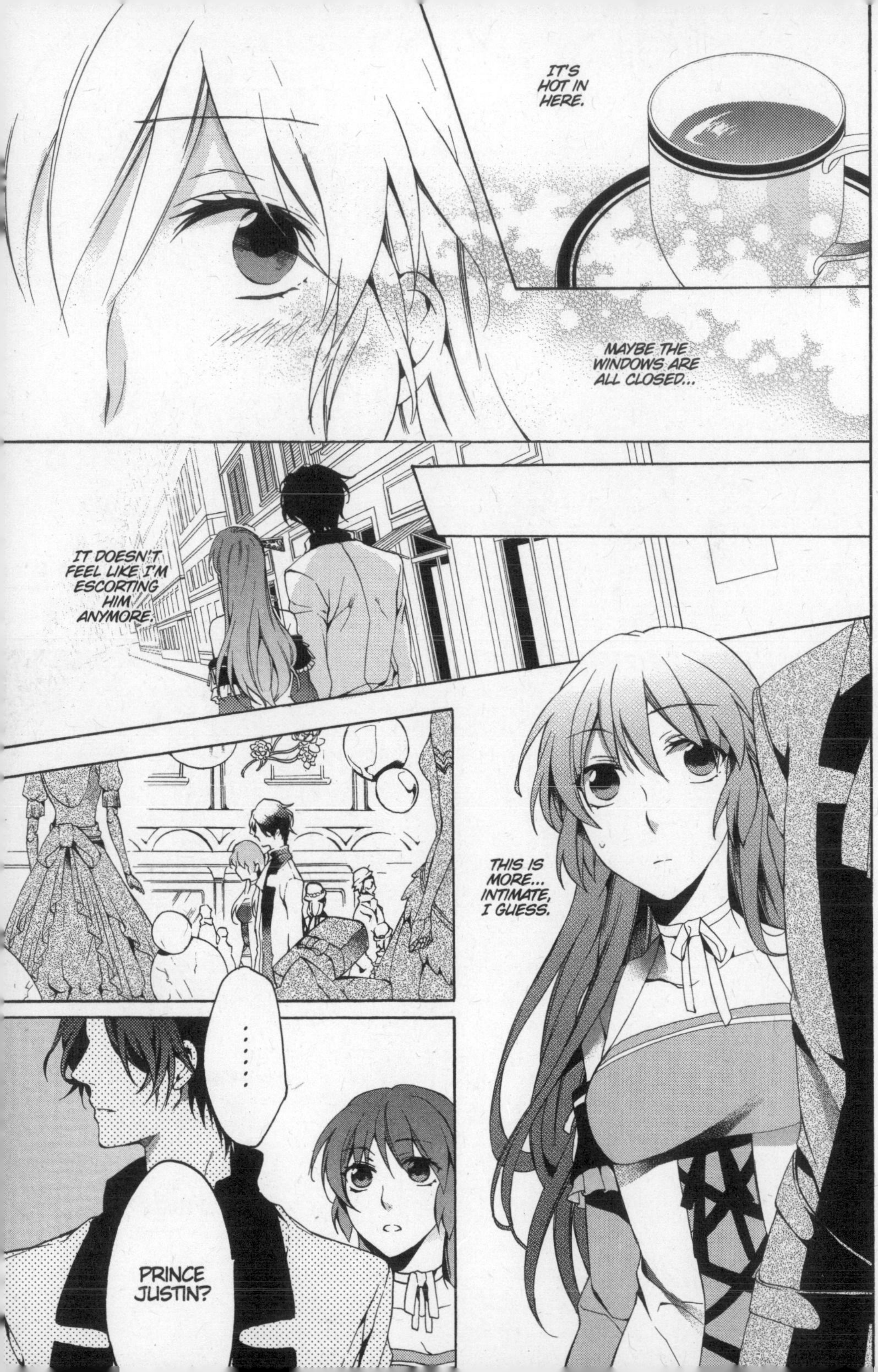
IT'S HOT IN HERE.
MAYBE THE WINDOWS ARE ALL CLOSED...
IT DOESN'T FEEL LIKE I'M ESCORTING HIM ANYMORE.
THIS IS MORE... INTIMATE, I GUESS.
......
PRINCE JUSTIN?

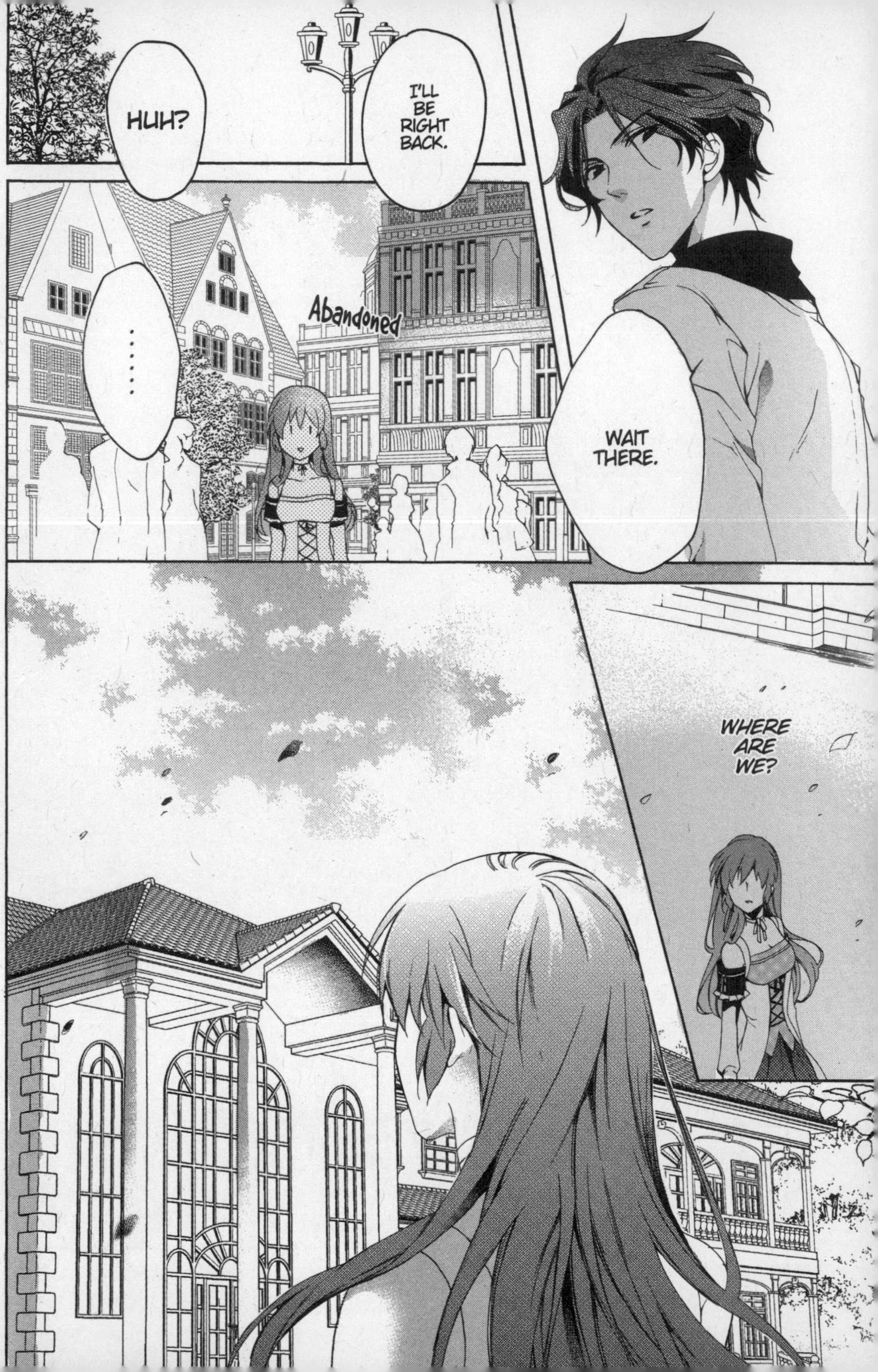
I'LL BE RIGHT BACK.
WAIT THERE.
HUH?
......
Abandoned
WHERE ARE WE?

CRIMSON EMPIRE
CIRCUMSTANCES TO SERVE A NOBLE

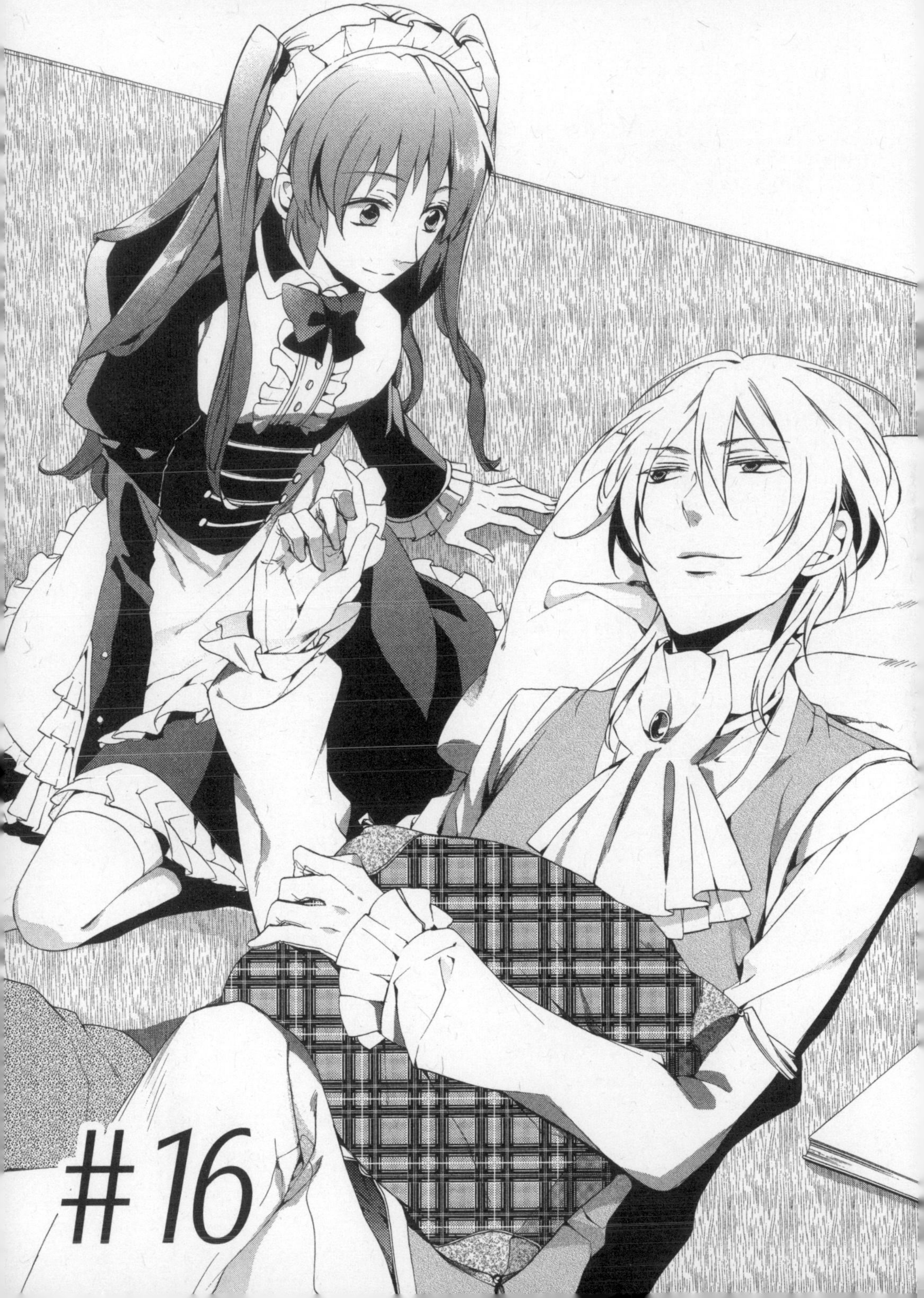
#16

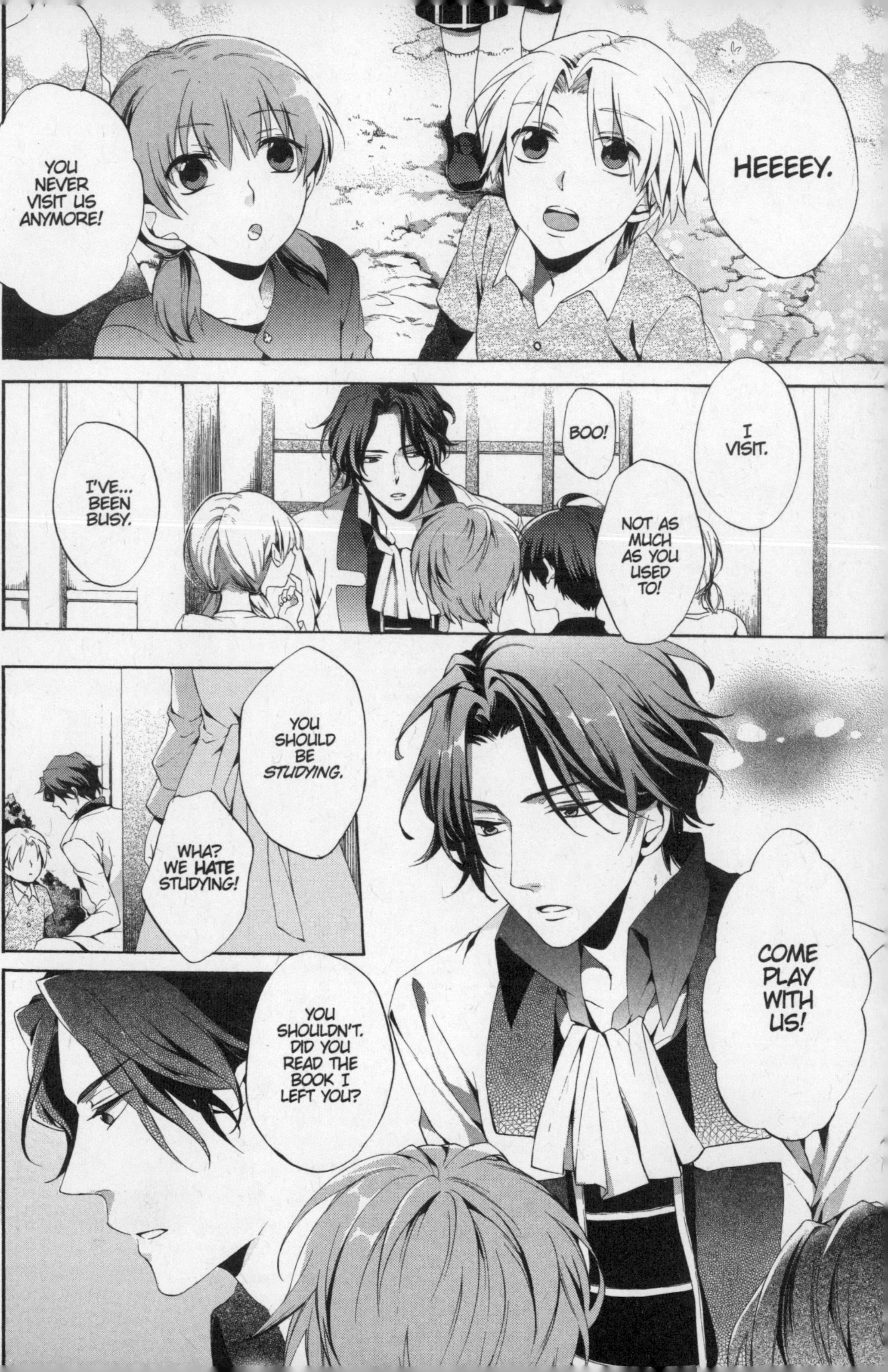
HEEEEY.
YOU NEVER VISIT US ANYMORE!
I VISIT.
BOO!
NOT AS MUCH AS YOU USED TO!
I'VE... BEEN BUSY.
COME PLAY WITH US!
YOU SHOULD BE STUDYING.
WHA? WE HATE STUDYING!
YOU SHOULDN'T. DID YOU READ THE BOOK I LEFT YOU?

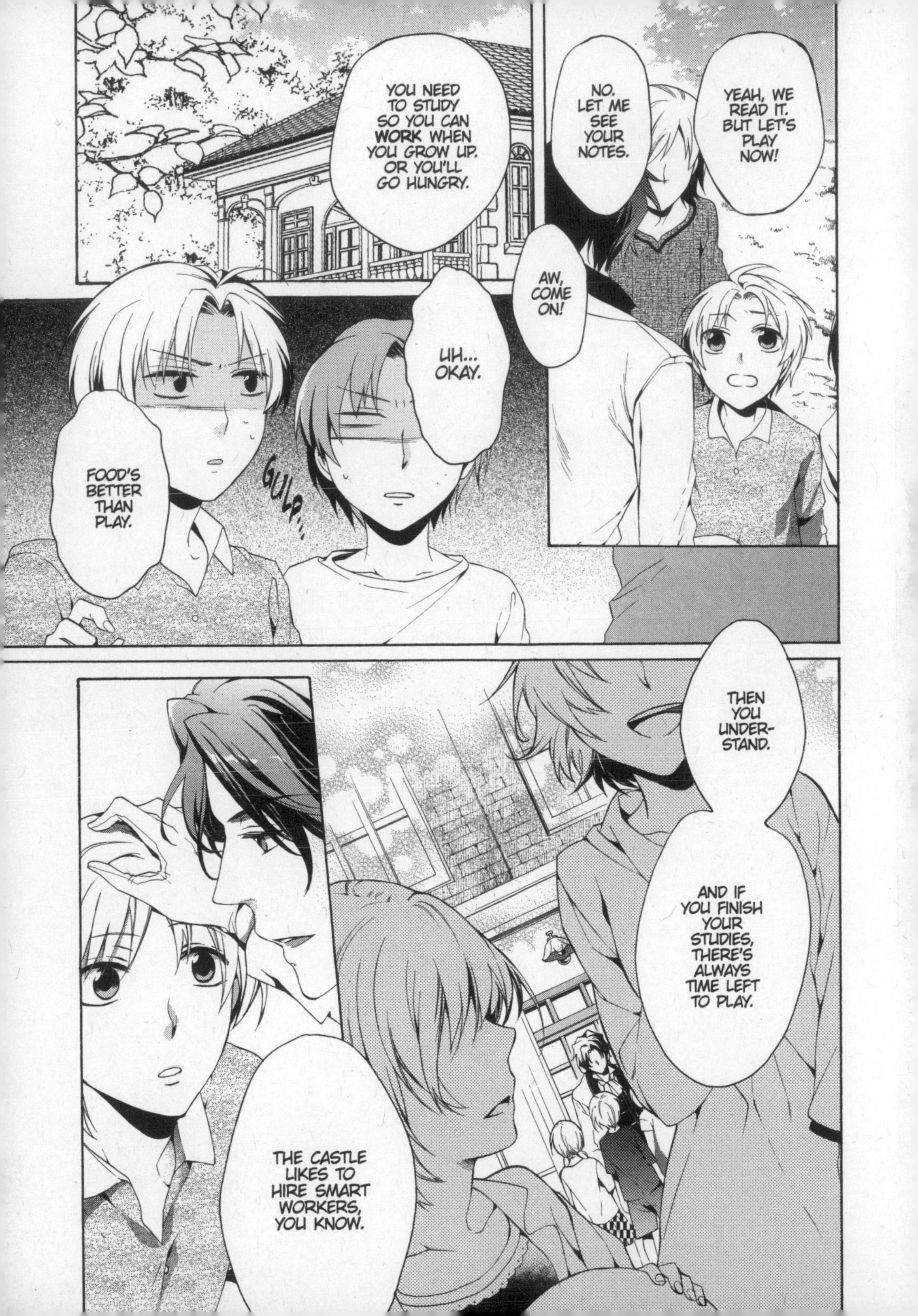
YEAH, WE READ IT. BUT LET'S PLAY NOW!
NO. LET ME SEE YOUR NOTES.
AW, COME ON!
YOU NEED TO STUDY SO YOU CAN **WORK** WHEN YOU GROW UP. OR YOU'LL GO HUNGRY.
UH... OKAY.
GULP...
FOOD'S BETTER THAN PLAY.
THEN YOU UNDER-STAND.
AND IF YOU FINISH YOUR STUDIES, THERE'S ALWAYS TIME LEFT TO PLAY.
THE CASTLE LIKES TO HIRE SMART WORKERS, YOU KNOW.

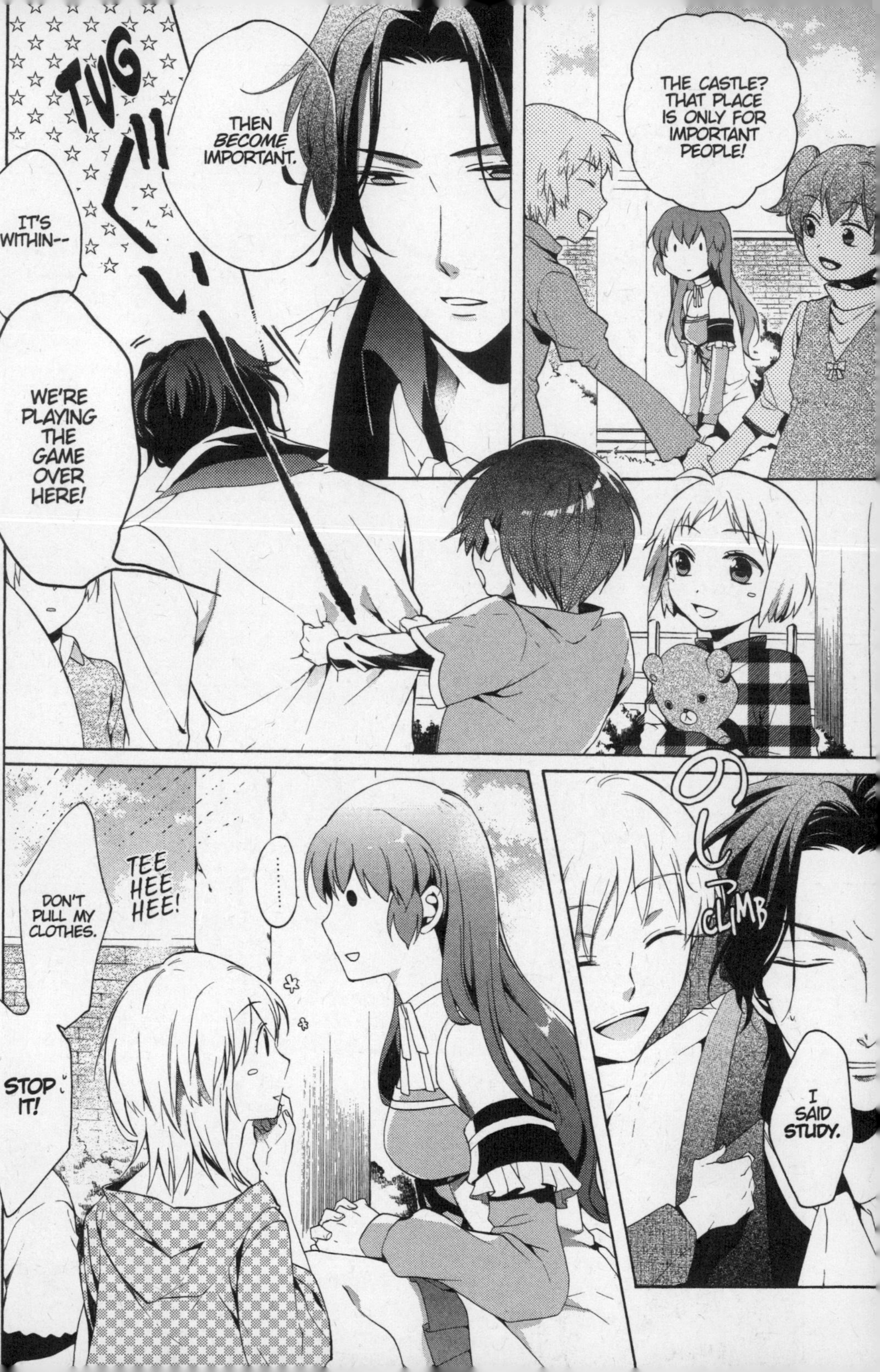
THE CASTLE? THAT PLACE IS ONLY FOR IMPORTANT PEOPLE!
THEN BECOME IMPORTANT.
IT'S WITHIN--
TUG
WE'RE PLAYING THE GAME OVER HERE!
CLIMB
I SAID STUDY.
......
TEE HEE HEE!
DON'T PULL MY CLOTHES.
STOP IT!

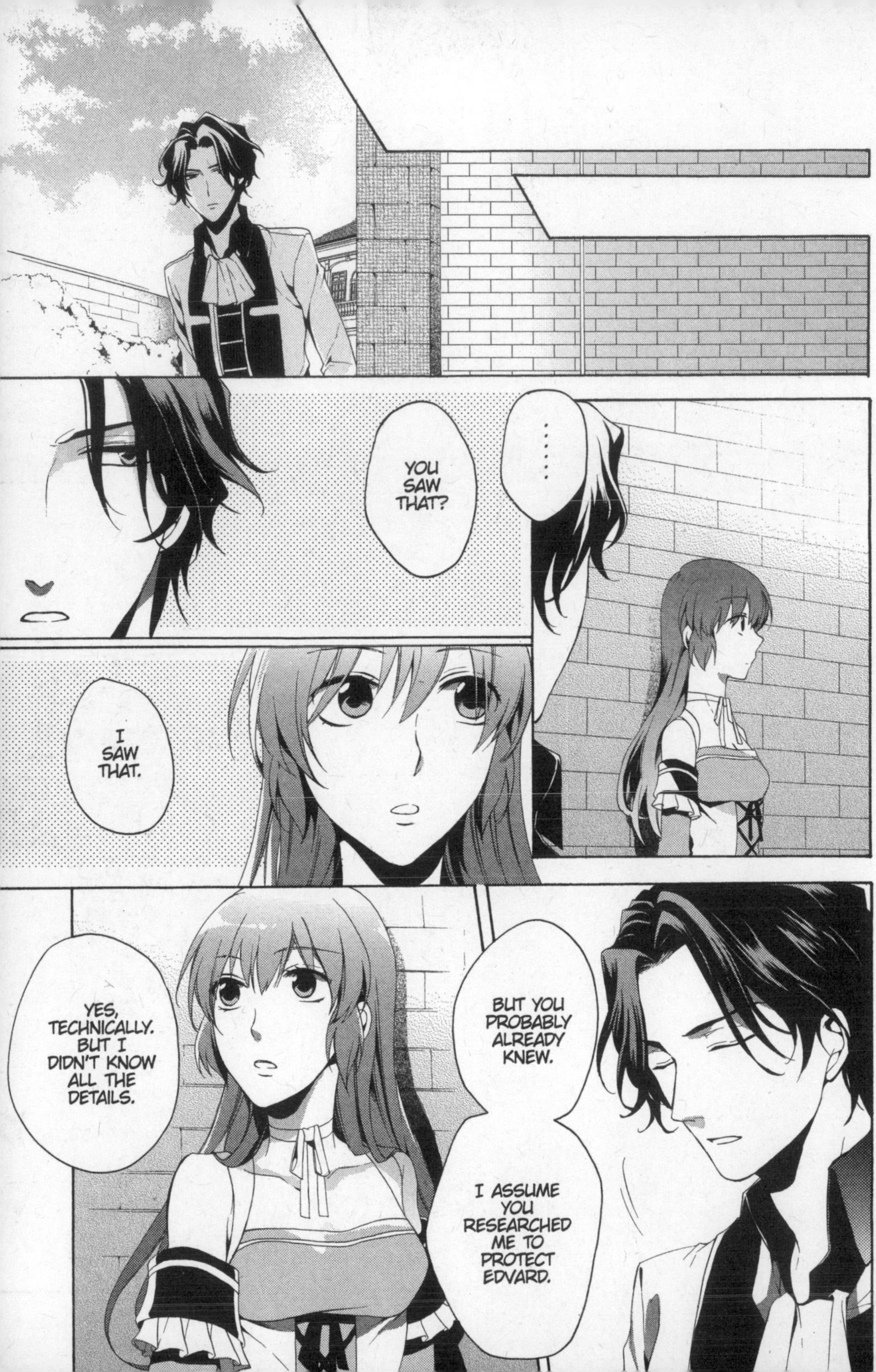
......
YOU SAW THAT?
I SAW THAT.
BUT YOU PROBABLY ALREADY KNEW.
I ASSUME YOU RESEARCHED ME TO PROTECT EDVARD.
YES, TECHNICALLY. BUT I DIDN'T KNOW ALL THE DETAILS.

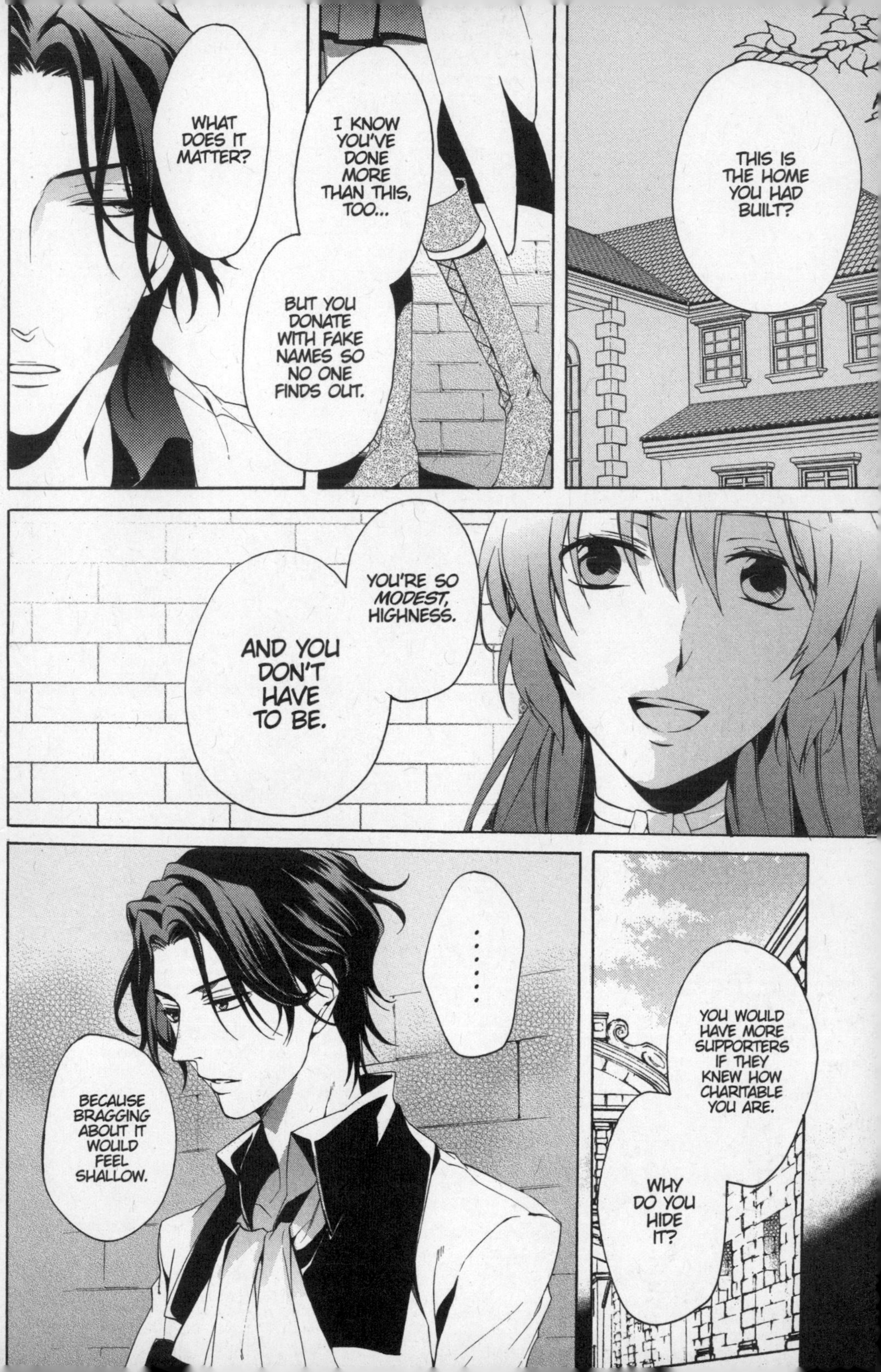
THIS IS THE HOME YOU HAD BUILT?
I KNOW YOU'VE DONE MORE THAN THIS, TOO...
BUT YOU DONATE WITH FAKE NAMES SO NO ONE FINDS OUT.
WHAT DOES IT MATTER?
YOU'RE SO *MODEST*, HIGHNESS.
AND YOU DON'T HAVE TO BE.
YOU WOULD HAVE MORE SUPPORTERS IF THEY KNEW HOW CHARITABLE YOU ARE.
WHY DO YOU HIDE IT?
......
BECAUSE BRAGGING ABOUT IT WOULD FEEL SHALLOW.

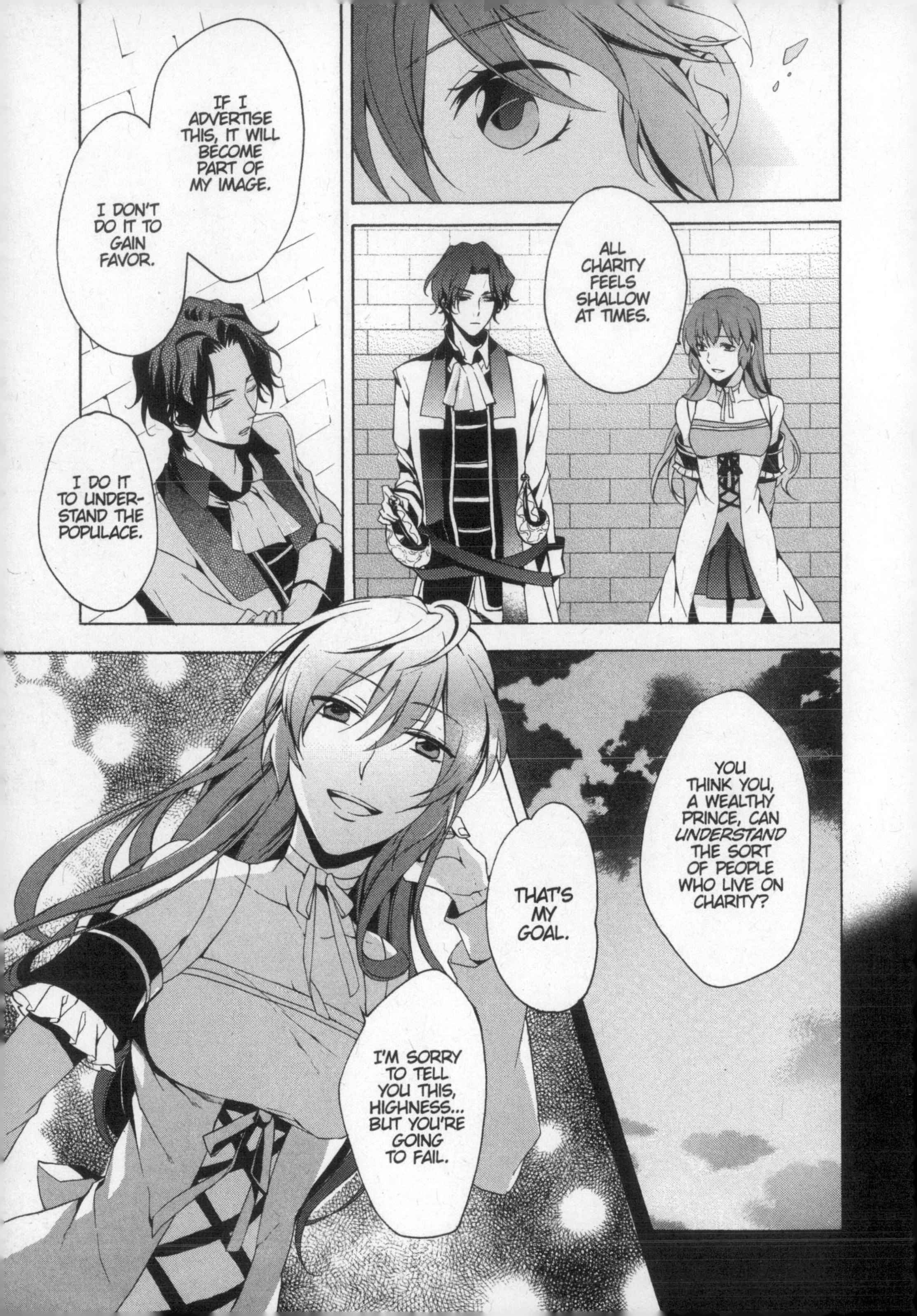
ALL CHARITY FEELS SHALLOW AT TIMES.
IF I ADVERTISE THIS, IT WILL BECOME PART OF MY IMAGE.
I DON'T DO IT TO GAIN FAVOR.
I DO IT TO UNDER-STAND THE POPULACE.
THAT'S MY GOAL.
YOU THINK YOU, A WEALTHY PRINCE, CAN *UNDERSTAND* THE SORT OF PEOPLE WHO LIVE ON CHARITY?
I'M SORRY TO TELL YOU THIS, HIGHNESS... BUT YOU'RE GOING TO FAIL.

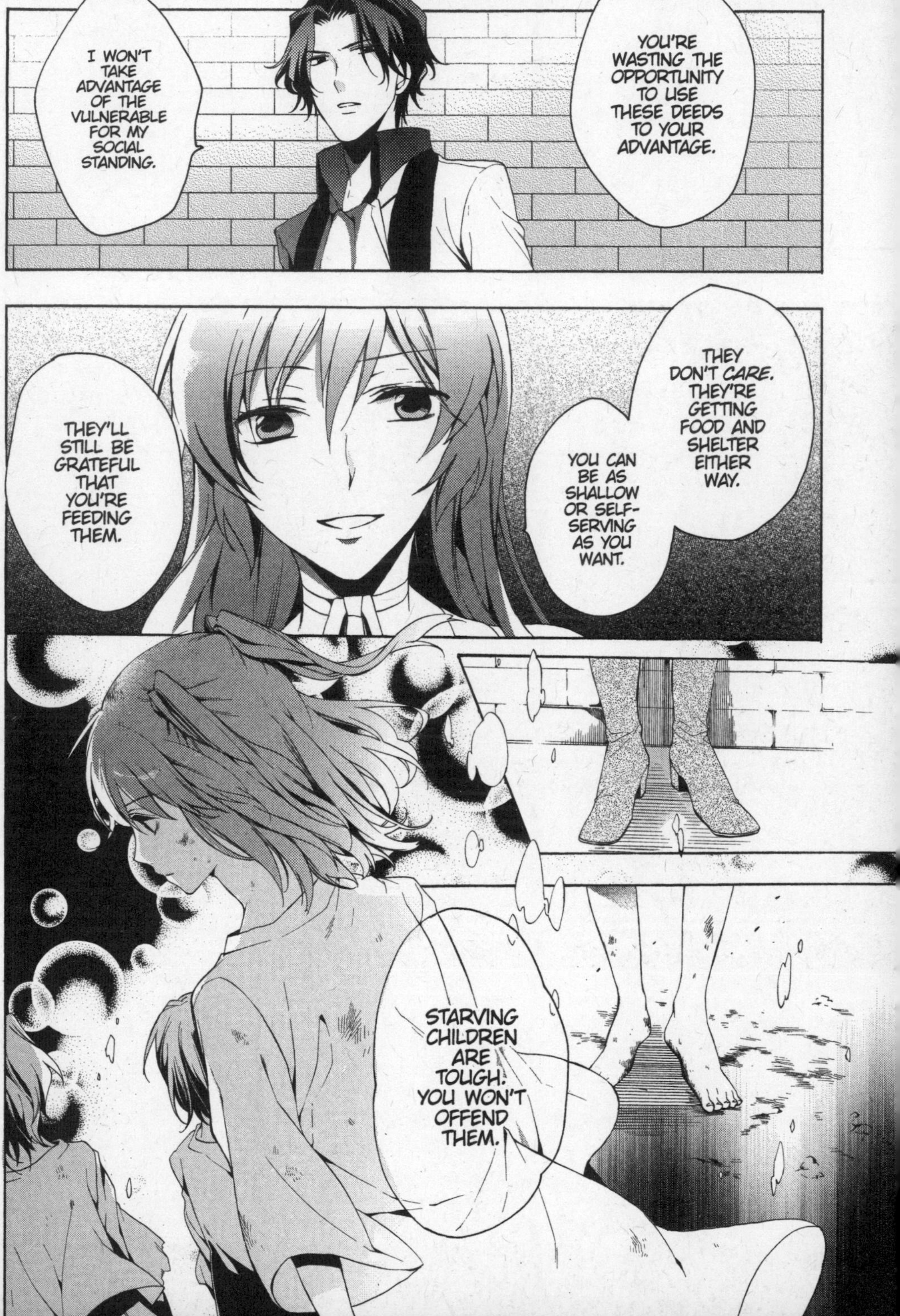
YOU'RE WASTING THE OPPORTUNITY TO USE THESE DEEDS TO YOUR ADVANTAGE.
I WON'T TAKE ADVANTAGE OF THE VULNERABLE FOR MY SOCIAL STANDING.
THEY DON'T CARE. THEY'RE GETTING FOOD AND SHELTER EITHER WAY.
YOU CAN BE AS SHALLOW OR SELF-SERVING AS YOU WANT.
THEY'LL STILL BE GRATEFUL THAT YOU'RE FEEDING THEM.
STARVING CHILDREN ARE TOUGH. YOU WON'T OFFEND THEM.

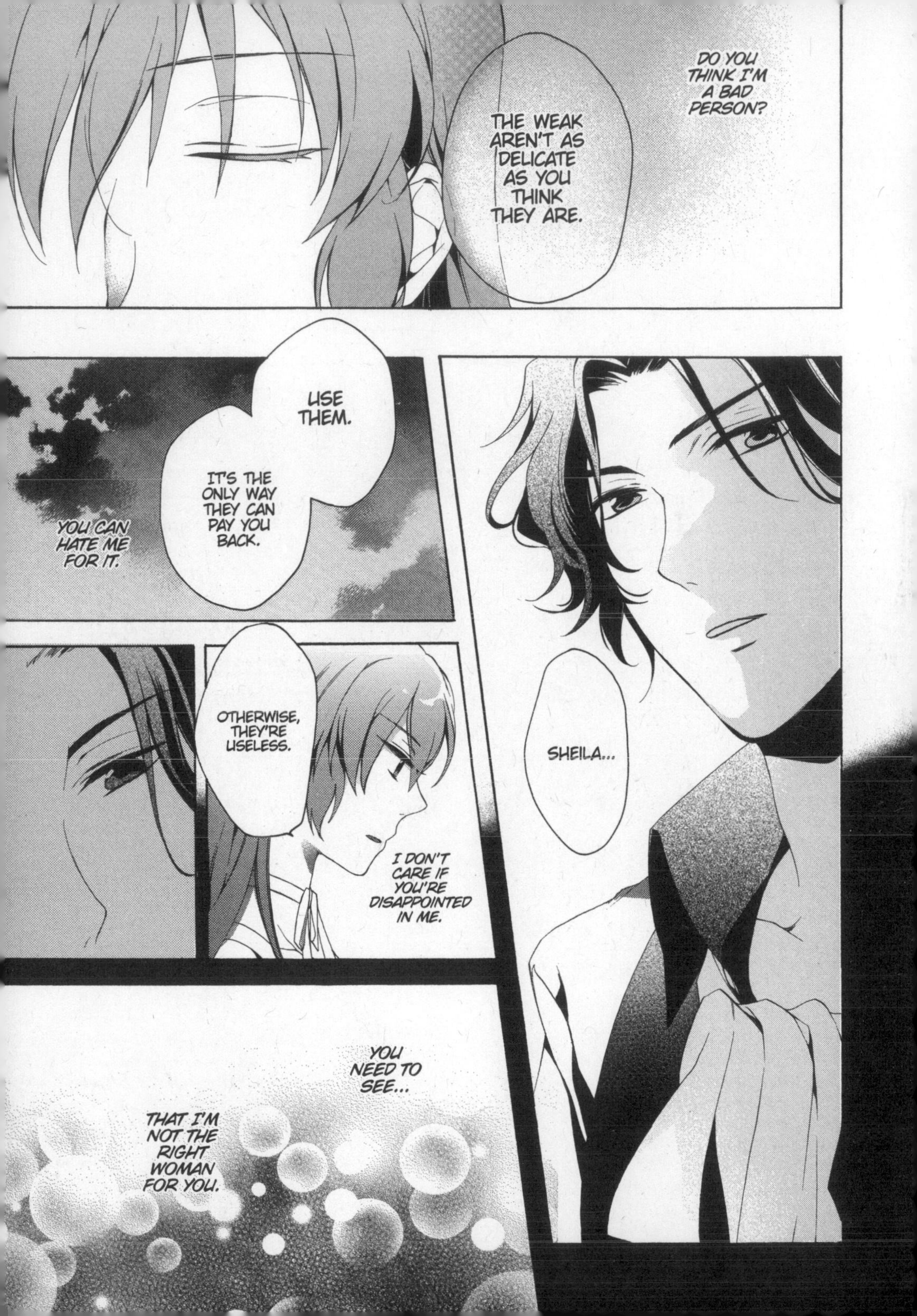
DO YOU THINK I'M A BAD PERSON?
THE WEAK AREN'T AS DELICATE AS YOU THINK THEY ARE.
SHEILA...
USE THEM.
IT'S THE ONLY WAY THEY CAN PAY YOU BACK.
YOU CAN HATE ME FOR IT.
OTHERWISE, THEY'RE USELESS.
I DON'T CARE IF YOU'RE DISAPPOINTED IN ME.
YOU NEED TO SEE...
THAT I'M NOT THE RIGHT WOMAN FOR YOU.

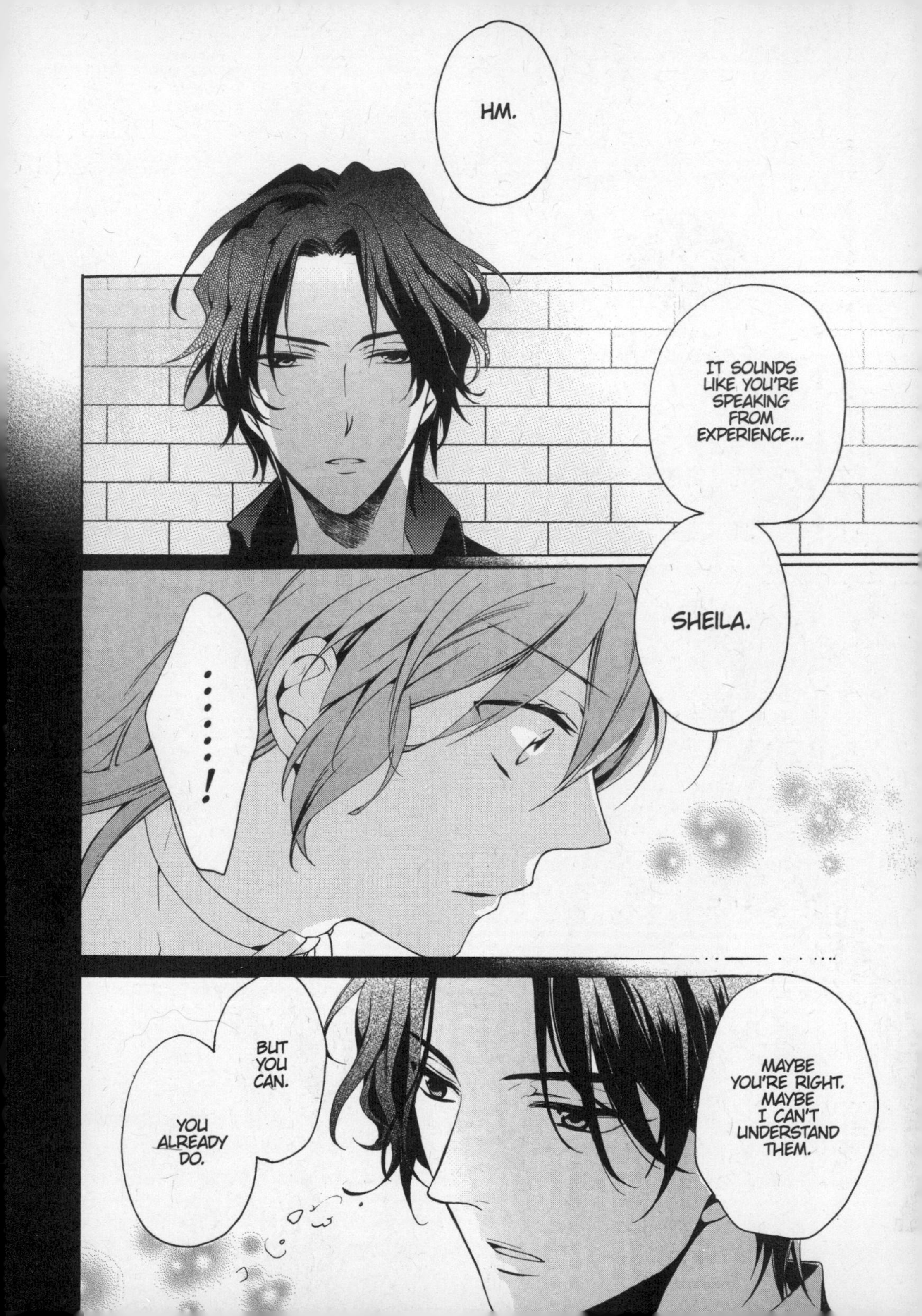
HM.
IT SOUNDS LIKE YOU'RE SPEAKING FROM EXPERIENCE...
SHEILA.
......!
MAYBE YOU'RE RIGHT. MAYBE I CAN'T UNDERSTAND THEM.
BUT YOU CAN.
YOU ALREADY DO.

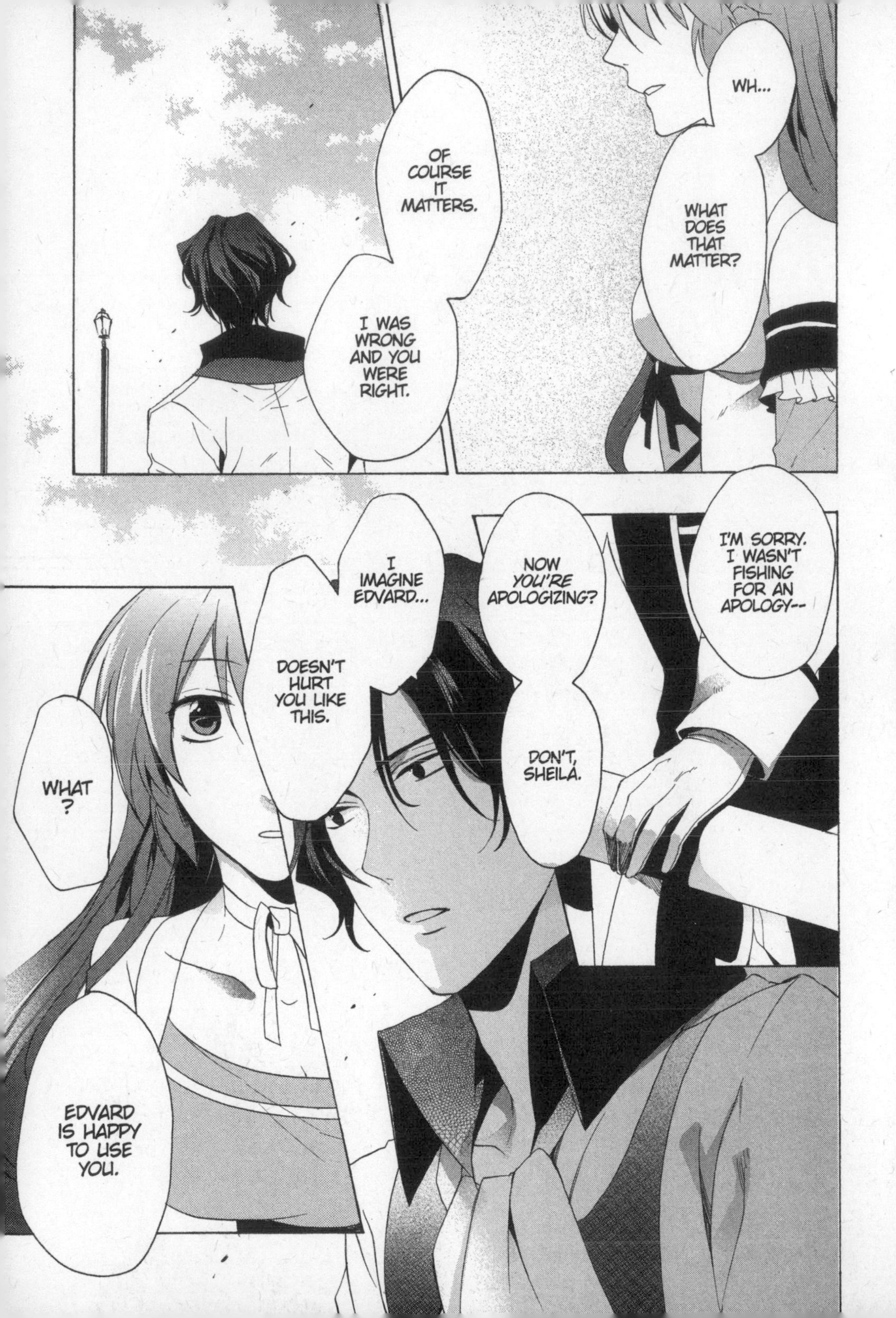
WH...
WHAT DOES THAT MATTER?
OF COURSE IT MATTERS.
I WAS WRONG AND YOU WERE RIGHT.
I'M SORRY. I WASN'T FISHING FOR AN APOLOGY--
NOW *YOU'RE* APOLOGIZING?
DON'T, SHEILA.
I IMAGINE EDVARD...
DOESN'T HURT YOU LIKE THIS.
WHAT?
EDVARD IS HAPPY TO USE YOU.

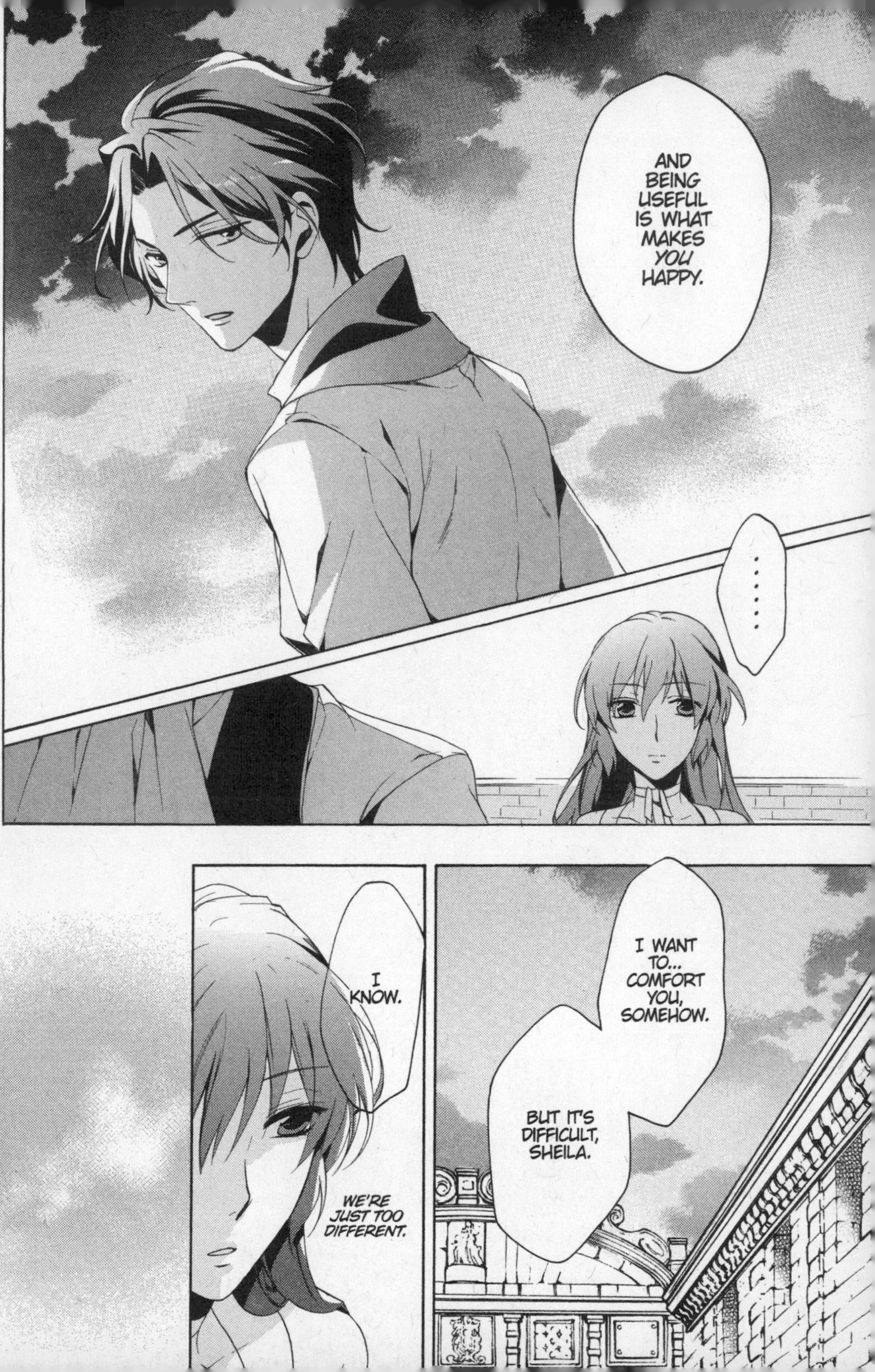
AND BEING USEFUL IS WHAT MAKES YOU HAPPY.
......
I WANT TO... COMFORT YOU, SOMEHOW.
BUT IT'S DIFFICULT, SHEILA.
I KNOW.
WE'RE JUST TOO DIFFERENT.

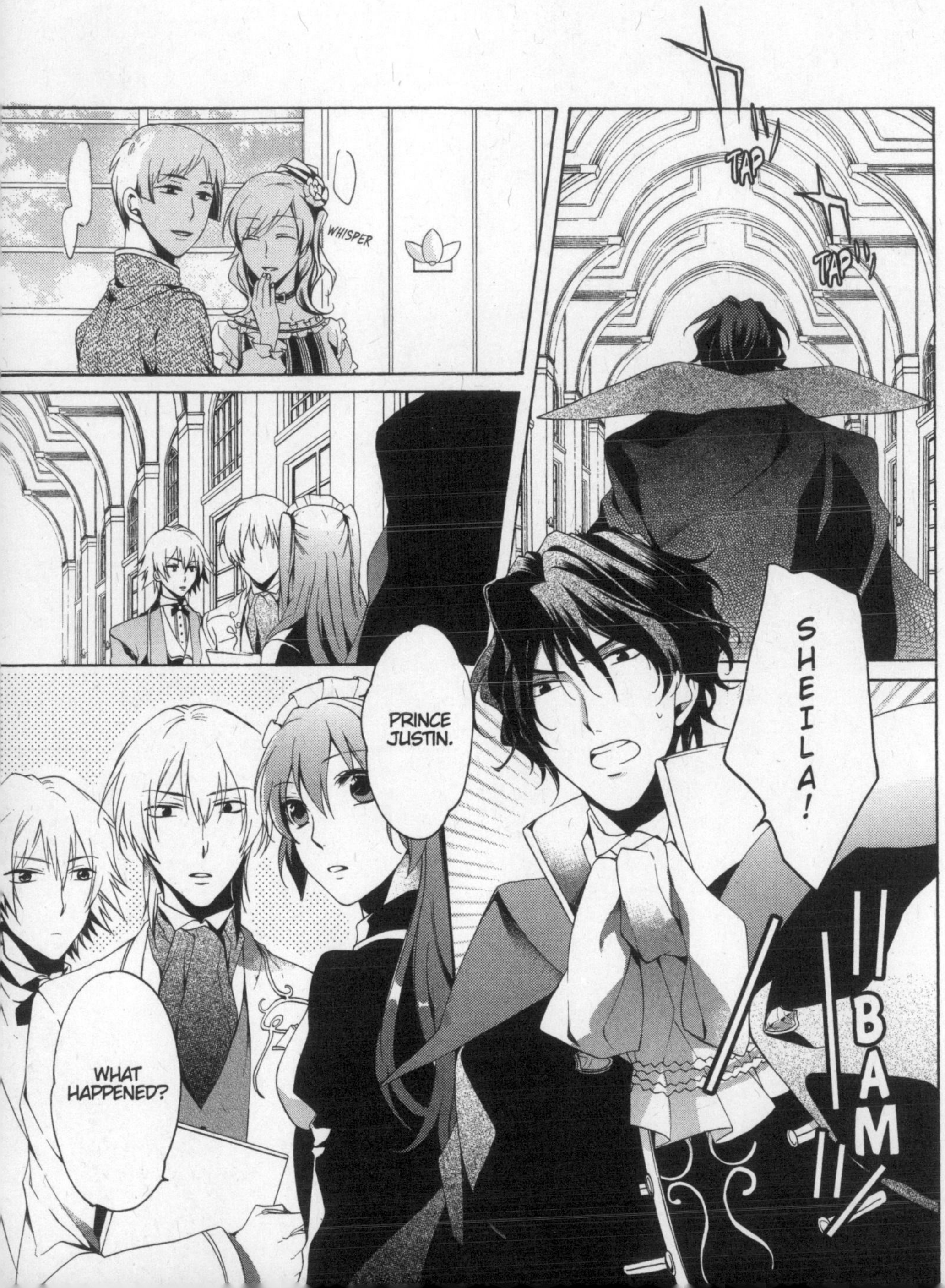
TAP
TAP
SHEILA!
BAM
WHISPER
PRINCE JUSTIN.
WHAT HAPPENED?

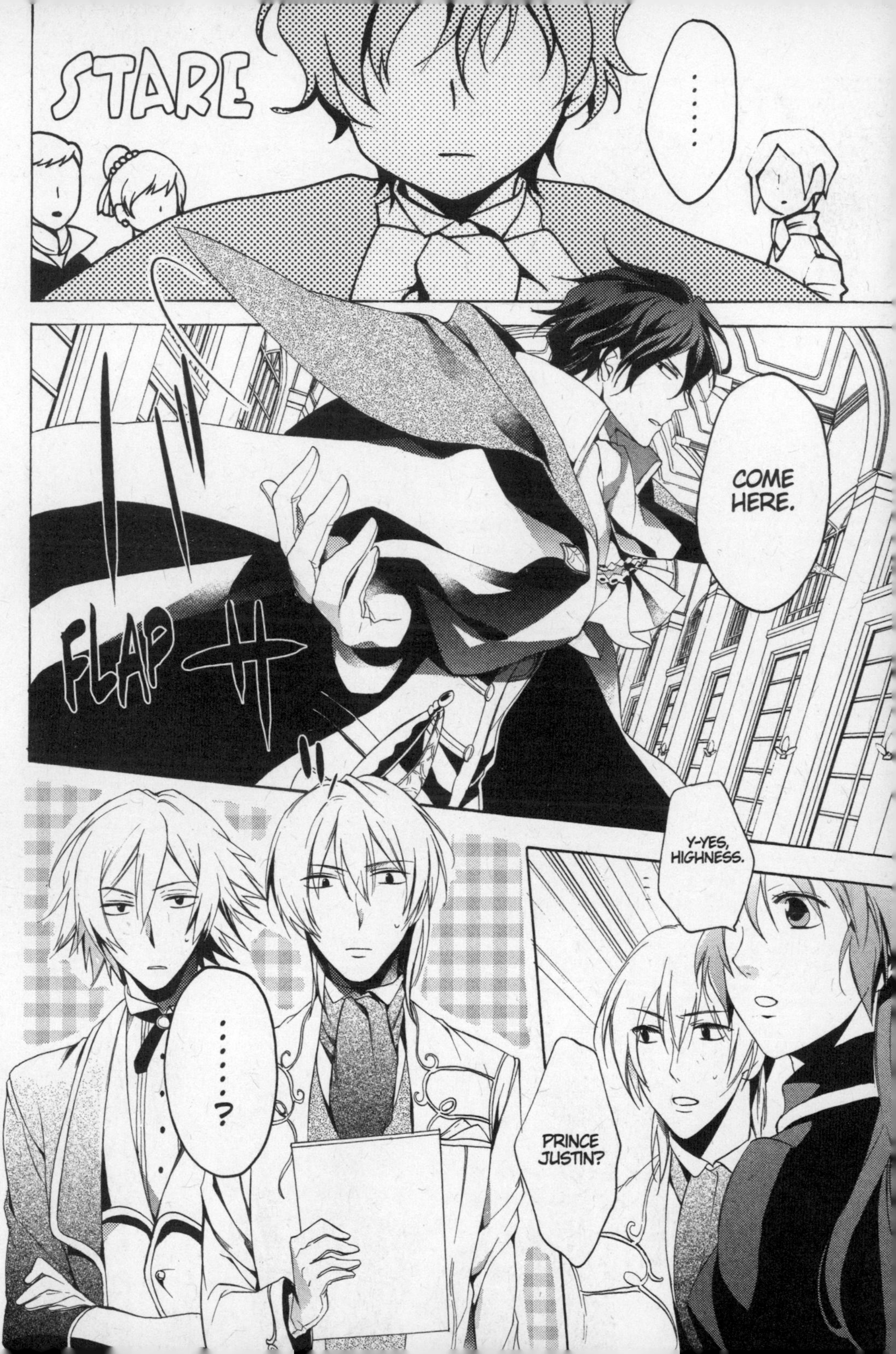
......
STARE
COME HERE.
FLAP
!!
Y-YES, HIGHNESS.
PRINCE JUSTIN?
......?

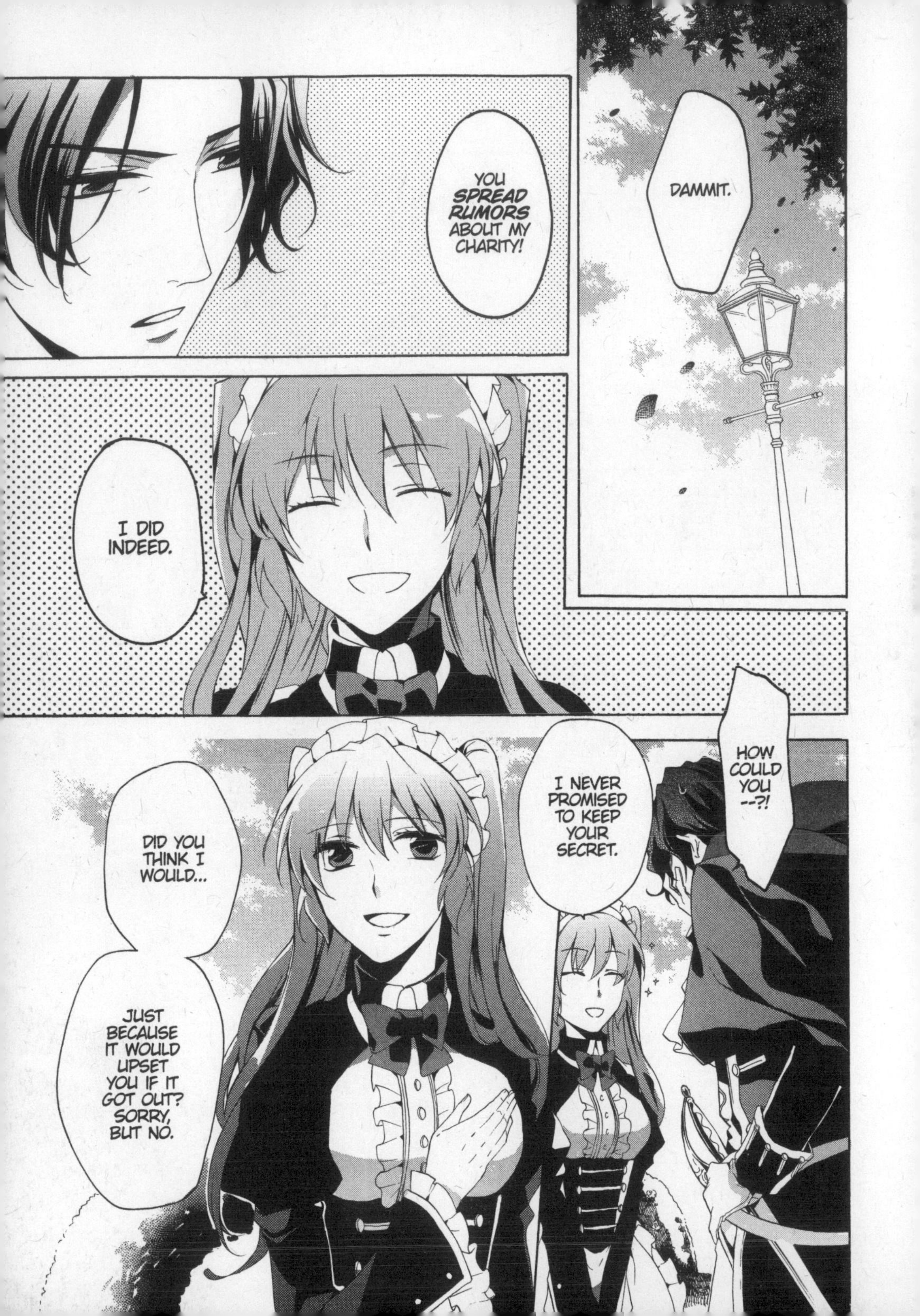
DAMMIT.
YOU SPREAD RUMORS ABOUT MY CHARITY!
I DID INDEED.
HOW COULD YOU --?!
I NEVER PROMISED TO KEEP YOUR SECRET.
DID YOU THINK I WOULD...
JUST BECAUSE IT WOULD UPSET YOU IF IT GOT OUT? SORRY, BUT NO.

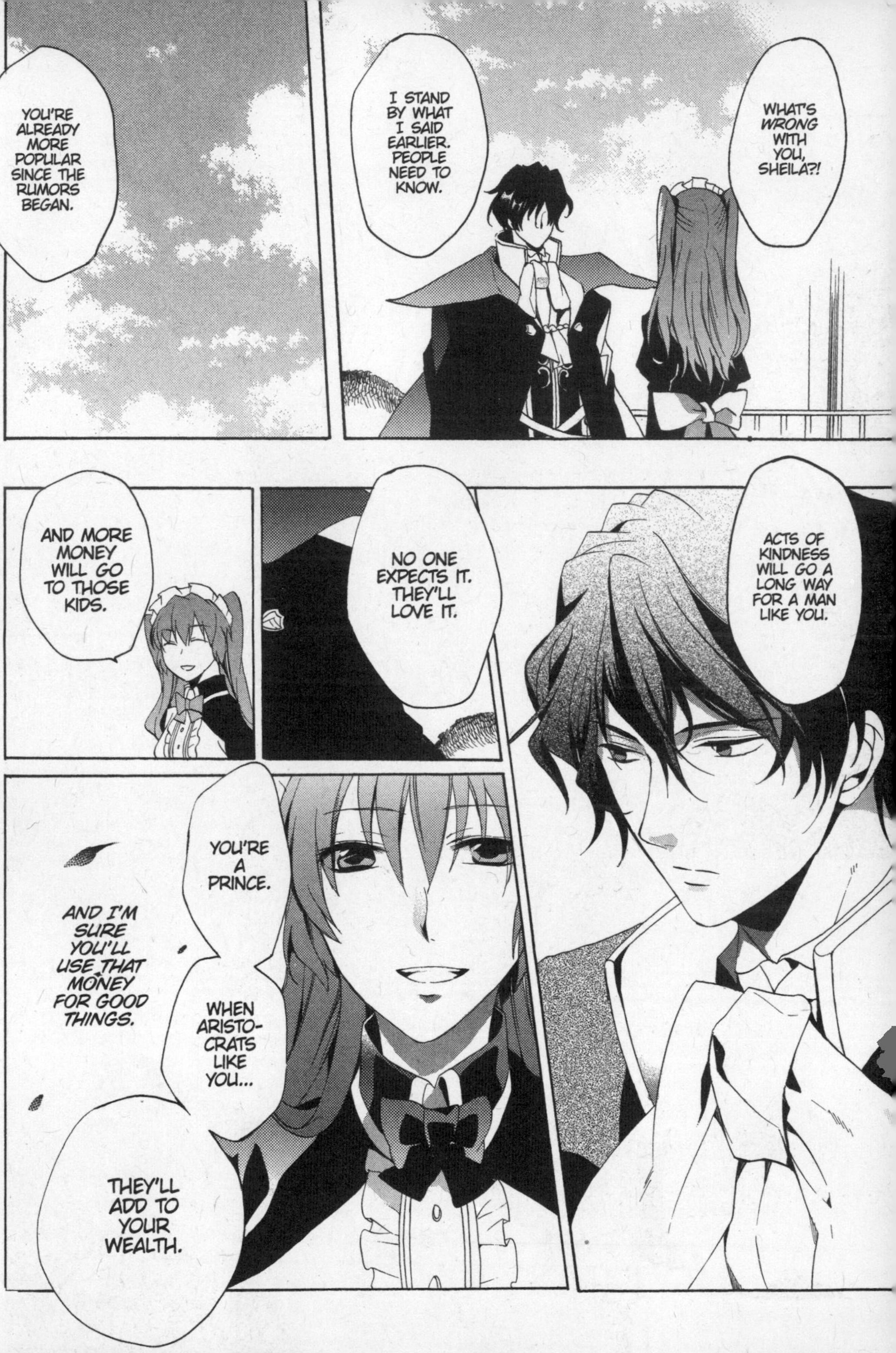
WHAT'S WRONG WITH YOU, SHEILA?!
I STAND BY WHAT I SAID EARLIER. PEOPLE NEED TO KNOW.
YOU'RE ALREADY MORE POPULAR SINCE THE RUMORS BEGAN.
ACTS OF KINDNESS WILL GO A LONG WAY FOR A MAN LIKE YOU.
NO ONE EXPECTS IT. THEY'LL LOVE IT.
AND MORE MONEY WILL GO TO THOSE KIDS.
YOU'RE A PRINCE.
AND I'M SURE YOU'LL USE THAT MONEY FOR GOOD THINGS.
WHEN ARISTO-CRATS LIKE YOU...
THEY'LL ADD TO YOUR WEALTH.

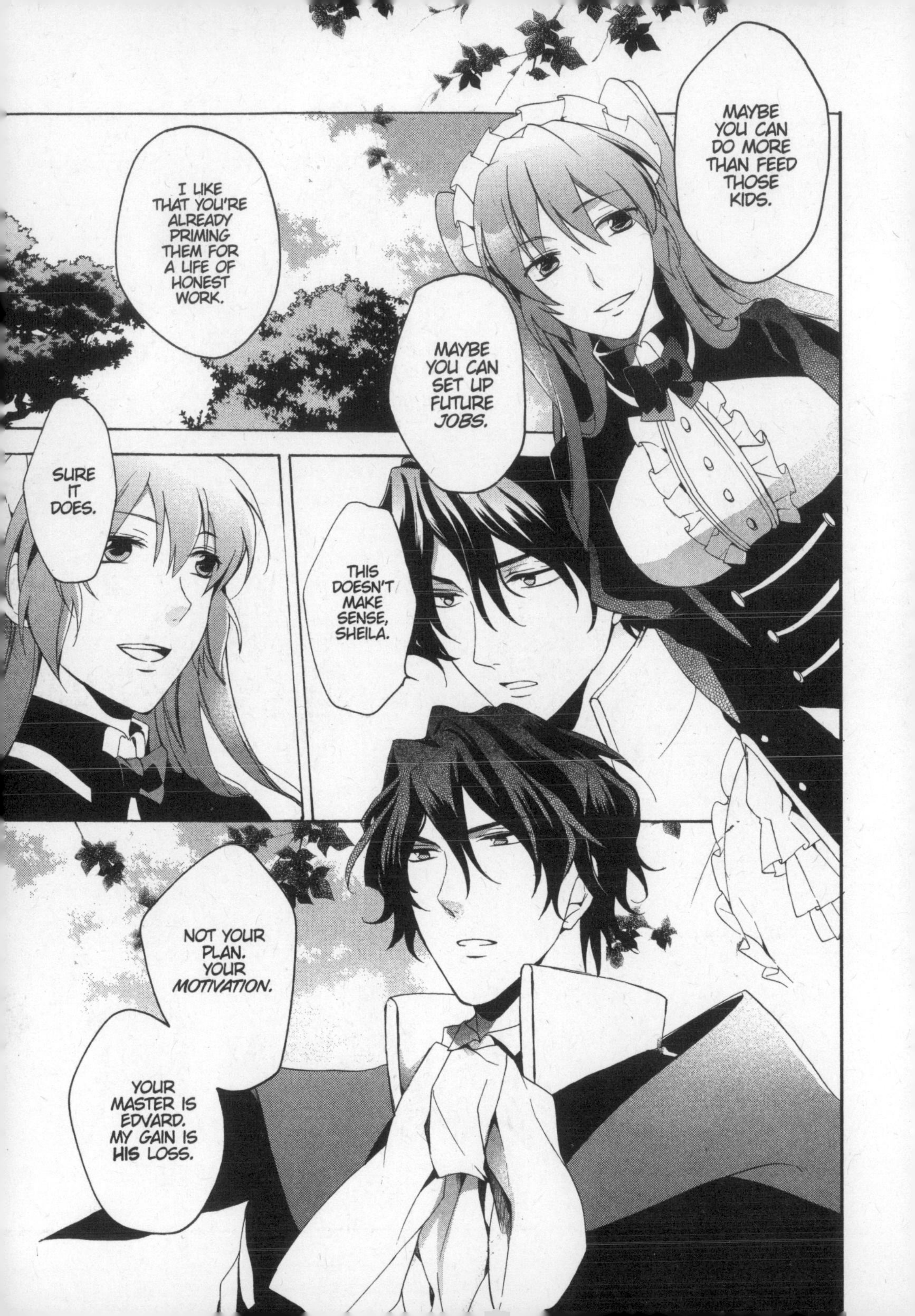
MAYBE YOU CAN DO MORE THAN FEED THOSE KIDS.
MAYBE YOU CAN SET UP FUTURE *JOBS.*
I LIKE THAT YOU'RE ALREADY PRIMING THEM FOR A LIFE OF HONEST WORK.
THIS DOESN'T MAKE SENSE, SHEILA.
SURE IT DOES.
NOT YOUR PLAN. YOUR *MOTIVATION.*
YOUR MASTER IS EDVARD. MY GAIN IS HIS LOSS.

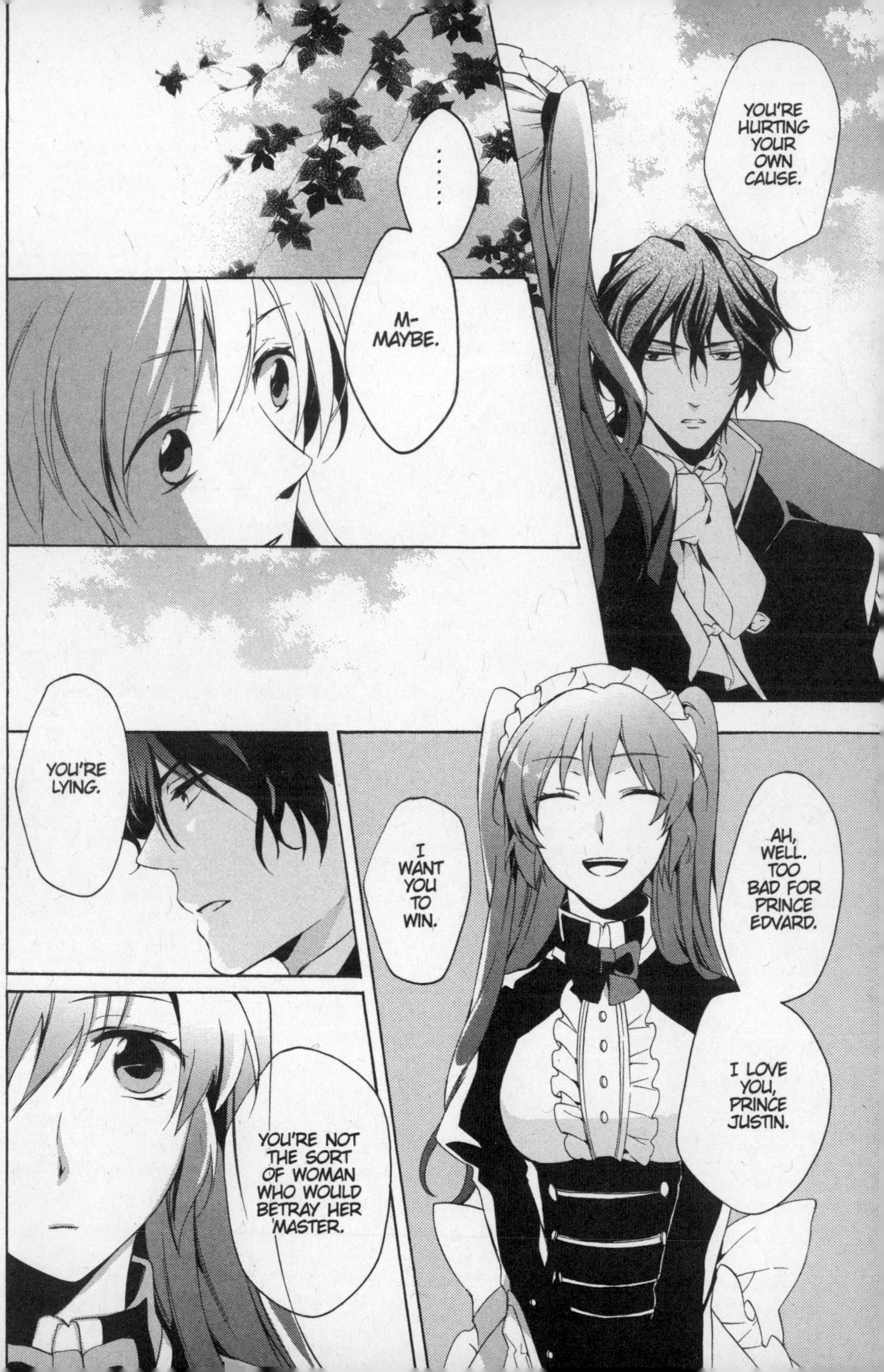
YOU'RE HURTING YOUR OWN CAUSE.
......
M-MAYBE.
AH, WELL. TOO BAD FOR PRINCE EDVARD.
I WANT YOU TO WIN.
I LOVE YOU, PRINCE JUSTIN.
YOU'RE LYING.
YOU'RE NOT THE SORT OF WOMAN WHO WOULD BETRAY HER MASTER.

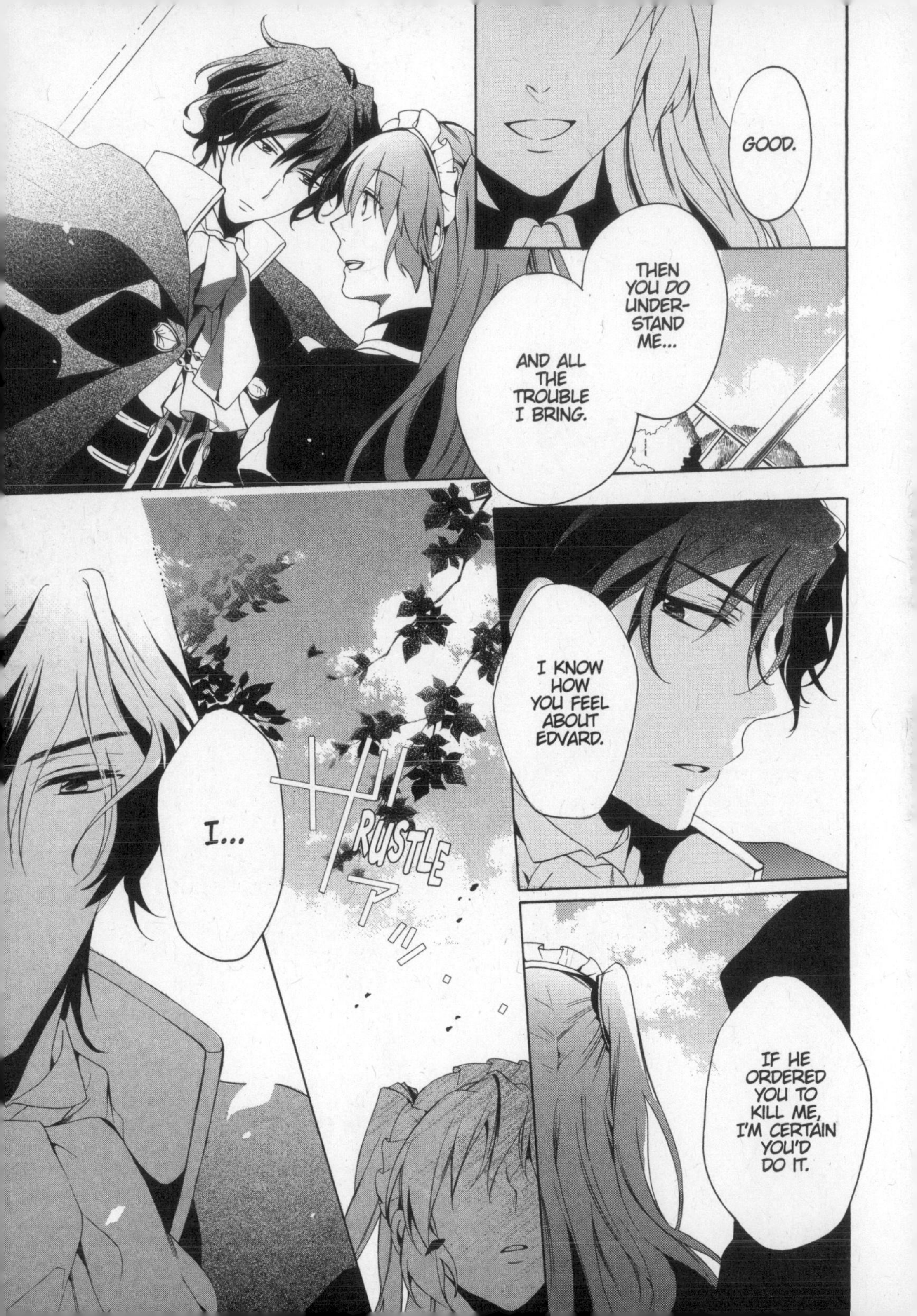
GOOD.
THEN YOU DO UNDERSTAND ME...
AND ALL THE TROUBLE I BRING.
I KNOW HOW YOU FEEL ABOUT EDVARD.
IF HE ORDERED YOU TO KILL ME, I'M CERTAIN YOU'D DO IT.
I...
RUSTLE

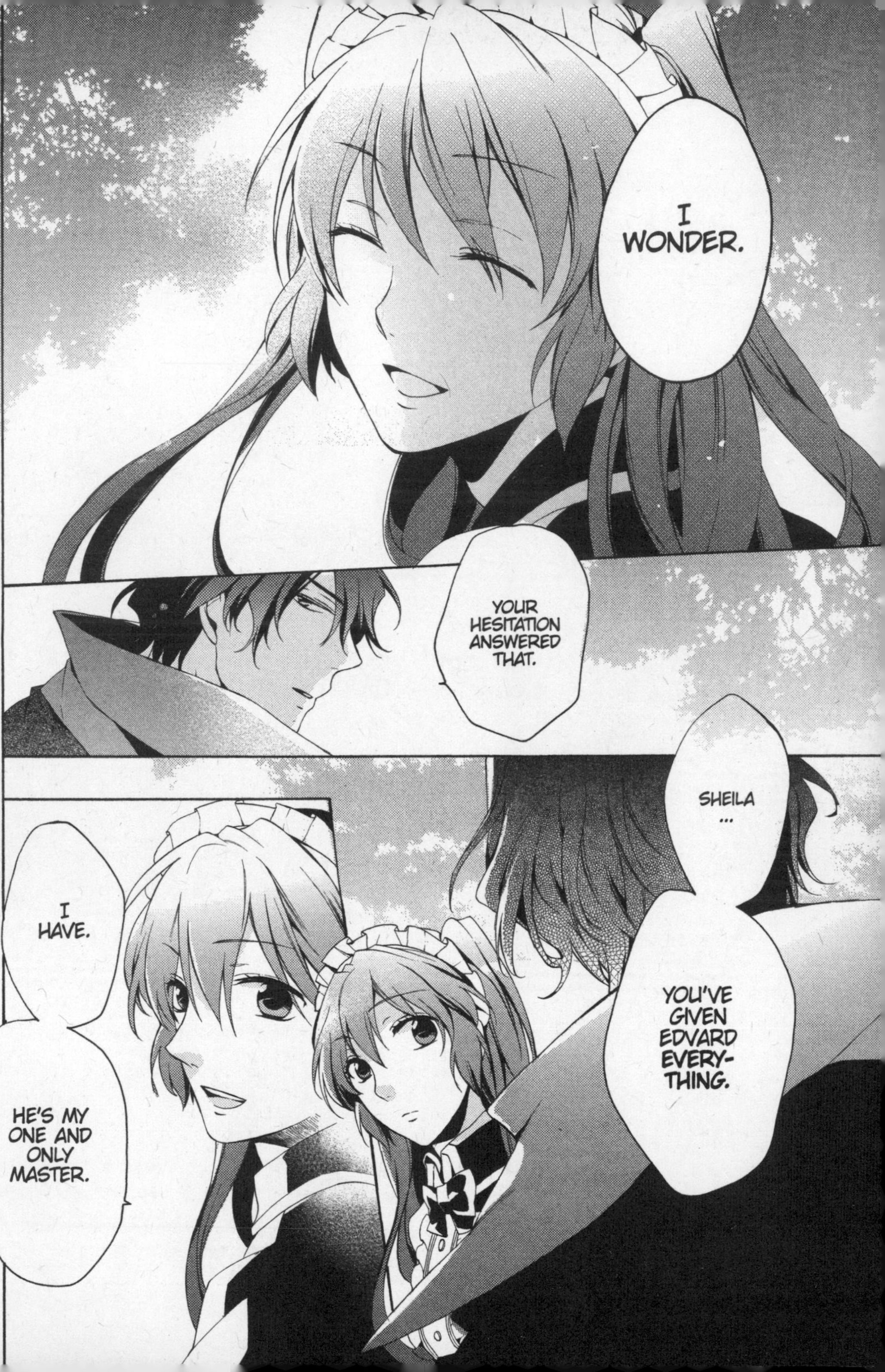
I WONDER.
YOUR HESITATION ANSWERED THAT.
SHEILA ...
YOU'VE GIVEN EDVARD EVERY-THING.
I HAVE.
HE'S MY ONE AND ONLY MASTER.

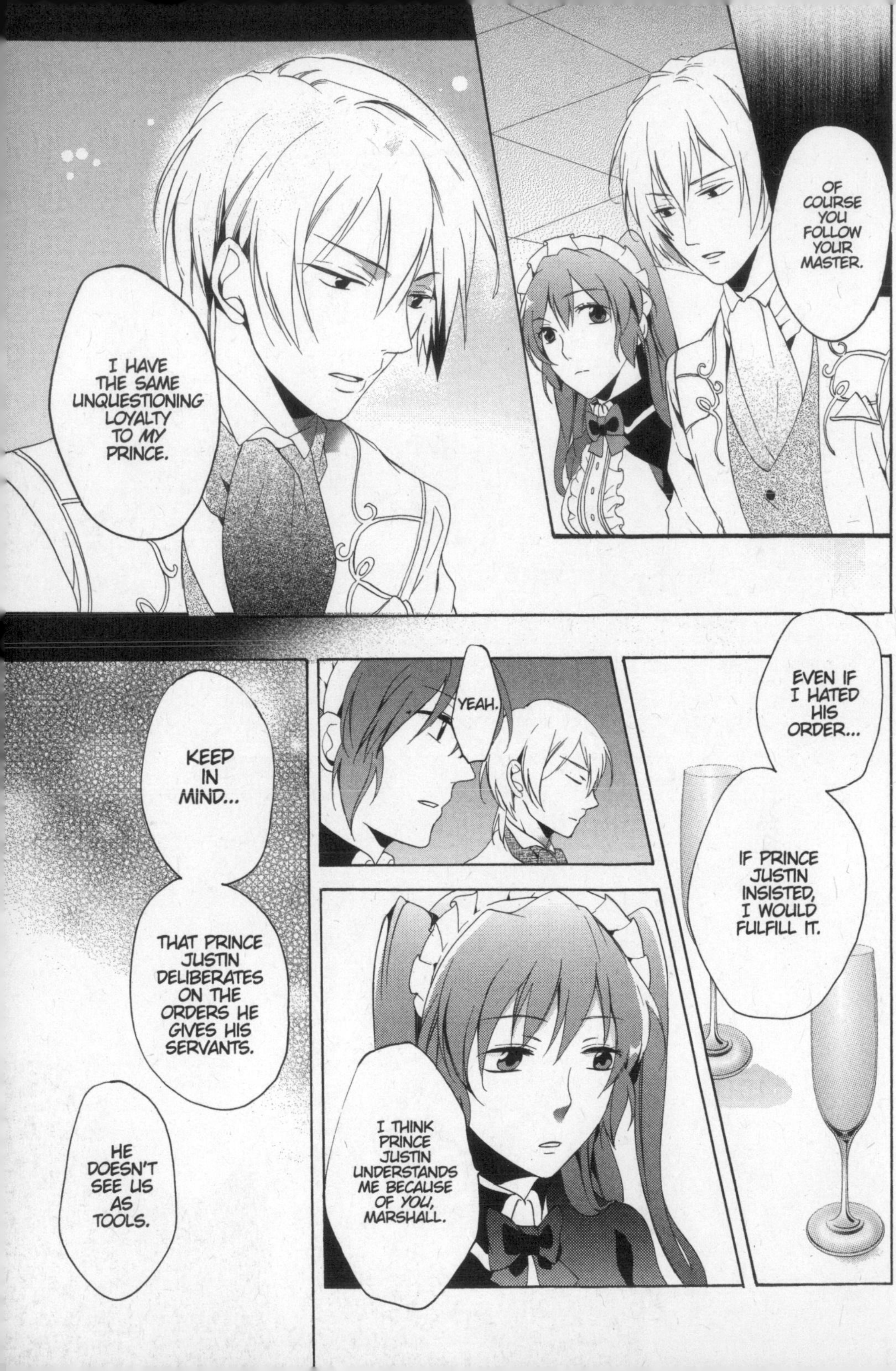
OF COURSE YOU FOLLOW YOUR MASTER.
I HAVE THE SAME UNQUESTIONING LOYALTY TO *MY* PRINCE.
EVEN IF I HATED HIS ORDER...
IF PRINCE JUSTIN INSISTED, I WOULD FULFILL IT.
YEAH.
I THINK PRINCE JUSTIN UNDERSTANDS ME BECAUSE OF *YOU*, MARSHALL.
KEEP IN MIND...
THAT PRINCE JUSTIN DELIBERATES ON THE ORDERS HE GIVES HIS SERVANTS.
HE DOESN'T SEE US AS TOOLS.

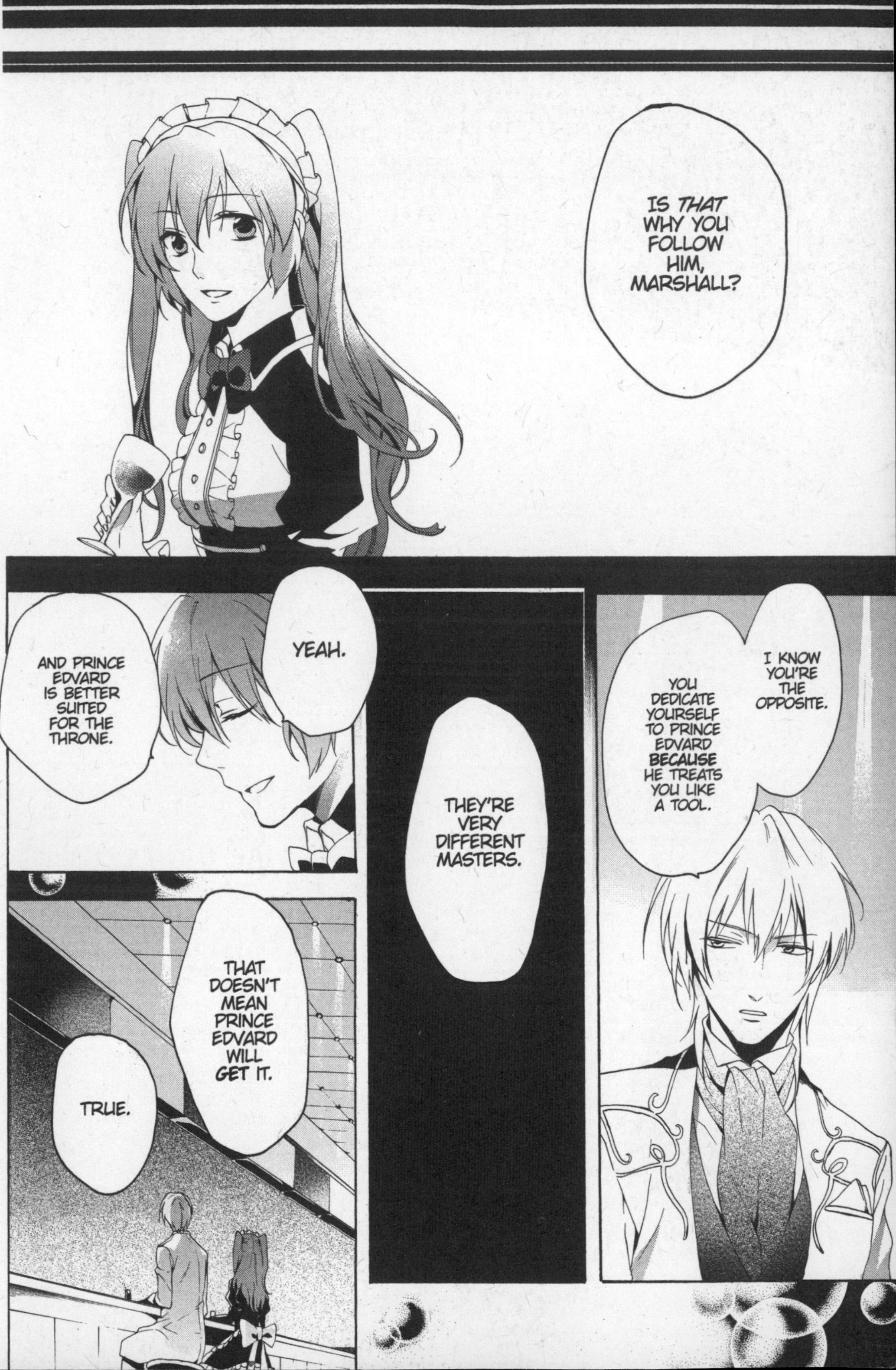
IS *THAT* WHY YOU FOLLOW HIM, MARSHALL?
I KNOW YOU'RE THE OPPOSITE.
YOU DEDICATE YOURSELF TO PRINCE EDVARD BECAUSE HE TREATS YOU LIKE A TOOL.
THEY'RE VERY DIFFERENT MASTERS.
YEAH.
AND PRINCE EDVARD IS BETTER SUITED FOR THE THRONE.
THAT DOESN'T MEAN PRINCE EDVARD WILL GET IT.
TRUE.

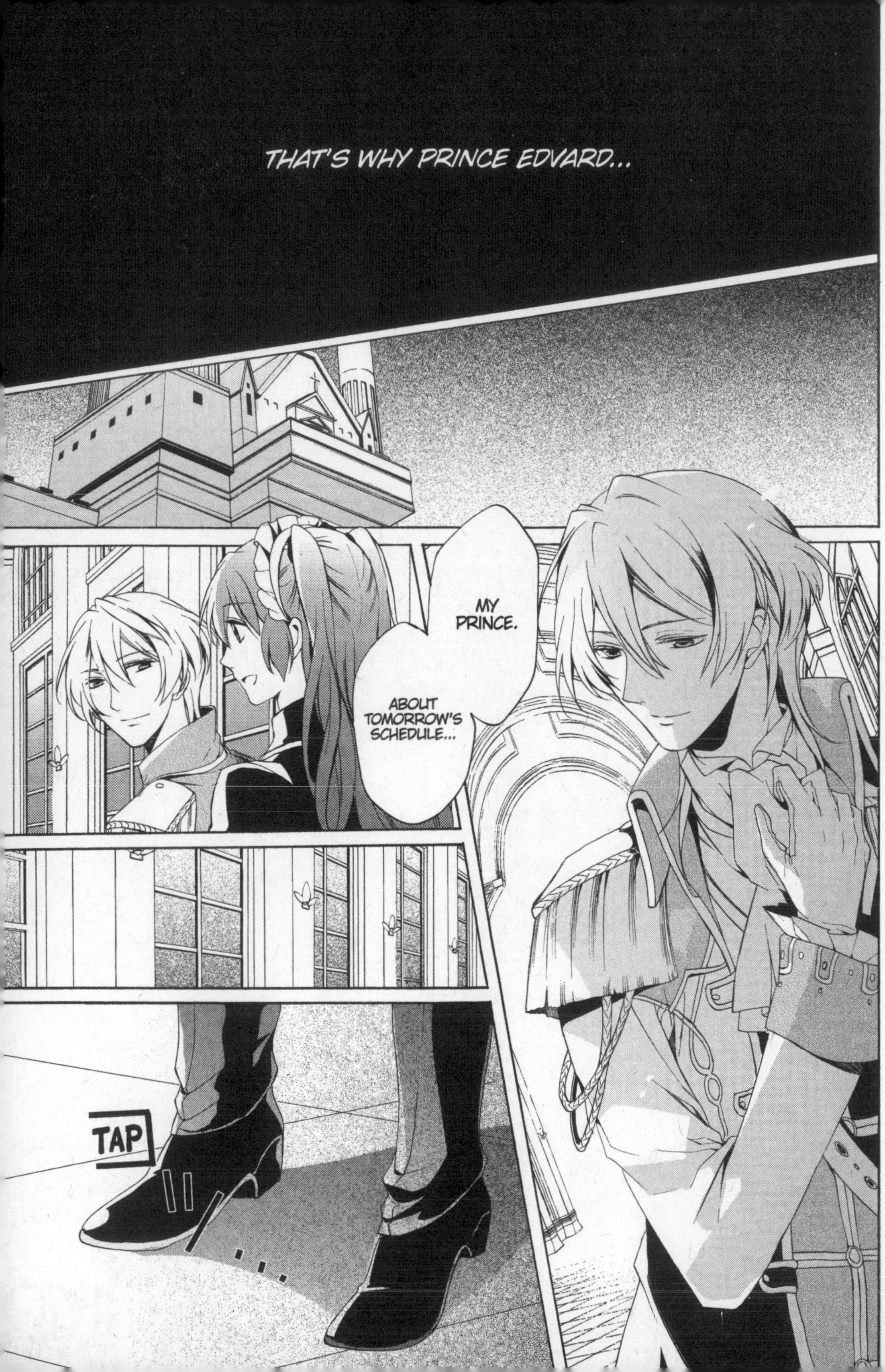
THAT'S WHY PRINCE EDVARD...
MY PRINCE.
ABOUT TOMORROW'S SCHEDULE...
TAP
...

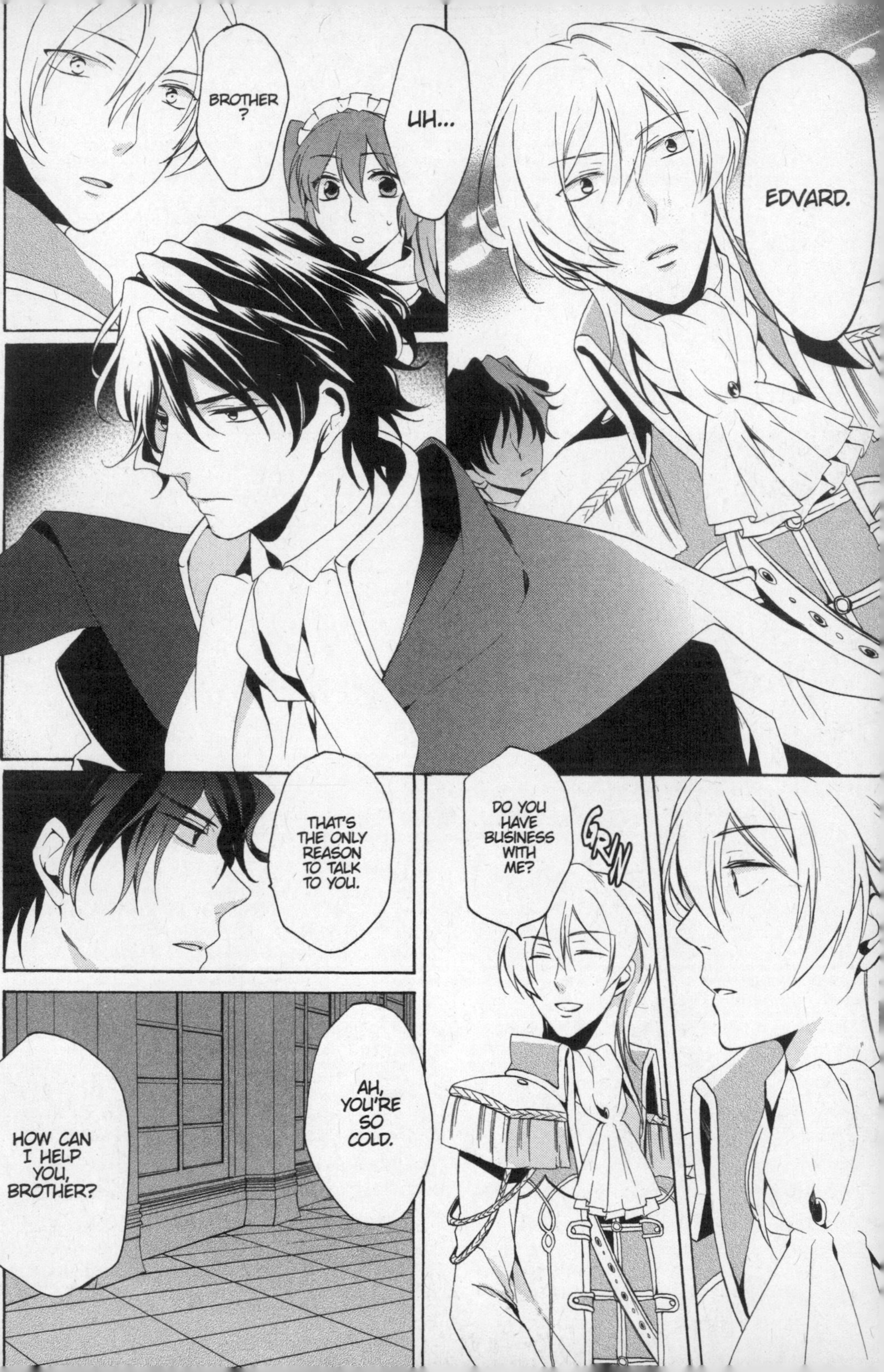
EDVARD.
UH...
BROTHER?
DO YOU HAVE BUSINESS WITH ME?
GRIN
THAT'S THE ONLY REASON TO TALK TO YOU.
AH, YOU'RE SO COLD.
HOW CAN I HELP YOU, BROTHER?

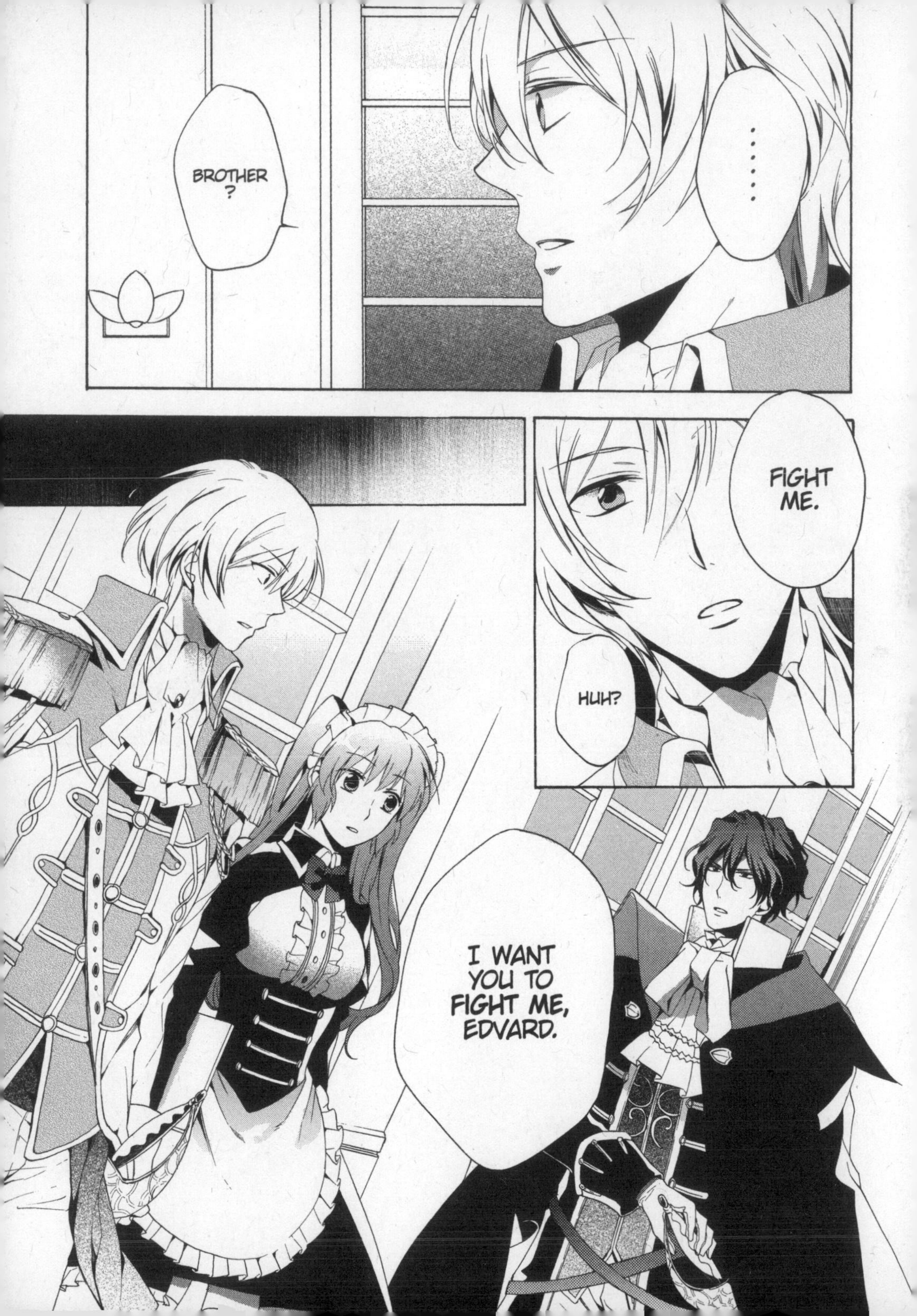
……
BROTHER?
FIGHT ME.
HUH?
I WANT YOU TO FIGHT ME, EDVARD.

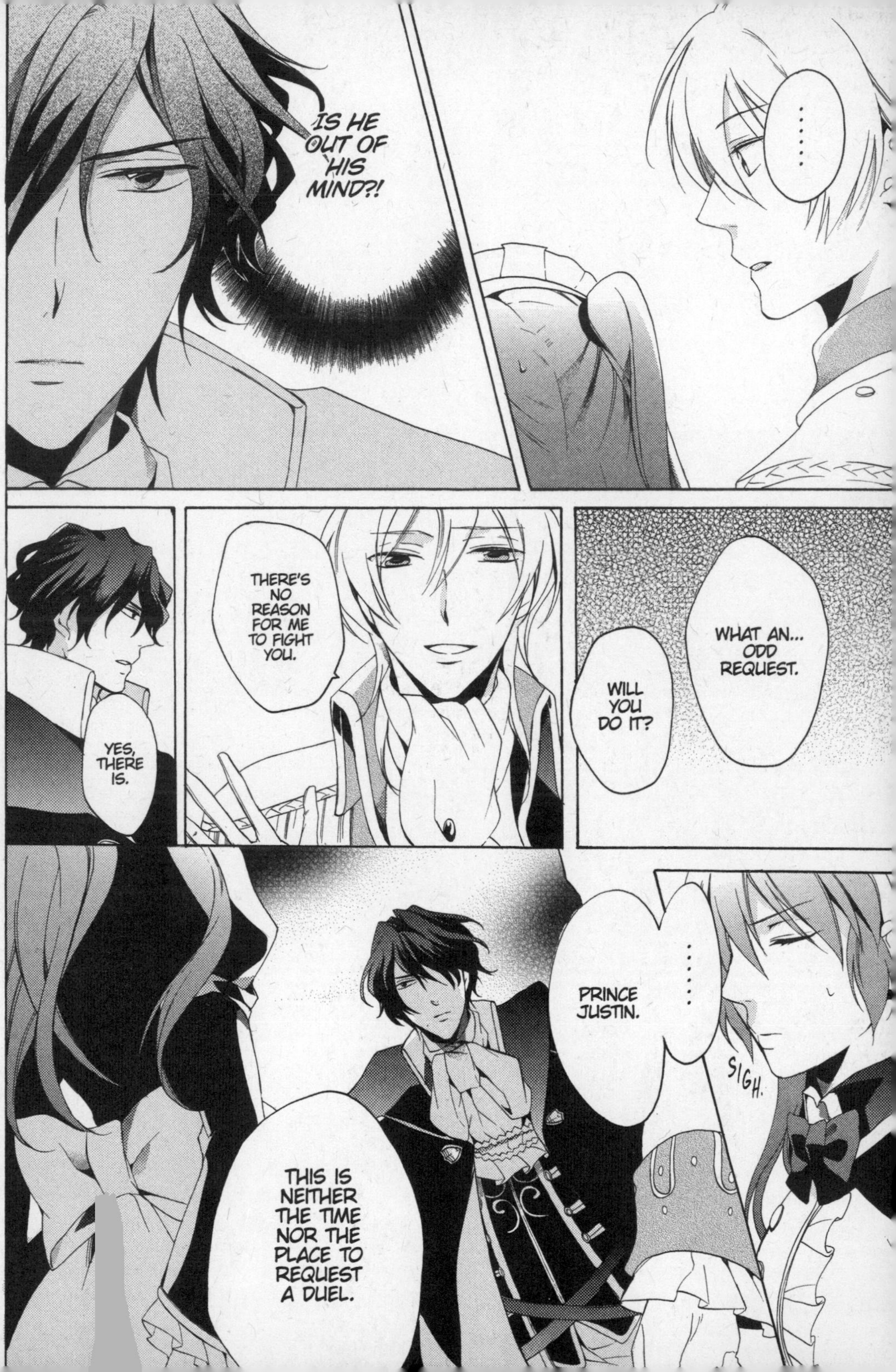
……
IS HE OUT OF HIS MIND?!
WHAT AN... ODD REQUEST.
WILL YOU DO IT?
THERE'S NO REASON FOR ME TO FIGHT YOU.
YES, THERE IS.
……
PRINCE JUSTIN.
SIGH.
THIS IS NEITHER THE TIME NOR THE PLACE TO REQUEST A DUEL.

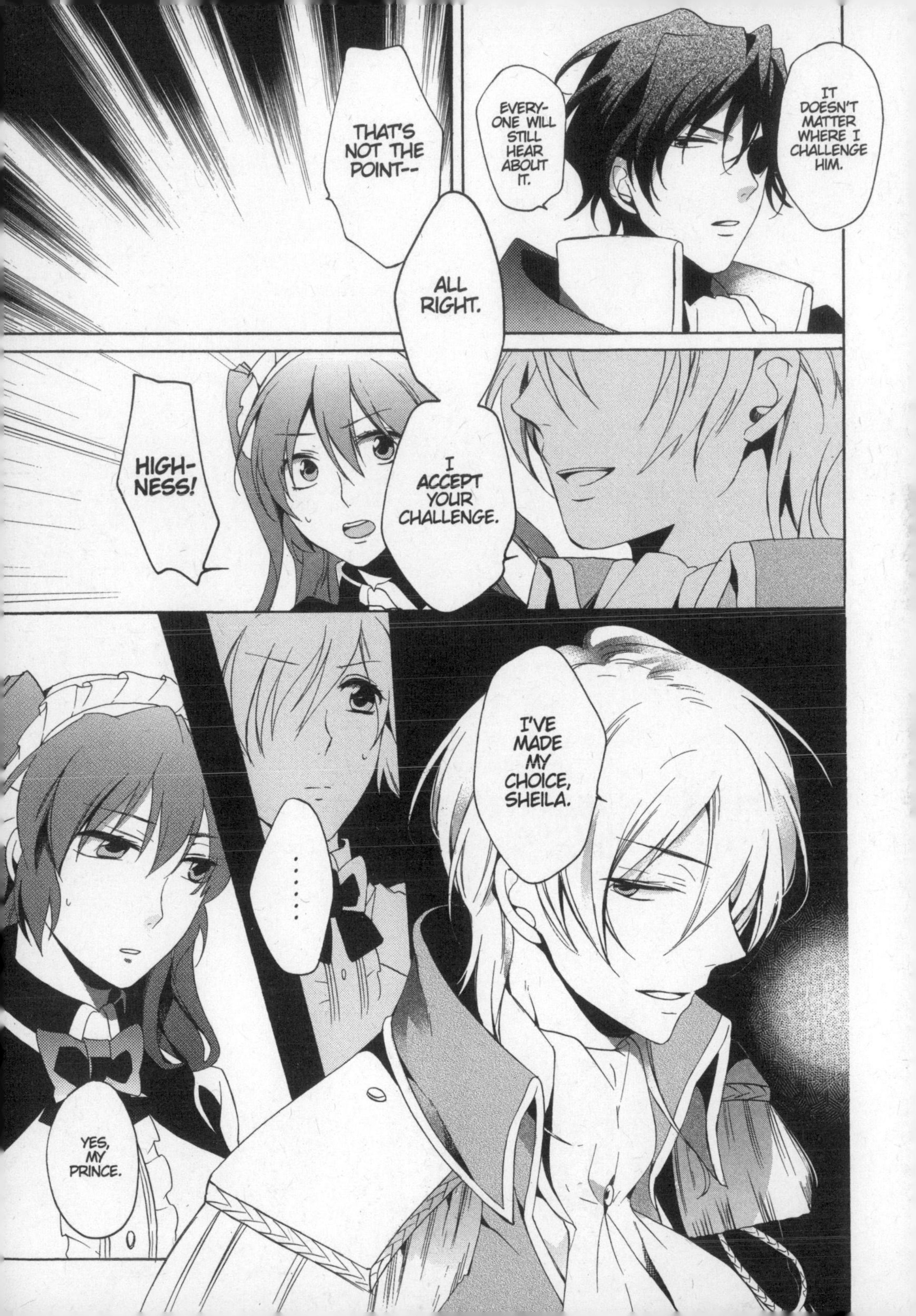
IT DOESN'T MATTER WHERE I CHALLENGE HIM.
EVERY-ONE WILL STILL HEAR ABOUT IT.
THAT'S NOT THE POINT--
ALL RIGHT.
I ACCEPT YOUR CHALLENGE.
HIGH-NESS!
I'VE MADE MY CHOICE, SHEILA.
......
YES, MY PRINCE.

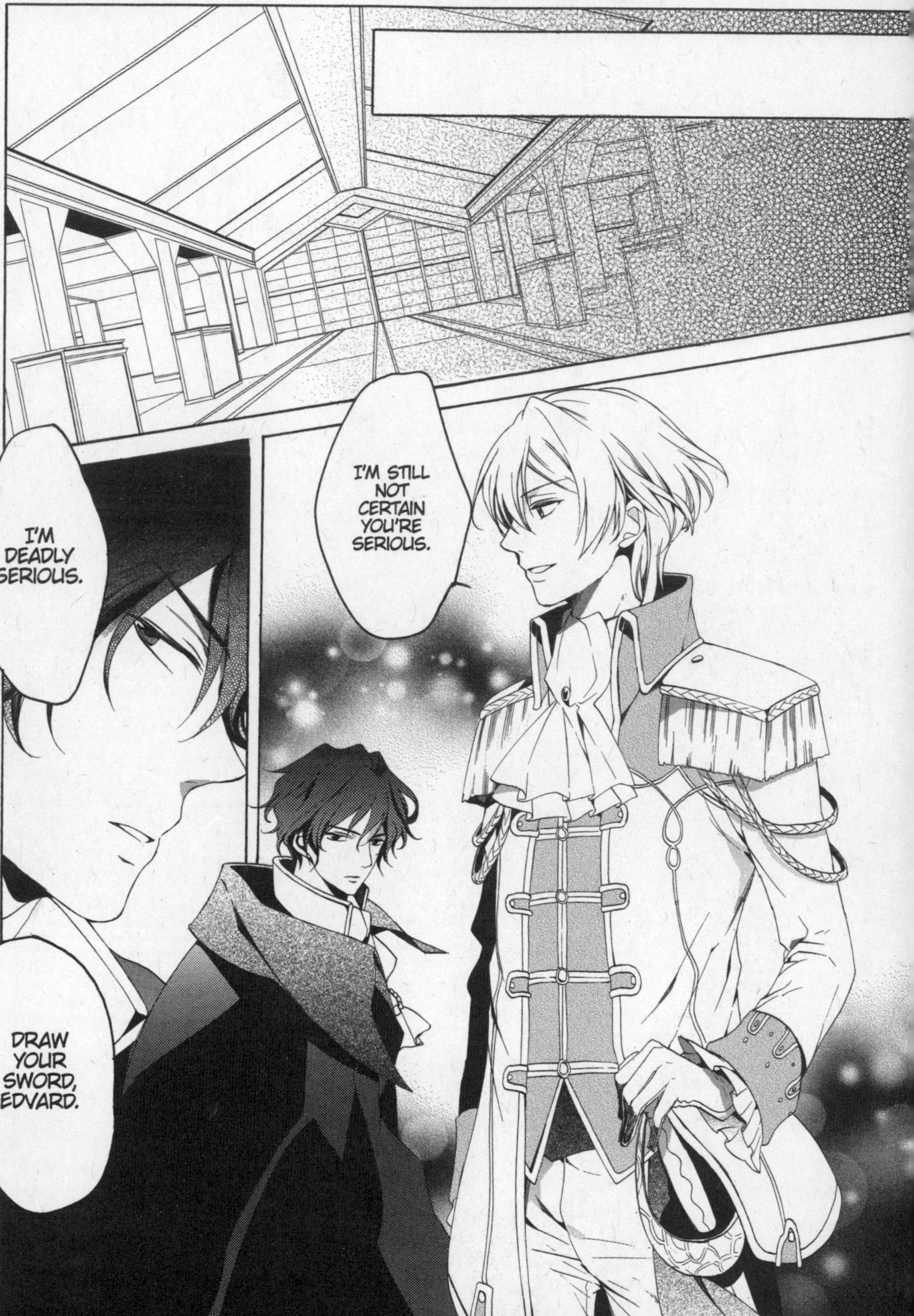
I'M STILL NOT CERTAIN YOU'RE SERIOUS.
I'M DEADLY SERIOUS.
DRAW YOUR SWORD, EDVARD.

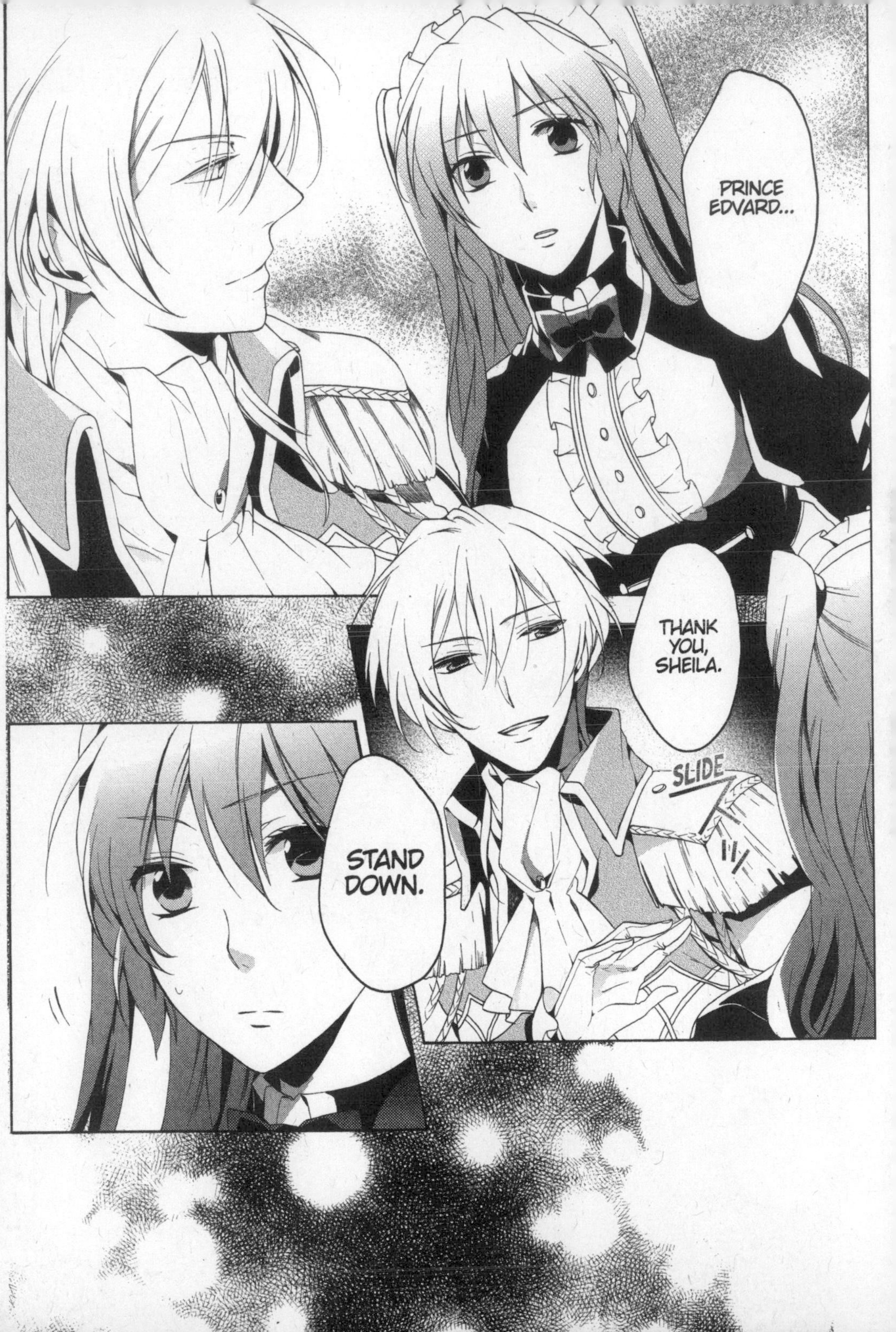
PRINCE EDVARD...
THANK YOU, SHEILA.
SLIDE
STAND DOWN.

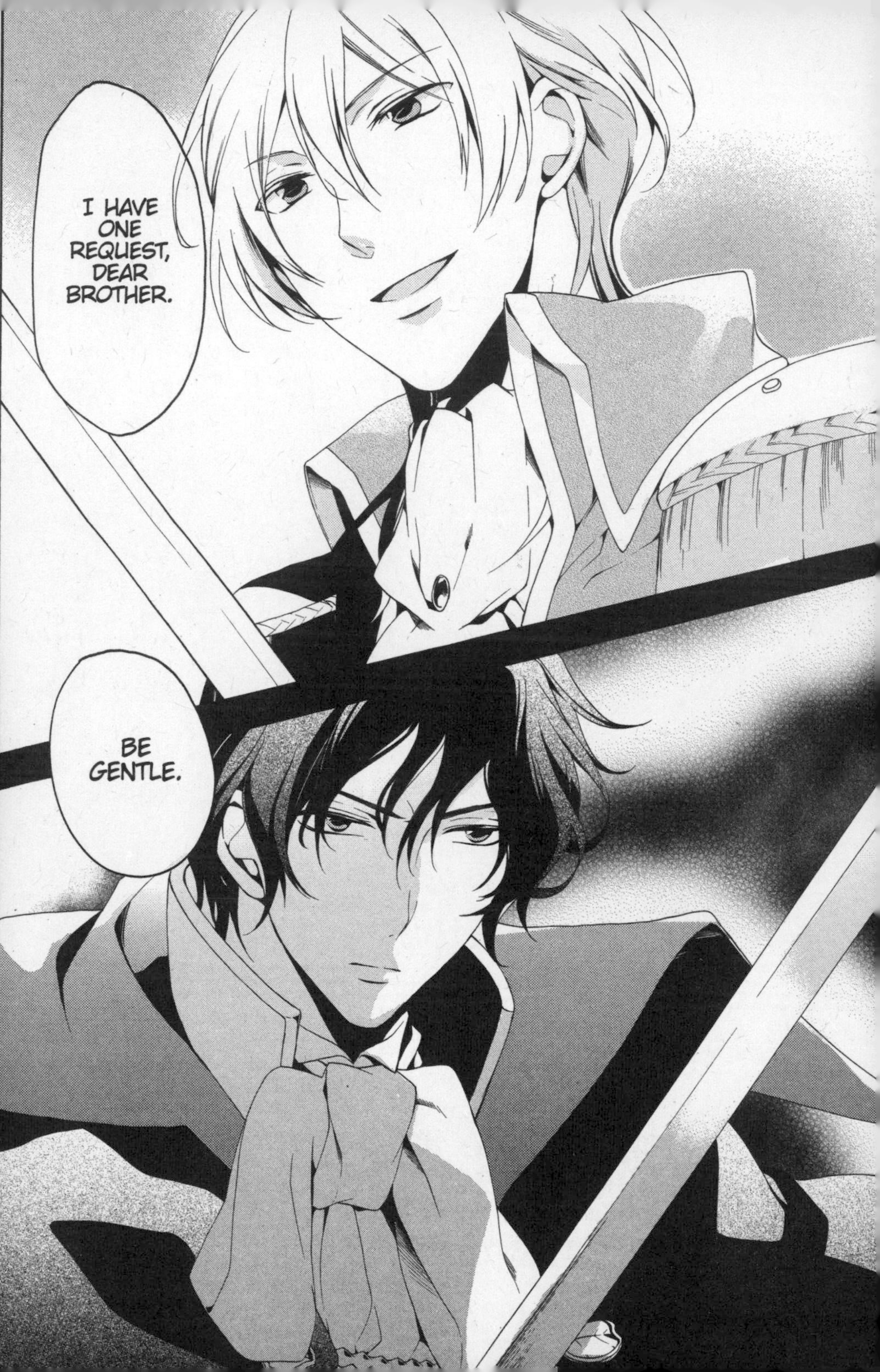
I HAVE ONE REQUEST, DEAR BROTHER.
BE GENTLE.

CRIMSON EMPIRE

Circumstances to serve a noble

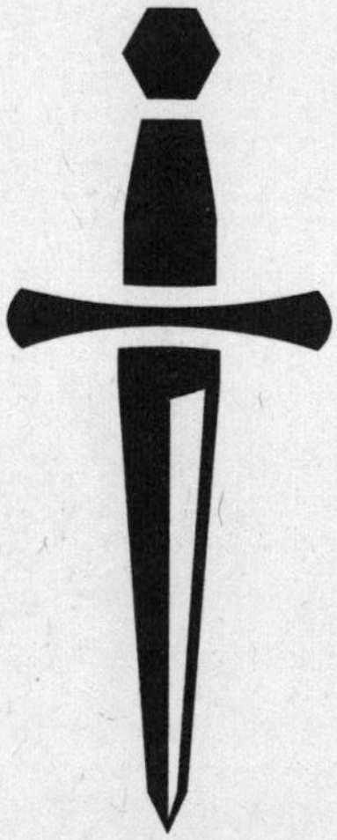

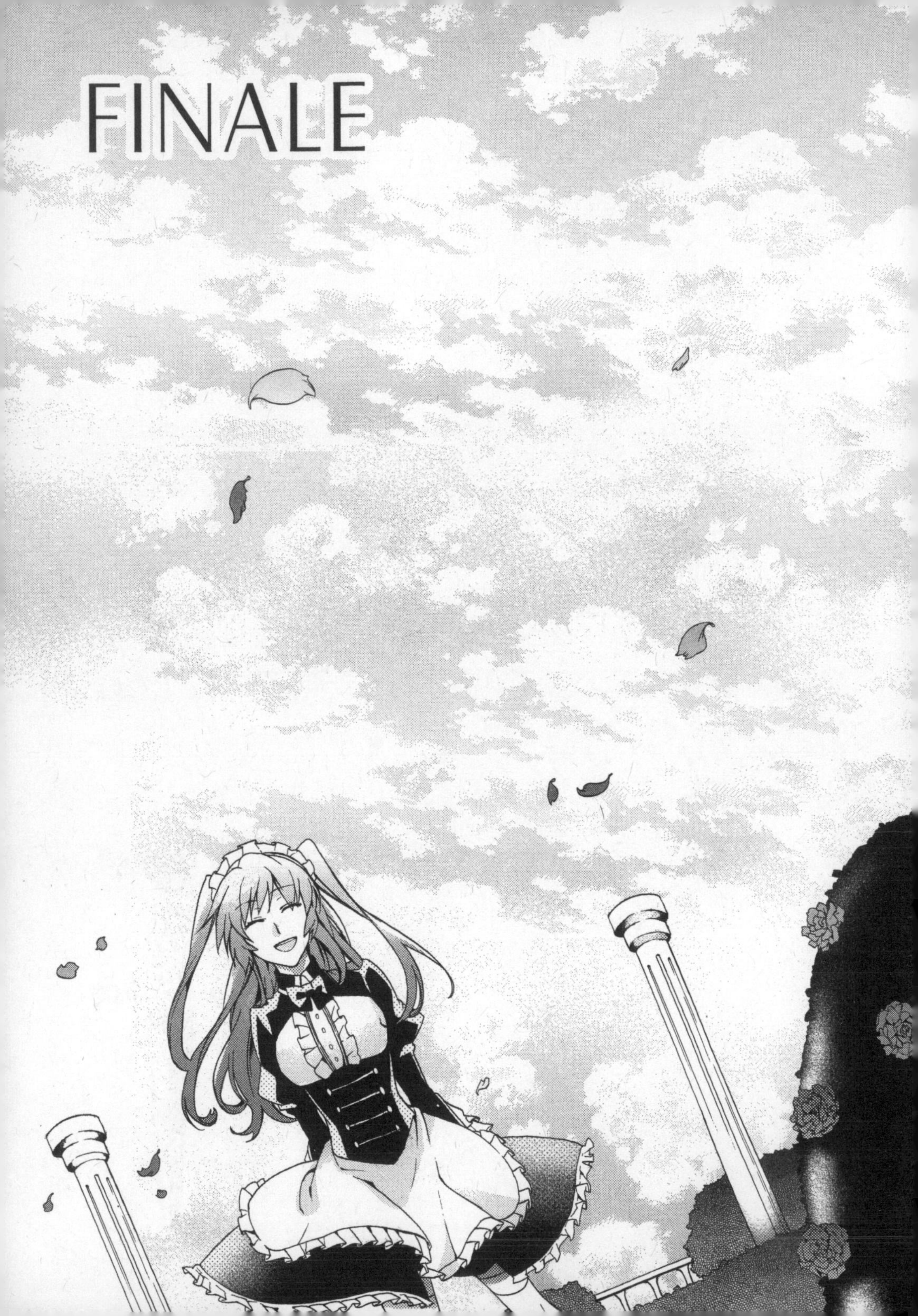
FINALE

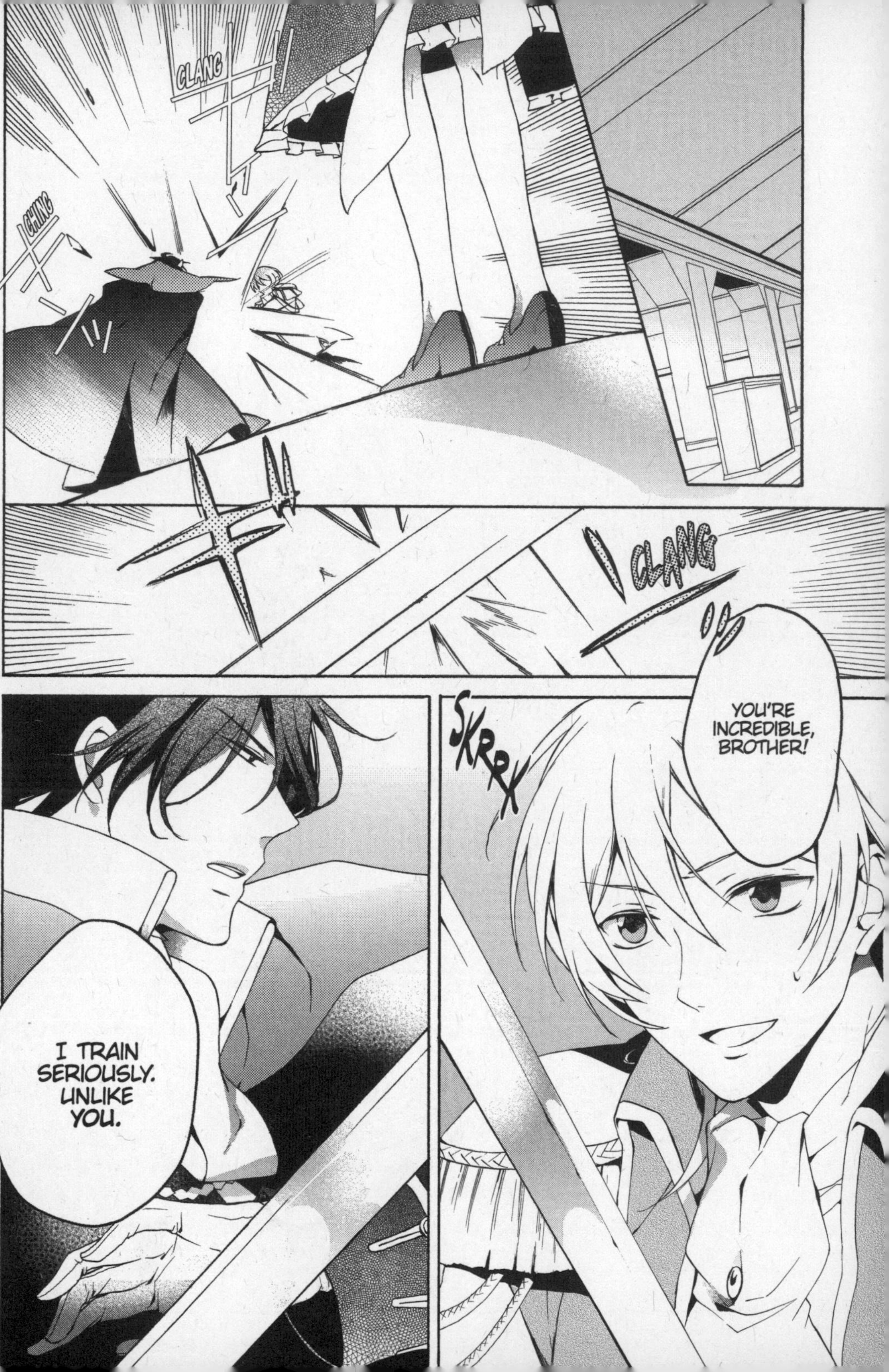
CLANG
CHING
CLANG
SKRRK
YOU'RE INCREDIBLE, BROTHER!
I TRAIN SERIOUSLY. UNLIKE YOU.

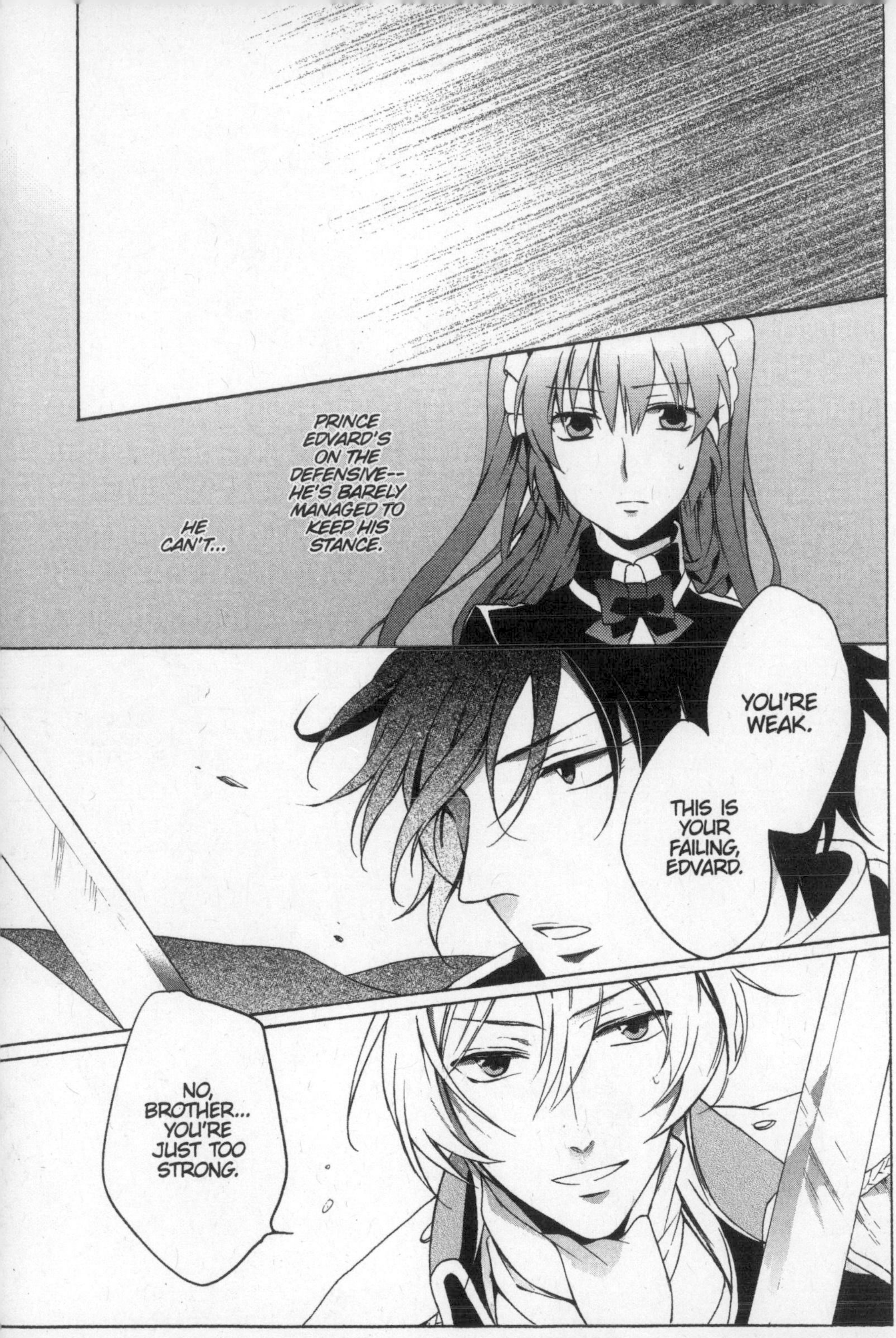
PRINCE EDVARD'S ON THE DEFENSIVE-- HE'S BARELY MANAGED TO KEEP HIS STANCE.
HE CAN'T...
YOU'RE WEAK.
THIS IS YOUR FAILING, EDVARD.
NO, BROTHER... YOU'RE JUST TOO STRONG.

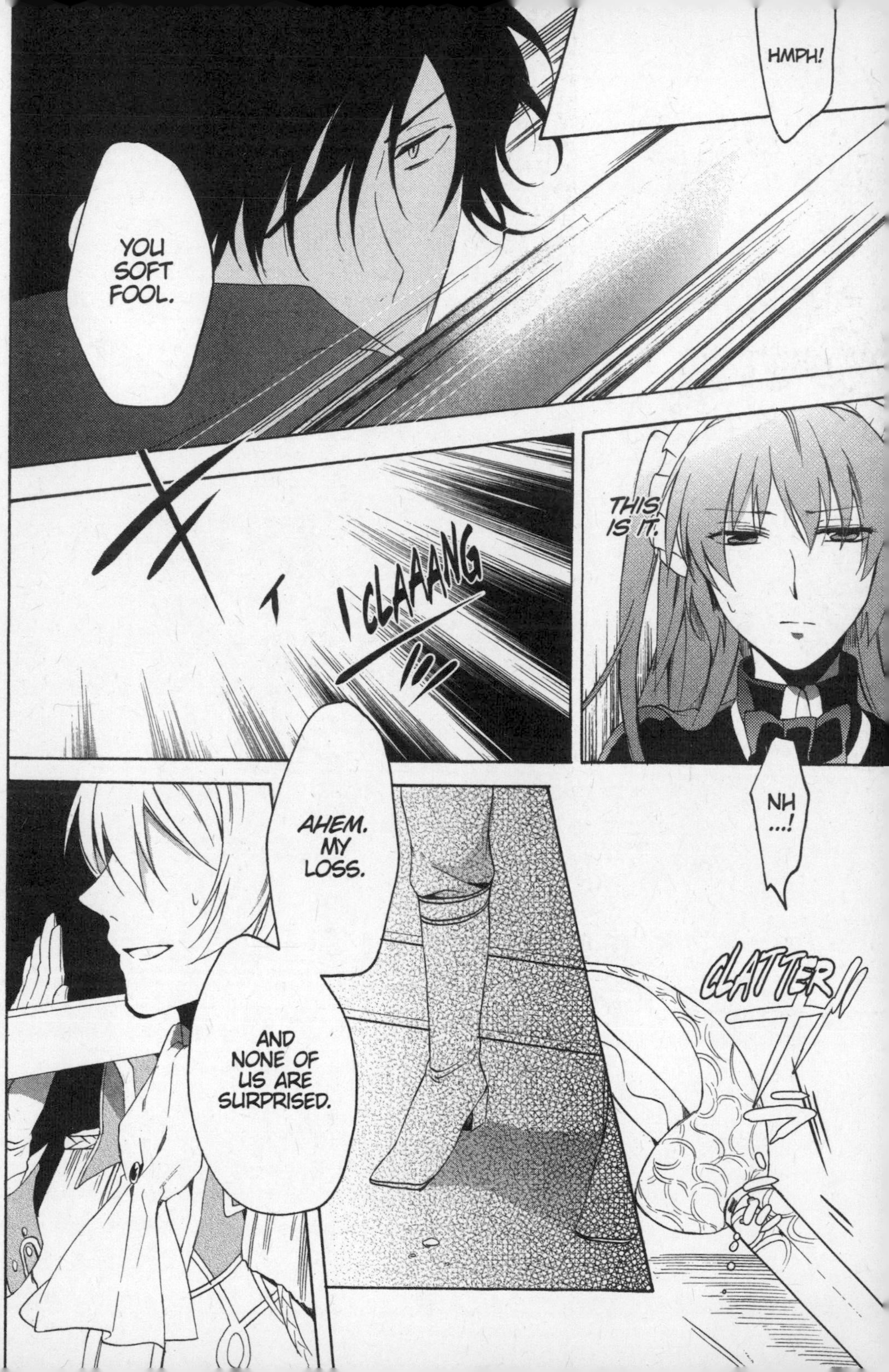
HMPH!
YOU SOFT FOOL.
THIS IS IT.
CLAAANG
NH ...!
CLATTER
AHEM. MY LOSS.
AND NONE OF US ARE SURPRISED.

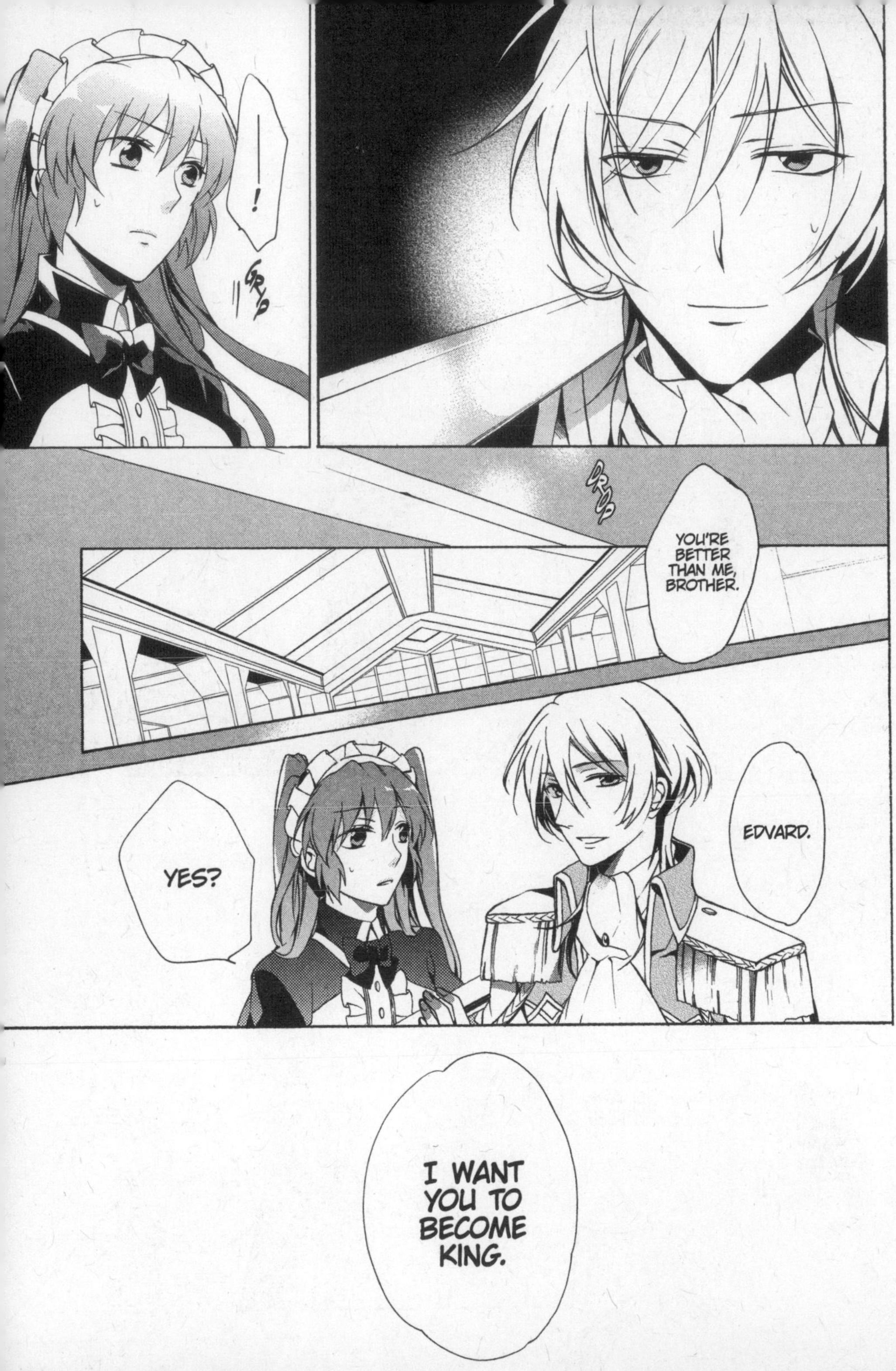
!
GRIP
DROP
YOU'RE BETTER THAN ME, BROTHER.
EDVARD.
YES?
I WANT YOU TO BECOME KING.

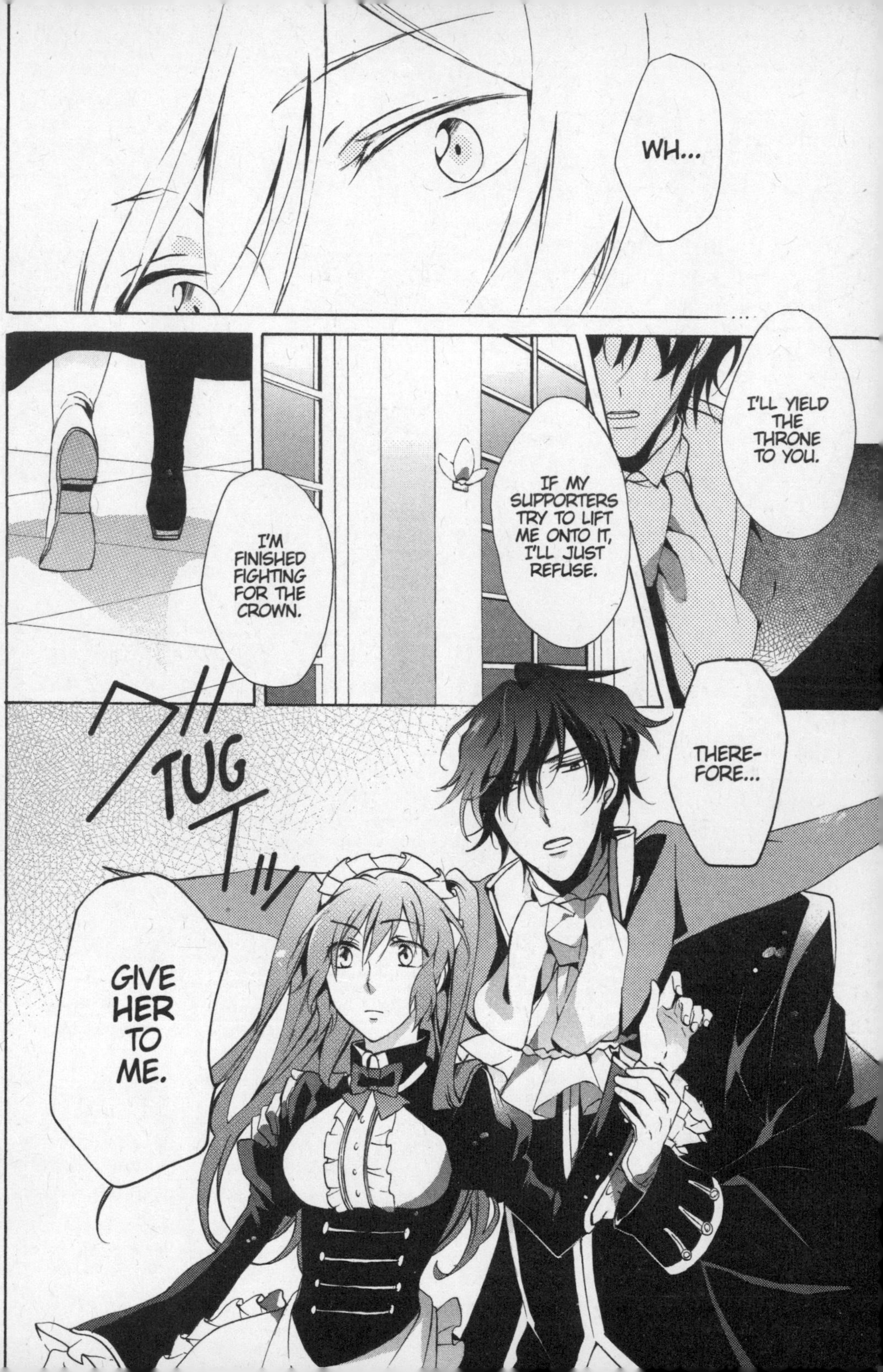
WH...
....
I'LL YIELD THE THRONE TO YOU.
IF MY SUPPORTERS TRY TO LIFT ME ONTO IT, I'LL JUST REFUSE.
I'M FINISHED FIGHTING FOR THE CROWN.
THERE-FORE...
TUG
GIVE HER TO ME.

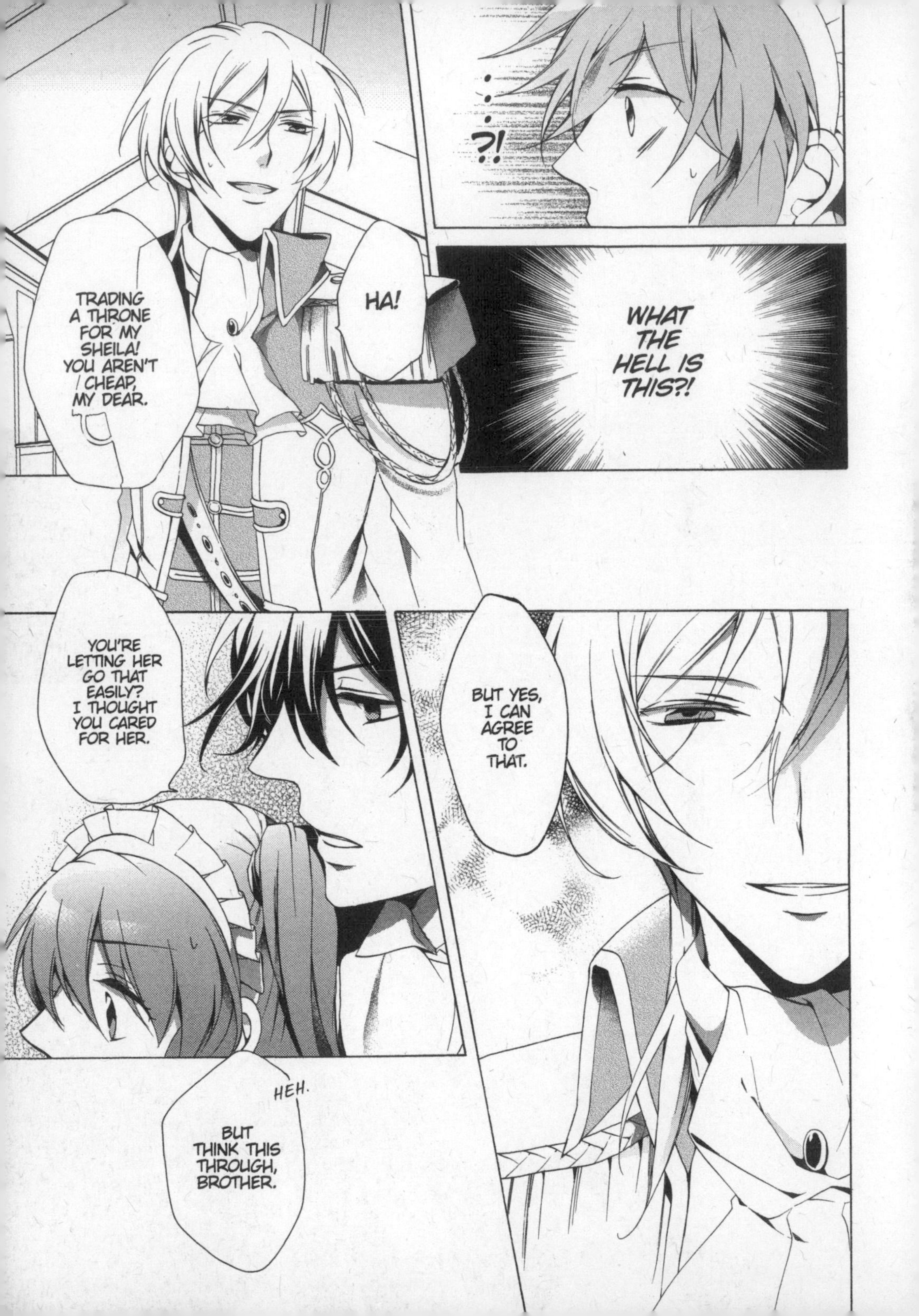

...?!
WHAT THE HELL IS THIS?!
HA!
TRADING A THRONE FOR MY SHEILA! YOU AREN'T CHEAP, MY DEAR.
BUT YES, I CAN AGREE TO THAT.
YOU'RE LETTING HER GO THAT EASILY? I THOUGHT YOU CARED FOR HER.
HEH.
BUT THINK THIS THROUGH, BROTHER.

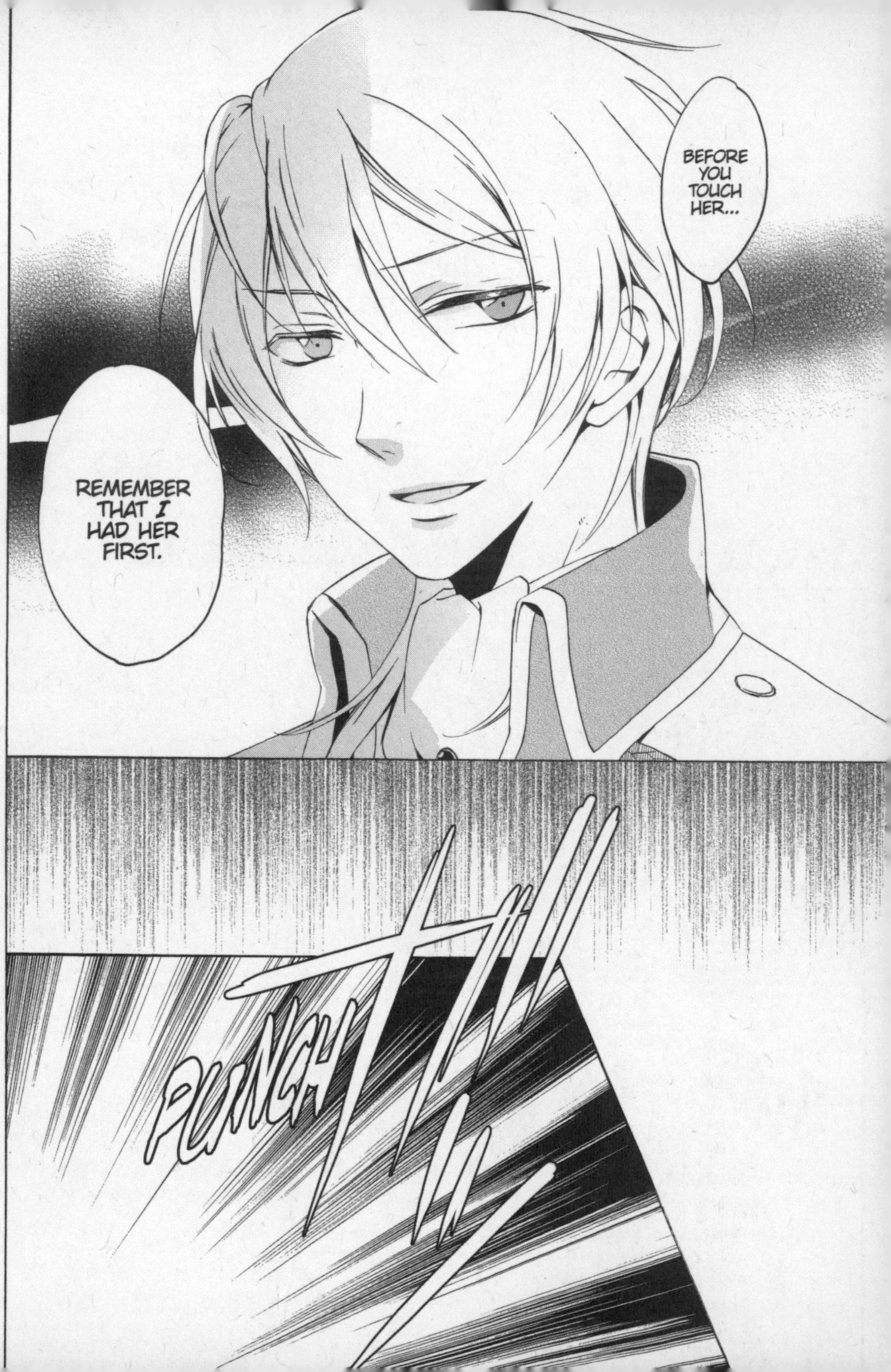
BEFORE YOU TOUCH HER...
REMEMBER THAT I HAD HER FIRST.
PUNCH

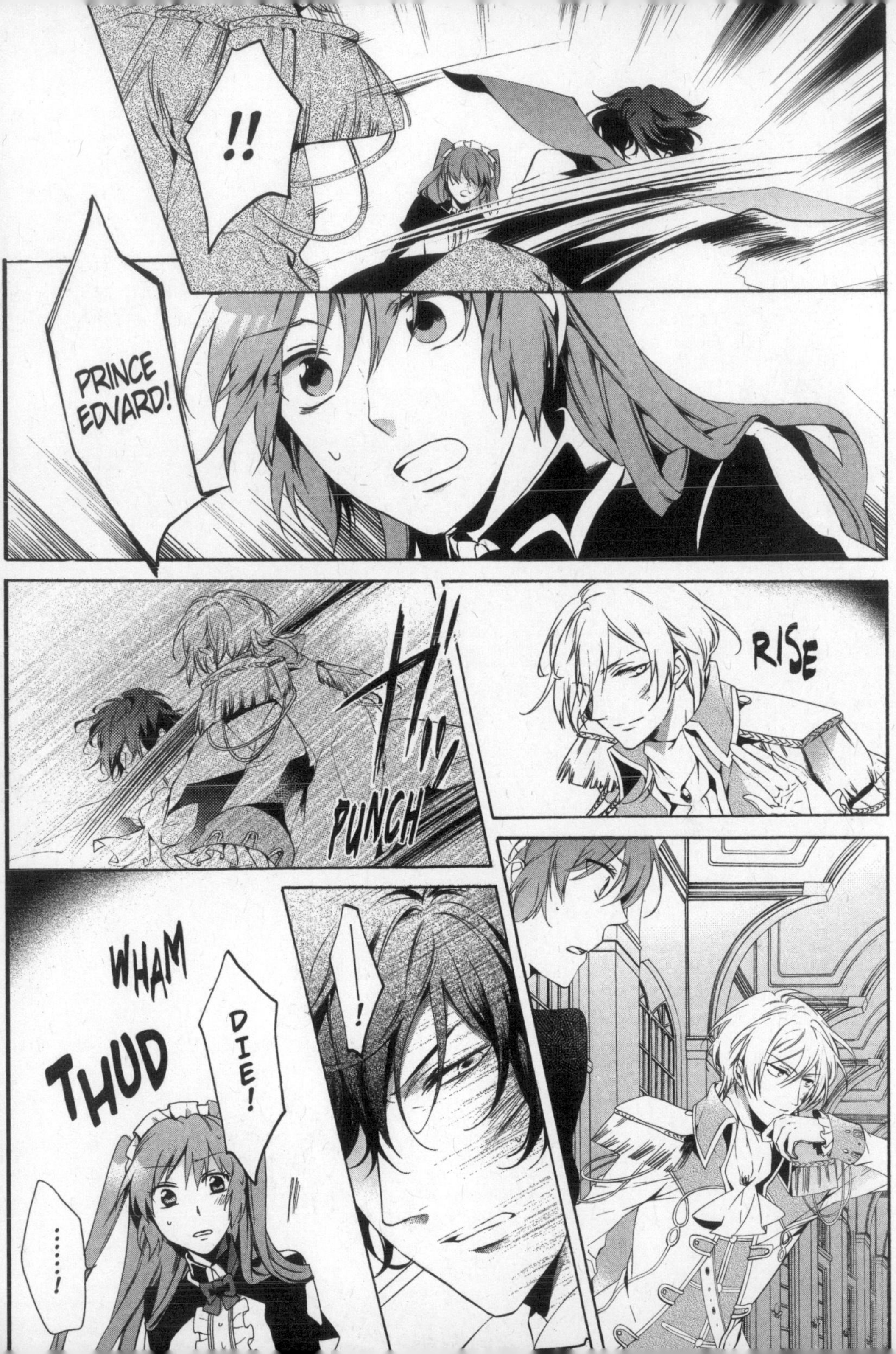
!!
PRINCE EDVARD!
RISE
PUNCH
!
WHAM
THUD
DIE!
......!

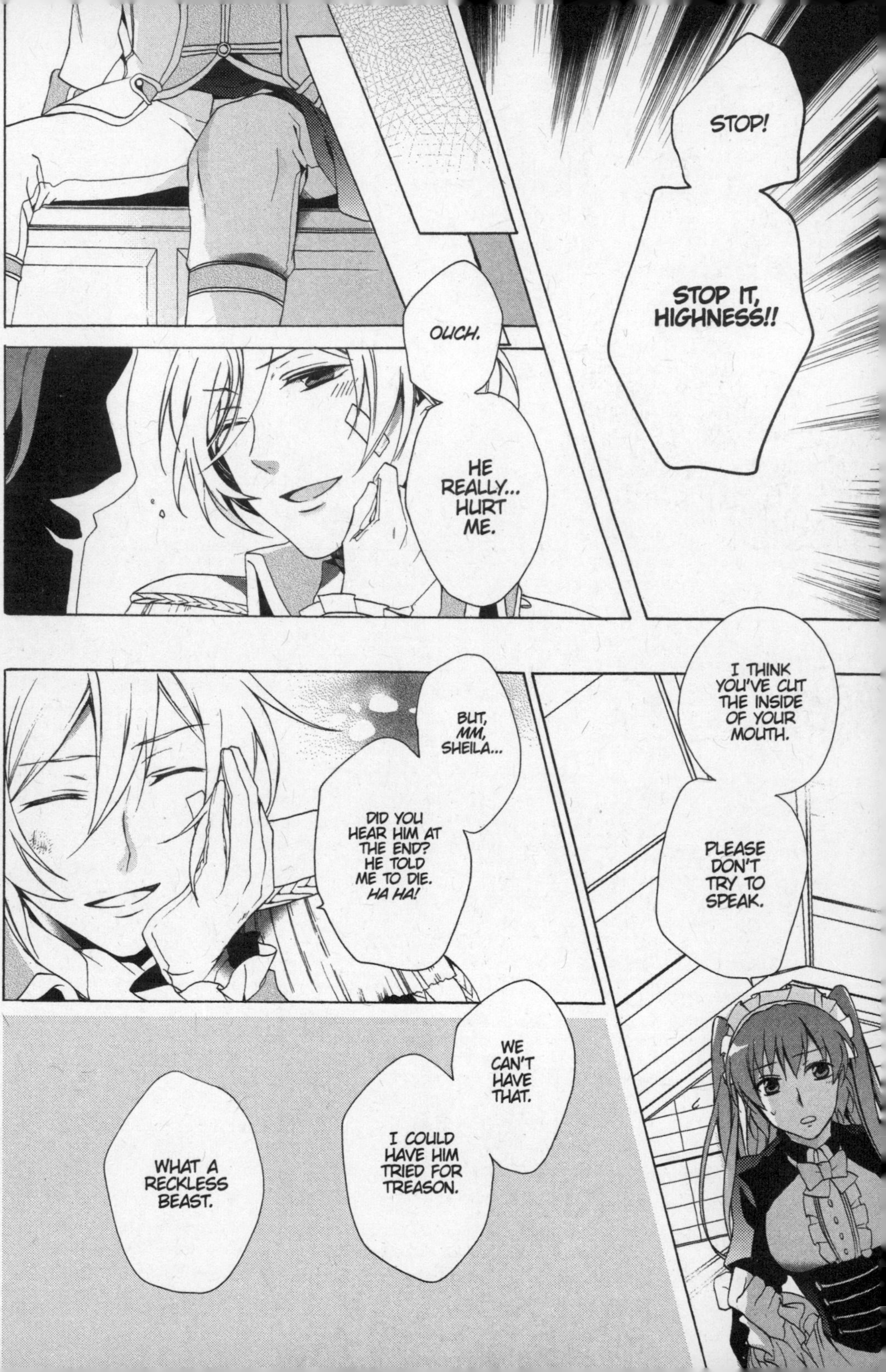
STOP!
STOP IT, HIGHNESS!!
OUCH.
HE REALLY... HURT ME.
I THINK YOU'VE CUT THE INSIDE OF YOUR MOUTH.
PLEASE DON'T TRY TO SPEAK.
BUT, MM, SHEILA...
DID YOU HEAR HIM AT THE END? HE TOLD ME TO DIE. *HA HA!*
WE CAN'T HAVE THAT.
I COULD HAVE HIM TRIED FOR TREASON.
WHAT A RECKLESS BEAST.

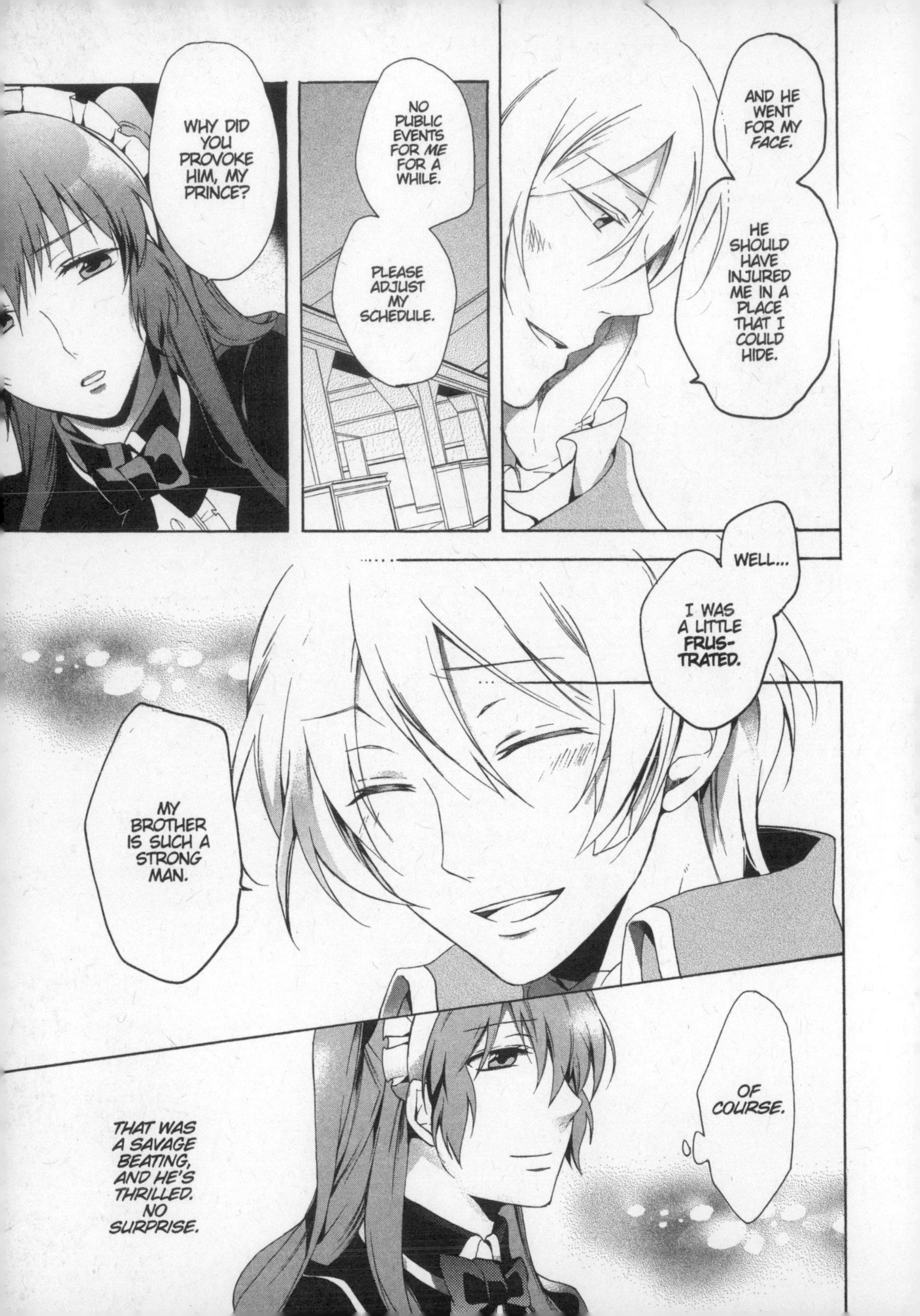
AND HE WENT FOR MY FACE.
HE SHOULD HAVE INJURED ME IN A PLACE THAT I COULD HIDE.
NO PUBLIC EVENTS FOR ME FOR A WHILE.
PLEASE ADJUST MY SCHEDULE.
WHY DID YOU PROVOKE HIM, MY PRINCE?
......
WELL...
I WAS A LITTLE FRUS-TRATED.
...
MY BROTHER IS SUCH A STRONG MAN.
OF COURSE.
THAT WAS A SAVAGE BEATING, AND HE'S THRILLED. NO SURPRISE.

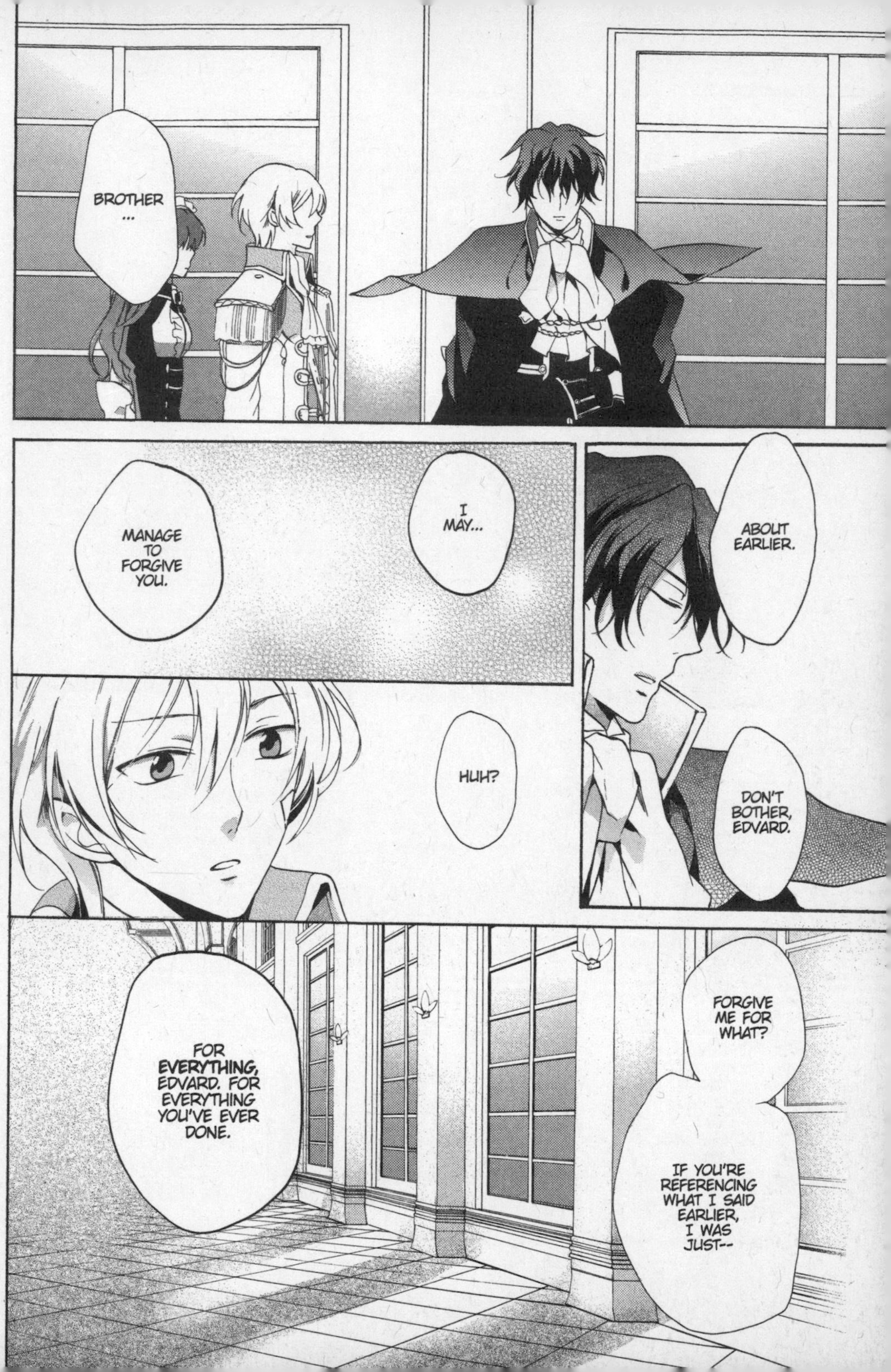
BROTHER ...
ABOUT EARLIER.
DON'T BOTHER, EDVARD.
I MAY...
MANAGE TO FORGIVE YOU.
HUH?
FORGIVE ME FOR WHAT?
IF YOU'RE REFERENCING WHAT I SAID EARLIER, I WAS JUST--
FOR EVERYTHING, EDVARD. FOR EVERYTHING YOU'VE EVER DONE.

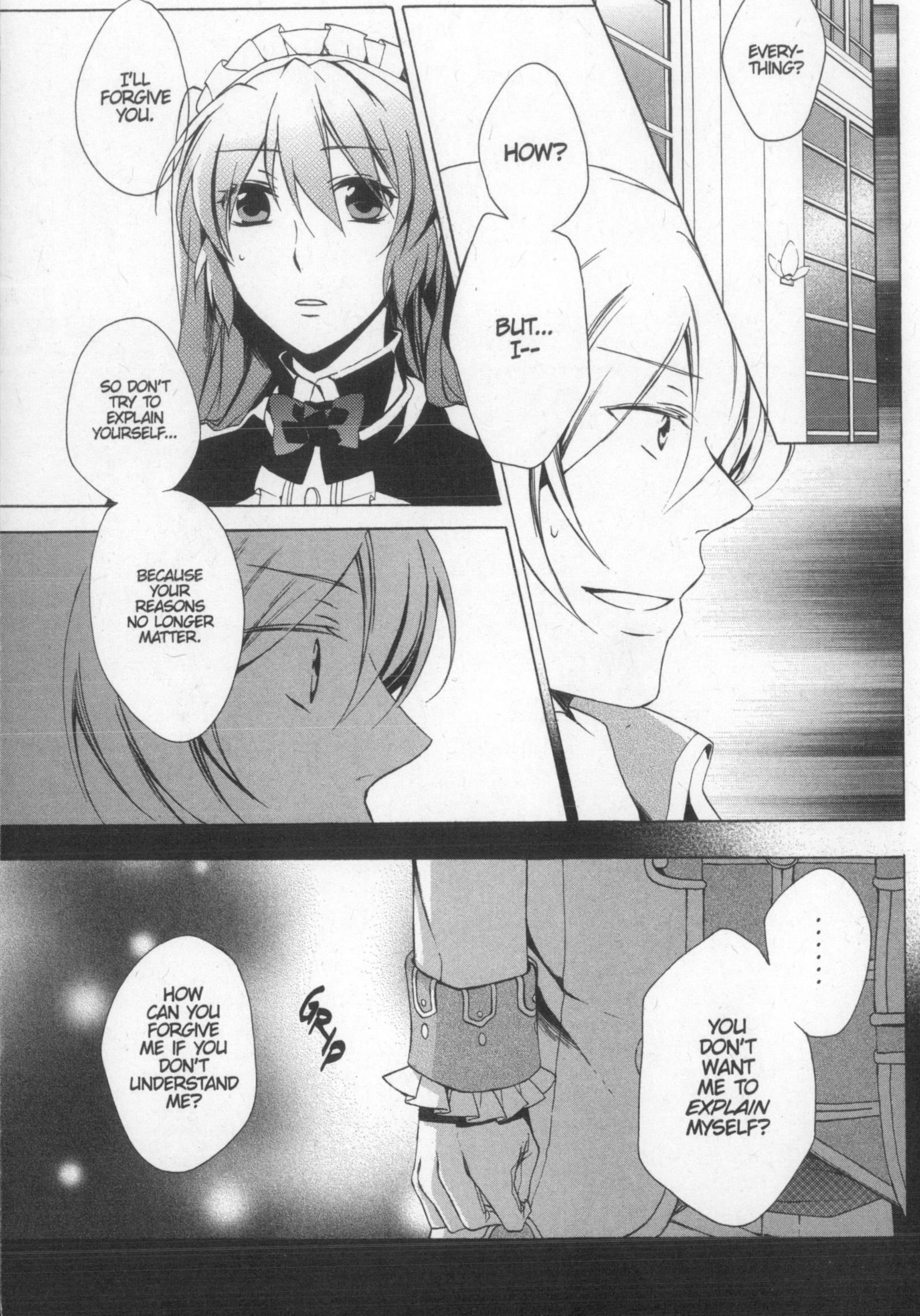
EVERY-
THING?
HOW?
BUT... I--
I'LL FORGIVE YOU.
SO DON'T TRY TO EXPLAIN YOURSELF...
BECAUSE YOUR REASONS NO LONGER MATTER.
......
YOU DON'T WANT ME TO *EXPLAIN* MYSELF?
GRIP
HOW CAN YOU FORGIVE ME IF YOU DON'T UNDERSTAND ME?

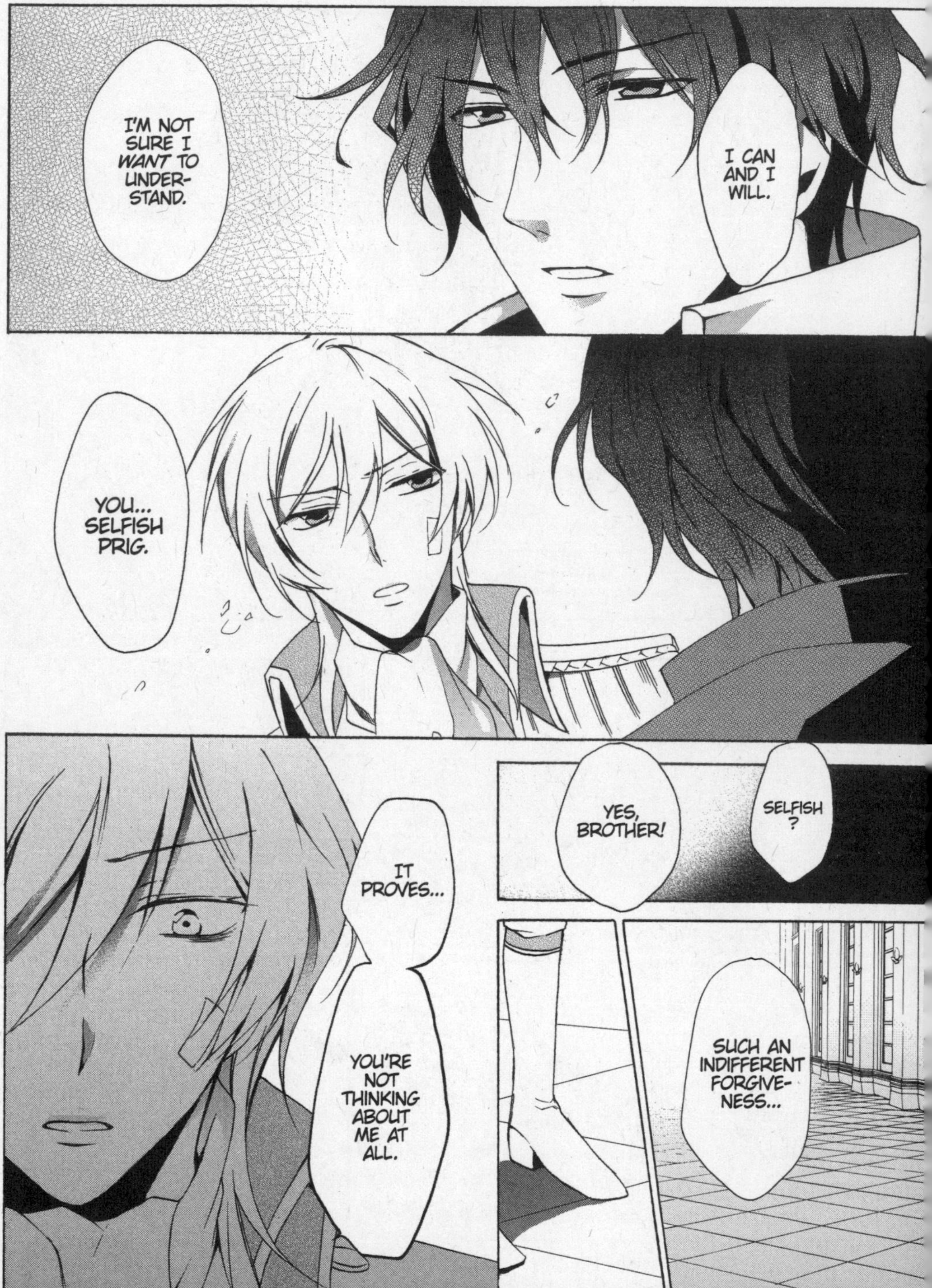
I CAN AND I WILL.
I'M NOT SURE I *WANT* TO UNDER-STAND.
YOU... SELFISH PRIG.
SELFISH?
YES, BROTHER!
SUCH AN INDIFFERENT FORGIVE-NESS...
IT PROVES...
YOU'RE NOT THINKING ABOUT ME AT ALL.

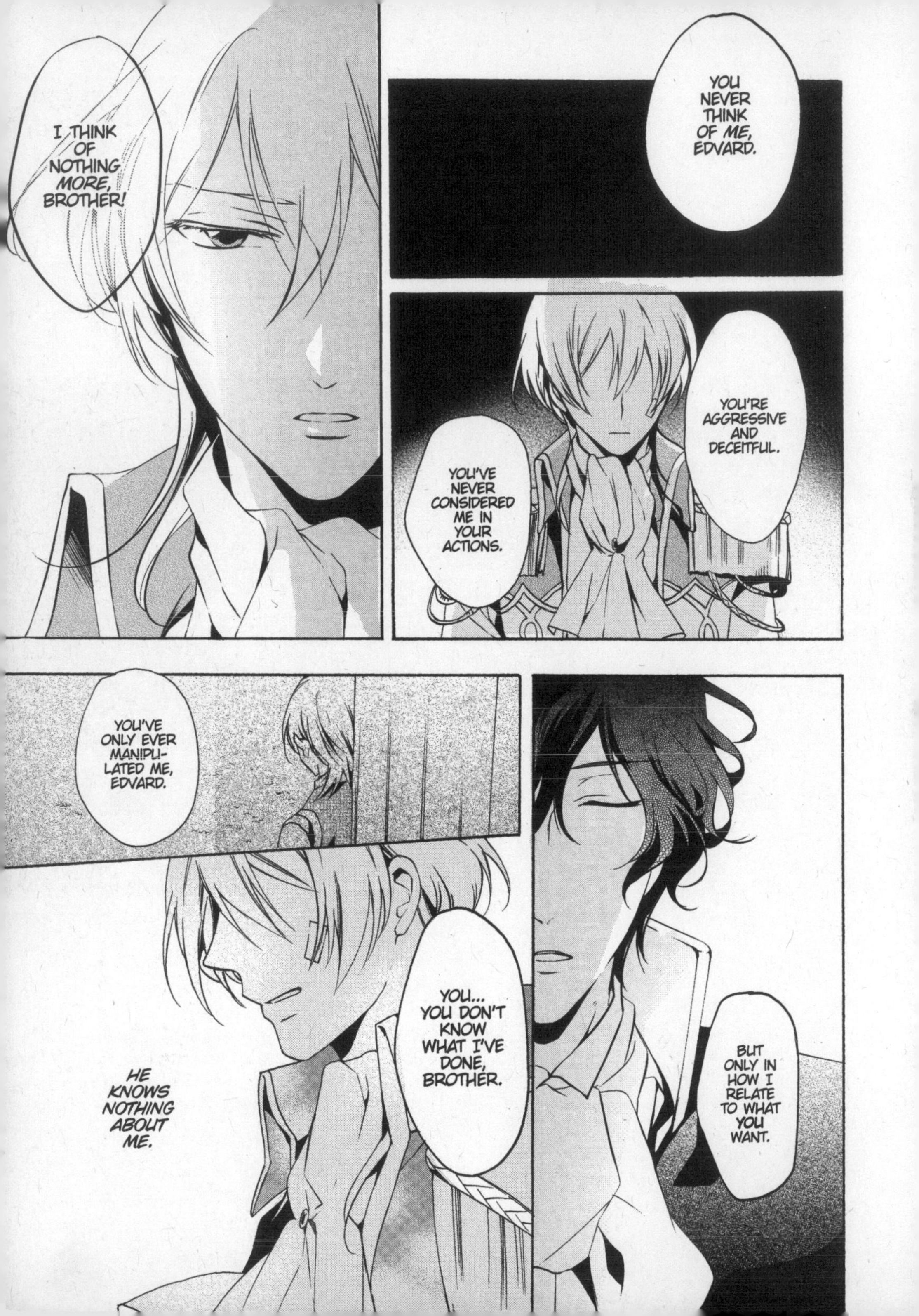
YOU NEVER THINK OF *ME*, EDVARD.
YOU'RE AGGRESSIVE AND DECEITFUL.
YOU'VE NEVER CONSIDERED ME IN YOUR ACTIONS.
I THINK OF NOTHING *MORE*, BROTHER!
BUT ONLY IN HOW I RELATE TO WHAT YOU WANT.
YOU'VE ONLY EVER MANIPU-LATED ME, EDVARD.
YOU... YOU DON'T KNOW WHAT I'VE DONE, BROTHER.
HE KNOWS NOTHING ABOUT ME.

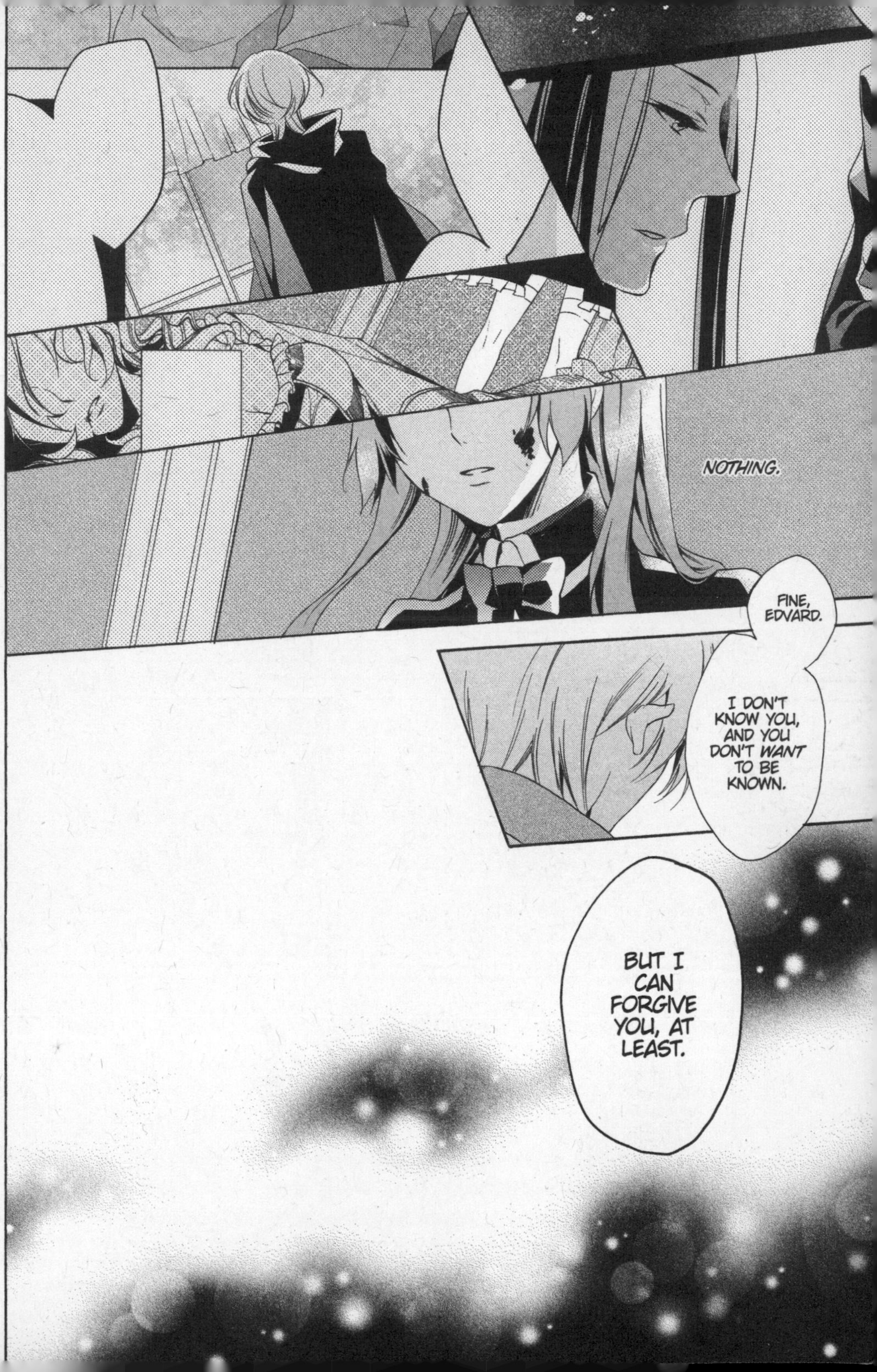
NOTHING.
FINE, EDVARD.
I DON'T KNOW YOU, AND YOU DON'T *WANT* TO BE KNOWN.
BUT I CAN FORGIVE YOU, AT LEAST.

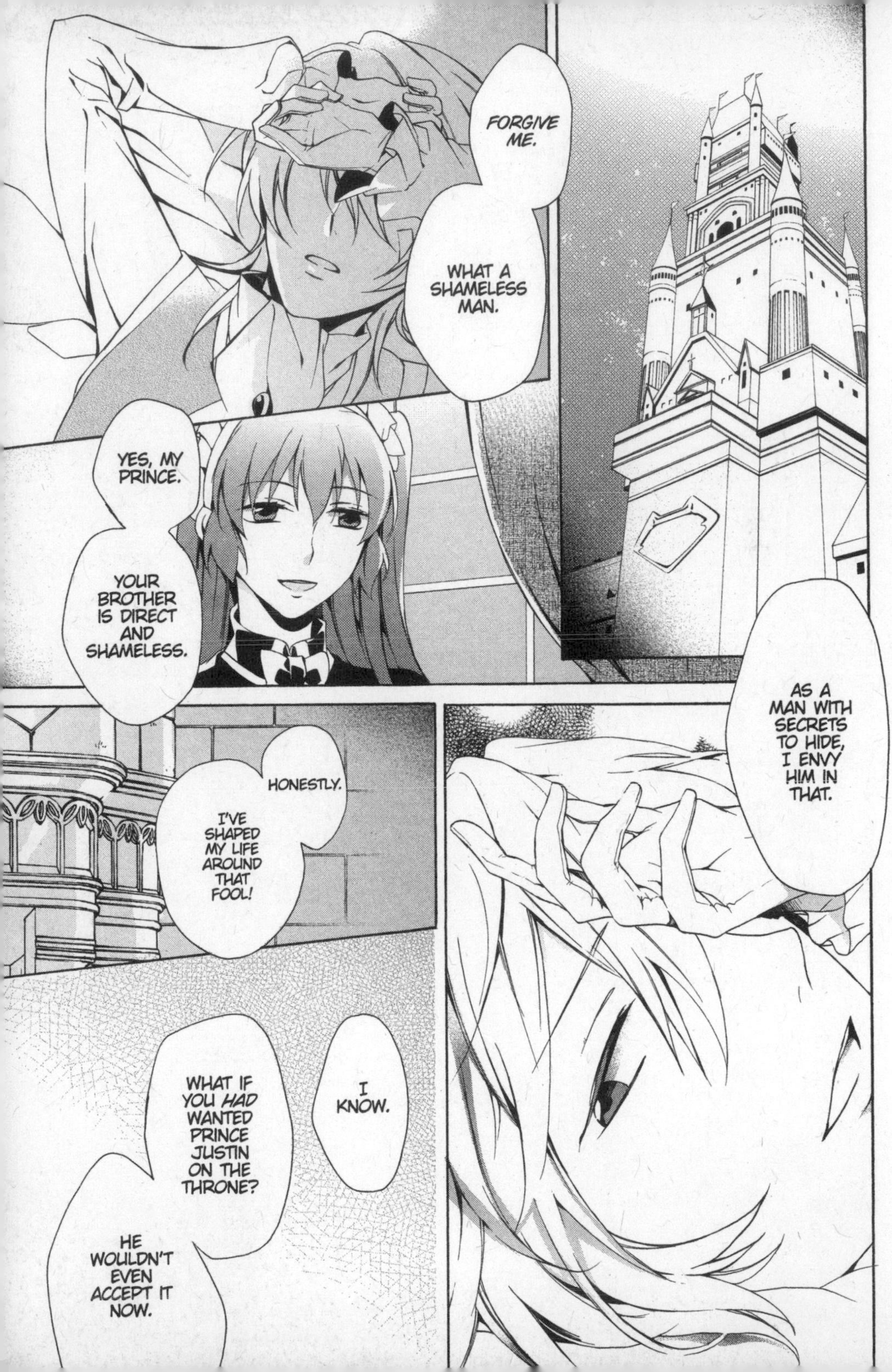
FORGIVE ME.
WHAT A SHAMELESS MAN.
YES, MY PRINCE.
YOUR BROTHER IS DIRECT AND SHAMELESS.
AS A MAN WITH SECRETS TO HIDE, I ENVY HIM IN THAT.
HONESTLY.
I'VE SHAPED MY LIFE AROUND THAT FOOL!
I KNOW.
WHAT IF YOU *HAD* WANTED PRINCE JUSTIN ON THE THRONE?
HE WOULDN'T EVEN ACCEPT IT NOW.

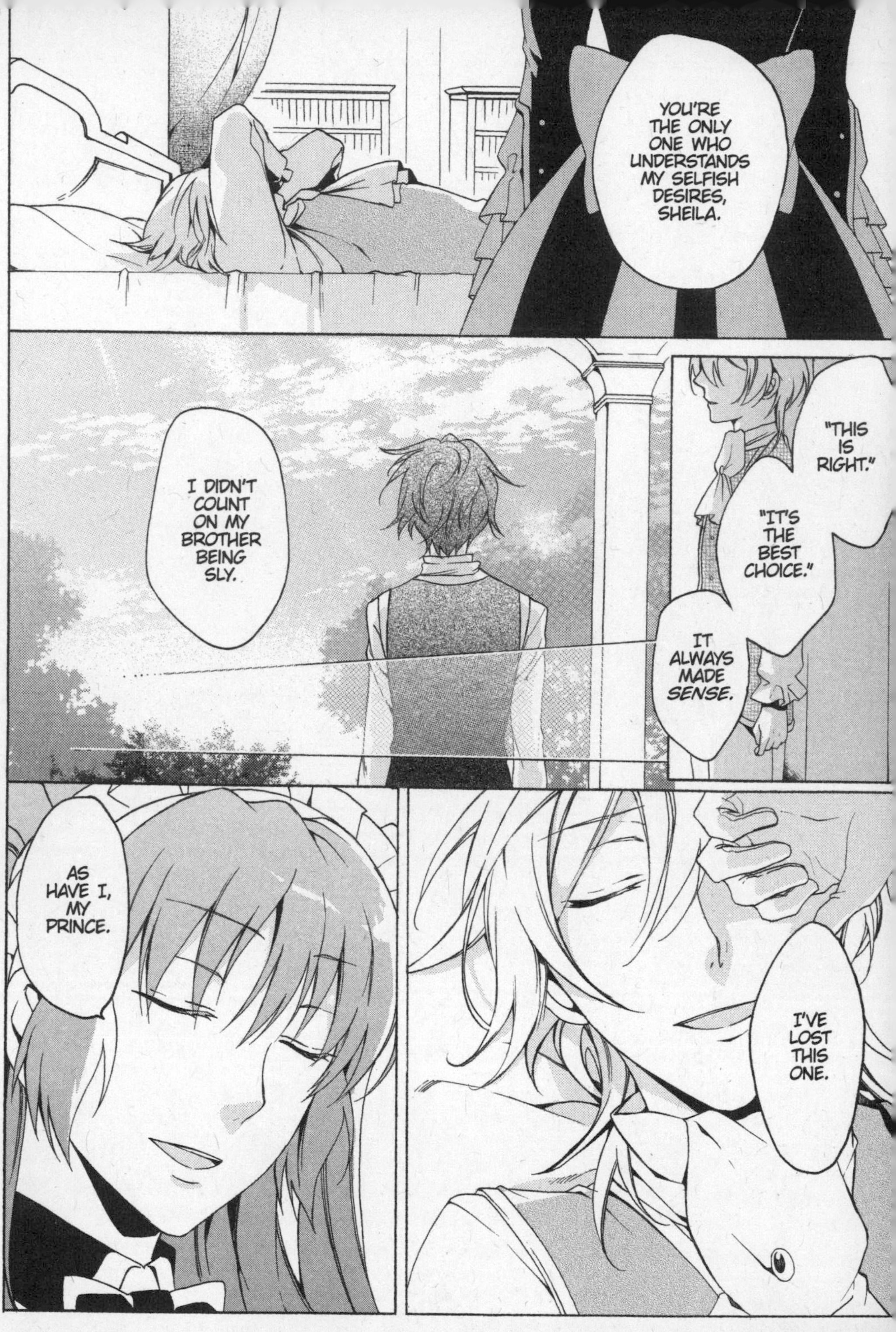
YOU'RE THE ONLY ONE WHO UNDERSTANDS MY SELFISH DESIRES, SHEILA.
"THIS IS RIGHT."
"IT'S THE BEST CHOICE."
IT ALWAYS MADE SENSE.
I DIDN'T COUNT ON MY BROTHER BEING SLY.
I'VE LOST THIS ONE.
AS HAVE I, MY PRINCE.

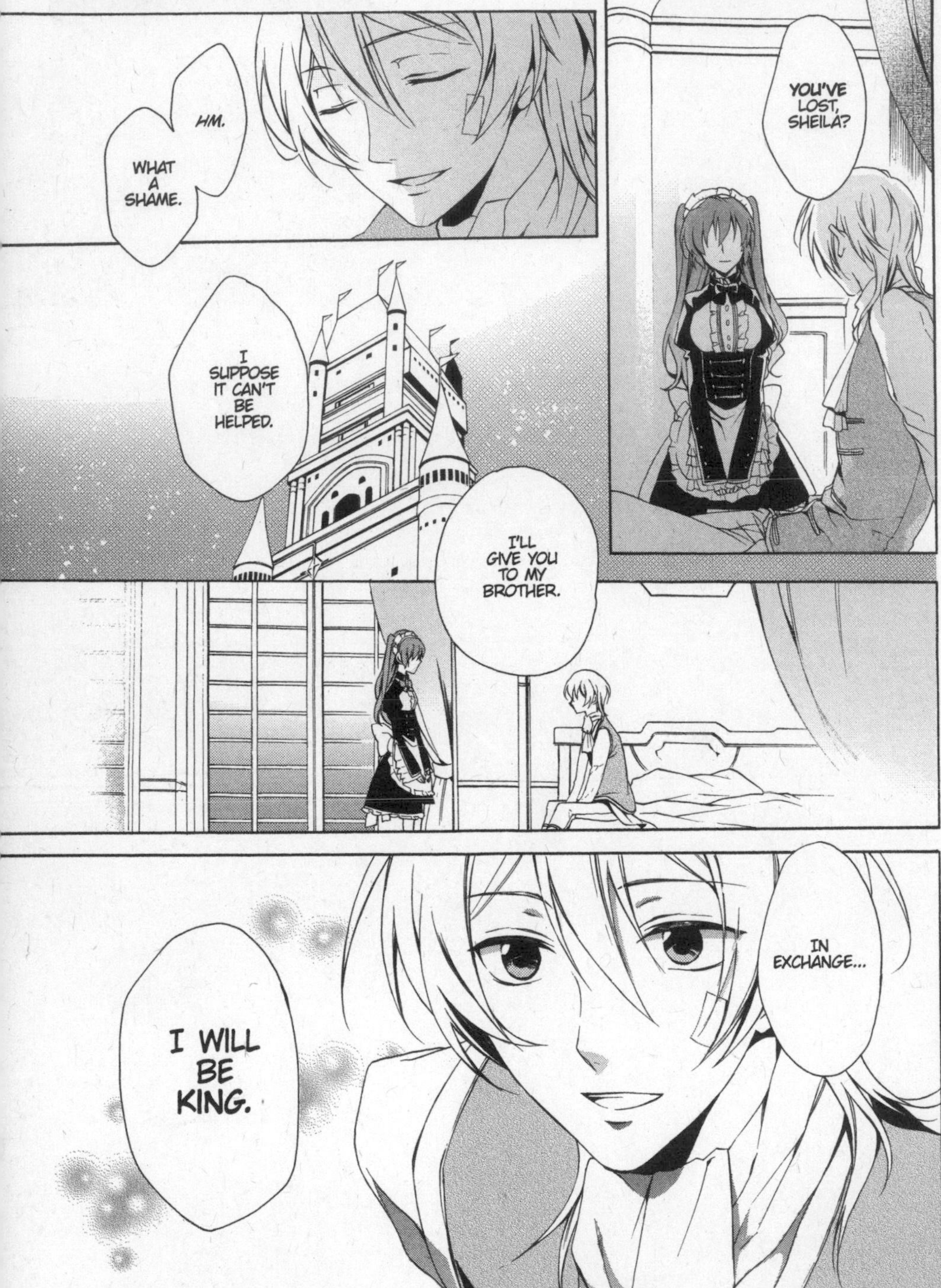
YOU'VE LOST, SHEILA?
HM.
WHAT A SHAME.
I SUPPOSE IT CAN'T BE HELPED.
I'LL GIVE YOU TO MY BROTHER.
IN EXCHANGE...
I WILL BE KING.

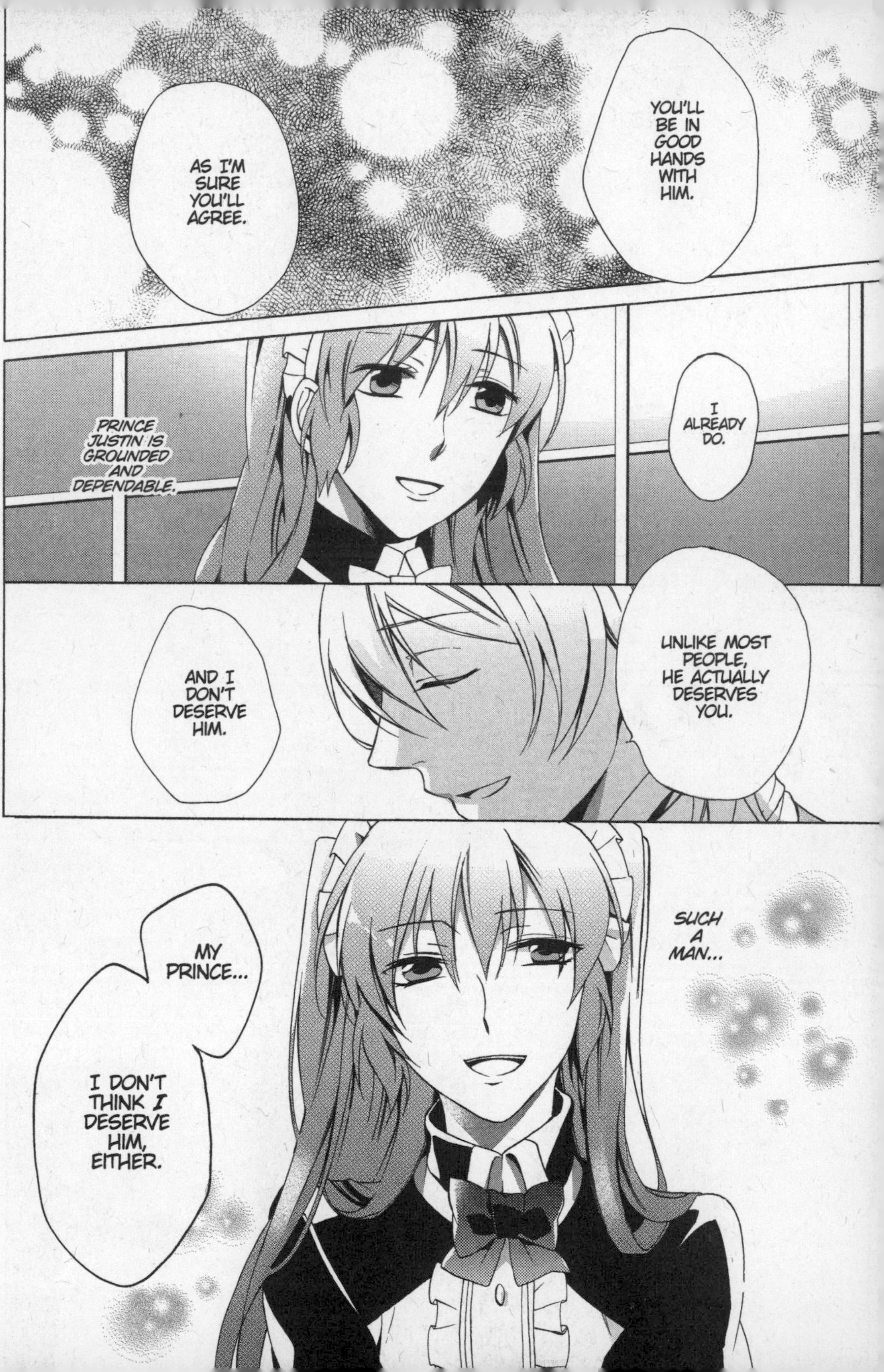
YOU'LL BE IN GOOD HANDS WITH HIM.
AS I'M SURE YOU'LL AGREE.
I ALREADY DO.
PRINCE JUSTIN IS GROUNDED AND DEPENDABLE.
UNLIKE MOST PEOPLE, HE ACTUALLY DESERVES YOU.
AND I DON'T DESERVE HIM.
SUCH A MAN...
MY PRINCE...
I DON'T THINK *I* DESERVE HIM, EITHER.

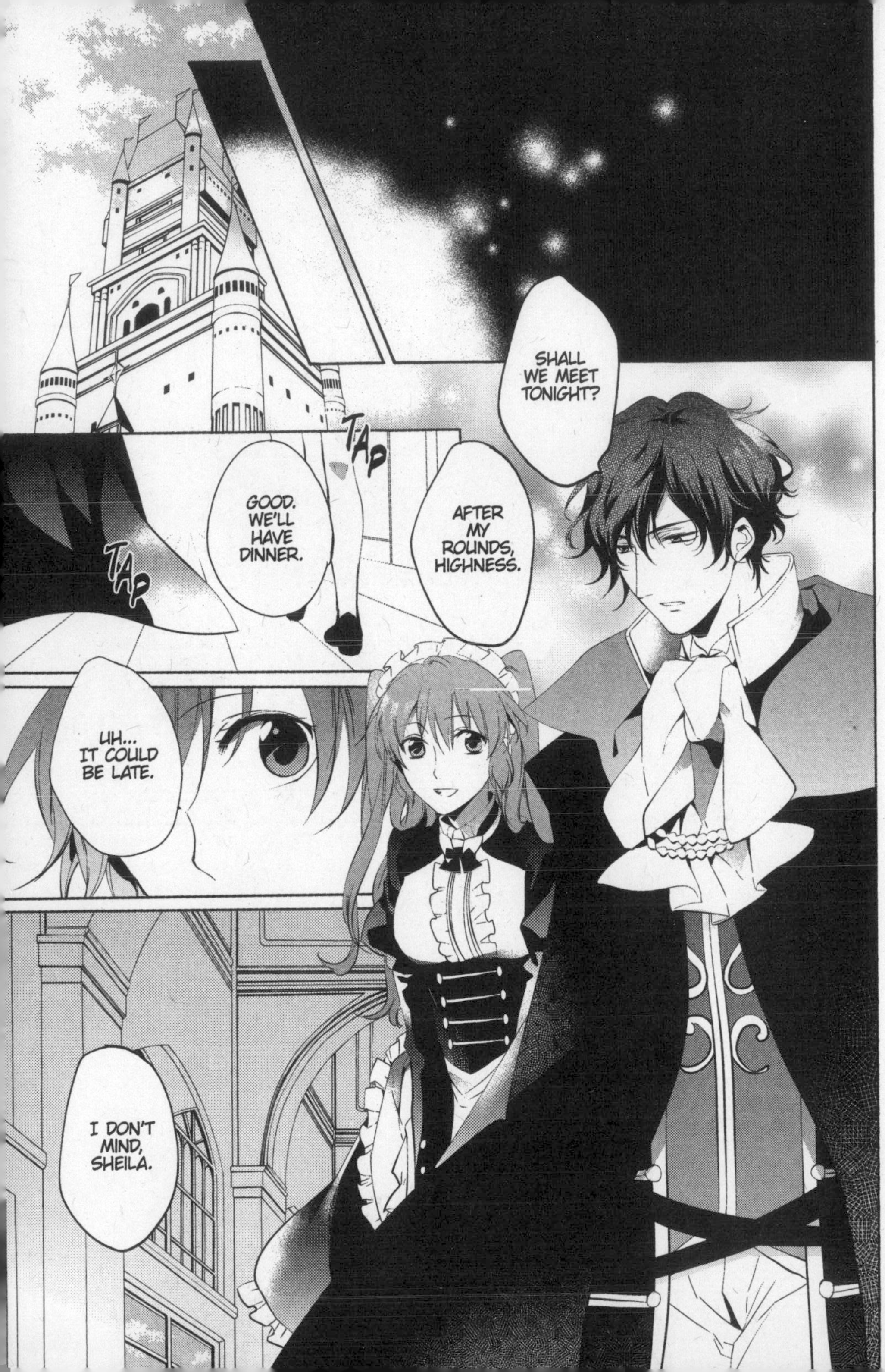
SHALL WE MEET TONIGHT?
AFTER MY ROUNDS, HIGHNESS.
TAP
GOOD. WE'LL HAVE DINNER.
TAP
UH... IT COULD BE LATE.
I DON'T MIND, SHEILA.

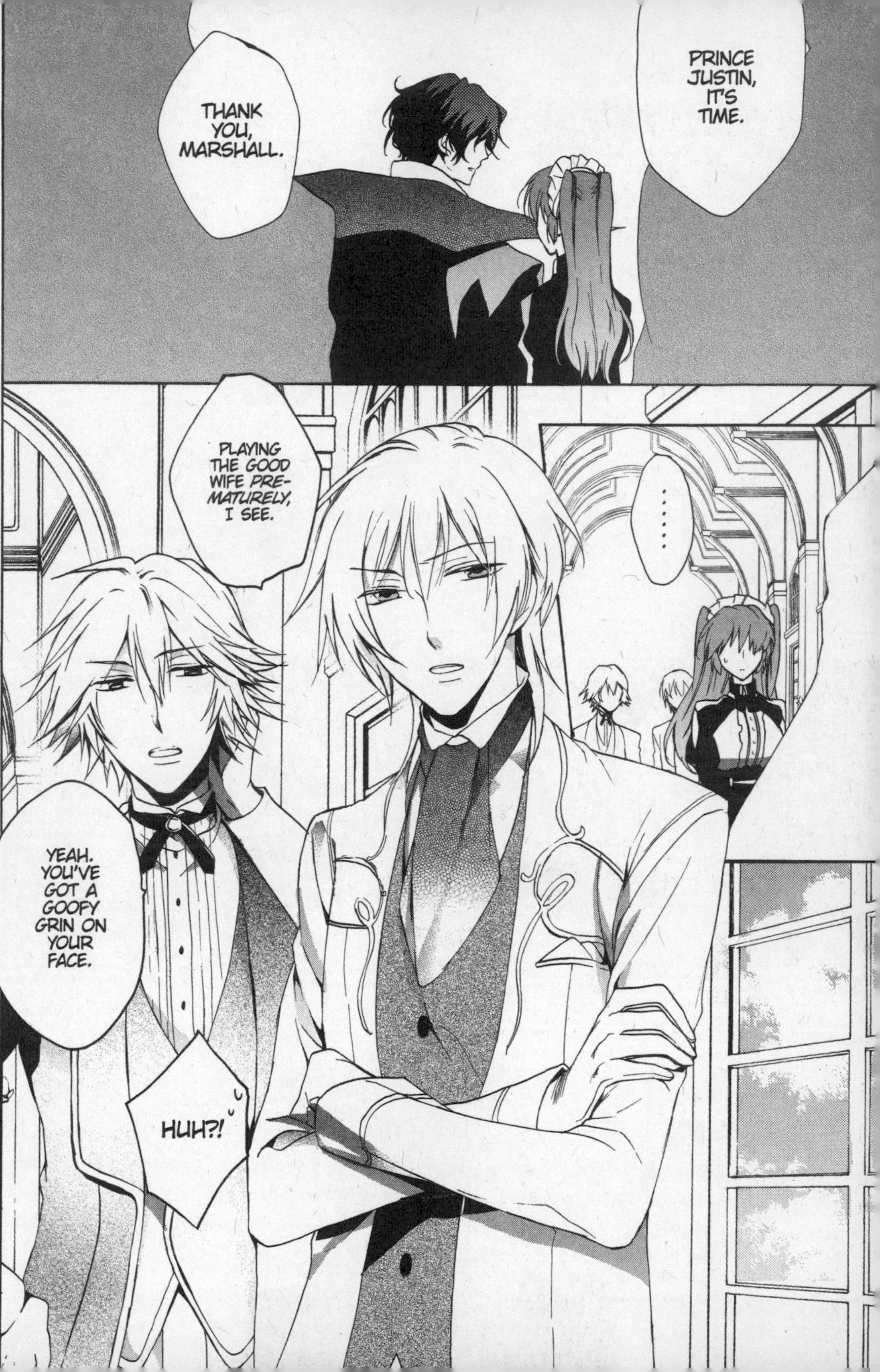
PRINCE JUSTIN, IT'S TIME.
THANK YOU, MARSHALL.
......
PLAYING THE GOOD WIFE PRE-MATURELY, I SEE.
YEAH. YOU'VE GOT A GOOFY GRIN ON YOUR FACE.
HUH?!

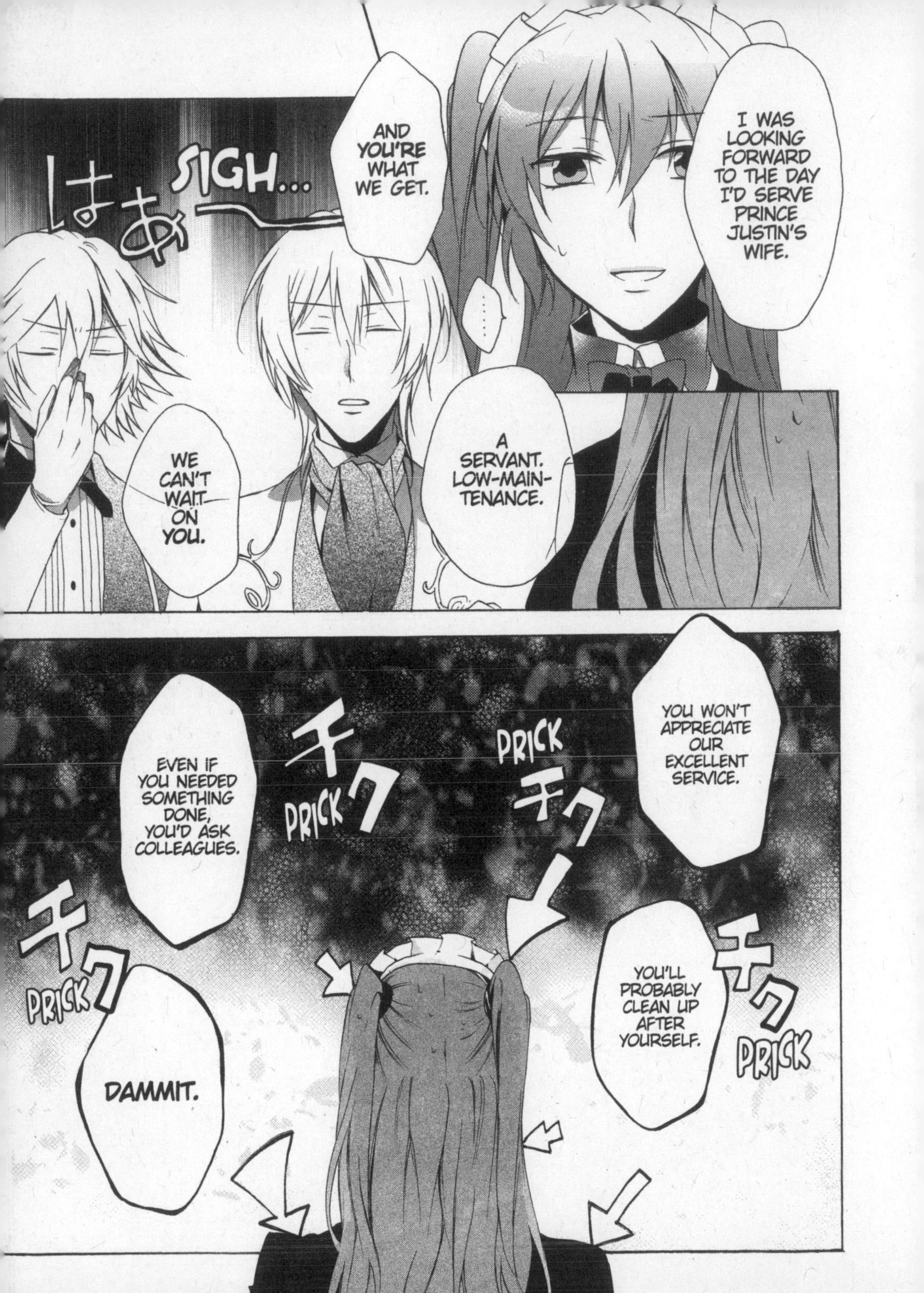
I WAS LOOKING FORWARD TO THE DAY I'D SERVE PRINCE JUSTIN'S WIFE.
AND YOU'RE WHAT WE GET.
......
はぁー SIGH...
A SERVANT. LOW-MAIN-TENANCE.
WE CAN'T WAIT ON YOU.
YOU WON'T APPRECIATE OUR EXCELLENT SERVICE.
PRICK チクッ
チク PRICK
EVEN IF YOU NEEDED SOMETHING DONE, YOU'D ASK COLLEAGUES.
YOU'LL PROBABLY CLEAN UP AFTER YOURSELF.
チク PRICK
チク PRICK
DAMMIT.

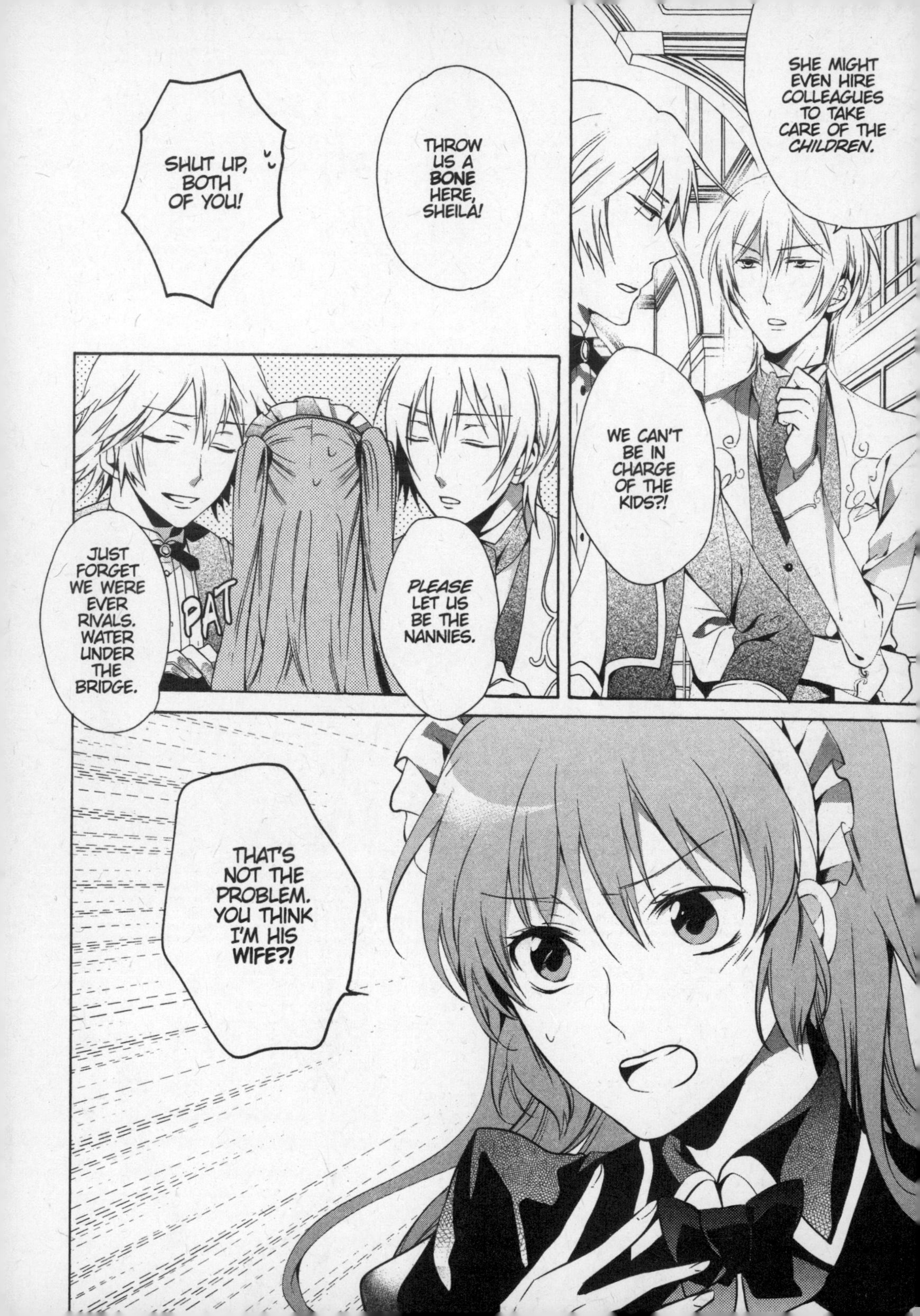

SHE MIGHT EVEN HIRE COLLEAGUES TO TAKE CARE OF THE *CHILDREN.*
WE CAN'T BE IN CHARGE OF THE KIDS?!
THROW US A BONE HERE, SHEILA!
SHUT UP, BOTH OF YOU!
PLEASE LET US BE THE NANNIES.
JUST FORGET WE WERE EVER RIVALS. WATER UNDER THE BRIDGE.
PAT
THAT'S NOT THE PROBLEM. YOU THINK I'M HIS WIFE?!

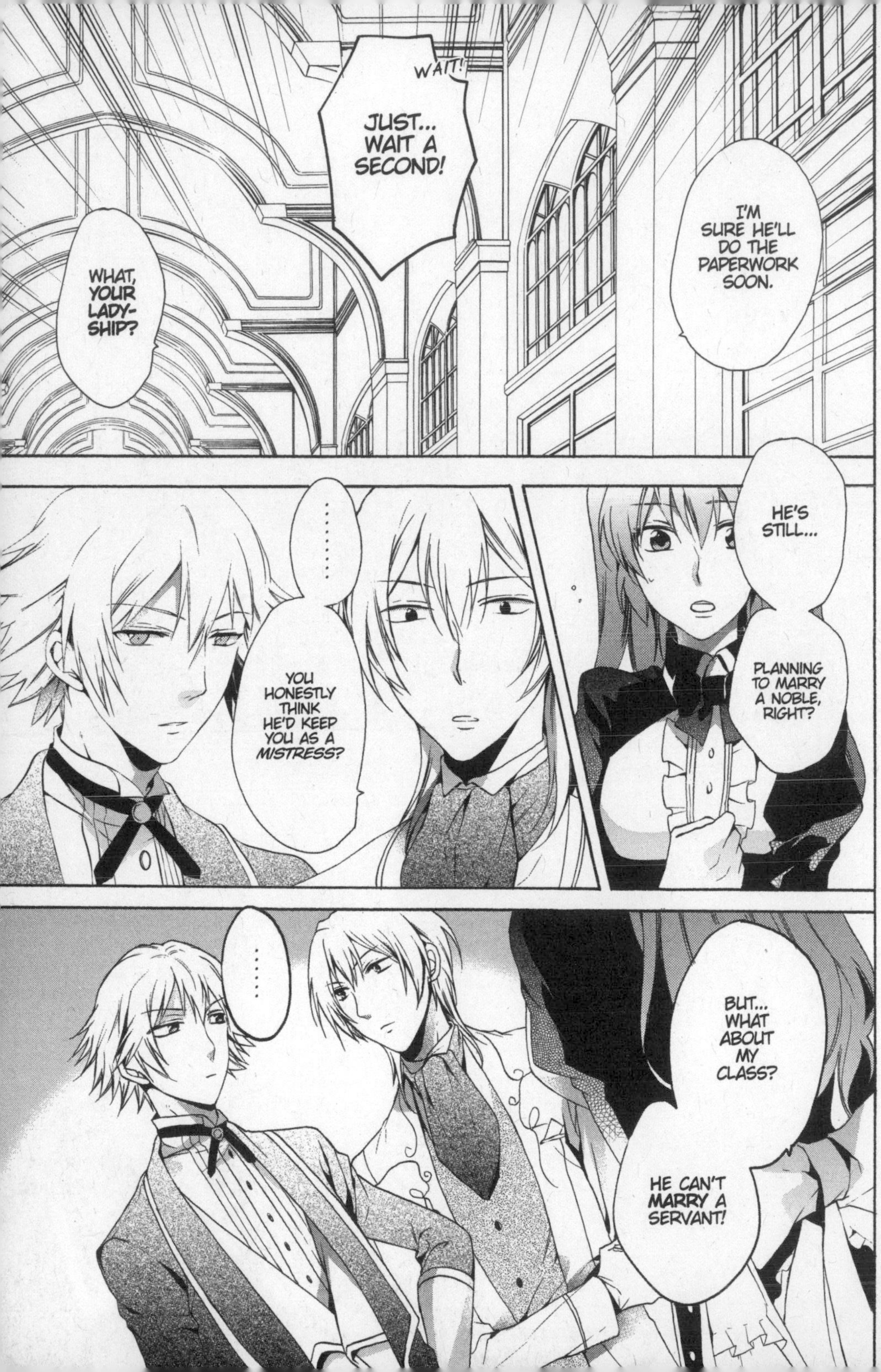
I'M SURE HE'LL DO THE PAPERWORK SOON.
WAIT!
JUST... WAIT A SECOND!
WHAT, YOUR LADY-SHIP?
HE'S STILL...
PLANNING TO MARRY A NOBLE, RIGHT?
......
YOU HONESTLY THINK HE'D KEEP YOU AS A *MISTRESS*?
BUT... WHAT ABOUT MY CLASS?
HE CAN'T MARRY A SERVANT!
......

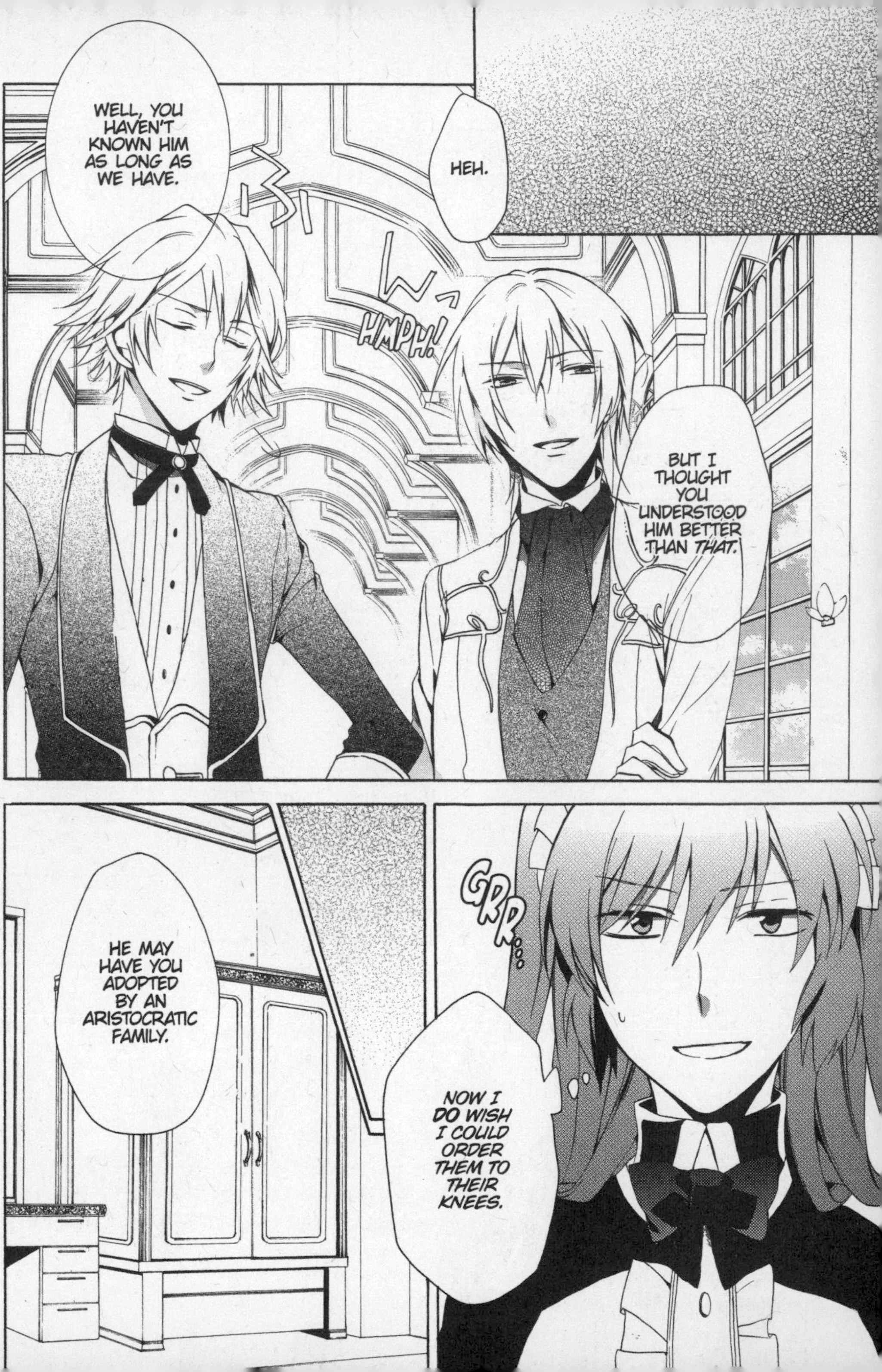
HEH.
WELL, YOU HAVEN'T KNOWN HIM AS LONG AS WE HAVE.
HMPH!
BUT I THOUGHT YOU UNDERSTOOD HIM BETTER THAN *THAT*.
GRR...
NOW I DO WISH I COULD ORDER THEM TO THEIR KNEES.
HE MAY HAVE YOU ADOPTED BY AN ARISTOCRATIC FAMILY.

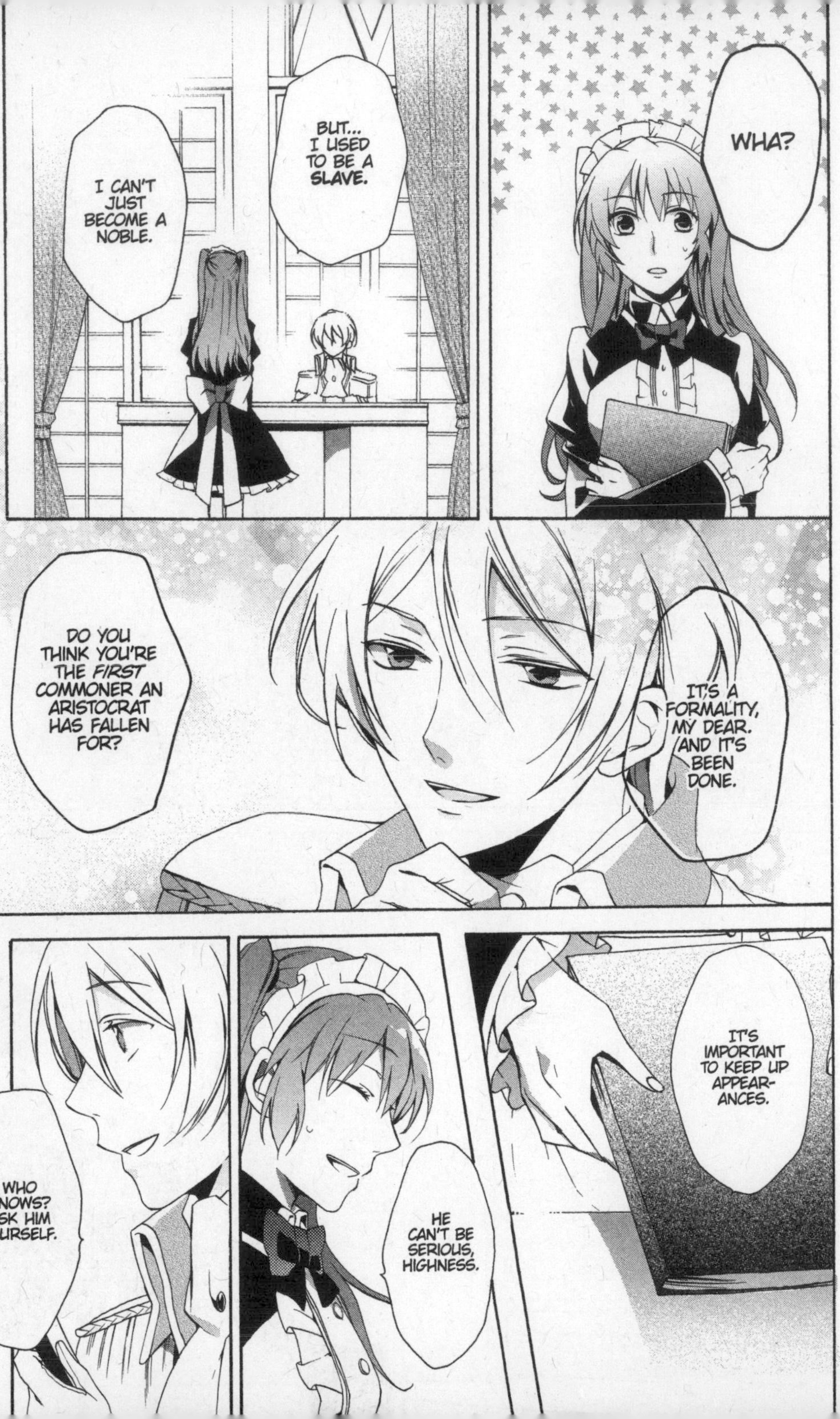
WHA?
BUT... I USED TO BE A SLAVE.
I CAN'T JUST BECOME A NOBLE.
IT'S A FORMALITY, MY DEAR. AND IT'S BEEN DONE.
DO YOU THINK YOU'RE THE *FIRST* COMMONER AN ARISTOCRAT HAS FALLEN FOR?
IT'S IMPORTANT TO KEEP UP APPEAR-ANCES.
HE CAN'T BE SERIOUS, HIGHNESS.
WHO KNOWS? ASK HIM YOURSELF.

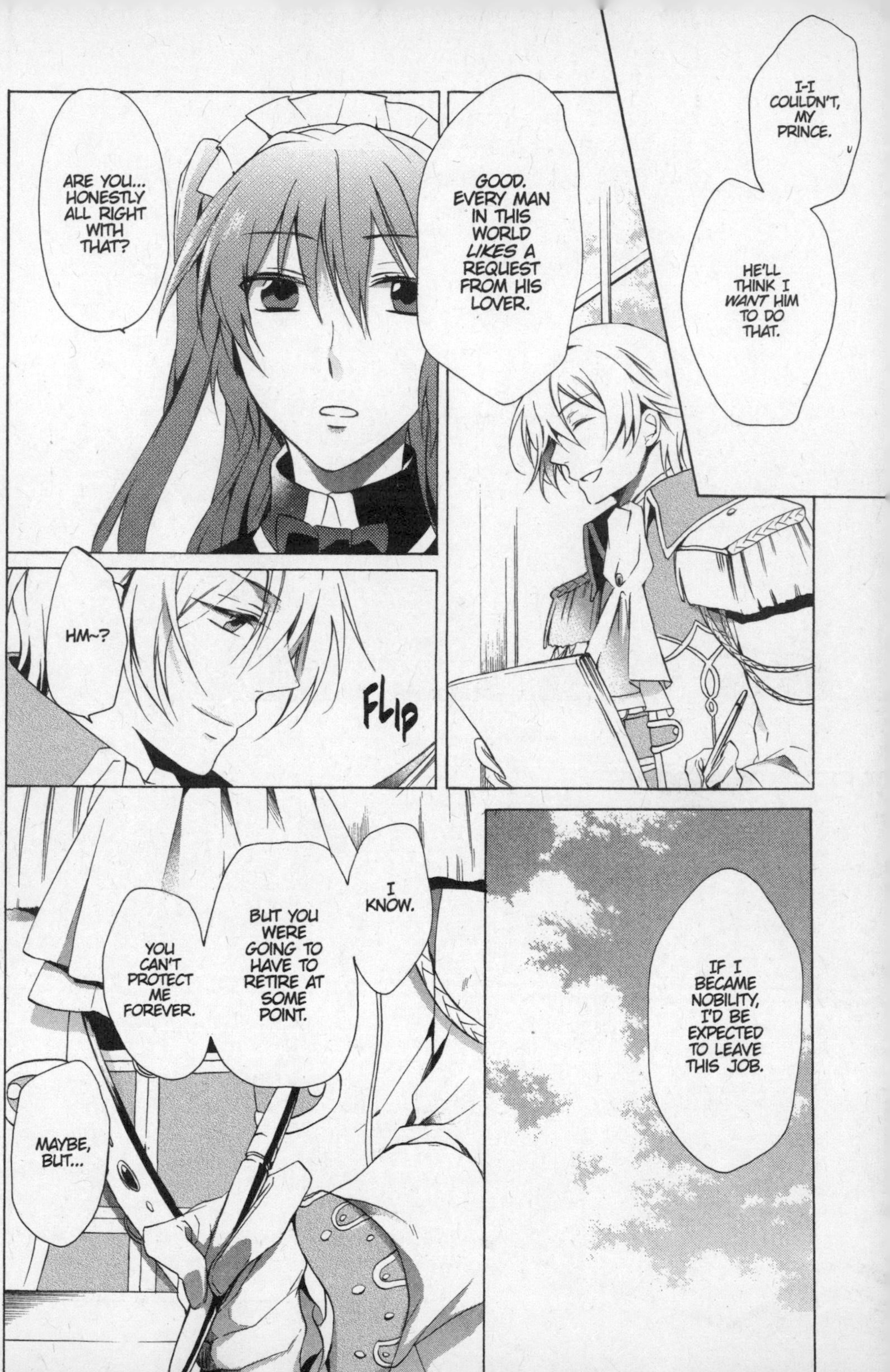
I-I COULDN'T, MY PRINCE.
HE'LL THINK I *WANT* HIM TO DO THAT.
GOOD. EVERY MAN IN THIS WORLD *LIKES* A REQUEST FROM HIS LOVER.
ARE YOU... HONESTLY ALL RIGHT WITH THAT?
HM~?
FLIP
IF I BECAME NOBILITY, I'D BE EXPECTED TO LEAVE THIS JOB.
I KNOW.
BUT YOU WERE GOING TO HAVE TO RETIRE AT SOME POINT.
YOU CAN'T PROTECT ME FOREVER.
MAYBE, BUT...

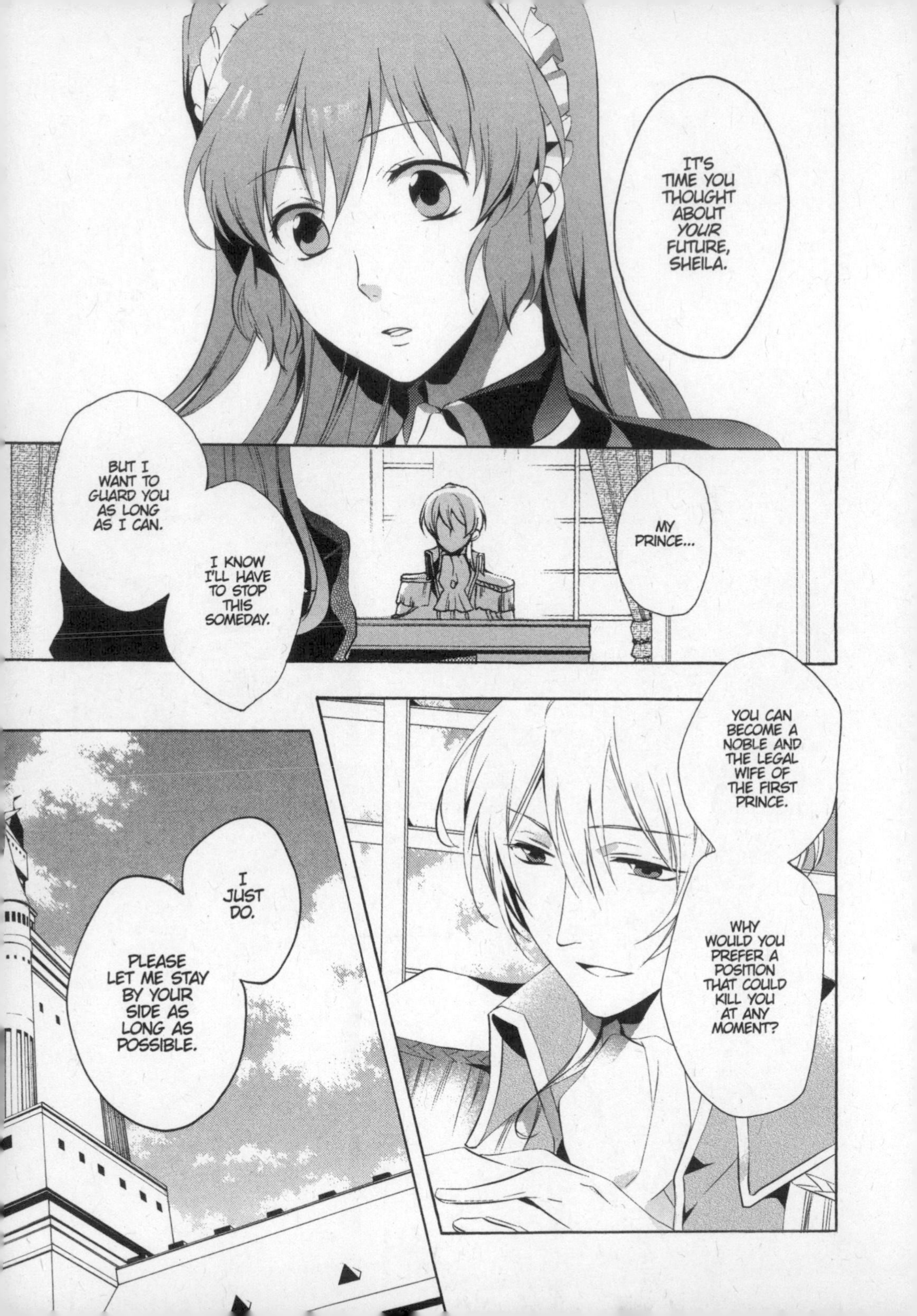
IT'S TIME YOU THOUGHT ABOUT *YOUR* FUTURE, SHEILA.
MY PRINCE...
BUT I WANT TO GUARD YOU AS LONG AS I CAN.
I KNOW I'LL HAVE TO STOP THIS SOMEDAY.
YOU CAN BECOME A NOBLE AND THE LEGAL WIFE OF THE FIRST PRINCE.
WHY WOULD YOU PREFER A POSITION THAT COULD KILL YOU AT ANY MOMENT?
I JUST DO.
PLEASE LET ME STAY BY YOUR SIDE AS LONG AS POSSIBLE.

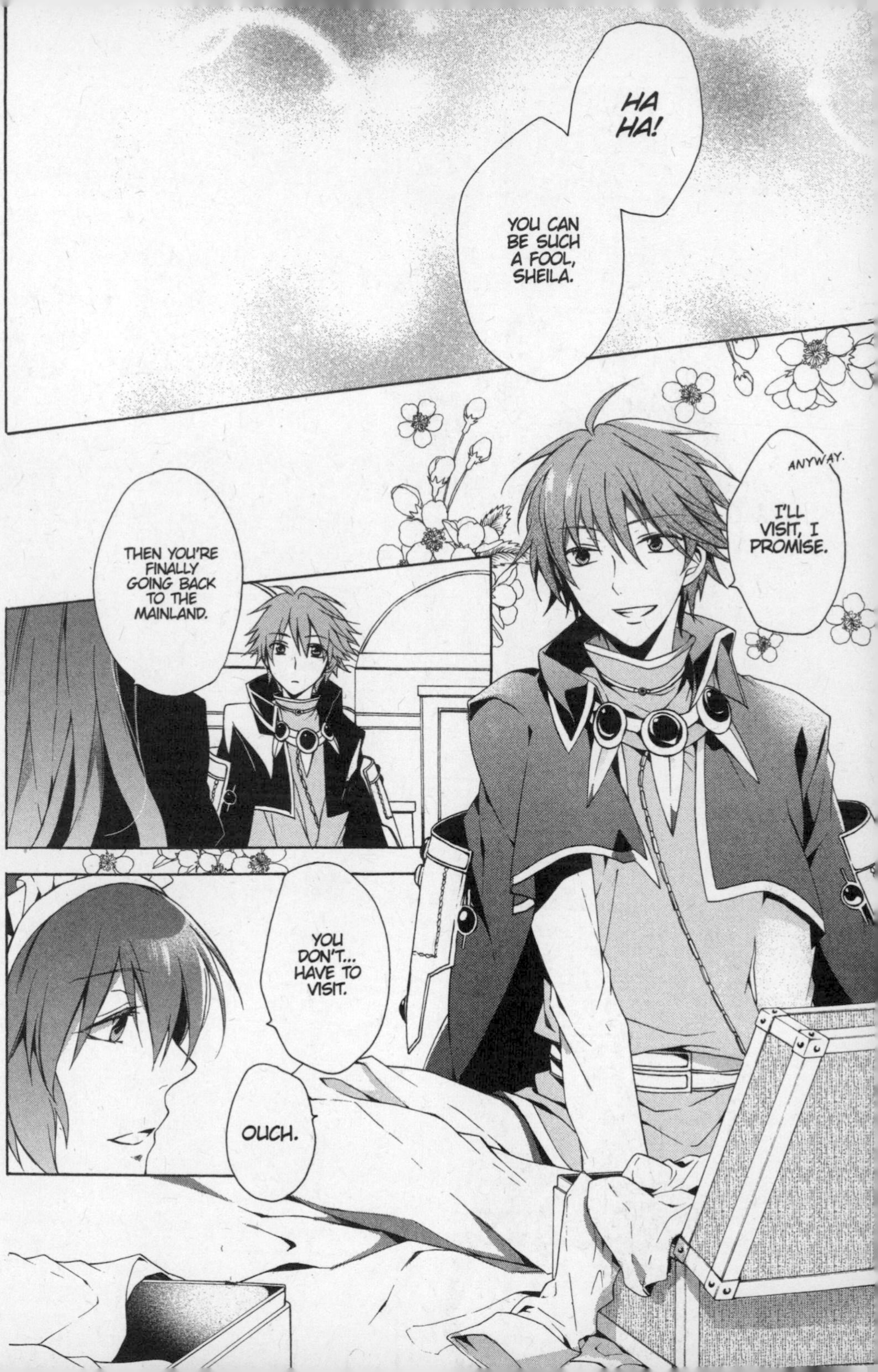
HA HA!
YOU CAN BE SUCH A FOOL, SHEILA.
ANYWAY.
I'LL VISIT, I PROMISE.
THEN YOU'RE FINALLY GOING BACK TO THE MAINLAND.
YOU DON'T... HAVE TO VISIT.
OUCH.

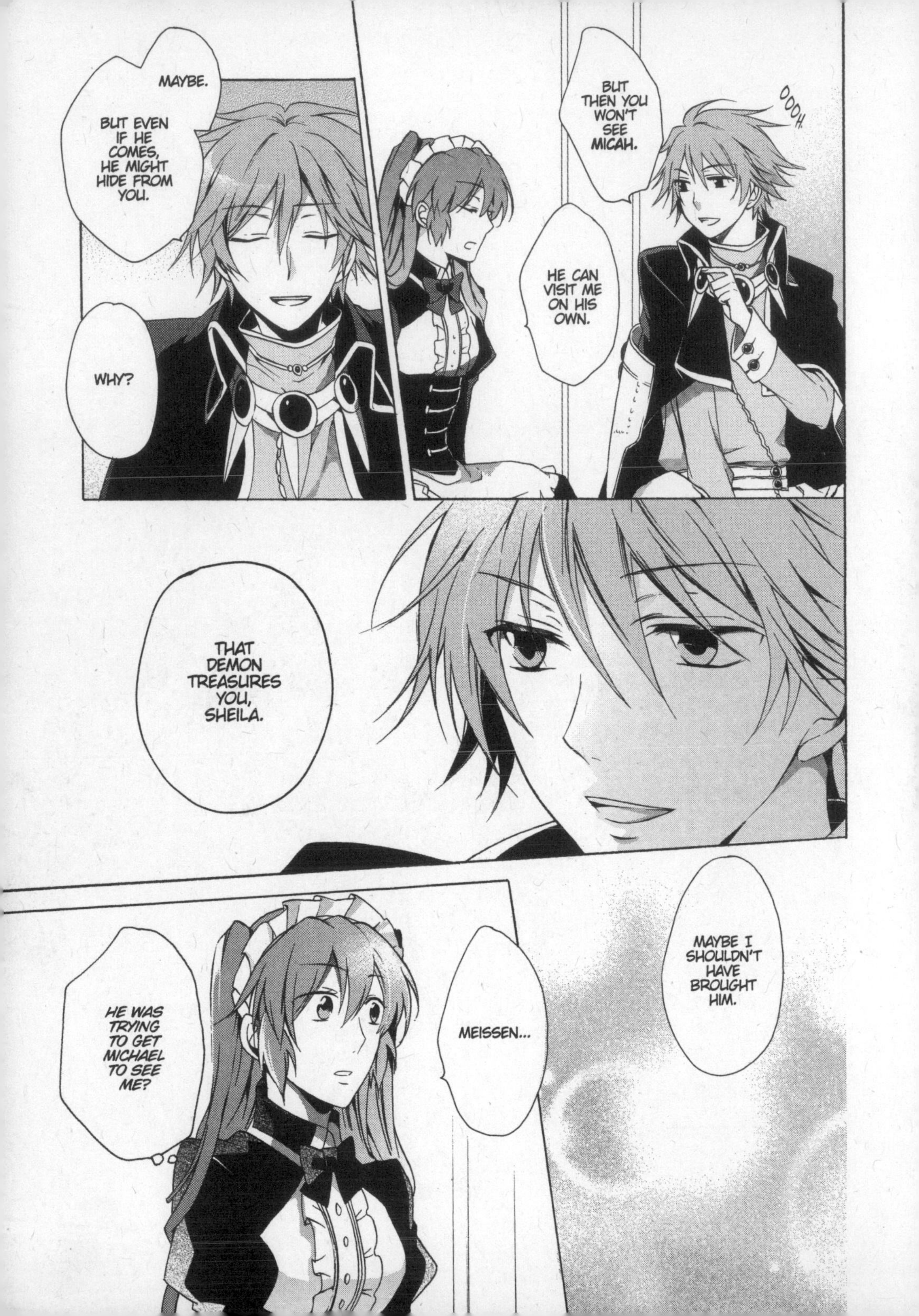
OOOH.
BUT THEN YOU WON'T SEE MICAH.
HE CAN VISIT ME ON HIS OWN.
MAYBE.
BUT EVEN IF HE COMES, HE MIGHT HIDE FROM YOU.
WHY?
THAT DEMON TREASURES YOU, SHEILA.
MAYBE I SHOULDN'T HAVE BROUGHT HIM.
MEISSEN...
HE WAS TRYING TO GET MICHAEL TO SEE ME?

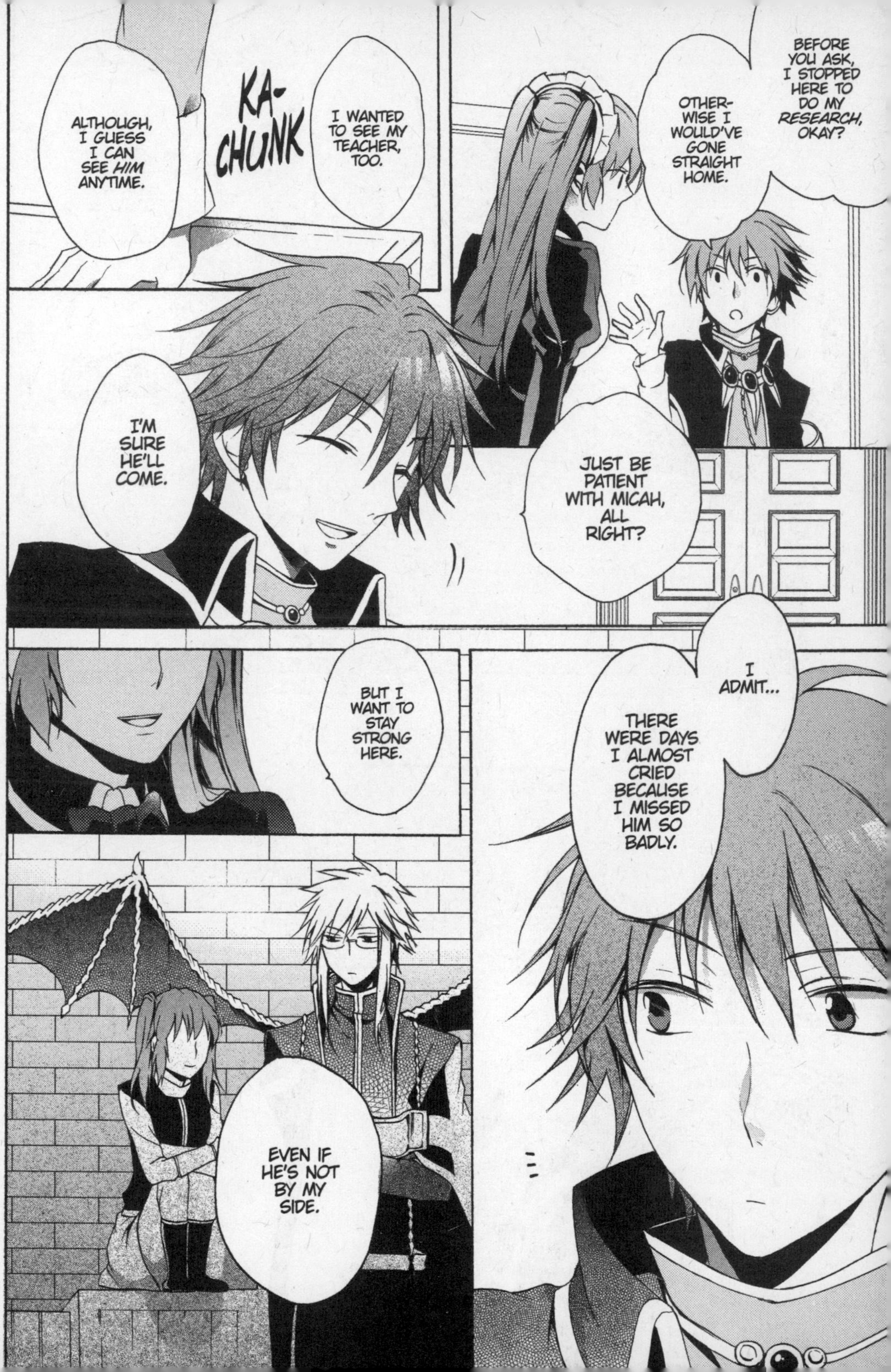
BEFORE YOU ASK, I STOPPED HERE TO DO MY *RESEARCH*, OKAY?
OTHERWISE I WOULD'VE GONE STRAIGHT HOME.
I WANTED TO SEE MY TEACHER, TOO.
KA-CHUNK
ALTHOUGH, I GUESS I CAN SEE *HIM* ANYTIME.
JUST BE PATIENT WITH MICAH, ALL RIGHT?
I'M SURE HE'LL COME.
I ADMIT...
THERE WERE DAYS I ALMOST CRIED BECAUSE I MISSED HIM SO BADLY.
BUT I WANT TO STAY STRONG HERE.
EVEN IF HE'S NOT BY MY SIDE.

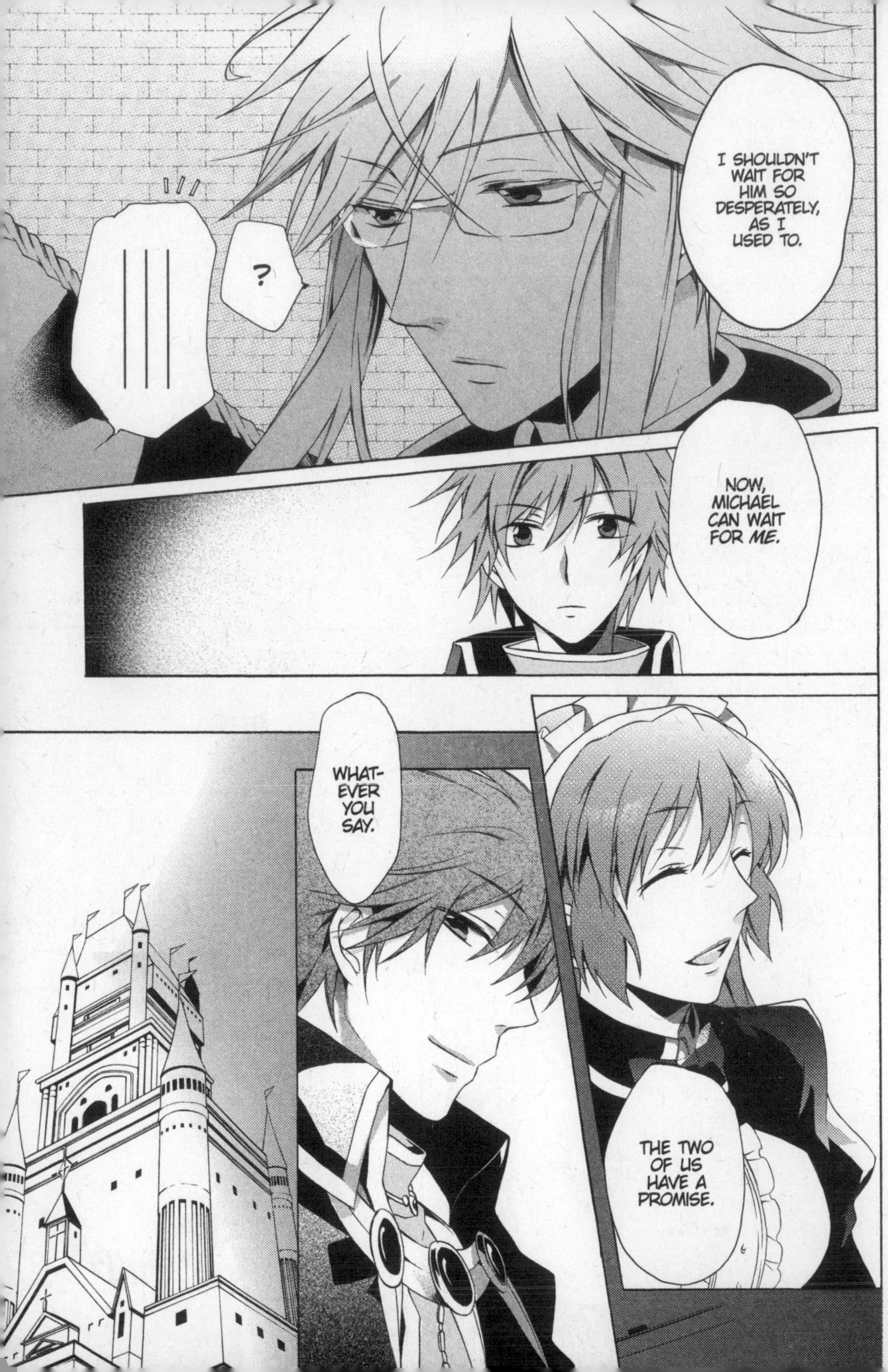
I SHOULDN'T WAIT FOR HIM SO DESPERATELY, AS I USED TO.
?
NOW, MICHAEL CAN WAIT FOR ME.
THE TWO OF US HAVE A PROMISE.
WHAT-EVER YOU SAY.

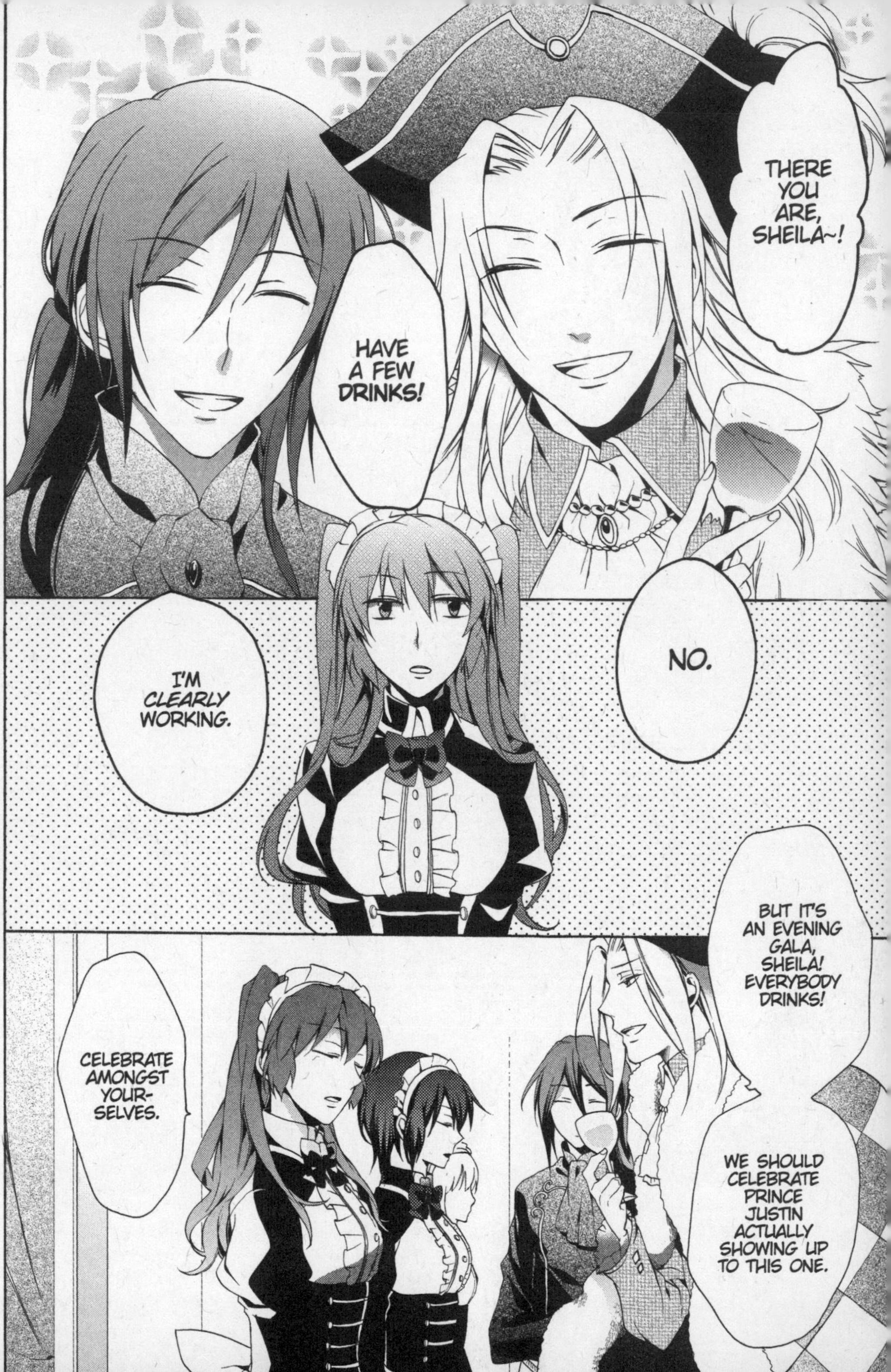
THERE YOU ARE, SHEILA~!
HAVE A FEW DRINKS!
NO.
I'M CLEARLY WORKING.
BUT IT'S AN EVENING GALA, SHEILA! EVERYBODY DRINKS!
WE SHOULD CELEBRATE PRINCE JUSTIN ACTUALLY SHOWING UP TO THIS ONE.
CELEBRATE AMONGST YOUR-SELVES.

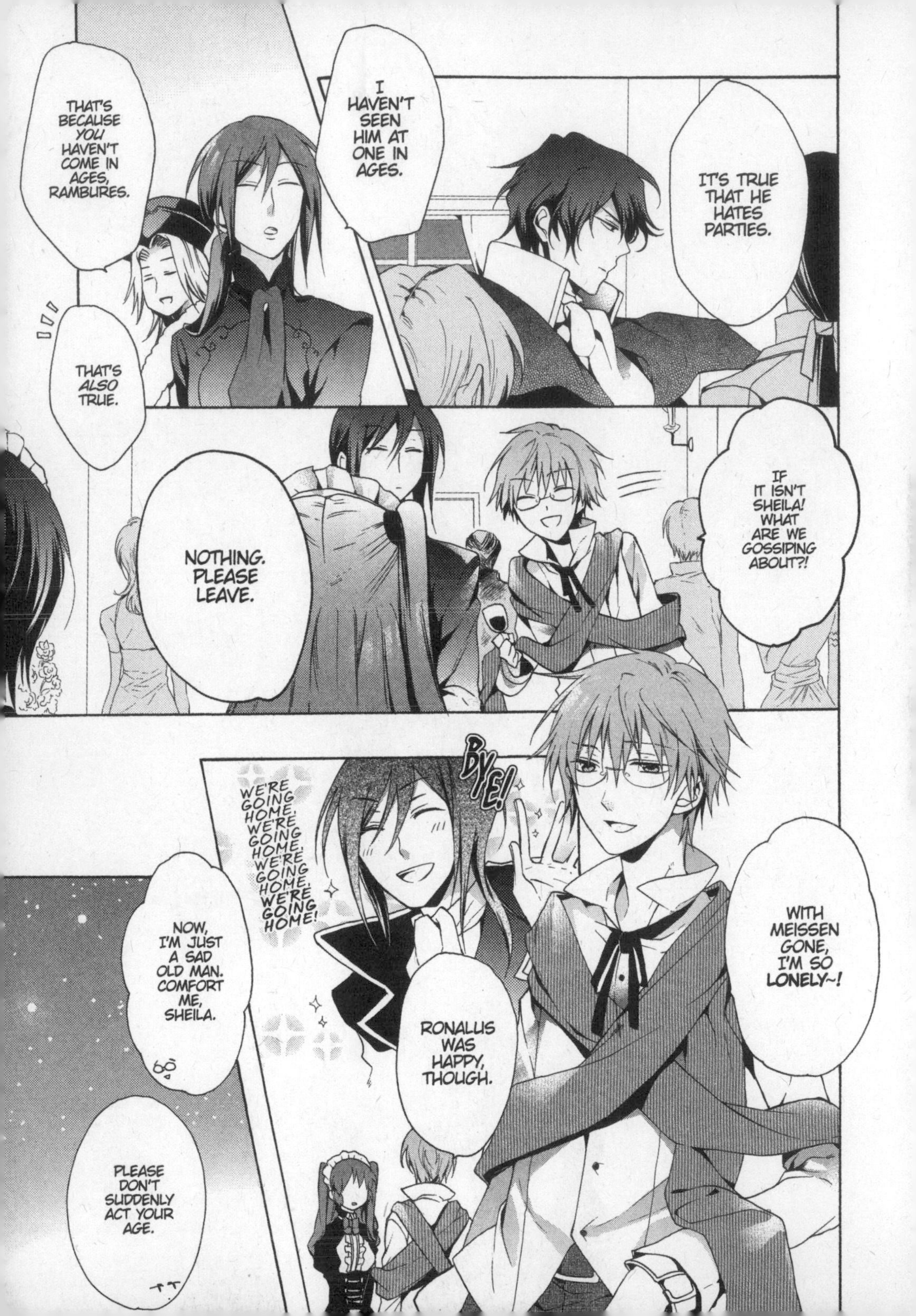
IT'S TRUE THAT HE HATES PARTIES.
I HAVEN'T SEEN HIM AT ONE IN AGES.
THAT'S BECAUSE YOU HAVEN'T COME IN AGES, RAMBURES.
THAT'S ALSO TRUE.
IF IT ISN'T SHEILA! WHAT ARE WE GOSSIPING ABOUT?!
NOTHING. PLEASE LEAVE.
BYE!
WE'RE GOING HOME, WE'RE GOING HOME, WE'RE GOING HOME, WE'RE GOING HOME!
WITH MEISSEN GONE, I'M SO LONELY~!
RONALUS WAS HAPPY, THOUGH.
NOW, I'M JUST A SAD OLD MAN. COMFORT ME, SHEILA.
PLEASE DON'T SUDDENLY ACT YOUR AGE.

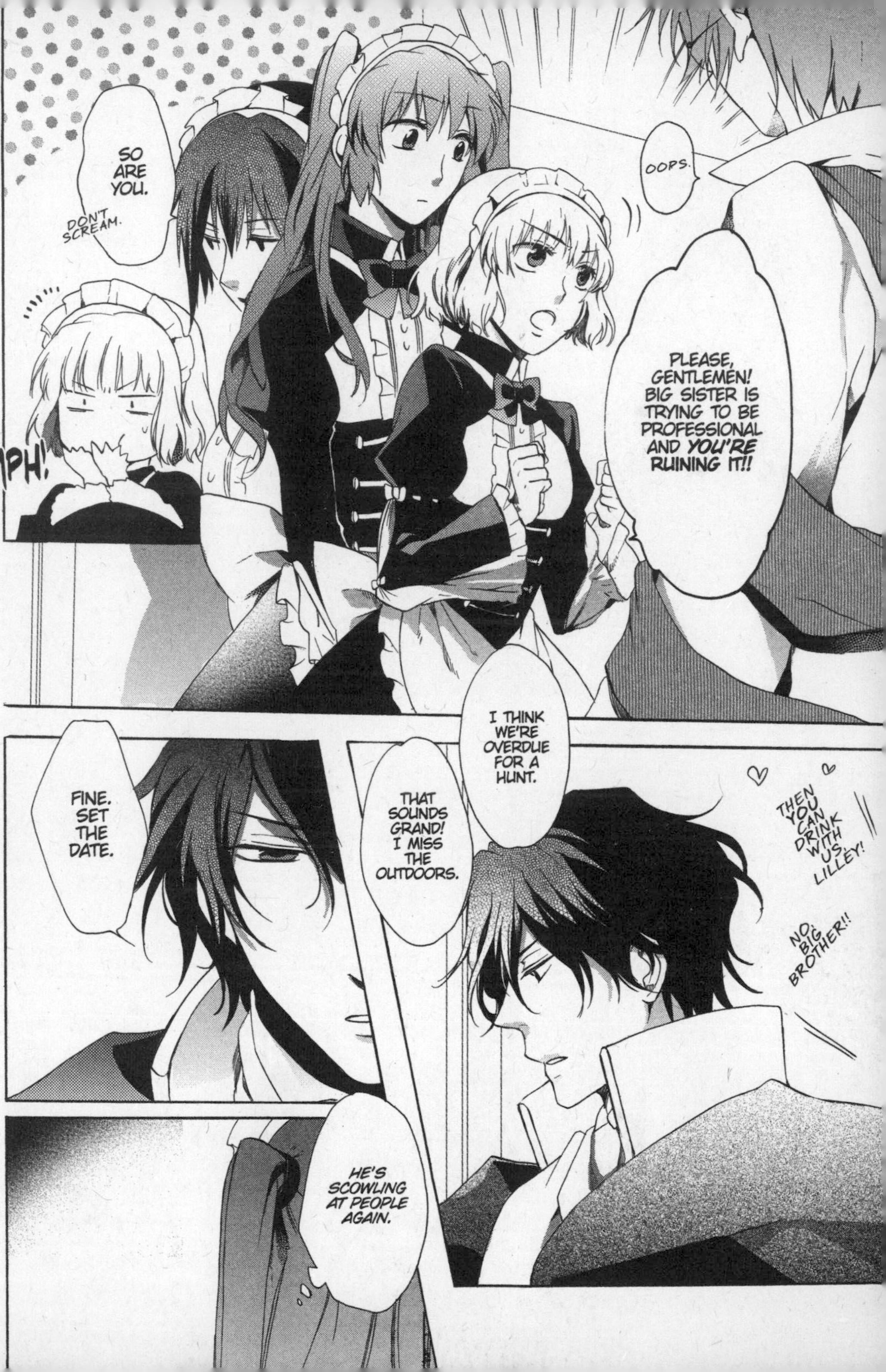
OOPS.
PLEASE, GENTLEMEN! BIG SISTER IS TRYING TO BE PROFESSIONAL AND YOU'RE RUINING IT!!
SO ARE YOU.
DON'T SCREAM.
MMPH!
I THINK WE'RE OVERDUE FOR A HUNT.
THAT SOUNDS GRAND! I MISS THE OUTDOORS.
THEN YOU CAN DRINK WITH US, LILLEY!
NO, BIG BROTHER!!
FINE. SET THE DATE.
HE'S SCOWLING AT PEOPLE AGAIN.

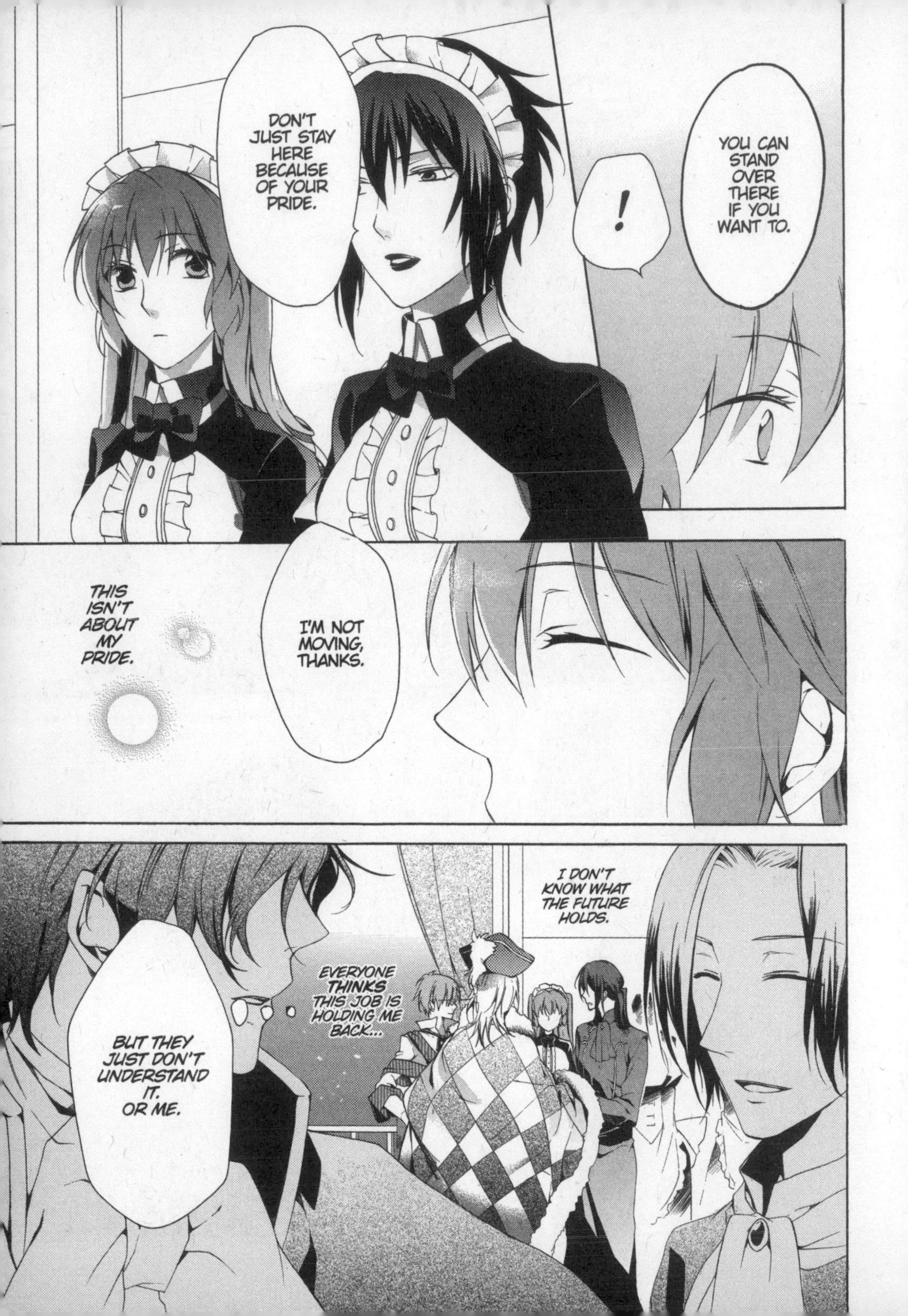
YOU CAN STAND OVER THERE IF YOU WANT TO.
!
DON'T JUST STAY HERE BECAUSE OF YOUR PRIDE.
I'M NOT MOVING, THANKS.
THIS ISN'T ABOUT MY PRIDE.
I DON'T KNOW WHAT THE FUTURE HOLDS.
EVERYONE THINKS THIS JOB IS HOLDING ME BACK...
BUT THEY JUST DON'T UNDERSTAND IT. OR ME.

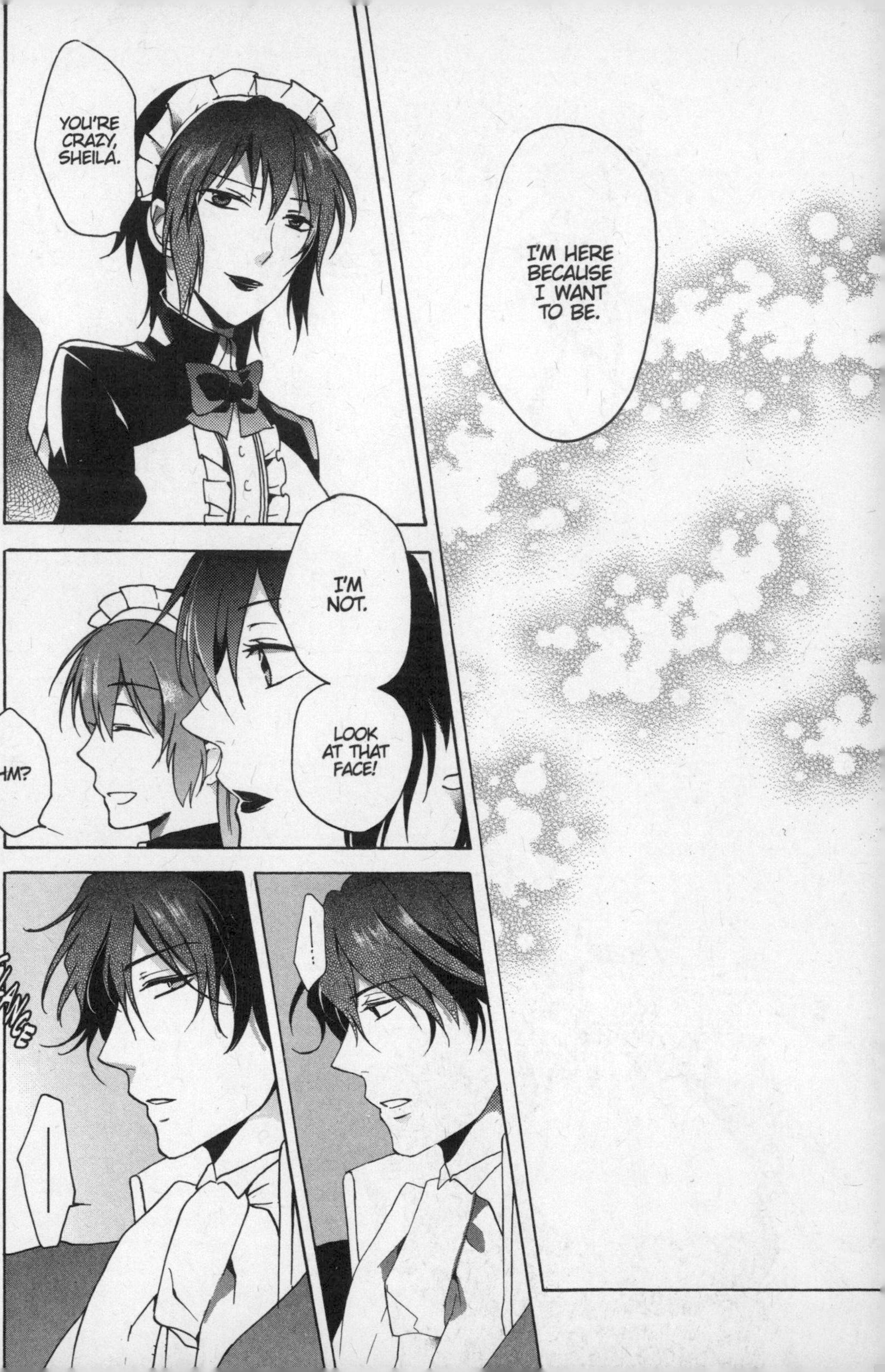
I'M HERE BECAUSE I WANT TO BE.
YOU'RE CRAZY, SHEILA.
I'M NOT.
LOOK AT THAT FACE!
HM?
!..
GLANCE

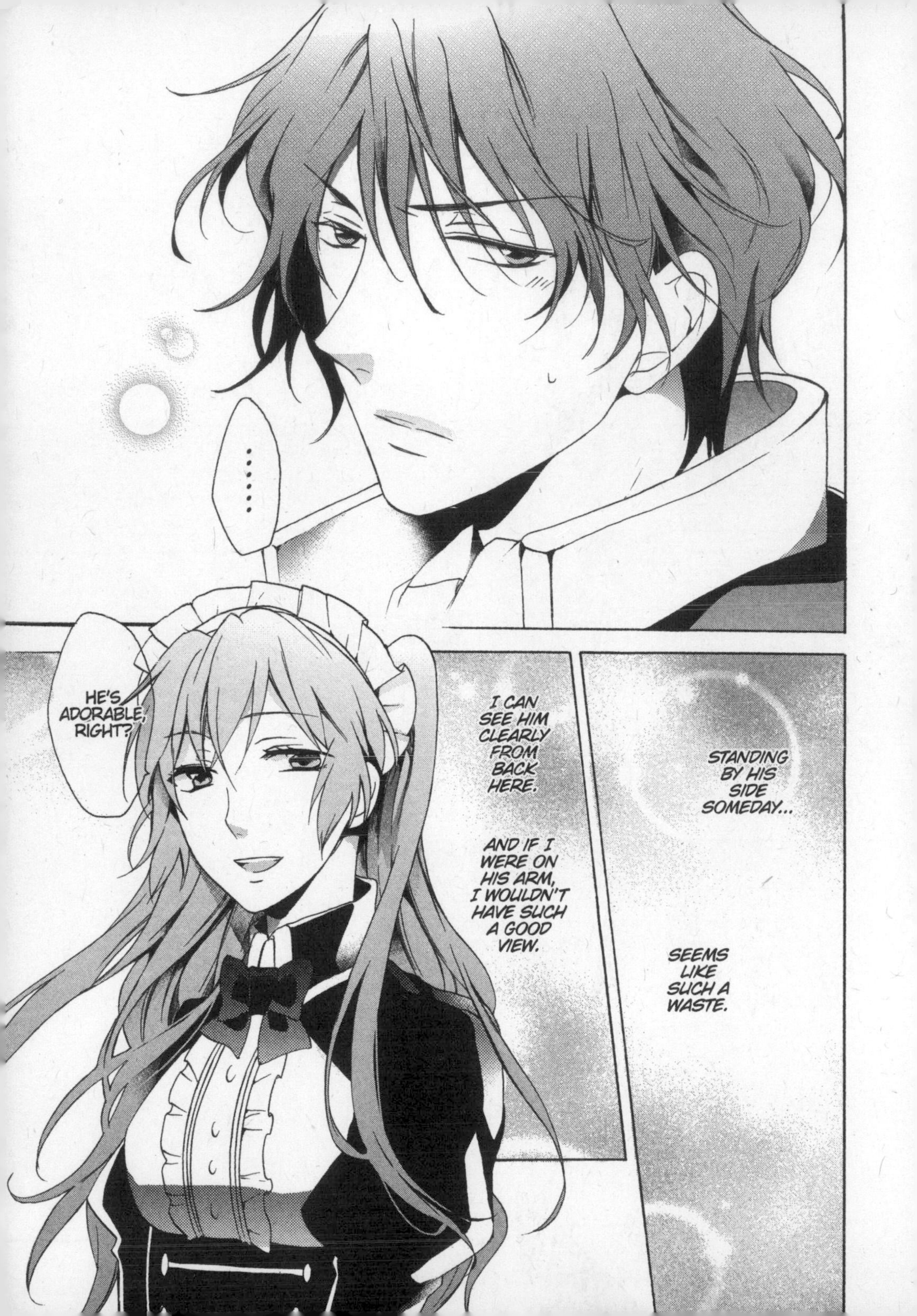
......
STANDING BY HIS SIDE SOMEDAY...
SEEMS LIKE SUCH A WASTE.
I CAN SEE HIM CLEARLY FROM BACK HERE.
HE'S ADORABLE, RIGHT?
AND IF I WERE ON HIS ARM, I WOULDN'T HAVE SUCH A GOOD VIEW.

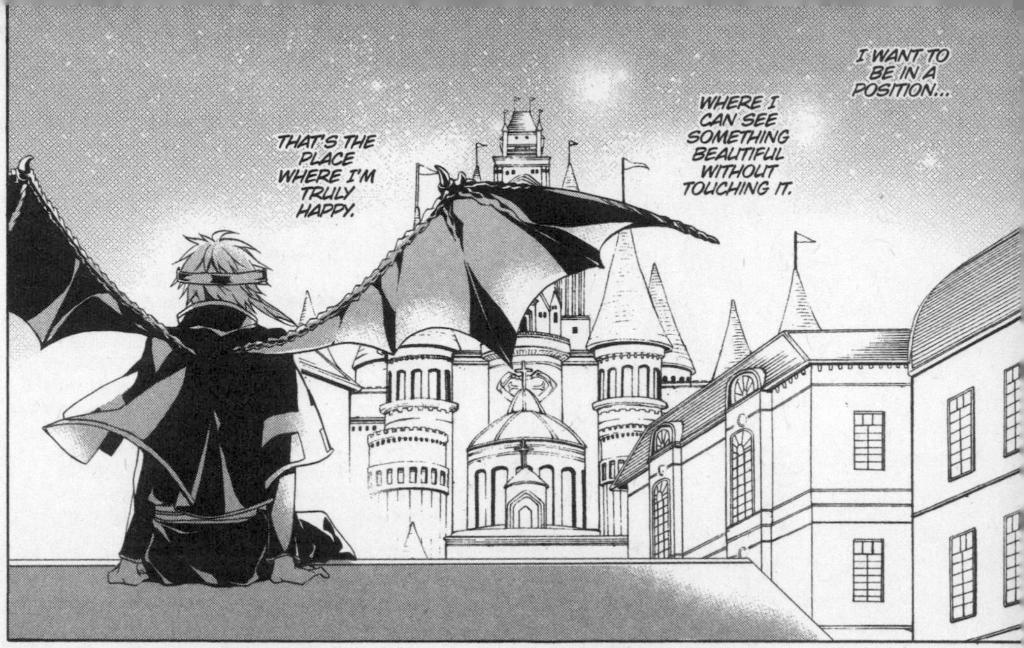
I WANT TO BE IN A POSITION...
WHERE I CAN SEE SOMETHING BEAUTIFUL WITHOUT TOUCHING IT.
THAT'S THE PLACE WHERE I'M TRULY HAPPY.

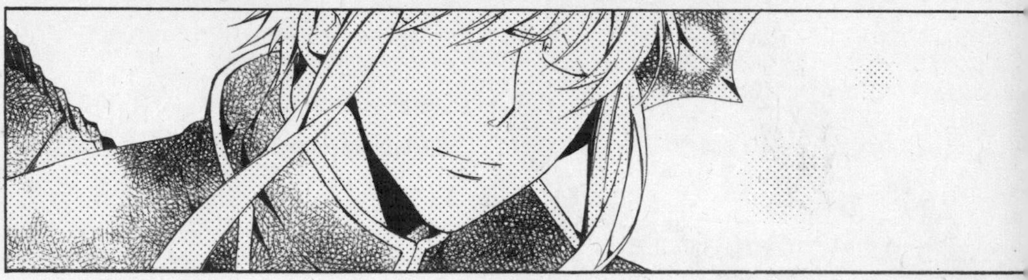

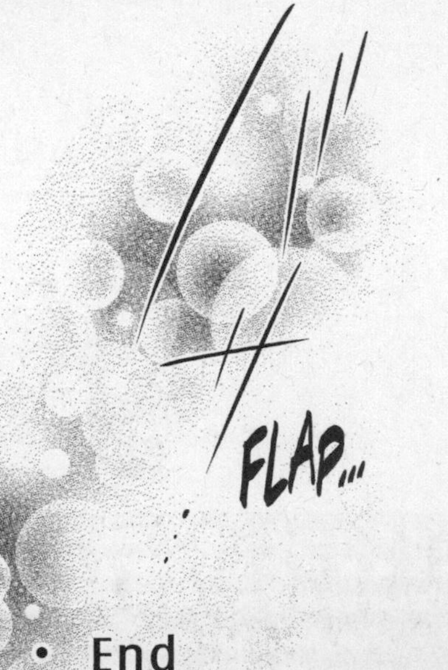
FLAP...

Crimson Empire • End